INTRODUCTION TO

FAMILY DEVELOPMENT

FIRST EDITION

Edited by Chalandra M. Bryant

University of Georgia

cognella® | ACADEMIC PUBLISHING

Bassim Hamadeh, CEO and Publisher
Michael Simpson, Vice President of Acquisitions
Jamie Giganti, Senior Managing Editor
Miguel Macias, Graphic Designer
Zina Craft, Senior Field Acquisitions Editor
Gem Rabanera, Project Editor
Elizabeth Rowe, Licensing Coordinator
Berenice Quirino, Associate Editor
Kat Ragudos, Interior Designer

Cover image copyright © Depositphotos/monkeybusiness.
        copyright © Depositphotos/spotmatikphoto.
        copyright © Depositphotos/fotoluminate.
        copyright © iStockphoto LP/Vladmax.
        copyright © Depositphotos/Wavebreakmedia.

Printed in the United States of America

ISBN: 978-1-5165-0640-8 (pbk) / 978-1-5165-0641-5 (br)

ABOUT THE CONTRIBUTORS

Dr. Mary Crawford is a Professor of Psychology at the University of Connecticut. She taught previously at West Chester University of Pennsylvania. Throughout her career, she has addressed gender and communication; she has paid particular attention to feminism. In her book, *Methods for Studying Gender*, she highlighted research methods for feminist psychologists.

Dr. Jeanne Flora is a Professor of Communications at New Mexico State University. She has written about relationship development, family conflict, and interpersonal communication.

Dr. John Iceland is a Professor of Sociology and Demography at The Pennsylvania State University. His areas of research include social demography, immigration, residential segregation, and poverty.

Dr. Michelle R. Kaufman is a Social Psychologist who studies gender and sexual risk behavior. At Johns Hopkins University, she serves as a research and evaluation officer in the Bloomberg School of Public Health, Center for Communication Programs. She is also affiliated with the Center for AIDS Research and the Women's Health Research Group at Johns Hopkins.

Dr. Patrick H. Mooney is a Professor of Sociology at the University of Kentucky. He has written about the role of community engagement in building community food security, agricultural cooperation, and farm workers movements.

Dr. Stella M. Resko is a Professor of Social Work at Wayne State University. She has written about substance use among adolescents, intimate partner violence, and the emotional impact of conducting research on trauma.

Dr. Craig A. Rimmerman is a Professor of Political Science at Hobart and William Smith Colleges. His research has focused on public policy, political science, and sexual identity.

Dr. Christina M. Rodriguez is a Professor of Psychology at the University of Alabama Birmingham. She studies factors contributing to parental risk of physical abuse and abuse risk assessments.

Dr. Karen Saucier Lundy holds degrees in Nursing and Sociology. She has written books about community health nursing. She is a former Dean of the School of Nursing at Delta State University.

Dr. Stephen K. Sanderson is a Professor of Sociology at the University of California, Riverside. His research and teaching focuses on family, comparative-historical sociology, macrosociology, sociological theory, and social change.

Dr. Chris Segrin is a Professor in the Department of Communication at the University of Arizona. His research focuses on interpersonal relationships, relationship development, anxiety, and depression.

Dr. Gene H. Starbuck is a Professor Emeritus at Colorado Mesa University. This sociologist has published in the areas of gender, family, and human sexuality.

Dr. Keiko Tanaka is a Professor of Rural Sociology at the University of Kentucky. Her research addresses sustainable agriculture and food systems.

Paul Taylor was a political reporter for *The Washington Post* for over a decade. He has also served as the Pew Research Center's Executive Vice President, focusing on demography.

Timothy Taylor earned his M.A. at Stanford University where he studied public finance, economic history, and industrial organization.

Brett Wolff earned an M.A. in Sociology. As a Senior Extension Associate at the University of Kentucky, he organizes statewide sustainable agriculture events.

INTRODUCTION

The purpose of this book is to introduce readers to an array of topics related to families and family functioning. This book consists of seven units and sixteen chapters covering a wide range of issues affecting families and individuals in families. It begins by describing how marriages and families have changed over time and how attitudes about family differ across age groups. Family communication is addressed with a special focus on theoretical perspectives. Two chapters address gender, aspects of sexuality, and how communication is influenced by one's sex. This is followed by divorce, remarriage, family conflict, family stress, poverty, health, food insecurity, and obesity. Underlying some of the readings are theoretical frameworks—theory guides the study of many aspects of family relationships. Understanding families requires understanding the context in which they are embedded. Thus, culture, economic conditions, and stress are underscored.

Family has been defined in many ways. While reading, think about how you define family and what family means to you. A functional definition emphasizes what families do or what functions they serve. This refers to how families aid society (e.g., socialization of children) or how families aid its own members (e.g., emotional support). A structural definition emphasizes the makeup of a family. Families are diverse and complex. Even social scientists have struggled with the development of definitions that are flexible enough to reflect that diversity and complexity. It has be suggested that family is "a self-defined group of intimates who create and maintain themselves through their own interactions and their interactions with others; a family may include both voluntary and involuntary relationships" (Turner & West, 2013, p. 9). Others suggest that "family membership now is often socially constructed, defined by affective indicators (e.g., love, affection, close emotional ties) and instrumental connections (e.g., feelings of loyalty and obligation because of resources received)" (Chapman, Coleman, & Ganong, 2016, p. 634).   The United States Census Bureau has its own definition:

U.S.CENSUS BUREAU DEFINITION

A household contains one or more people. Everyone living in a housing unit makes up a household. One of the people who owns or rents the residence is designated as the householder. For the purposes of examining family and household composition, two types of households are defined: family and nonfamily.

A **family household** has at least two members related by birth, marriage, or adoption, one of whom is the householder.

A **nonfamily household** can be either a person living alone or a householder who shares the housing unit only with nonrelatives—for example, boarders or roommates. The nonrelatives of the householder may be related to each other

Jonathan Vespa, Jamie M. Lewis, and Rose M. Kreider, (2013). America's Families and Living Arrangements: 2012, *Current Population Reports, P20-570*, U.S. Census Bureau, Washington, DC. (https://www.census.gov/prod/2013pubs/p20-570.pdf)

Which definition reflects your view of family? Keep those definitions in mind as you read the chapters. Below is an outline of how the book is structured and features readers are to expect.

Unit 1: Marriages and Families: Then and Now consists of chapters written by Stephen K. Sanderson (Chapter 1, Marriage and Families); Paul Taylor (Chapter 2, Whither Marriage); Gene H. Starbuck and Karen Saucier Lundy (Chapter 3, Population and Family Planning; Chapter 4, Forming Intimate Relationships); and Craig A. Rimmerman (Chapter 5, Jilted at the Altar: The Debate Over Same-Sex Marriage). Chapter 1 provides a sociohistorical overview of family and marriage by explaining the evolution of the modern family as well as the contextual factors (e.g., industrialization, the Great Depression, war) that have shaped changes in the United States and other countries. Fertility rates across nations are also compared. Chapters 1 and 2 complement each other. Chapter 2 describes attitudes about family across age groups with a focus on Millennials and Generation Xers. Chapter 3 expands upon the topic of reproduction from a macrosocial level. World population growth over time is described. All three chapters address the demographic transition – thereby providing an opportunity for students and instructors to compare and contrast the manner in which the authors explain the topic. Chapter 4 covers the development of close relationships. The authors describe perceptions of love across cultures beginning with Ancient Greece and Rome. Chapter 5 is about same-sex marriage and the Defense of Marriage Act. Some of the key court cases are identified.

Unit 2: Family Communication consists of a chapter written by Chris Segrin and Jeanne Flora (Chapter 6, Theoretical Perspectives on Family Communication). This chapter consists of a very comprehensive review of numerous theories. Historical backgrounds are provided for each theory discussed, as well as information about the scholars who developed the theories.

Unit 3: Sex and Gender consists of chapters written by Mary Crawford and Michelle R. Kaufman (Chapter 7, Sex Differences Versus Social Processes in the Construction of Gender) and Richard A. Quantz (Chapter 8, Narratives of Sexuality, Adolescence, and Education). Chapter 7 explains the intersection of gender and language while Chapter 8 provides concise definitions of various terms such as transgender, intersexed, heterosexism, and heteronormativity. When reading these two chapters instructors should highlight the difference between gender and sex.

Unit 4: Marital Dissolution and Remarriage consists of a chapter written by Gene H. Starbuck and Karen Saucier Lundy (Chapter 9: Divorce and Rescripted Families). Numerous terms associated with marital dissolution are defined throughout this chapter. Dissolutions across various cultures and societies are described as well as divorce rates, reasons for divorce, outcomes of divorce, children of divorce, remarriage, and stepfamilies.

Unit 5: Family Violence consists of chapters written by Christina M. Rodriguez (Chapter 10, Parent-Child Aggression: Association with Child Abuse Potential and Parenting Styles) and Stella M. Resko (Chapter 11, Theoretical Perspectives on Intimate Partner Violence). Chapter 10 begins by distinguishing physical abuse from physical discipline and explaining Diana Baumrind's conceptualization of parenting styles (permissive, authoritarian, authoritative). This is followed by a research study exploring the associations between dysfunctional parenting styles, parent-child discipline, and abuse. This study provides students with the opportunity learn how measures are used to collect data from study participants. Chapter 12 describes numerous theories and how those theories are used to explain intimate partner violence. The theories are divided into three levels of analysis: macro, micro, and multidimensional.

Unit 6: Stress and Wellbeing consists of chapters written by Chris Segrin and Jeanne Flora (Chapter 12, Models of Family Stress and Coping), Timothy Taylor (Chapter 13, Poverty and Economic Inequality), and John Iceland (Chapter 14, Economic Well-Being). Chapter 12 identifies some of the various stressors families face and explains the impact stressors have on families. This chapter also contains some of the models used to explain stress such as the ABC-X Model and the Vulnerability-Stress-Adaptation Model. Chapters 13 and 14 complement each other. Chapter 13 explains how some families find themselves trapped in poverty, and it describes programs meant to help families in need. Chapter 14 takes a more macro approach by describing the economy of the United States, including the Great Recession. It illustrates changes in the gross domestic product (GDP) from 1790 to 2011 as well as changes in median household incomes and changes in poverty rates over the decades.

Unit 7: Health and Aging consists of chapters written by John Iceland (Chapter 15, Health and Mortality) and Keiko Tanaka, Patrick H. Mooney, and Brett Wolff (Chapter 16, Food Insecurity and Obesity in Rural America: Paradoxes of the Modern Agrifood System). Chapter 15 describes life expectancy changes, health by educational attainment, health disparities, factors contributing to obesity, aging, and leading causes of death by age. Chapter 16 also addresses obesity, but in greater detail and by underscoring the irony of obesity and food insecurity (hunger) occurring simultaneously.

APPENDICES

Four Appendices are located at the end of the book. Appendix A contains Marriage Rates by State; Appendix B, National Marriage and Divorce Rate Trends; Appendix C, Remarriage in the United States, and Appendix D, How the Census Bureau Measures Poverty and Poverty Guidelines. Appendices A, B and C are meant to supplement Chapter 9 (Divorce and Rescripted Families). Appendix D is meant to supplement Chapter 13 (Poverty and Economic Inequality).

KEY TERMS

Each chapter begins with a list of terms used in the chapter. This list is provided to highlight terms that students may want to look up before proceeding with the readings.

Questions for Review, Reflection, and Discussion

A section called "Questions for Review, Reflection, and Discussion" is located at the end of each chapter. Those questions can be used in study groups, or they can be used by the instructor to generate in-class conversations about the topics covered.

ADDITIONAL READINGS

For those of you who would like to learn more about the topics covered, a list of Additional Readings has been provided for each chapter. Those readings can be used for class presentations, or they can be used to help students expand literature reviews that they may need to write. Instructors can use the Additional Readings to supplement their lectures or to assign special projects to students.

FOR INSTRUCTORS ONLY

QUIZ BANK

Quiz Questions in the form of Multiple Choice and True/False are available as well as Short Answer Quiz Questions. Please note that the "Questions for Review, Reflection, and Discussion" can also be used as Quiz Questions.

REFERENCES

Chapman, A., Coleman, M., & Ganong, L. (2016). "life my grandparent, but not": A qualitative investigation of skip-generation stepgrandchild-stepgrandparent relationships. Journal of Marriage and Family, 78, 634-643.

Turner, L.H. & West, R. (2013). Perspectives on family communication (4th ed).. New York, NY: McGraw-Hill.

UNIT 1

MARRIAGES AND FAMILIES: THEN AND NOW

KEY TERMS

Joint Family

Stem Family

Demographic Transition

Below-Replacement Fertility

Primogeniture

1

MARRIAGE AND FAMILIES

By Stephen K. Sanderson

Most readers of this book live in a society whose family system is based on strong affection and close companionship between spouses and in which the basis of marriage is romantic love rather than economics or family lineage. Young people expect to choose a spouse free from family dictates, and to have a close companionate and sexual relationship with that person. Yet this mode of family and marital life is unique to the modern world. Nowhere before about the seventeenth or eighteenth century in the West was family and marital life organized in this fashion. This chapter tells the story of how this type of family was born and how it evolved into its current state.

THE TRADITIONAL FAMILY IN ASIA AND EUROPE

In traditional China and India, as in nearly all agrarian societies, the extended family has been the basic residential unit. The household can be either a *joint family* or a *stem family*. A joint family consists of three generations living together under a common roof, pooling resources, and headed by the eldest male. All of the brothers live together, along with their fathers, sons, and in-marrying wives, and inherit equally at the father's death. A stem family is a segment of a joint family; it consists of a couple, their unmarried minor children, and one married son and his wife. Under this system, only one son (usually the oldest) inherits the farm and continues to live with his parents. Other sons normally leave the household and work for others as, say, farmhands or servants; in some cases they join monasteries. Both joint and stem families have been found in China and India, but the joint family has been more common (Therborn 2004).

Family relations in European societies have differed in important ways from those in China and India—indeed, from those in most of the rest of the world. The differences date as far back as Roman times. Many Roman families were nuclear families, and there was more emphasis on the conjugal relationship between husband and wife than in Asia (Goody 1990). There appears to have been a more affectionate relationship between spouses than was the norm in other agrarian societies. In Asia and elsewhere, marriage typically occurred early, with girls being married off at puberty and boys somewhat later. But in Rome, marriage occurred later, sometimes much later.

The feudal society that gradually formed in the centuries after the collapse of the Roman Empire was overwhelmingly rural, with peasants of various levels engaged in subsistence farming. Within this context, the stem family, with inheritance determined by primogeniture, was the norm. Here, as noted above, Europe was distinct as well, for in the rest of Eurasia the joint family was far more common, and all males of the household inherited land equally.

Moving ahead to more recent times, we find that the European family, or at least the Western European family, retained its distinctiveness. Göran Therborn (2004) refers to a "rule of universal marriage" that prevailed throughout the non-Western world at the beginning of the twentieth century. Nearly all women married, and they married very young. In China, for example, only one-tenth of 1 percent of women aged thirty-four or older had not married. In India, 96 percent of women aged twenty to twenty-four were married, many of them having married much earlier. The average age of marriage for Indian girls was thirteen, but in some of the states of North India, the age of betrothal was eleven. Marriage was also universal in the Dutch East Indies and in the Muslim world. In Egypt, for example, 94 percent of girls had married by age twenty-nine, with most of these having married before age twenty (Therborn 2004).

In Eastern Europe we find essentially the same universal marriage pattern, although the age of marriage was somewhat higher. In 1900 only about 2 percent of women never married, and the average age of marriage was just over twenty. But in Western Europe, things were different. Some 13 percent of women never married, and the average age at marriage was just under twenty-six. Western Europe was also characterized by greater sexual informality: more premarital pregnancies, more births out of wedlock, and more cohabitation in place of marriage (Therborn 2004). This Western/Eastern divide was not a recent development; it probably existed as early as the late Middle Ages (Macfarlane 1978, 1986).

THE EVOLUTION OF THE MODERN FAMILY SYSTEM

Sociologists of the 1950s and 1960s interested in the evolution of the modern family attributed the new developments largely to the effects of industrialization (Goode 1963). However, some of the most important changes, such as the shift from extended to nuclear family households, began well before the Industrial Revolution. Arthur Alderson and Stephen Sanderson (1991) studied European family patterns in the sixteenth century, drawing on research undertaken by numerous historians of the family (in particular Laslett 1977, 1983, and Laslett and Wall 1972; see Sanderson 1995, Table 16.1). They found that in the more economically advanced parts of Europe, nuclear families predominated. In England and northern France, an average of 81 percent of people were living in nuclear family households. In Belgium the average for two villages was 77 percent. Colonial America exhibited the same pattern, with a striking 97 percent of families organized as nuclear families. In eastern Europe, which was much less economically developed, the nuclear family was in the minority. In Russia, Serbia, Estonia, and Hungary taken together, only 39 percent of people were living in nuclear families. Here the extended family was still dominant. In Serbia the most common family unit was the *zadruga*, a large extended household containing perhaps three or four nuclear families under the control of a patriarch and functioning as a single economic unit. Any given *zadruga* could contain as many as thirty people. In the Russian Baltic province of Kurland, there was a similar type of extended household, the *Gesind*, whose average size was about fourteen members (Shorter 1975). In European societies with intermediate levels of development—Italy, southern France, Austria, and Germany—slightly more than half the population was living in nuclear households. The rest were living in extended households, but in this case the smaller stem family household rather than the joint households common in eastern Europe (Shorter 1975).

Other important changes also began early (Shorter 1975; Stone 1979). The traditional European family was largely an economic and reproductive unit. Companionate marriage with strong affection between husband and wife existed, but it was usually not the principal basis for marriage. This was to change. Children increasingly rejected arranged marriages and, indeed, any interference by their parents in the choice of a spouse. Romantic love increased in importance as the basis for choosing a spouse and for holding a marriage together. This "sentimental revolution" in marriage, as Edward Shorter (1975) has called it, carried over to the relationships between parents and children. Mothers began to breast-feed their children rather than send them out to wet nurses, and they also showed increasing concern with advice on good child-rearing practices. Sexual behavior changed as well. A great increase in premarital sex seems to have occurred, for we see a marked rise in rates of illegitimacy. Marital sex also seemed to have become more common and to have received more erotic significance.

One of the most important aspects of the transition to the modern family was the emergence of romantic love as the basis for marriage. Romantic love has no doubt existed in all societies (Jankowiak and Fisher 1992), but in no society before the seventeenth or eighteenth century has it played the predominant role in the selection of marriage partners. The rise of romantic love as the basis for marriage was a revolutionary phenomenon (Coontz 2005), of which there were really two aspects. First, as noted above, young people increasingly demanded the right to their own free choice of a spouse. Second, the marriage itself came increasingly to be seen as an affective rather than an economic unit, one held together by the sentimental attachment of the spouses rather than by economic considerations. The tie between the spouses became one in which affection was of paramount significance. They were becoming companions sharing a long life together. Spouses (and courting partners) began to idealize their loved ones and to prefer their company to that of everyone else. They spent countless hours with each other, called each other by special terms of endearment, and expressed their attachment in poetry, literature, and song. One of the most interesting features of eighteenth- and nineteenth-century literature, for instance, was the rise of the romantic novel, a telling symbolic expression of the great family change that was occurring.

Hardly less important was the corresponding change in relations between the family and the outside world, which Shorter has called "the rise of domesticity." The traditional family was lacking in privacy or "separateness" from the rest of society. The type of family that most of us live in today—a private social unit relatively isolated from the rest of society—scarcely existed. Outsiders interacted freely with members of the household, and the relations between family members and outsiders were sometimes as close as the relations among the family members themselves. But in the seventeenth, eighteenth, and nineteenth centuries, the family was becoming increasingly private and the boundaries between it and the rest of society more and more closely drawn. By the middle of the nineteenth century, the family had become a unit insisting upon its private existence and its separation from the outside world. Shorter (1975: 227–228) characterizes the rise of domesticity in the following way:

> Domesticity, or the family's awareness of itself as a precious emotional unit that must be protected with privacy and isolation from outside intrusion, was the third great spearhead of the great onrush of sentiment in modern times. Romantic love detached the couple from communal sexual supervision and turned them towards affection. Maternal love created a sentimental nest within which the modern family would ensconce itself, and it removed many women from involvement with community life. Domesticity, beyond that, sealed off the family as a whole from its traditional interaction with the surrounding world. The members of the family came to feel far more solidarity with one another than they did with their various age and sex peer groups. We know in practical terms when domesticity is present if, like the French, people begin removing their names from the front doors to insure that no one will knock; if, as in Germany, long Sunday walks through the woods begin to tear Papa from his card games; and if, as happens everywhere, people begin spending greater proportions of their time at home.

In the view of many, the evolution of the modern family was largely a product of the vast shift taking place during these centuries toward a highly commercialized, capitalist society (Shorter 1975; Stone 1979; Zaretsky 1976; Lasch 1977). Shorter (1975: 258–259) links the rise of capitalism to the modern family revolution through the rise of economic individualism:

> Laissez-faire marketplace organization, capitalist production, and the beginnings of proletarianization among the work force were more important than any other factors in the spread of sentiment.
>
> . . . How did capitalism help cause that powerful thrust of sentiment among the unmarried that I have called the romance revolution? . . . The logic of the marketplace

positively demands individualism: the system will succeed only if each participant ruthlessly pursues his own self-interest, buying cheap, selling dear, and enhancing his own interests at the cost of his competitors (i.e., his fellow citizens). Only if this variety of economic egoism is internalized will the free market come up to the high expectations of its apologists, for if people let humanitarian or communitarian considerations influence their economic behavior, the market becomes inefficient; the weak cease to be weeded out. Thus, the free market engraves upon all who are caught up in it the attitude: "Look out for number one."

. . . Egoism that was learned in the marketplace became transferred to community obligations and standards, to ties to the family and lineage—in short, to the whole domain of cultural rules that regulated familial and sexual behavior.

. . . So capitalism exerted its impact upon romantic love through involvement in the market labor force: economic individualism leads to cultural egoism; private gratification becomes more important than fitting into the common weal; the wish to be free produces the illegitimacy explosion.

As for the increasing separation of the family from the outside world, Christopher Lasch (1977) has suggested that the private family of the eighteenth and nineteenth centuries emerged as a kind of shelter into which people could escape from the increasingly harsh realities of the outside world. The family became, in Lasch's memorable phrase, a "haven in a heartless world." The heartless world that Lasch has in mind is the competitive capitalist marketplace. The intensely competitive character of the work environment created the need for a refuge in which people could recover from the slings and arrows of the work world so as to be able to enter it again. As Lasch (1977: xix) has put it, "As business, politics, and diplomacy grow more savage and warlike, men seek a haven in private life, in personal relations, above all in the family—the last refuge of love and decency."

THE CONTEMPORARY FAMILY REVOLUTION

Lasch has also suggested, however, that in the past several decades, the family has been under so much stress that it is having increasing difficulty fulfilling its role as a refuge from the competitive workplace. Whether this is actually true or not, the Western family since the early 1960s has undergone profound changes. These involve both the relations between husbands and wives and those between parents and their adolescent children.

RECENT CHANGES IN MARITAL RELATIONSHIPS

Since the 1960s there has been a marked increase in cohabitation, as either a prelude to marriage or an alternative to it. In the United States, for example, there were 523,000 unmarried couples in 1970, but this increased to 1.59 million in 1980, to 2.9 million in 1990, and to 4.2 million in 1998. In France in the 1980s, 65 percent of first unions were cohabitations, a rate more than twice that of ten years earlier. In Canada in the early 1970s, 16 percent of first unions were cohabitations, but that had increased to 51 percent by the late 1980s. In England in the 1960s, about 25 percent of couples had cohabited before marriage, but by the 1990s the figure had risen dramatically to some 70 percent. In other Western European countries, we find similar patterns. In Austria in the 1990s, 40 percent of first unions for women in the age cohort twenty-five to twenty-nine were cohabitations; corresponding figures for Switzerland and Germany are 37 and 46 percent, respectively. The country that leads the modern industrial world in the rate of cohabitation is Sweden, and by a wide margin. Fully 96 percent of Swedish women who had married by the late 1970s had first cohabited, and cohabitation in Sweden is today a virtually universal practice. In fact, cohabitation is so pervasive in Sweden that having one's first child in a cohabiting relationship has become the norm (*International Encyclopedia of Marriage and Family* 2003; Cherlin 1992).

Divorce has also become much more common in the past several decades. The divorce rate has actually been rising since the mid-nineteenth century, but it experienced a real surge beginning in the early 1960s. Table 1.1 gives divorce rates for eight industrial countries from 1965 to 2000. We can clearly see that in the two decades between 1965 and 1986, divorce rates soared. After that they either leveled off or rose more slowly. The United States has the highest divorce rate of any country in the Western world, although its rate had leveled off by 2000 and in 2008 had actually dropped, from 6.2 to 5.2. Other Western countries whose divorce rates declined or remained flat between 2000 and 2008 include Sweden, the Netherlands, Germany, and Denmark (US Bureau of the Census 2012). However, some of these figures can be misleading in the sense that they underestimate the rate at which couples are breaking up. Many cohabiting couples break up before ever marrying, and obviously these are not included in divorce statistics.

It has often been said that this upheaval in marital relationships has been the result of fundamental changes in values and attitudes with regard to family life. This

TABLE 1.1: DIVORCE RATES IN EIGHT INDUSTRIAL SOCIETIES, 1965–2000			
Country	**1965**	**1986**	**2000**
United States	2.5	6.2	6.2
United Kingdom	0.8	3.6	4.0
Canada	0.5	3.2	3.4
Sweden	1.2	3.0	3.8
Germany	1.0	2.3	3.5
France	0.7	2.3	3.0
Japan	0.8	1.6	3.1
Italy	Not legal	0.4	1.0

Note: Figures represent the number of divorces per 1,000 persons.

Sources: Levitan, Belous, and Gallo (1988); US Bureau of the Census (2012).

explanation, though, has little to commend it. Even if true, it would be trivial, for we would still be faced with the problem of explaining why these attitudes and values have changed in the first place. But the explanation does not even appear to be true. Recent survey and opinion poll evidence suggests that familial attitudes and values did not begin to change until the late 1960s or early 1970s, whereas the recent behavioral changes in question really began in the early 1960s. It thus seems that changes in values and attitudes have actually followed rather than generated behavioral changes (Cherlin 1992).

Andrew Cherlin (1992) suggests that these recent trends are due to fundamental economic changes involving the participation of women in the labor force. The trends correspond very closely to the dramatic increase in the proportion of married women with dependent children who work full-time outside the household. As women have entered the labor force in much larger numbers, their economic power has been substantially amplified, and this has reduced their dependence on their husbands. They are therefore much less likely to stay in an unhappy marriage. In the past women often felt they had little chance to end an unsatisfactory marriage because they would have had great difficulty supporting themselves and their children on their own. But this has now changed dramatically, and with these changes in the balance of power, women's expectations of marriage have changed. They demand much more from it and are likely to end it quickly when it does not live up to their hopes. And, in fact, wives are much more likely than husbands to initiate divorce. Men's expectations have changed correspondingly, and with both men and women now heavily involved in their careers, the pressures on marriages are even greater.

This is probably part of the story, but the family historian Stephanie Coontz (2005) gives things a different twist. For her, the roots of the recent changes were planted as early as the eighteenth century and are the logical outcome of the emergence of romantic love as the principal basis of marriage. Love became not only the main motive for marriage but the very basis for human fulfillment and happiness in general. As Coontz (2005: 162) remarks, "By the middle of the nineteenth century there was near unanimity in the middle and upper classes throughout Western Europe and North America that the love-based marriage . . . was a recipe for heaven on earth." She adds that "the Victorians were the first people in history to try to make marriage the pivotal experience in people's lives and married love the principal focus of their emotions, obligations, and satisfactions" (2005: 177). And it was not just love that mattered. Sex came to matter too, and all the more as time wore on.

And yet there were people who saw the hazards in the new forms of marriage and intimacy. As early as the 1920s, a number of observers warned that love-based marriage contained serious contradictions and tensions because people's expectations for it were unrealistically high, and such tensions could not be contained forever. Indeed, even in the 1920s they were already starting to erupt. The Great Depression and World War II slowed things for a while, but the war was followed by a quarter century of great economic boom and prosperity, and the love-based marriage reemerged with a vengeance. In the 1950s and early 1960s, it was the uppermost concern of most young women, and to such an extent that it was often joked that the reason women were going to college in greater numbers was to get their MRS degrees.

But the critics were proved right; it was not to last. As Coontz remarks (2005: 228), "In the 1970s, when the inherent instability of the love-based marriage reasserted itself, millions of people were taken completely by surprise. Having lost any collective memory of the convulsions that occurred when the love match was first introduced and the crisis that followed its modernization in the 1920s, they could not understand why this kind of marriage, which they thought had prevailed for thousands of years, was being abandoned by the younger generation." In essence, the dramatic changes that began in the 1960s had long been preordained. Throughout most of human history, marriage has served largely economic and reproductive ends; little more was expected of it. But the love revolution changed everything. In Coontz's words, it was love that killed the modern family.

RECENT CHANGES IN PARENT-CHILD RELATIONS

The current family revolution involves a change not only in marital relations but in the whole character of relations between parents and their children, especially adolescent children. These relations have been changing for a very long time, but in the past four decades the changes have accelerated markedly. The changes are in the direction of an increasing loss of parental control over children and an increasing separation of parents and children into two distinct worlds. As Shorter (1975) suggests, children are now caught up in an elaborate youth subculture that plays at least as much a role in shaping their basic values as do the teachings of their parents. Parents seem to be increasingly irrelevant as educators and teachers of the young, and many youth seem to view their parents (and members of the older generation generally) as having little of value to transmit to them. According to Shorter (1975: 276–277), we are witnessing

> a fundamental shift in the willingness of adolescents to learn from their parents. In the 1960s, relations between the generations started to undergo the same evolution that kinship had earlier undertaken: from function to friendship. In the heyday of the modern nuclear family, the prime burden of transmitting values and attitudes to teenage children fell upon the parents, and the rules of the game were learned in the cloistered intimacy of countless evenings about the hearth. But as the post-modern family rushes down upon us, parents are losing their role as educators. The task passes instead to the peers, and with its transfer passes as well a sense of the family as an institution continuing over time, a chain of links across the generations. The parents become friends (an affective relationship), not representatives of the lineage (a functional relationship). If this is so, we are dealing with an unprecedented pattern.

Shorter has suggested that there are two things at work here. The children have been pulled away by the massive development of an independent youth culture, but they also seem to have been pushed out of the family as a result of the fundamental changes it has undergone. Putting it candidly, many parents simply do not have the time for their children that they once did. Given that the dual-career family has become a significant form of family life, it is difficult for either parent to have the time that was once available for intensive socialization and upbringing (Hochschild 1997). Hence the closeness between parents and their children so characteristic of days gone by is more and more missing now, and that makes the pull of the adolescent subculture all the more enticing.

These changes have been exacerbated by another set of changes: increases in births to unmarried women and in single-parent households. Table 1.2 indicates how common out-of-wedlock childbirth has become since 1970. In the 1950s and even into the early 1960s, pregnancy outside marriage was usually regarded as scandalous. In those days before legal abortion, unmarried pregnant women were often hidden away by their families or sent to special homes designed to shield them from the prying eyes of friends and neighbors. After birth, the baby would often be given up for adoption. Those days are long gone. As Table 1.2 shows, in 1970 only a small minority of births were to unmarried women, but from that point on, everything exploded. In 2008 in a number of industrial societies, 40 percent or more of children were born to women who were not married to the children's fathers. And because this has become so common, it is no longer considered scandalous. Many people do not accept it, of course, but its former stigma has been largely lifted. (Japan stands out as a glaring exception.)

Naturally, with many more births to unmarried women, single-parent households have become increasingly common. As can be seen in Table 1.3, there were few single-parent households in 1980 (and certainly even fewer in preceding decades), but by 2008 they had come to comprise a significant proportion of all households. David Popenoe (1993) contends that these data understate the matter because they pertain to single-parent families at only one point in time. If we look at the likelihood that children will live in a single-parent family *at some point* in their childhood or adolescence, the changes appear much more striking. As Popenoe (1993: 531) points

TABLE 1.2: BIRTHS TO UNMARRIED WOMEN, 1970–2008

Country	1970	1980	1990	2000	2008
United States	11	18.4	28.0	33.2	40.6
Canada	10	12.8	24.4	28.3	27.3
Denmark	11	33.2	46.4	44.6	46.2
France	7	11.4	30.1	43.6	52.6
Germany	6	—	15.1	23.4	32.1
Italy	2	4.3	6.5	9.7	17.7
Japan	1	0.8	1.1	1.6	2.1
Netherlands	2	4.1	11.4	24.9	41.2
Sweden	18	39.7	47.0	55.3	54.7
United Kingdom	8	11.5	27.9	39.5	43.7

Note: Numbers are percentages.

Source: US Bureau of the Census (1995, 2012).

TABLE 1.3: SINGLE-PARENT HOUSEHOLDS, 1980–2008

Country	1980	1990	2000	2008
United States	19.5	24.0	27.0	29.5
Canada	12.7	16.2	23.5	24.6
Denmark	13.4	17.8	18.4	21.7
France	10.2	13.2	17.4	19.8
Germany	—	15.2	17.6	21.7
Ireland	7.2	10.7	17.4	22.6
Japan	4.9	6.5	8.3	10.2
Netherlands	—	9.6	13.0	16.0
Sweden	11.2	17.4	21.4	18.7
United Kingdom	13.9	19.4	20.7	25.0

Note: Numbers represent the percentage of all households that are single-parent households.

Source: US Bureau of the Census (2012).

out with respect to the United States, "Of children born between 1950 and 1954, only 19% of whites (48% of blacks) had spent some time living in single-parent families by the time they reached age 17. But for white children born in 1980, this figure was projected by one estimate to be 70% (94% for black children)."

FROM LARGE FAMILIES TO SMALL

THE DEMOGRAPHIC TRANSITION

Another major change is the reduction in family size. Few parents today have more than two or three children, whereas 150 years ago they may have had four, five, or even six. The long-term shift from larger to smaller families is known as the *demographic transition* (Harris and Ross 1987; cf. Handwerker 1986), which occurred in the more advanced societies mostly between 1870 and 1930 and in less-developed societies later in the twentieth century.

Why have birth rates dropped so much in modern industrial societies? The most common answer is the introduction of modern birth control technologies. This may be part of the story, but much more has to be going on. For one thing, we know that when people become aware of modern birth control methods, they do not always use them. They must therefore have reasons for keeping their childbearing rates high. In addition, in many societies in Europe and North America in the nineteenth century, fertility levels had already started to decline before modern birth control methods became available (Knodel and van de Walle 1979).

Some demographers have emphasized the role of mortality rates, especially rates of infant and child mortality. When infants and children are likely to die early in life, people need to have "surplus" children in order to reach a desired completed family size. If a couple desires to have, say, three children who live to reproductive age, they may need to have one, two, or even three additional children in order to achieve this objective. In this theory, fertility tracks mortality.

Another theory emphasizes the status of women. Where women are highly subordinated, as they most often are in agrarian societies, fertility will be high, but as women's status improves with industrialization, fertility will drop. This argument is based on the assumption that women generally wish to have fewer children than their husbands because the burdens of child care fall disproportionately on mothers. Where women's status is low, their husbands can compel them to have more children, but when women acquire a more equal status, they gain a greater voice in childbearing decisions (Dyson and Moore 1983; Malhotra, Vanneman, and Kishor 1995; Murthi, Guio, and Dreze 1995).

Yet another theory suggests that fertility levels are adjusted primarily to the economic value of children's labor (Boserup 1981; Harris and Ross 1987). This theory says that in agrarian societies, children tend to be economic assets because they perform a range of useful services that benefit the family. But as societies industrialize and people move into towns and cities, these services no longer exist to be performed by anyone, and children turn from economic assets into economic liabilities. The economic costs of children force people to have fewer, perhaps many fewer.

Stephen Sanderson and Joshua Dubrow (2000) attempted to test these theories by performing a series of statistical analyses on samples of societies between 1910 and 1990. The year 1910 was about the midpoint of the demographic transition. Looking at sixteen European societies, they found that the infant mortality rate was far and away the strongest determinant of the fertility rate. Fertility was significantly lower in those societies whose infant mortality rates were lower. The economic value of children's labor could be assessed by looking at the percentage of the labor force working in either agriculture or manufacturing. This did not play any role in fertility rates. Unfortunately, the role of women's empowerment could not be tested because at the time no one had gotten around to constructing indexes to measure it.

Then the authors considered more recent fertility rates for a set of societies at various levels of economic development. For both 1960 and 1990, the rate of infant mortality was the strongest determinant of fertility, and the level of female empowerment was the second strongest. Neither the percentage of the labor force working in agriculture nor that of the population living in urban areas had any effect. A limitation of this research was the small number of societies considered (between forty-two and sixty-three, only about a third of the world's total). Therefore, an additional set of analyses was carried out using a much larger group of contemporary nation-states (145) for the year 2008. The results turned out to be essentially the same. The infant mortality rate was once again the most important determinant of the fertility rate, and female empowerment was also important. The percentage of the labor force in agriculture played some role, but it was relatively minor.

Bear in mind, however, that the decision to have fewer children reflects more than greater female empowerment and changing levels of infant and child survival. Modern societies are organized in radically different ways from earlier agrarian societies. One of the most dramatic changes accompanying industrialization has been the development of mass education and skills-based competitive labor markets (H. Kaplan 1996). If one's children are going to become successful in today's world, they have to be educated and prepared to compete with other people's children. Unless one is quite well off, affording this becomes difficult if one has, say, six, seven, or eight children. Better to have one or two (perhaps three) and invest intensively in each.

A "SECOND" DEMOGRAPHIC TRANSITION

In the past half century birth rates have continued to decline, reaching levels far lower than anyone ever anticipated. We are now entering a very different demographic era, one of *below-replacement fertility* (sometimes called *low-low fertility*) (Frejka and Ross 2001; Chesnais 2001). For a population to remain stable over time, the overall fertility rate must be around 2.1 children per woman in her reproductive lifetime in highly developed countries with low mortality and long lifespans. For less-developed countries with higher mortality and shorter lifespans, below-replacement fertility ranges from approximately 2.5 to 3.3, and for the world as a whole it is about 2.33. Above these levels population grows, and below them it declines. Roughly half of the world's countries have now reached below-replacement levels. Most of these are not yet losing population because of something called the population-lag effect, but within a couple of generations this will begin to happen. Table 1.4 shows selected countries that in 2010 were below replacement level (using the global level of 2.33 as the cutoff point), along with some that are still above replacement. In order to show a trend, 1993 fertility levels are also shown. All modern industrial societies, with the exception of Israel, are below replacement, some far below. The lowest fertility rates in the world are now concentrated in East and Southeast Asia: South Korea has a rate of 1.22; Japan, 1.20; Taiwan, 1.15; Singapore, 1.10; and Hong Kong, 1.04. But many less-developed countries are now below replacement, and others are edging ever closer. As can be seen from the table, the fertility rate in Surinam is 1.97; in Vietnam, 1.93; in Iran, 1.89; and in Mauritius, 1.80. Notice also the extent to which fertility rates have declined in some places. India's fertility rate, for example, was 3.80 in 1993, but by 2010 it had declined to 2.65. This is extremely significant because India is the world's second-largest country with over 1 billion people and was, in the fairly recent past, experiencing very rapid population growth. Within twenty years it could very well be below replacement level. Honduras, one of the poorest countries in Latin America, is another striking case: its fertility rate was 5.16 in 1993 but had dropped to 3.17 in 2010. And the fertility rate in the very poor African country of Djibouti has declined even more dramatically, from 5.98 to 2.79.

Demographers are not of one mind in explaining why childbearing has plummeted to such low levels, but I see three major forces at work. First, the high cost of children continues to escalate. Children have become extremely expensive to rear, especially as more and more young people attend college and as college expenses skyrocket. Children may not have been economic assets in earlier agrarian societies, but now they have become extreme economic liabilities. Their greater cost has led to adjustments in childbearing. In essence, parents have

TABLE 1.4: FERTILITY LEVELS IN SELECTED COUNTRIES, 1993 AND 2010

Country	1993	2010
Below replacement		
United States	2.08	2.06
Surinam	2.64	1.97
Vietnam	3.62	1.93
Iran	4.68	1.89
Mauritius	2.32	1.80
Denmark	1.67	1.74
Sweden	2.31	1.67
Canada	1.83	1.58
China	2.10	1.54
Spain	1.33	1.47
Russia	1.89	1.41
Poland	2.04	1.29
South Korea	1.77	1.22
Japan	1.54	1.20
Taiwan	—	1.15
Singapore	1.87	1.10
Hong Kong	1.27	1.04
Above replacement		
Niger	7.64	7.68
Ethiopia	6.91	6.07
Benin	6.62	5.40
Madagascar	6.22	5.09
Senegal	6.20	4.86
Guinea-Bissau	7.10	4.58
Zimbabwe	4.78	3.66
Pakistan	5.84	3.28
Honduras	5.16	3.17
Libya	4.72	3.01
Djibouti	5.98	2.79
India	3.80	2.65
Kyrgyzstan	3.69	2.64
Bahrain	3.76	2.47
United Arab Emirates	4.12	2.41

Sources: Central Intelligence Agency (2010, online version); Allen (2006).

adapted themselves to children's increased costs by increasing their investment in the well-being of each child—by trading the *quantity* of children for their *quality* (Cleland 2001; Kaplan and Lancaster 2000).

Second, the women's movement has completely upset the applecart in terms of gender roles and relations. In 1950 only about 12 percent of married women with young children were in the labor force, but now close to two-thirds are. Moreover, many women are keen to have high-powered careers. Children interfere with such aspirations, often greatly. Highly ambitious women will at the very least postpone childbearing, and many will decide not to have children at all. A large-scale survey of British women undertaken in 1999 divided women into three categories based on their lifestyle preferences: home-centered women, for whom family life and children were the main priorities; work-centered women, whose most important priority was employment or some equivalent activity in the public sphere; and adaptive women, who wanted to combine the preferences of the first two groups. The fertility level of the home-centered women was 1.28; of the adaptive women, 1.02; and of the work-centered women, only 0.61, or less than half that of the home-centered women (Hakim 2003).

Finally, modern societies have become increasingly affluent; hedonistic gratification and attention to the self have become paramount for many individuals. For those who are most vigorously pursuing these goals, children are often thought of as nuisances, as little "rugrats" who cannot be bothered with because they get in the way. As the demographer Jean-Claude Chesnais (2001: 258) expresses it, "The consumer-goods society, strongly supported by advertising, tends to produce a marked preference for the present or the short-term future. In such a context, individuals hesitate to make long-term and irreversible commitments such as to family-building and childbearing. Individual independence and personal freedom become key values: enjoying life . . . is the basic rule of consumerism." He adds that "marriages and consensual unions are centered on new objectives that are more egocentric: the pursuit of personal happiness and self-fulfillment are at the top of the list" (2001: 258).

THE MODERN FAMILY: CHANGE OR DECLINE?

For decades social scientists and laypersons have debated whether the family in modern industrial societies is in a state of decline. Indeed, the debate seems to be renewed in each new generation. David Popenoe (1988, 1993) notes that sociologists have for many years generally argued that the idea of family decline is a myth. The family has been changing to adapt to new circumstances, they say, but this does not mean that it is weakening or losing importance. Popenoe himself, however, challenges this view and claims that the family in the late twentieth and early twenty-first centuries is in fact in a rather profound state of decline. By decline Popenoe (1988: xii) means that "the institution of the family is growing weaker; it is losing social power and functions, losing influence over behavior and opinion, and generally becoming less important in life." Popenoe delineates twelve indicators of family decline, some of which are already familiar from previous discussions:

1. There has been a retreat from marriage. Many couples postpone it, and an increasing number do not marry at all.
2. Marriages break up more easily and are far less durable and stable.
3. Cohabitation has dramatically increased, either as a form of trial marriage or as a substitute for marriage. But it has performed poorly as trial marriage; research shows that married couples who first cohabited are more likely to divorce than married couples who did not cohabit.

4. The modern family is less cohesive and less capable of controlling the behavior of its individual members; it has lost power to other social groups, such as the state, the mass media, schools, and peer groups.

5. Families have become smaller, with fewer children and more single- parent families.

6. Families today engage in fewer joint activities; they do fewer things as a unit.

7. Meaningful contact time between parents and children has diminished (parents often rationalize this by claiming that they spend "quality time" with their children).

8. Families today have less time for the development and maintenance of family-centered routines and activities, such as those that revolve around mealtime, bedtime, birthdays, and holidays.

9. Children have entered an era of less regular contact with relatives outside the nuclear family.

10. As a result of the greater degree of marital breakup, children suffer increasing anxiety about the possibility of a breakup and increased anxiety when a breakup does occur.

11. At one time children had a close association with the work of their parents and could develop mental models of the occupational roles of adulthood; this is less true today, and children live increasingly in their own separate world.

12. Familism—the emphasis on the family as an important social institution—has weakened and has been increasingly replaced by values relating to individual self-fulfillment and egalitarianism.

To Popenoe's comments can be added Christopher Lasch's contention that one of the most disturbing aspects of the recent family changes is the increasing inability of the family to function as a haven or refuge, a development that Shorter has referred to as the "destruction of the nest." The family seems to be increasingly losing its capacity to shelter the young and adult males from the extreme pressures of competition in an advanced capitalist civilization, and it is exposing females more and more to these pressures. With the increase in the number of single-parent families, things are only made worse.

Arlie Russell Hochschild (1997) puts this in perspective. In her research on the work and family lives of employees in a modern American corporation, she found, much to her dismay, that people's work and family lives are in a sense the reverse of what they were decades ago. Work life has become the refuge, and stress is concentrated in the family. Both parents put in workdays of ten hours or longer and often say that they prefer work life to family life. As a result, the pace of family life has accelerated markedly. Parents have less time to devote to the emotional needs of children. Hochschild relates the appalling story of a young boy whose parents were scheduled to give presentations at work on a day in which a medical emergency developed and the boy had to be taken to the hospital. The parents were then faced with a dilemma—which they resolved in favor of giving their presentations rather than being with their son!

And yet many sociologists do not see the family changes of the late twentieth century in such negative terms. For example, Randall Collins (1988: 499) has said that "the family is not fundamentally weakening under all this change" and in "some respects it is even stronger than before." Collins (1988: 499) adds,

> One thing that is indicated by the trend toward divorce, remarriages, and multiplicity of family styles is that individuals now form families predominantly as a matter of personal preference for marriage. Love has become more important, not less. People make their marriages more for love, now that they are less coerced into depending upon a family economically. . . . Children, too, are apparently recipients of more love than before. There are fewer children per family, and their births are more carefully chosen. This actually makes children more important to their parents, not less. . . .
> . . . Although it lives with strains, nevertheless the family seems to be in better shape than ever.

Why do Popenoe and Collins draw such different conclusions from basically the same set of facts? The only conceivable answer, I believe, is that they approach these facts from different political perspectives. Popenoe has a rather conservative outlook, unusual for a sociologist, whereas Collins has the liberal outlook that is the norm in sociology. As Cherlin (1992: 138) has remarked, when they examine the various dimensions of family change, "liberal defenders of family change focus on the emotionally enhanced relationships between adults and on the increased autonomy of women, [whereas] conservatives focus on instability and on children." In other words, Collins concludes that the family is not weakening because he approves of many of the changes it has undergone, whereas Popenoe sees the family as under siege because he wants to return to the recent past when familism was a stronger value and families exerted stronger control over their members.

Both Popenoe and Collins have important points to make. Certainly many aspects of family change in recent decades, such as skyrocketing divorce rates and the alarming rise in the number of female-headed households, are cause for concern, but other aspects of family change, such as greater individual autonomy and increasing opportunities for women, seem very positive. On this matter, as on others, we cannot have our cake and eat it too. In the not-too-distant past of the societies of the West, the family was a powerful and, in some respects, coercive institution, dictating the lives of its individual members, and the relations between husbands and wives and parents and children were much colder and more formal. (In the early twentieth century a common expression was "Children should be seen and not heard," and fathers often gave their sons no choice in their career paths.) Indeed, the family still functions in this way across much of the world, as it did throughout a good deal of human history. If we value the increased autonomy and possibilities for individuality that family change brings, as well as the greater warmth between husbands and wives and parents and children—and many members of Western societies do—then we have to be willing to acknowledge that, despite the losses, there are also gains.

REFERENCES

Alderson, Arthur S., and Stephen K. Sanderson. 1991. "Historical European household structures and the capitalist world-economy." *Journal of Family History* 16:419–432.

Boserup, Ester. 1981. *Population and Technological Change*. Chicago: University of Chicago Press.

Cherlin, Andrew J. 1992. *Marriage, Divorce, Remarriage*. 2nd ed. Cambridge, MA: Harvard University Press.

Chesnais, Jean-Claude. 2001. "Comment: A march toward population recession." *Population and Development Review* 27(Supplement): 255–259.

Cleland, John. 2001. "The effects of improved survival on fertility: A reassessment." *Population and Development Review* 27(Supplement): 60–92.

Sanderson. 1988. *Sociology of Marriage and the Family: Gender, Love, and Property*. 2nd ed. New York: Nelson-Hall.

Coontz, Stephanie. 2005. *Marriage, a History: How Love Conquered Marriage*. New York: Penguin Books.

Dyson, Tim, and Mick Moore. 1983. "On kinship structure, female autonomy, and demographic behavior in India." *Population and Development Review* 9:35–60.

Frejka, Tomas, and John Ross. 2001. "Paths to sub-replacement fertility: The empirical evidence." *Population and Development Review* 27(Supplement): 213–254.

Goode, William J. 1963. *World Revolution and Family Patterns*. New York: Free Press.

Goody, Jack. 1990. *The Oriental, the Ancient, and the Primitive: Systems of Marriage and the Family in the Pre-industrial Societies of Eurasia*. Cambridge: Cambridge University Press.

Hakim, Catherine. 2003. "A new approach to explaining fertility patterns: Preference theory." *Population and Development Review* 29:349–374.

Handwerker, W. Penn. 1986. "The modern demographic transition: An analysis of subsistence choices and reproductive consequences." *American Anthropologist* 88:400–417.

Harris, Marvin, and Eric B. Ross. 1987. *Death, Sex and Fertility: Population Regulation in Preindustrial and Developing Societies*. New York: Columbia University Press.

Hochschild, Arlie R. 1997. *The Time Bind: When Work Becomes Home and Home Becomes Work*. New York: Henry Holt.

International Encyclopedia of Marriage and Family. 2003. "Cohabitation." Online at www.encyclopedia.com/topic/Cohabitation.aspx.

Jankowiak, W. R., and E. F. Fisher. 1992. "A cross-cultural perspective on romantic love." *Ethnology* 31:149–155.

Kaplan, Hillard S. 1996. "A theory of fertility and parental investment in traditional and modern human societies." *Yearbook of Physical Anthropology* 39:91–135.

Kaplan, Hillard S., and Jane B. Lancaster. 2000. "The evolutionary economics and psychology of the demographic transition to low fertility." In Lee Cronk, Napoleon Chagnon, and William Irons (eds.), *Adaptation and Human Behavior: An Anthropological Perspective*. New York: Aldine de Gruyter.

Knodel, John, and Etienne van de Walle. 1979. "Lessons from the past: Policy implications of historical fertility studies." *Population and Development Review* 5:217–245.

Lasch, Christopher. 1977. *Haven in a Heartless World: The Family Besieged*. New York: Basic Books.

Laslett, Peter. 1977. *Family Life and Illicit Love in Earlier Generations*. Cambridge: Cambridge University Press.

———. 1983. "Family and household as work group and as kin group: Areas of traditional Europe compared." In Richard Wall, Jean Rodin, and Peter Laslett (eds.), *Family Forms in Historic Europe*. Cambridge: Cambridge University Press.

Laslett, Peter, and Richard Wall. 1972. *Household and Family in Past Time*. Cambridge: Cambridge University Press.

Macfarlane, Alan. 1978. *The Origins of English Individualism: The Family, Property, and Social Transition*. Oxford, UK: Basil Blackwell.

———. 1986. *Marriage and Love in England: Modes of Reproduction, 1300–1840*. Oxford, UK: Basil Blackwell.

Malhotra, Anju, Reeve Vanneman, and Sunita Kishor. 1995. "Fertility, dimensions of patriarchy, and development in India." *Population and Development Review* 21:281–305.

Murthi, Mamta, Anne-Catherine Guio, and Jean Dreze. 1995. "Mortality, fertility, and gender bias in India: A district-level analysis." *Population and Development Review* 21:745–782.

Popenoe, David. 1988. *Disturbing the Nest: Family Change and Decline in Modern Societies*. Hawthorne, NY: Aldine de Gruyter.

———. 1993. "American family decline, 1960–1990: A review and appraisal." *Journal of Marriage and the Family* 55:527–555.

Sanderson. 1995. *Social Transformations: A General Theory of Historical Development*. Oxford, UK: Blackwell.

Sanderson, Stephen K., and Joshua Dubrow. 2000. "Fertility decline in the modern world and in the original demographic transition: Testing three theories with cross-national data." *Population and Environment* 21:511–537.

Shorter, Edward. 1975. *The Making of the Modern Family*. New York: Basic Books.

Stone, Lawrence. 1979. *The Family, Sex and Marriage in England, 1500–1800*. Abr. ed. New York: Harper and Row.

Therborn. 2004. *Between Sex and Power: Family in the World, 1900–2000*. London: Routledge. Thernstrom, Stephan, and Abigail Thernstrom. 1997. *America in Black and White: One Nation, Indivisible*. New York: Simon and Schuster.

U.S. Bureau of the Census. 2012. *Statistical Abstract of the United States*. Washington, DC: US Government Printing Office.

Zaretsky, Eli. 1976. *Capitalism, the Family, and Personal Life*. New York: Harper and Row.

QUESTIONS FOR REVIEW, REFLECTION, AND DISCUSSION

1. What occurred during the transition to the modern family? How did people begin to view marriage?
2. How would you describe cohabitation trends in the United States since the 1960s?
3. How do the divorce rates of the United States compare to the divorce rates of other industrialized societies?
4. What role does labor-force participation play in shaping marriage trends? What did Andrew Cherlin suggest?
5. How does Stephanie Coontz explain changes in marriage trends? Compare her ideas to those of Andrew Cherlin.
6. Do you think that love makes marriages stronger or weaker? Why? To what degree will (or did) love play a role in your decision to marry?
7. Do you think that children are more likely to listen to and learn from their peers than their parents? Why?

ADDITIONAL READINGS

Cooke, L. P. and Baxter, J. (2010). Families in international context: Comparing institutional effects across Western societies. *Journal of Marriage and Family*, 72(3), 516–36.

Coontz, S. (2006). *Marriage, a history: How love conquered marriage*. New York, NY: Viking.

Cherlin, A. J. (2009). *The marriage-go-round: The state of marriage and the family in America today*. New York, NY: Knopf.

Lundberg, S. and Robert, P.A. (2015). The evolving role of marriage: 1950-2010. *The Future of Children*, 25(2), 29–50.

Stacey, J. (2011). *Unhitched: Love, marriage and family values from West Hollywood to Western China*. New York, NY: NYU Press.

KEY TERMS

Millennials

Gen Xers

Silent Generation

Friends with Benefits

2

WHITHER MARRIAGE

By Paul Taylor

Sixty years ago *Ladies' Home Journal* launched "Can This Marriage Be Saved?," an advice column that has become the longest-running and most widely read standing feature in magazine publishing history. Its "riveting true stories" about marriages in trouble chronicle the everyday stresses that take their toll on the world's most enduring social institution: "He's Always Obsessing About Money"; "The Holidays Make Me Crazy"; "Our Sex Life Is Stale"; "My Stepdaughter Is Ruining Our Marriage"; "We Can't Get Pregnant"; "He Told Our Secrets Online"; "Home Renovations Are Wrecking Us"; and so on. The column is a cornucopia of commonsense advice, but if its mission has been to save marriages, it has been a massive bust. Back when it launched, nearly three-quarters of all adults in the US were married. Now just half are.

Lots of particular marriages fail for lots of particular reasons. But nowadays it's the institution itself that's in big trouble. And the biggest problem isn't that people who try marriage are failing at it. It's that fewer are trying at all.

Marriage's loss of customers has occurred among all age groups, but it's most acute among Millennials. Today just 20% of adults ages 18 to 29 are married, compared with 59% in 1960. During the past half century, the median age at first marriage has risen by about six years for both men and women.

Are today's young adults abandoning marriage or merely delaying it? The weight of history would suggest the latter. In one form or another, marriage has been a social foundation upon which virtually all of the world's cultures and civilizations have been built. Institutions that have endured for thousands of years don't disappear overnight—do they?

FIGURE 2.1.

Marriage Loses Market Share, 1960–2011

% of adults 18 and older, by current marital status

Source: Pew Research Center analysis of Decennial Census (1960–2000) and American Community Survey data (2008–2011), IPUMS

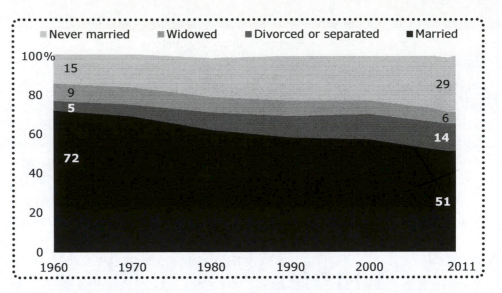

Time will tell. For now, it's notable that marriage is in retreat not just in the US but in nearly all developed (and some less developed) countries across the world. The trend is most advanced in Scandinavia, where cohabitation has for all intents and purposes replaced marriage. (But cohabiting unions there are much more durable than those in the US—so much so that a child born to cohabiting parents in Sweden has less of a chance of experiencing his or her parents' breakup than does a child born to *married* parents in the US, according to sociologist Andrew Cherlin.)

In the US, meantime, large swaths of the public—led by Millennials—express doubts about the long-term viability of the institution. In a 2010 Pew Research survey, nearly 4 in 10 (39%) Americans—and 44% of Millennials—agreed that marriage is becoming obsolete. When the same question was posed to voters by *Time* magazine back in 1978, when divorce rates were peaking, just 28% agreed.

This doesn't mean that today's young people don't want to marry. Most still do. If history is a guide, most eventually will. That same 2010 survey also found that 70% of unmarried Millennials say they would like to get married one day. So what's holding them back?

To borrow an old joke about politics: three things—money, money, and I can't remember the third. The retreat from marriage is above all a class-based phenomenon. Back in 1960, there was just a 4 percentage point gap (76% versus 72%) in marriage rates between college graduates and those with a high school diploma or less. By 2011, the gap had ballooned to 17 percentage points (63% versus 46%). The same disparities are found by income and race; over the past half century the greatest declines in marriage rates have been among minorities and those at the lower end of the income scale—categories that overlap.

It's not that people in these groups lack the motivation to marry. If anything, it's that they place marriage on too high a pedestal. The Pew Research survey found that among the unmarried, there are no differences by education or income in the desire to get married. But the survey also found that the less education and income people have, the more likely they are to say that to be a good marriage prospect, a person must be able to support a family financially. In effect, they create an economic prerequisite for marriage that they themselves can't meet.

Their doubts can be self-fulfilling. Marriage has always been associated with positive economic outcomes—not just because it's an efficient way to allocate and combine labor (yes, two can live more cheaply than one), but because the marital commitment itself tends to promote values and behaviors associated with economic success—constancy, responsibility, persistence, an inclination for pragmatic compromise. On top of that, our tax laws provide lots of benefits to married couples. When people from all walks of life get married in roughly equal shares, marriage spreads these economic and behavioral rewards in roughly equal measure up and down the socioeconomic ladder. But in a world where a disproportionate share of those who tie the knot enter marriage already enjoying the head start of a good education and healthy economic prospects, it's easy to see how the marriage gap and the income gap reinforce each other. That's exactly what has been happening for decades.

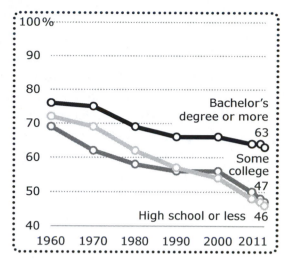

FIGURE 2.2.

Share Married, by Educational Attainment

% of adults 18 and older

Source: Pew Research Center analysis of Decennial Census (1960–2000) and American Community Survey data (2008–2011), IPUMS

Demographers estimate that 8 in 10 adults will eventually marry, but the typical American today spends less of his or her adult life in a marriage than at any time in modern history—and a record 28% of all US households are now headed by a single person. Marriage, in short, has lost its cultural hegemony. It was once the mandated path to adulthood; it's now a lifestyle choice.

The shift is most visible among Millennials, who value marriage somewhat less than the next youngest adult generation, the Gen Xers, did back when they were the age Millennials are now. Just 30% of Millennials say having a successful marriage is one of the most important things in life. Back in 1997, 35% of Gen Xers felt that way about marriage. And there's an even bigger disparity between the two generations in their views of parenthood—but that one runs in the opposite direction. Some 52% of Millennials say being a good parent is one of the most important things in life, compared with 42% of Gen Xers who said the same back when they were the age Millennials are now.

Our entertainment culture mirrors and reinforces these changes. In the first several decades of television, the family sitcom ruled the ratings roost. All of the iconic shows— *Ozzie and Harriet, Leave It to Beaver, My Three Sons, Father Knows Best, The Cosby Show,* etc.—revolved around the foibles of everyday life in a tight-knit nuclear family. Dad was both the authority figure and the butt of endless jokes about his clumsiness in matters of the heart and hearth. But the humor was always loving, and it was impossible to miss the meta-message: people, this is how you're supposed to live!

In more recent times, television has done an about-face on marriage. With the excep tion of the hilariously dysfunctional *Simpsons,* it has been a long time since a happily married nuclear television family grabbed and held the prime-time zeitgeist. Instead television has served up a steady diet of relationship shows, buddy shows, and parenthood shows—*Friends, Seinfeld, Sex and the City, Desperate Housewives, The Good Wife, Two and a Half Men, Parenthood.* When marriage appears at all on the small screen, it's usually as a bridge too far, a cautionary tale, or a full-on calamity.

One need not sentimentalize marriage. The good old Ozzie and Harriet marriages included a lot of relationships that were loveless, or worse. In the days when adults felt overwhelming social pressure to get and stay married, the rate of domestic violence within marriage was an estimated 30% higher than now.[1] And while the great majority of 1950s-era wives never faced that sort of abuse, many felt trapped in other ways. The women's liberation movement drew much of its energy from women who wanted more from life than a wife-as-homemaker marriage.

Half a century later, adults of both genders have their doubts that a person needs to be married to lead a fulfilling life. A 2010 Pew Research survey asked respondents whether they thought it was easier for a married person or a single person to find happiness. About 3 in 10 (29%) said it was easier for married people while just 5% said it was easier for single people. But a sizable majority—62%—said it makes no difference. Even among married people, a majority said marriage has no bearing on one's prospects for happiness.

These findings are notable for a couple of reasons beyond their decidedly lukewarm embrace of the joys of married life. One is a big gender disparity. Some 38% of men say it's easier to find happiness as a married person, compared with just 22% of women—providing some data underpinnings to the folk wisdom and social science that say marriage is a better deal for men than women.

Even more intriguing, however, is that the public appears to be undervaluing the contribu-tion marriage makes to happiness. Pew Research surveys often begin by asking respondents, "Generally, how would you say things are these days in your life—would you say you are very happy, pretty happy, or not too happy?" In the survey profession, this is known as a door-opener question; its main goal is to get respondents comfortable with doing the interview. But because there's quite a cottage industry these days in happiness research, the responses have value in their own right, especially since we can deconstruct the nationwide sample to analyze the various correlates of happiness.

It turns out that happiness and marriage make a great couple. In one recent survey, 36% of married people say they are very happy, while just 22% of unmarried people say the same. These results rarely vary by more than a few percentage points from survey to survey. But they should be kept in perspective. Marriage is correlated with other traits that are also correlated with happiness—such as high income, religiosity, and good health. In other words, the kind of people inclined to be married are the kind of people inclined to be happy.

However, this still leaves open the possibility that marriage in and of itself also helps in life's happiness sweepstakes. One way to test that proposition is through a statistical technique known as regression analysis, which measures the strength of the linkage between a variable of interest (in this case, marriage) and an outcome of interest (in this case, happiness), while holding all other variables constant. Our regression analysis finds that, all else equal, marriage increases one's likelihood of being very happy—by 12%. That might not sound like much. But consider: Gender, race, ethnicity, education and age are among the many characteristics that have no independent statistical impact whatsoever on a person's likelihood of being very happy. Marriage is among a small circle of traits—including good health, high income, and strong religious observance—for which there is an independent impact.

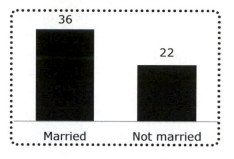

FIGURE 2.3.

Is Marriage Bliss?
% "very happy" by marital status

Source: Pew Research Center survey, Nov. 2012, N=12, 511 US adults

The irony, of course, is that the very public that affirms a link between marriage and happiness doesn't seem to be reading its own memos. Marriage helps make people happier, yet fewer people are marrying. Why?

WHY IS MARRIAGE IN RETREAT?

Most theories about the decline of marriage start with the impact of structural changes to the economy. The most important of these—the movement of women in the workforce—undid the equilibrium of the male breadwinner/female homemaker template for marriage that had prevailed since the industrial era. At the same time, the development of a postindustrial, knowledge-based economy has diminished the job prospects and earning power of less-educated men, creating a "marriage market mismatch" at the lower end of the socioeconomic scale. In the old marriage marketplace, a woman needed a husband for financial security. In the new marriage marketplace, fewer women have that need, and fewer men can cater to it.

Other theories focus on the more intimate realms of marriage. Until not too long ago, marriage was the only socially and morally acceptable gateway to sexual partnerships. The introduction of the birth control pill in the early 1960s helped to pry much of this regulatory authority over sex away from marriage. Adultery remains a taboo, but in an era of "friends with benefits," sex among unmarried or never-married adults carries little if any stigma. This has complicated the case for marriage—and not just because sexual desires can now be respectably accommodated without lifetime commitments, but also because it has increased the demand on marriage to provide something even more precious than sex. More so than ever, people want a spouse to be their lifelong companion, emotional soul mate, partner in the journey toward self-fulfillment. Marriage, in a word, is supposed to be built on love.

But as social historian Stephanie Coontz has observed, love may be the undoing of marriage.[2] At the very least, it has injected an unstable element into the suddenly fragile heart of an age-old institution. For most of its 5,000-year history, marriage had little to do with love. Across cultures and centuries, it thrived as a way to propagate the species; establish people's place in the social and economic order; acquire in-laws; organize productive activity along gender lines; extract labor from the young; and distribute resources from parents to children. Only in the eighteenth century, with the spread of market economies and the Enlightenment, did love and mutual self-fulfillment start to enter into marital bargain. Today, arguably, they're the dominant part. But love can be fickle and self-fulfillment a high bar. Can an institution built on love be as durable as one built on the stouter stuff of economic self-interest? As a society, we're conducting that experiment right now. So far, the answer appears to be no.

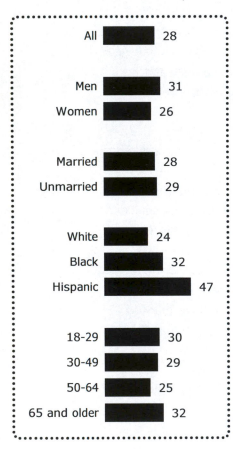

FIGURE 2.4.

Only One True Love?

% who agree

Source: Pew Research Center, Oct. 2010, N=2, 691 US adults

In the middle of the twentieth century, the anti-Nazi German theologian Dietrich Bonhoeffer sent a congratulatory letter to some newlyweds of his acquaintance. It contained an aphorism about marriage that reflected an old-fashioned view of the institution. "It is not your love that sustains the marriage," he wrote, "but from now on, the marriage that sustains your love." Today one would be hard-pressed to find that sentiment expressed anywhere in Western literature or culture. "If you were to write the same letter to newlyweds now, I don't think they'd have a clue what you were talking about," said David Blanken-horn, founder and president of the Institute for American Values, a nonpartisan think tank whose mission, among others, is to try to restore what he calls the "fractured" institution of marriage.

Other groups have also taken up that challenge, but their contributions so far have been mainly in the realm of diagnosis, not cure. A 2013 research paper, "Knot Yet: The Benefits and Costs of Delayed Marriage," did a wonderful job showing how young adults view marriage as a "capstone" rather than "cornerstone" arrangement—"something they do after they have all their other ducks in a row, rather than a foundation for launching into adulthood and parenthood."[3] Given this new cultural framework for marriage, it's no surprise that it's the high-achieving young adults who are most likely to get hitched. "Marriage has become a status symbol," writes Cherlin, "a highly regarded marker of a successful personal life. . . . Something young adults do after they and their live-in partners have good jobs and a nice apartment."[4] He noted that in 2012, according to a study by *Brides* magazine, 36% of newlyweds paid the entire cost of their wedding receptions, and an additional 26% contributed to the cost.

THE STIGMA OF SINGLE PARENTHOOD

As marriage rates have declined, the reaction of the American public for the most part has been a do-your-own-thing shrug of acceptance. That's not the case, however, for the most important consequence of the decline in marriage—the sharp rise in births outside of marriage. Of all the structural changes on the marriage and family front in recent decades, this one has drawn the most negative reaction by far from the public.

In 2011, 41% of all births in the US were to unmarried mothers, up from just 5% in 1960. Many might assume this has been driven by a surge in teenage births. To the contrary, the teen birthrate (births per 1,000 women ages 15 to 19) in the US today has dropped by more than 60% from its peak in 1957; it is now at the lowest level since the US government started tracking such data in 1940. As recently as 1990, teenage girls accounted for more births in the US than did women ages 35 and older. Now the reverse is true. Teenage mothers today give birth to about 10% of all babies, and 18% of babies born outside of marriage. They may or may not be having more sex than their same-age counterparts of previous generations, but thanks to the widespread use of contraception, they're having fewer kids.

So then, who's having children out of wedlock? Mostly, women in their 20s and 30s. Until not too long ago, marriage and parenthood were linked milestones on the journey to adulthood. And if they happened out of sequence—that is, if a single woman got pregnant—a "shotgun wedding" was the culturally prescribed remedy. This custom now seems quaint. Nowadays an estimated 6 in 10 single mothers have live-in boyfriends when they give birth, about double the rate among unmarried mothers a generation ago. However, these cohabiting unions tend to be of short duration—only about half survive until the child's 5th birthday.

Nonmarital births have also soared in many of the world's other developed countries, for many of the same reasons. But the US is an outlier in its combination of high nonmarital birthrates, high divorce rates, and high turnover in cohabiting relationships. As a result of all these trends, Cherlin says that a teenager in the US has a smaller likelihood than a teenager in any other country in the world of living in a household with both biological parents.

A large body of social science research shows that, on average and controlling for other factors, children have better outcomes in life if raised by both parents than if raised by just one. They are healthier, do better academically, get into less trouble as adolescents, are less likely to drop out of high school or become teenage parents, are less prone to substance abuse or criminal behavior, and are more successful in their jobs and careers.[5]

Policy experts of all ideological stripes accept these findings—and so, as we'll see in a moment, does the public. Yet the topic of single parenthood gets very little public attention these days. It has been politically and racially fraught for decades, ever since Daniel Patrick Moynihan penned the controversial 1965 report "The Negro Family: The Case for National Action." Moynihan, who went on to become UN Ambassador, a US senator from New York, and one of the nation's leading public intellectuals, was at the time a young assistant secretary of labor in the Johnson administration, which was pressing ahead with its ambitious civil rights agenda and its "War on Poverty." Moynihan's thesis was that progress toward racial equality

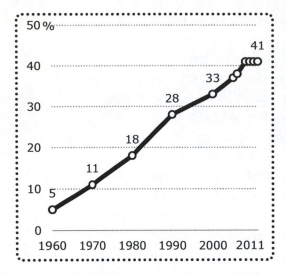

FIGURE 2.5.

Share of Births to
Unmarried Women,
1960–2011

Source: National Center for
Health Statistics data

would be held back because so many black children were being raised by single mothers. He argued that such families were a by-product not just of the "tangle of pathologies" in poor communities, but of a matriarchal family culture among blacks that traced its roots to slavery.

Critics denounced the report for what they deemed its "blame-the-victim" take on poverty and racial inequality; supporters welcomed it as an unvarnished dose of truth. The Johnson administration went ahead and ramped up funding for Aid to Families with Dependent Children, a welfare program that provided cash support to poor single mothers. But the program quickly became a lightning rod for conservatives who said it created incentives for nonmarital motherhood and promoted a culture of dependence. Ronald Reagan, among many others, inveighed against "welfare queens" to good effect on the campaign trail. In 1996 President Bill Clinton joined with a Republican- controlled Congress to kill AFDC and enact a stripped-down replacement, a move that has taken much of the toxicity out of the political debate over welfare policies. Since then, the national conversation about single parenthood has pretty much disappeared.

But single parenthood itself hasn't. Indeed, what's notable about this brief retrospective are the data that attracted Moynihan's notice in 1965. He sounded the alarm because the out-of-wedlock birthrate among blacks had risen to an estimated 25%. Half a century later, the rate is 72%. Among Latinos, the rate is 53%. Among whites, 29%. What once seemed shocking has become mainstream. Perhaps that's why it draws so little public attention. Or perhaps it's that elites—mindful of the stir the Moynihan report triggered decades ago—find the whole subject to be uncomfortable. "I know of no other set of important findings [about the poor outcomes of children raised by single parents] that are as broadly accepted by social scientists . . . and yet are so resolutely ignored by network news programs, editorial writers for the major newspapers, and politicians of both political parties," wrote conservative scholar Charles Murray in his 2012 book, *Coming Apart.*[6]

The overall verdict from the public about the rise of single parenthood is an emphatic thumbs down. Asked in 2010 whether each of seven demographic changes affecting the composition of families were good or bad for society, 69% said the rise in single women having children was bad, while just 4% said it was good—by far the most negative reading on any of the trends. In 2013, when the question was asked in a slightly different form, 64% said the rising number of children born to unmarried mothers was a big problem for society, 19% said it was a small problem, and 13% said it was not a problem.

However, there are some notable generational differences in these attitudes. Among adults ages 50 and older, 74% say unwed motherhood is a big problem; among adults

18 to 29, just 42% say the same. Along these same lines, a majority of the public (61%) believes that a child is more likely to grow up happy in a home with both a mother and a father, but there are generational differences here too. Silent Generation adults are more likely than Millennials (75% versus 53%) to say this. Also, men are more likely than women (67% versus 54%) to feel this way. And more Hispanics (72%) and blacks (65%) say this than do whites (57%)—more evidence that when it comes to single parenthood, attitudes and behaviors do not always move in sync with one another.

Nonmarital births aren't the only reason more children are being raised by single parents. Divorce has become much more prevalent over the past half century, though rates have declined somewhat in recent decades after peaking in the 1970s and 1980s. Most experts trace the divorce explosion to the same mix of economic and cultural factors that have produced the delayed marriage phenomenon: if marriage is supposed to be mainly about finding love and self-actualization, it's a destination that some share of the married population won't be able to reach.

Divorce is never a happy outcome, but Americans cast a much less disapproving eye on it than they do on nonmarital births. A majority (58%) of the public says that divorce is preferable to maintaining an unhappy marriage, and an even bigger majority—67%—says that if a marriage is very unhappy, the children are better off when the parents get divorced.

Contrary to public perceptions, divorce rates have been declining for several decades. Part of this is simple math: people can't divorce if they don't marry. But rates of divorce have also declined somewhat among married couples. This is likely related to the changing demographics of marriage. Divorce rates have always been highest among couples who marry young and couples at the lower end of the socioeconomic scale. There are fewer of those marriages now. And so as marriage has become more confined to the land of the "haves," divorce has receded.

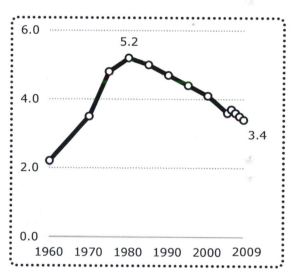

FIGURE 2.6.

Trend in Divorce Rate, 1960–2009

Number of divorces per 1,000 population

Source: US Department of Commerce, *Statistical Abstract of the United States: 2012*, published 2011

GRAY DIVORCE

At the same time, however, there has been a sharp rise in "gray divorce"—a Boomer-driven phenomenon exemplified by the breakup in 2010 of the 40-year marriage of former vice president Al Gore and his wife, Tipper. A half century ago, only 2.8% of adults older than age 50 were divorced; by 2011, that share had risen to 15.4%. For the first time in history, more Americans ages 50 and older are divorced than widowed (13.5%).[7]

Family scholar Susan L. Brown has done research showing that divorce has been migrating north on the age pyramid for several decades. Just 1 in 10 people who got divorced in 1990 were ages 50 or older, she reports; now more than 1 in 4 new divor-cees are in that age group. Boomers have been at the heart of the divorce explosion throughout all phases of their adult lives. Forty years ago they tended to marry young and divorce young. Now they're more likely than previous generations to divorce later in life (in part because their remarriages are at a relatively high risk of ending in divorce). Given all this, Brown finds that that 1 in 3 Boomers are currently single—which leaves many of them economically and socially vulnerable on the cusp of old age.[8]

But gray divorce may also be a by-product of more positive social trends—for example, advances in the quality of life of older adults and changes in women's roles, opportunities, and expectations. "The extension of the active, healthy life span is a big part of this," said Coontz. "If you are a healthy 65, you can expect another pretty healthy 20 years. So with the kids gone, it seems more burdensome to stay in a bad relationship, or even one that has gone stale." Most divorces among older adults, as among younger adults, are initiated by women, leading Coontz to observe: "Another big factor is that with their increased work experience and greater sense of their own possibilities, [women] are less willing to just 'wait it out.' We expect to find equality, intimacy, friendship, fun and even passion right into what people used to see as the 'twilight years.'"[9]

WHAT'S A FAMILY?

As marriage has receded, family forms have changed. Back when *Ladies' Home Journal* launched its advice column, the preeminent family unit of the mid-twentieth century—mom, dad, and the kids—pretty much had the stage to itself. No longer. Families now come in all shapes, sizes, and constellations: single parent, multigen-erational, same sex, different race, step, blended, tangled.

Given the breadth and sweep of these changes, it's reasonable to ask: Just who belongs in the family album these days and who doesn't? As Figure 2.7 shows, a majority considers most of the constellations discussed in this chapter to be a family.

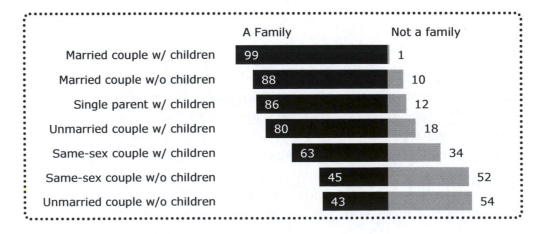

FIGURE 2.7.

Is This a Family?

% saying each grouping

is ...

Note: Question wording: "As I read you a list of different arrangements, please tell me whether you consider each to be a family or not?"

Source: Pew Research Center survey, Oct. 2010, N=2, 691 US adults

Not surprisingly, traditional marriage and parenthood top the list. However, the public is also ready to confer family status on groupings it doesn't always approve of. For example, nearly 9 in 10 say a single parent with a child is a family, and more than 6 in 10 say the same about a same-sex couple raising a child. Younger adults are more expansive than older adults with all of these definitions. Thus, the broader boundaries of family would seem to be both culturally and demographically ascendant.

But that doesn't mean all relatives are created equal. In 2010, Pew Research did a survey in which we asked people how obligated they would feel to provide either financial help or care-giving to a relative who had a serious problem. (Each respondent was asked only about the category of relative he or she has, as determined by questions asked earlier in the survey.)

Obviously, these are highly individual matters, but as Figure 2.8 illustrates, some overall patterns emerge. The biblical injunction to honor thy mother and father hasn't been lost on the American public: parents top the list (we didn't ask about young children because we took it as a given that everyone would say they are obligated to help them). From there the rankings descended in a crisp stair-step pattern: grown child, grandparent, sibling, in-law. Steprelatives don't fare as well as biological relatives. But all rank above "your best friend"—which was the lone nonrelative on the list.

All of this suggests that in the face of massive social and demographic change, kinship is still a preeminent element of people's lives. Yes, the institution of marriage is in retreat; yes, the makeup of families is changing; and yes, the public disapproves of the decoupling of marriage and parenthood. But through it all, family remains the center of most people's universe.

Three-quarters of adults say their family is the most important element of their lives. There are very few differences by demographic group. And when asked about the future of the institution of marriage and family in this country, two-thirds say they are optimistic—again, with little variance in responses by age, race, or gender. That same question tested the public's optimism about other key institutions, values, and behaviors that impact the nation's well- being. None rose to the level of family and marriage.

However, the public's upbeat view of the future of marriage finds few takers in the community of scholars and policy advocates who track its faltering fortunes. "I suspect marriage as we have known it is not coming back," writes Isabel V. Sawhill of the Brookings Institution.[11] Social commentator Kay S. Hymowitz concurs, noting that even if a national movement to take up the challenge of restoring marriage were to somehow

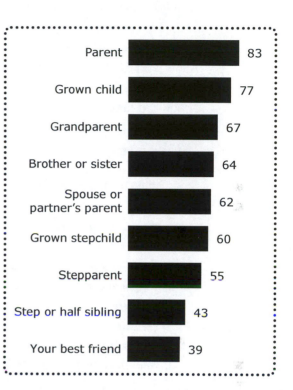

Parent	83
Grown child	77
Grandparent	67
Brother or sister	64
Spouse or partner's parent	62
Grown stepchild	60
Stepparent	55
Step or half sibling	43
Your best friend	39

FIGURE 2.8.

Ranking the Relatives

% who say they feel "very obligated" to provide needed financial assistance or caregiving to their ...

Note: Each respondent was asked only about relatives he or she has. Question wording: "Suppose someone you know had a serious problem and needed either financial help or caregiving. How obligated would you feel to provide assistance if that person were your [NAME ON LIST]: Would you feel very obligated, somewhat obligated, not too obligated or not at all obligated?"

Source: Per Research Center survey, Oct. 2010, N=2,691 US adults

emerge, "the policy levers are few."[12] At a subdued Brookings symposium in 2013 built around the "Knot Yet" report, Douthat of the *New York Times* struck the closest thing to a hopeful note. He pointed out that over the past several decades, as family instability has grown, many of the dire social consequences that were presumed to be an inevitable by-product—youth crime, high school dropouts, teen pregnancy, etc.—have ameliorated rather than worsened. "[The decline of marriage] may have a negative impact on human flourishing," he said, "but it hasn't dragged us into the kind of abyss that scolds and conservatives usually like to threaten people with." That's not exactly a ringing endorsement of the status quo, but it's a useful reminder of the resilience of the human spirit and human institutions. Looking ahead, as the Boomers grow older and the social safety net grows smaller, that resilience will be put to the test as the nation struggles to figure out how best to care for its elderly at a time when a growing share will have fractured families to which they are only loosely attached.

ENDNOTES

1. See Stephanie Coontz, *The Way We Never Were: American Families and the Nostalgia Trap* (New York: Basic Books, 1993).
2. See Stephanie Coontz, *Marriage, A History: How Love Conquered Marriage* (New York: Penguin Books, 2005).
3. Kay Hymowitz et al., "Knot Yet," the National Marriage Project at the University of Virginia, the National Campaign to Prevent Teen and Unplanned Pregnancy, and the Relate Institute, 2013.
4. Andrew Cherlin, "In the Season of Marriage, a Question: Why Bother?" *New York Times,* April 27, 2013.
5. For a summary of findings in this field, see the chapter on marriage (Chapter 8) in Charles Murray, *Coming Apart* (New York: Crown Forum, 2012).
6. Ibid., p. 158.
7. Sam Roberts, "Divorce after 50 Grows More Common," *New York Times,* September 20, 2013.
8. Susan L. Brown, "A 'Gray Divorce' Boom," *Los Angeles Times,* March 31, 2013.
9. Coontz was quoted in "Divorce after 50 Grows More Common," by Sam Roberts, *New York Times,* September 20, 2013.
10. Ross Douthat, "Marriage Looks Different Now," *New York Times,* March 30, 2013.
11. Isabel V. Sawhill, "Restoring Marriage Will Be Difficult," Brookings Institution, December 20, 2012.
12. Quoted at a Brooking Institution symposium, March 2013.

QUESTIONS FOR REVIEW, REFLECTION, AND DISCUSSION

1. Who is having children out of wedlock?
2. What was "Aid to Families with Dependent Children"? What happened to that program?
3. How do you feel about single women having children? Why do you feel that way?
4. This chapter mentions Dr. Susan L. Brown and Dr. Isabel V. Sawhill. Do a little investigative work and find out who they are. What do they study/research? What have they written about over the past few years?

ADDITIONAL READINGS

Hill, H. D. 2007. Steppin' out: Infidelity and sexual jealousy. In *Unmarried couples with children*, eds. Kathryn Edin and Paula England, 104–32. New York, NY: Russell Sage Foundation.

Lundberg, S., Pollak, R.A., & Stearns, J.E. (2016). Family inequality: Diverging patterns in marriage, cohabitation, and childbearing. National Bureaus of Economic Research (NBER) Working Paper 22078. NBER Working Paper Series.

Martinez, G. M., Daniels, K. & Chandra, A. (2012). Fertility of men and women aged 15–44 years in the United States: National survey of family growth, 2006–2010. *National Health Statistics Reports* 51. Hyattsville, MD: National Center for Health Statistics.

McLanahan, S., & Sawhill, I. (2015). Marriage and child wellbeing revisited: Introducing the issue. *The Future of Children*, 25(2), 3–9.

KEY TERMS

Fertility

Fecundity

Latent Fertility Regulation

Manifest Fertility Regulation

Contraception

Abortion

Abstinence

Hysterectomy

Ovariectomy

Vasectomy

Relinquishment

Adoption

Polygyny

3

POPULATION AND FAMILY PLANNING

By Gene H. Starbuck and Karen
Saucier Lundy

PRELUDE

Mitra, 10, lives in Calcutta, India. She was the fourth of six surviving children who live with their aging mother and father. They belong to a laboring caste, and her father is not able to work as hard as he used to. Although Mitra gets hungry sometimes, her family usually has enough rice to eat, and they are able to pay the rent on their two-room apartment.

Mitra is usually happy. She likes playing with the other children in the neighborhood. She is glad she is not in the untouchable caste, and she hopes that next time she will be born to a Brahmin, the upper caste.

When Mitra's oldest brother got married and he and his wife had a baby, the apartment seemed too crowded. But she was unhappy when they moved out; she misses having the baby around. She wants lots of children when she grows up and hopes that her father will find her a good man to marry.

Mitra has heard about places where only a few people live and where married couples only have one or two children. Mitra can't understand how people could live like that. Maybe they had done something horrible in their last life.

Are you as influenced by your social context as is Mitra?

This chapter provides information about reproduction, society, and individual choice. It will also mention the host of new technologies available today and the challenge to our social and personal values and norms raised by the technological changes.

In 2006, the fertility rate in this crowded Tunisian City is 1.74 per woman. In India, it is 2.73, and in the United States it is 2.09 per woman. In many sub-Saharan African countries, the rate varies from 4 to more than 7 per woman.

Thinking Ahead How many children would you like to have? Why? What social forces have affected this very personal decision of yours? Would adopting a child serve the same purposes for you as having a biological offspring? Why, why not? Is finding someone with similar views on these issues important in your mate-selection decisions?

Our sociological imagination would help us place ourselves in a particular sexual script at a particular time. It would help us see that even such a personal thing as how many children we would like to have is affected by the society in which we live. In turn, the number of children we, collectively, give birth to significantly affects our society.

In this chapter, we will first look at the issue of reproduction from a macrosocial level in terms of forces that affect population growth and control. We will then cover the methods available today either to reduce fertility or to increase the chances of having a child. The chapter ends with an introduction to some of the legal, moral, and ethical issues involved with family planning.

CULTURE AND REPRODUCTIVE REGULATION

Fertility: Actual number of births to a woman.

Fecundity: A biological potential of lifetime childbearing.

As macrolevel measures of reproduction, the **fertility** rate is the actual number of births while **fecundity** is a potential. Rarely does the fertility rate approach the fecundity rate, although it comes close among some groups. The Hutterites, a communal religious group in the northern Great Plains of the United States and in southern

Alberta, Canada, have approached the maximum reproduction rate. In 1954, Eaton and Mayer found that Hutterite women between 45 and 54 years of age had averaged 10.6 children per woman. Only for short periods of time have entire societies maintained such high fertility rates.

Preindustrial societies tended to have lifetime fertility levels of 6 or 7 children per woman, well below the fecundity rate (Haub & Riche, 1994). Both conscious and nonconscious birth control practices limited the actual number of offspring. The unconscious, or hidden, practices that lower fertility rates constitute **latent fertility regulation.** Practices used with the conscious purposes of limiting fertility are referred to as **manifest fertility regulation.**

LATENT FERTILITY REGULATION

Family formation norms are one form of latent fertility regulation. Polygyny, for example, may tend to reduce overall fertility rates because each married women would be less likely to have sexual intercourse as often (Hern, 1991). Polygyny was not instituted for the purpose of reducing fertility, so that is an example of latent fertility regulation.

Marital economic exchanges and age at first marriage also affect fertility rates. It takes time to accumulate a dowry or bridewealth. Some families are never able to accumulate enough to provide their offspring enough wealth to afford the marriage. When that was combined with a sexual morality that prohibited nonmarital sexual intercourse, lowered fertility for the society resulted. Even when a couple did marry, the average age at first marriage would be relatively old. This would reduce the number of children a woman would have in a lifetime. Societies with higher divorce rates also tend to have lower fertility rates, especially where remarriage rates are low (Clark, 1992).

Norms that make sexual intercourse forbidden at various times can lower the fertility rate. Many societies have had taboos about having sexual relations when women are breast feeding. While breast-feeding itself provided some contraceptive protection, the taboo would further reduce the odds of conception. This increased the time that would pass before a woman would have another child and, hence, lower her lifetime fertility.

Throughout the Middle Ages, bishops and popes in the Catholic Church, while generally pronatalist, imposed several temporal bans on sexual intercourse. Christians were to abstain during Lent, the 40 days before Easter; during Advent, the four weeks before Christmas; on various Ember Days; on Sundays, the Lord's Days; and on Fridays (Kissling, 1994). Couples who followed all these rules would abstain about 180 days each year—almost half of the year.

Latent forms of fertility control have always affected fertility rates. So have other factors, such as maternal death rates and the supply of nutritional requirements. While these were all unintentional, some actions were taken specifically to affect population levels.

Latent fertility regulation: Cultural practices that affect fertility without conscious intent by individuals.

Manifest fertility regulation: Practices used by persons with the conscious intent of affecting fertility.

MANIFEST FERTILITY CONTROL

Individuals in most societies have practiced various forms of manifest fertility control, or family planning. Some practices were designed to increase fertility; many cultures have potions, spells, prayers, charms, rituals, saints, or other customs to which individuals could turn when children were desired. Other practices were designed to limit fertility. For the most part, neither fertility-enhancement nor fertility-limiting practices were extremely effective until modern times.

Although the discovery of sperm and its exact part in conception did not occur until the late 17th century, earlier human groups recognized that sexual intercourse and semen were somehow necessary for procreation. This knowledge was applied in several ways in attempts to prevent conception. Egyptian sources, from as long ago as 1850 BC, describe vaginal plugs of honey, gum acacia, and crocodile dung (Fathalla, 1994). The acidity of the mixture probably had some spermicidal effect, and the plug would operate like the modern sponge in both absorbing sperm and acting as a barrier.

Coitus interruptus: The practice of attempting to prevent conception in which the penis is withdrawn from the vagina before ejaculation.

Coitus interruptus is a very old form of birth control. This and many other methods had at least some effectiveness, and their availability meant that there was some desire, especially among women, to regulate fertility. Abortion and infanticide have also long been used for fertility regulation (Daly & Wilson, 1984; Tannahill, 1980).

While family planning decisions are personal, social forces such as modes of production influence the decisions made by individuals and couples. In less industrialized countries, pronatalist attitudes remain prominent. This has implications for the entire world as concern grows about overpopulation and environmental depletion.

DEMOGRAPHIC TRANSITION THEORY

Editorial Commentary: Gerhard E. Lenski (1924-2015) was a Professor of Sociology at the University of North Carolina-Chapel Hill. He wrote, *Power & Privilege: A Theory of Social Stratification* (1966) and *Ecological-Evolutionary Theory: Principles and Applications* (2005). Jean Lenski died in 1994.
Gerhard Lenski, Jean Lenski, and Patrick Nolan co-authored the book *Human Societies: An Introduction to Macrosociology*. Later editions of that book were written by Patrick and Gerhard.

Thomas Robert Malthus is sometimes called the father of demography. He was born in 1776, as the industrial revolution dawned. Already productivity was increasing, and many social analysts were optimistic about improvements in the human condition. Not so Mr. Malthus. In his "Essay on the Principle of Population," he argued that a society's ability to produce children will always exceed the society's ability to increase the production of food and other products necessary for survival. As a consequence, overpopulation would always be a problem, and wars, disease, and starvation would be a permanent part of human life (Elwell, 1999).

Malthus's pessimistic essay was published in 1798 and went through seven editions, each one using more mathematics to prove his point. His argument was an influence on much of early demography and on the ecological-evolutionary theories of the Lenskis (Elwell, 1999). His perspective is also echoed by Paul Ehrlich (1976; 1997) and others who today are concerned about the "population explosion."

Later demographers began to develop more sophisticated analyses. The initial version of a theory of demographic transition was advanced in 1929 by Warren Thompson. He suggested that the more industrialized nations were able to increase their production fast enough to keep up with increasing populations but that the rest of the world was likely to remain in the conditions predicted by Malthus.

Several versions of a theory of demographic transition were later developed. All used the two basic facts of birth rates and death rates to determine overall population levels (see Figure 3.1). European nations had gone through three stages of economic development; the suggestion is that other societies, too, might go through the same process.

In the primary economic stage, all productive activity was directed toward providing basic necessities like food and shelter. This stage included hunting-gathering and agricultural modes of production. In these societies, there was a precarious balance between birth rates and death rates, both of which were high. Population levels were low and unstable for some groups. Agricultural societies were generally able to support a larger population than hunting-gathering ones, but at the global level, populations were relatively sparse and constant for most of human history.

Because of the constant threat that a society would die out if death rates exceeded birthrates for any significant period, successful agrarian societies became quite pronatalist. This value was espoused in the major world religions. Christianity, Judaism, Islam, and Hinduism all have mechanisms to encourage families to have large numbers of children. Commands such as "be fruitful and multiply" developed in the primary stage.

In the secondary economic stage, increasing amounts of productive activities were directed toward manufacturing. In Western Europe, the death rate began to fall in about 1750, which roughly coincides with the beginning of the industrial revolution

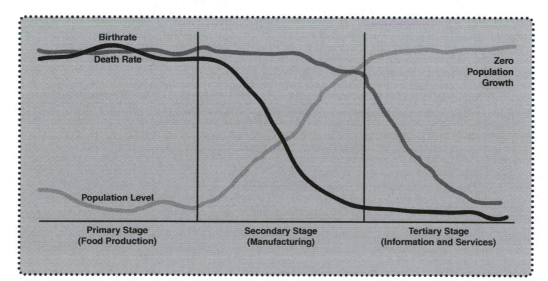

FIGURE 3.1.

Theory of Demographic Transition

Source: Suggested by Thompson, Warren. 1929. "Population," *American Journal of Sociology* 34(6): 959–75 and Handwerker, W. Penn. 1986. "Culture and Reproduction: Exploringt Micro & Macro LInkages." Pp. 1–29 in *Culture and Reproduction: An Anthropological Critique of Demographic Transition Theory*, edited by W. Penn Handwerker, Boulder, CO: Westview Press.

(Handwerker, 1986). Increased productivity provided better nutrition, and urban areas began to provide more sanitary living conditions.

In the next century, great strides were made in preventative medicine by such scientists as Louis Pasteur (1822–1895). The germ theory of disease replaced older ideas about what caused sickness. Widespread vaccines against smallpox, polio, and other killers followed over the next half century. The United States and other nations required that milk be pasteurized to prevent the spread of disease. Penicillin and other antibiotics were developed.

The germ theory of disease also lead to better sanitation systems in the major cities. Sewer systems were installed or improved, and concerted efforts were made to get rid of the conditions that bred rats, fleas, and other carriers of disease. In addition, nutrition and working conditions were improved.

These changes accelerated the drop in death rates while birthrates remained relatively high. A population explosion resulted. Between the time Malthus wrote and the beginning of World War I in the 20th century, the population of the United Kingdom grew from 10 million to 42 million. Had it not been for the mass migrations of millions to the Americas and elsewhere in the world, Europe might not have been able to increase its production enough to feed its growing population (Haub & Riche, 1994).

In about 1850, and considerably earlier in some parts of Europe, the fertility rate began to decline. In the 20th century, with the exception of the baby boom, the gradual decline continued. Several factors played a part. More and more people needed increasing numbers of years of formal education; this resulted in postponed marriages for many. Since they got married later, these women would have fewer children in a lifetime. Separation of women and men in the workforce and increasing numbers of women working outside the home played a part. The institutionalization of social security and other retirement plans reduced the necessity of the elderly to rely on large numbers of children to support them.

Perhaps the most important contributor to the decline in fertility rates was the fact that, especially in the cities, having children became a net economic cost, rather than a net labor benefit. On farms and ranches, children could begin to be economically productive at a fairly young age. This was not true in the cities, especially after the passage of child labor laws. Children still needed clothes, food, and school supplies; once they became self-supporting, they moved out of their parents' home.

Also, the drop in infant mortality meant that children were more likely to survive to adulthood, so fewer births were required to produce the same number of adult children. Increasingly wanting to limit their family size, couples used the technology available to do so. Fertility levels in Europe dropped from 7–10 lifetime births per woman, in early 19th century, to 2–4 by 1950 (Handwerker, 1986).

By the arrival of the tertiary economic stage, with economic activity focused on information and services, population growth had leveled off in most of the highly industrialized societies. Some countries have now apparently reached a point of zero population growth. This requires a prolonged period of time at replacement level, or about two children per couple.

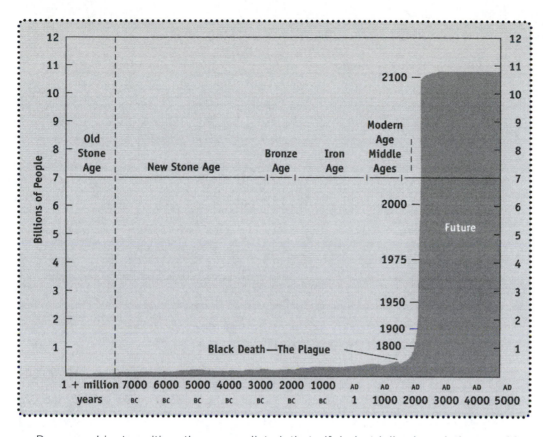

FIGURE 3.2.

World Population
Growth through
History

Source: Population
Reference Bureau; and
United Nations, *World
Population Projections
to 2100.*

Demographic transition theory predicted that, if industrialized societies would help the rest of the world to become more industrialized, other countries would go through the same kind of demographic transition. For a variety of reasons, however, many demographers now question that assumption (Cole, 1973; Handwerker, 1986; Goldscheider, 1992; Mazur, 1994).

At a global level, the world is still in the midst of a population explosion. In the thousands of years of human habitation of the earth, the total population did not reach 1 billion persons until about 1800. It reached 1.6 billion by 1900 and grew even more rapidly after that, reaching 2.5 billion in 1950 (Haub & Riche, 1994). World population now stands at 7.0 billion (Haub & Yanagishita, 2005). It is projected to reach 8.2 billion by 2025 (Haub & Yanagishita, 1996). Although birthrates have fallen in most of the countries of the world, they have not yet fallen to replacement level (see Figure 3.2).

If the world's population continues to grow at the present rate, it will double in 58 years. That growth, however will not be uniform throughout the world. Europe as a whole has stopped growing. **Doubling time** will be 116 years in North America, but only 50 years in South America and 25 years in Middle Africa, already the poorest region (see Table 3.1).

Doubling time: The number of years it would take a particular population to double in size if it continued to grow at a given rate. Doubling time at low rates of growth can be approximated by the formula (69/annual percentage growth rate) = doubling time in years.

TABLE 3.1: POPULATION DATA BY REGION AND SELECTED COUNTRIES, 2008

Region/ Countries	Population 2004 (Millions)	Births per 1,000	Deaths per 1,000	Infant Mortality per 1,000	Natural Increase %	Doubling Time, Years	GNI PPP per Capita, U.S. $
World	6,705.0	21	8	1.2	49.0	58.1	9,600
North America	338.0	14	8	0.6	7.0	115.9	44,790
United States	304.5	14	8	0.6	6.6	115.9	45,850
Canada	33.3	11	7	0.3	5.4	231.4	35,310
Central America	150.0	22	5	1.7	22.0	41.1	10,340
Mexico	107.7	20	5	1.6	19.0	43.7	12,580
Guatamala	13.7	34	6	2.8	34.0	25.1	4,120
South America	387.0	20	6	1.4	23.0	49.9	9,290
Brazil	195.1	20	6	1.3	24.0	53.7	9,370
Asia (exc. China)	4,052.0	19	7	1.2	45.0	58.1	5,780
China	1,324.7	12	7	0.5	23.0	139.0	5,370
Japan	127.7	9	9	—	2.8	NA	34,600
India	1,149.3	24	8	1.6	57.0	43.7	2,740
Northern Africa	197.0	26	7	1.9	45.0	36.8	4,760
Western Africa	291.0	42	15	2.6	96.0	27.0	1,480
Eastern Africa	301.0	41	15	2.5	81.0	28.1	940
Middle Africa	122.0	43	14	2.8	97.0	25.1	1,550
Sourthern Africa	55.0	24	16	0.8	48.0	87.0	9,140
Europe	736.0	11	11	—	6.0	NA	24,320
Sweden	9.2	12	10	0.2	2.5	246.9	35,840
United Kingdom	61.3	13	9	0.3	4.9	231.4	34,370
Germany	82.2	8	10	(0.2)	3.9	NA	33,820
Spain	46.5	11	9	0.2	3.7	346.9	30,110
Oceana	35.0	18	7	1.1	25.0	63.4	23,910
Australia	21.3	14	7	0.7	4.7	99.4	33,340
Papua-New Guinea	6.5	31	10	2.1	62.0	33.4	1,500

Source: Population Reference Bureau, 2009, World Population Data Sheet, www.prb.org/pdf08/08WPDS_Eng.pdf (doubling time calculated for this volume)

The population explosion in poorer nations is a result not of increased birthrates but of rapidly decreasing death rates. Part of the problem stems from good intentions. The Western world introduced modern vaccinations, sanitation, and other life-saving techniques to nations all over the world. The death rates dropped, but those nations were not able to increase their production of food and other necessities fast enough to feed the rapidly growing populations. The kinds of agricultural production in the United States are not feasible in many other parts of the world, either because of cultural differences or climatic differences.

While poorer societies as a whole might be better off if they had lower fertility rates, individual couples often see large families as the only chance they have of being supported in their old age. In addition, pronatalist religious and cultural beliefs encourage large families in many parts of the world. Table 3.1 reveals that the highly industrialized societies are at or near zero population growth; they have low infant mortality rates, low birthrates, and high consumption rates. Third World countries tend to have rapid growth rates, high infant mortality rates, high birthrates, and low consumption. Demographic transition has not occurred as many demographers had anticipated in most of the Third World.

Availability of family planning technology has allowed families in some Third World countries to plan their family size more accurately. Because many couples want large numbers of children, however, families remain larger than replacement level.

While not intentional, development attempts have sometimes increased the fertility rate by raising families' hopes of being able to provide for more children (Abernathy, 1993). Further complicating the issue is the provision of more Western medicine and sanitation that lowers infant mortality but causes populations to grow even faster.

FINDING OUT 3.1 GATHERING DEMOGRAPHIC INFORMATION

Most of the developed countries have a government agency that gathers and disseminates demographic information. In the United States there are a number of agencies that are involved, but the Census Bureau (http://www.census.gov) is the agency primarily responsible for that task. In addition to the national census taken every 10 years, the Census Bureau conducts hundreds of other studies related to population. Because the Census Bureau, a part of the U.S. Department of Commerce, is a government agency, the data it develops is not copyrighted and may be used without permission.

The Population Reference Bureau (http://www.prb.org) collects demographic data from all over the world. This is an important task because, in their words, "Population shapes almost every aspect of our lives. Population defines the need for resource allocations—where to build roads, schools, or hospitals. Population shapes political systems and helps determine economic vitality" (http://www.prb.org/inside/about_prb.htm).

The Population Reference Bureau employs social scientists, health care professionals, computer programmers, and other experts from around the world. Information is collected in a large library and serves as the basis for a number of publications distributed by the PRB. Information is made available to other researchers, journalists, government officials, middle school and high school educators, among others. The organization provides technical support to both government and private agencies.

The PRB is governed by a diverse board of trustees. Its funds come from a number of sources including government contracts, foundation grants, individual and corporate contributions, and the sale of their publications. The PRB has copyrights on its material, which may not be reprinted without permission.

Rather than simply advocating more development money, some demographers are taking a closer look at exactly what might cause a demographic transition in poorer nations.

Handwerker (1986:1) argued, "Fertility transition in the contemporary world comes about when personal material well-being is determined less by personal relationships than by formal education and skill training." This view advocates educational access for women, not only on grounds of gender equality but to help lower fertility rates (Sadik, 1994; De Barbieri, 1994). Pronatalism most directly affects women, since they are the ones who bear the children and provide most of their direct care. Lower fertility rates would improve the health of women, but in many societies, having children is the major source of a woman's status (McLaren, 1992).

The desire to limit family size is at least as important in regulating fertility rates as is the availability of modern contraceptive technology. That desire is influenced by a number of manifest and latent cultural factors. In the United States and other developed countries, the desire to separate the pleasure function of sexuality from the reproductive function has increased the demand for effective family planning technology (Giddens, 1992).

FERTILITY CHOICE IN CONTEMPORARY AMERICA

Important fluctuations have occurred in the American birthrate in the 20th century. The birthrate experienced a downturn in the 1930s, during the Great Depression. Because of the hard times, couples intentionally limited their births. In addition, couples were often separated for long periods of time as one partner, usually the husband, searched for work in other locations. The birthrate increased in the 1940s as the economy improved. The upward trend was interrupted briefly during America's heaviest involvement in the war, but it resumed sharply in 1946, after the war. This was the beginning of the baby boom. The boom tapered off in the mid-1960s. As Figure 3.3 indicates, the birthrate has generally continued to fall since 1950. There was a slight increase in the 1980s, peaking in 1990, as children of the baby boomers had their own children, and a continuing decline since then.

In contemporary North America and other postindustrial societies, the questions of whether to have children and how many to have are increasingly seen as matters

FIGURE 3.3.

Live Births per 1,000 Population, United States, 1950–2006

Source: U.S. Census Bureau. http://www.census.gov/prod/2004pubs/04statab/vitstat.pdf; *Statistical Abstract*, 2009, Table 77.

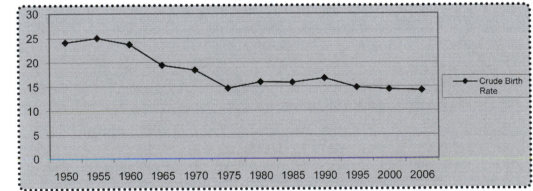

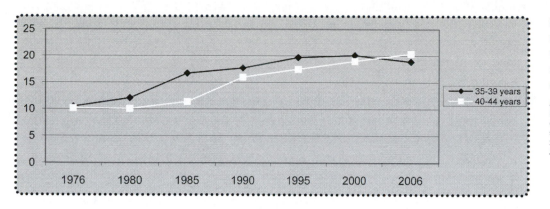

FIGURE 3.4.

Percent of Women Who Are Childless in 35–39 and 40–44 Age Groups, 1976–2006

Source: U.S. Census Bureau. http://www.census.gov/population/socdemo/fertility/tabH1.xls; *Stistical Abstract, 2009*, Table 90.

of choice. Results of surveys asking about "ideal" family size find that two children is the most common ideal in other postindustrial societies (Vandenheuvel, 1991). In the United States, also, two children is the most common ideal. Because a few people prefer large families, the mean average ideal is just over three children (Davis & Smith, 1998).

Pronatalism has weakened in the United States. Among all American women 18 to 34 years of age, 9.3% expect to have no births during their lifetime. That same figure applied to both Black and White women; 5.7% of Hispanic women expected to bear no children. The most highly educated women were most likely to expect to remain childless. (Census Bureau 1993:81).

Some who do not wish to have children have advocated replacing the term *childless* with the more positive-sounding term *child-free*. While being child-free by choice is increasing, there are couples who are involuntarily childless. More commonly, a couple drifts into childlessness (Heaton, Jacobson, & Holland, 1999). They are waiting until they are absolutely certain they want a child, or until they get their careers established, or for some other future event. Eventually, they wait so long that they become, or believe themselves to be, too old to have a child.

As Figure 3.4 indicates, the percentage of women remaining childless through their prime childbearing years has increased rapidly in postindustrial America. The percentage of childless women in their late 30s almost doubled from 1976 to 2006, when the figure stood at 18.9. In the early 40s group, 20.4% of women remained childless; very few of these will have their first child at a later age. We can soon expect that 20% or more of American women will never bear a child and that a large proportion of these will be the most highly educated, economically well off women.

Polenko, Scanzoni, and Teachman (1982) compared women who had children with various categories of childless women. Some had voluntarily decided to be child-free; some had not yet decided; some wanted children but were postponing the event; and some wanted children but were unable to have them. Compared with mothers, women without children in the voluntary, undecided, and postponing categories had somewhat greater marital satisfaction. These were often women who had other sources of satisfaction such as fulfilling careers. In couples who were involuntarily childless, both the husbands and wives felt considerable marital stress. The infertility issue created problems that spread to other aspects of their relationship (Abbey, Andrews, & Halman, 1992).

For fertile couples, remaining child-free requires the continued use of some form of contraception. In the next section, we will explore some of the common family planning methods used by couples to reduce the number of children they might have and to influence timing of childbirth. The section following that one covers methods used to increase family size.

FERTILITY REDUCTION METHODS

Contraception: Intentional prevention of impregnation.

Abortion: Termination of a pregnancy before the fetus can survive outside the uterus. **Spontaneous abortions** occur naturally and unintentionally; **induced abortions** are done intentionally.

Abstinence: The practice of refraining from indulging some appetite such as food, drink, or a particular sexual practice.

General abstinence: The practice of completely avoiding sexual intercourse.

Periodic abstinence: The practice of attempting to avoid conception by refraining from intercourse at certain times of the menstrual cycle.

Manifest forms of fertility reduction can be divided into two major types. **Contraception** is designed to prevent conception from occurring, while **abortion** prevents a fertilized egg from going through the full developmental process to live birth. In addition, although births are not prevented, family size can be limited by giving an infant up for adoption. Each of these approaches has a variety of specific techniques and varying degrees of social acceptability.

ABSTINENCE–BASED METHODS

Some approaches to reducing the probability of pregnancy rely on avoidance of some or all sexual activity, some or all of the time. Also known as *coitus abstentia,* **general abstinence** is the attempt to avoid sexual intercourse completely. This is not a practical method for married couples or others who wish to have a sexual relationship, but it is the approach most American parents would prefer their unmarried adolescents would use.

Contrary to popular belief, general abstinence is not 100% effective in the prevention of pregnancy. Every type of contraception has both a method failure rate and a user failure rate. Method failure occurs when a person using a contraceptive method does everything the method calls for, but pregnancy still results. User failure rates are based on the experience of typical users of the method in real life. Both failure rates are calculated as the percentage of women who get pregnant in a year while using the method (see Table 3.2).

In the case of general abstinence, a woman can practice the method perfectly but become pregnant as a result of rape or incest. Pregnancy that results from user failure of abstinence is much more common. A couple or individual might plan to practice abstinence but have sexual intercourse anyway because they get "carried away." Failure rates of this type are not typically calculated, but it is quite probable that user failure of general abstinence is a major cause of unwanted pregnancy among American adolescents. Since about one third of all births in the United States are to unmarried mothers, it would appear that abstinence user failure is quite high.

TABLE 3.2 CONTRACEPTIVE FAILURE RATES AND USAGE

Method	First-Year Failure Rates		Usage by Women Age 15–44	
	Perfect Use	Typical Use	Ever Used[1]	Current Use[2]
Pill	0.3	8.0	82.3	18.9
Female Sterilization	0.5	0.7	20.7	16.7
Male Condom	2.0	15.0	89.7	11.1
Male Sterilization	0.1	0.2	13.0	5.7
3–month injectable	0.3	3.0	16.8	3.3
1–month injectable	0.05	3.0	0.9	
Withdrawal	4.0	27.0	56.1	2.5
IUD	0.1–0.6	0.1–1.0	5.8	1.3
Periodic Abstinance	1.0–9.0	25.0	18.0	0.9
Implant	0.05	1.0		
Patch	0.3	8.0		
Diaphragm	6.0	16.0	8.5	0.2
Sponge	15.0	25.0	7.3	
Cervical Cap	18.0	24.0		
Female Condom	5.0	27.0	1.9	
Spermicides	18.0	29.0	19.4	
No Method	85.0	85.0		38.13

[1]Among women who have ever had sex.

[2]In last three months.

[3]Includes 18.1% who had not had sex in the last three months.

Sources: Failure rates from The Alan Guttmacher Institute, online at www.agi-usa.org/pubs/ fb_contra_use. *htm Source*: Usage rates from Centers for Disease Control, National Center for Health Statistics, 2004. *Use of Contraception and Use of Family Planning Services in the Unites States*: 1982–2002. Tables 1 and 3. Online at *www.cdc.gov/nchs/data/ad/ad350.pdf*

Also known as "natural family planning," "fertility awareness," and the "rhythm method," **periodic abstinence** is a very old family-planning technique. The basic idea of the method is to avoid sexual intercourse on and around the day of ovulation, so determining the time of ovulation is crucial. In the least restrictive of cases, use of the rhythm method would require abstinence for at least seven out of every 28 days, or one fourth of the couple's time together. Even longer periods of abstinence are suggested if the woman's period varies from a regular 28–day cycle.

Coitus Interruptus While abstinence methods generally assume that a couple does without sexual intercourse, it is technically only the ejaculation of sperm into the vagina that must be avoided for contraception to be successful. Coitus interruptus, now more commonly called early withdrawal, theoretically allows for sexual intercourse with decreased risk of pregnancy. While this is more effective than no contraception at all, it has a relatively high failure rate.

In what might also be considered a form of abstinence, a couple might engage in a number of noncoital sexual activities. Oral stimulation, manual stimulation, anal sex, and other activities that lead to noncoital orgasm are not usually considered contraceptive methods. They have very low method failure rates, but user failure rates are probably fairly high. Only if couples learn to define their sexual scripts in noncoital ways can alternative sexual expression be effective.

COITAL METHODS

For persons who want to enjoy less limited sexual behavior than the abstinence methods allow, a range of contraception techniques are available. These attempt to prevent pregnancy while allowing complete sexual intercourse, including ejaculation in the vagina.

Spermicide: An agent that kills sperm, especially as a contraceptive.

Spermicide is designed to kill sperm before they can produce conception. It is available in a variety of forms, including foam, jelly, cream, and suppository. Creams and gels should be used in conjunction with a diaphragm, while foam and suppositories are intended to be used alone or in conjunction with a condom.

Barrier methods are designed to block sperm from reaching the ovum. The most common of these is the male condom, varieties of which have been used for centuries. The diaphragm, another barrier method, is worn internally by the woman and is designed to block the sperm from passing through the cervix. A more recent product in the family of barrier methods is the female condom. Like the male version, the vaginal condom provides some protection against HIV infection and other STDs.

Intrauterine device (IUD): An object inserted into the uterus for the purpose of preventing pregnancy.

Centuries ago, Arab and Turkish camel drivers placed a pebble into a camel's uterus to prevent pregnancy on long desert trips. This was the first known use of an **intrauterine device (IUD).** The first human model, made of silkworm gut, was introduced in 1909, and the German physician Grafenberg produced an IUD made of gut and silver wire in the 1920s. Around the world today, it is estimated that 60 million women use an IUD; it is especially common in China, where there are an estimated 40 million users (Masters, Johnson, & Kolodny, 1992; Piotrow, Rinehart, & Schmidt, 1979).

Oral contraceptives, often referred to simply as "the pill," are available in two basic types. The combination pill contains synthetic versions of the hormones estrogen and progesterone. The most popular are the low-dosage combination pills, which contain considerably lower dosages of hormones than the original pills that revolutionized contraception when they were first made available in the 1960s. The less common and less effective minipill contains only the low-dosage progesterone-like compound.

In effect, the primary action of the pill is to trick the body into thinking it is pregnant so that ovulation does not occur. Conception is prevented because no egg is available for the sperm to find. Secondarily, the pill causes cervical mucus to become thick and acidic, creating a hostile environment for sperm so that even if an egg is released, live sperm is unlikely to reach it. Finally, the hormones render the uterine lining unsuitable for implantation of a fertilized egg, should the other two effects fail (Knox & Schacht, 1994). This last effect, although probably quite rare, does make the pill a possible **abortifacient,** if preventing a fertilized egg from implanting is considered abortion.

Although some are in the testing stage, there are no chemical contraceptives on the market designed for men. This is at least partly because it is easier to stop the release of one egg monthly than to stop the production of millions of sperm daily. Research has, however, found some chemicals with contraceptive promise. When taken by men, for example, Depo-Provera does decrease sperm production. Drawbacks are that production of sperm is not usually stopped completely. More seriously, the sex drive is significantly reduced (Bromwich & Parsons, 1990). Because of the effect of Depo-Provera on the libido, the drug has been referred to as "chemical castration" and has been suggested as a treatment or punishment for rapists. Because of such side effects, it is likely to be several years before an acceptable male chemical contraceptive is on the market in the United States.

When both female and male methods are included, permanent sterilization is the most popular method of birth control for American couples today. Women can become surgically sterile as a result of **hysterectomy** or **ovariectomy,** but these operations are generally used only for treatment of serious infections, cancer, or other major problems.

When surgery is done only for birth control, some variation of a **tubal ligation,** designed to make passage of an ovum through the fallopian tube impossible, is generally used. This popular "band-aid" surgery is relatively simple and leaves only a tiny scar in the navel. Although it is one of the safest forms of surgery, it is still surgery and can result in risk from the anesthetic, infection, bleeding, or from other rare complications.

Vasectomy, or surgical sterilization of the male, is cheaper, quicker, safer, and more effective than tubal ligation. General anesthetic is not necessary; the scrotum, not the abdominal cavity, is breached. There is, consequently, less chance of infection or dangerous bleeding.

Using methods that amount to major surgery, some physicians have reported a reversal rate for vasectomies of more than half; reversal for tubal ligations is more difficult and less often successful. Surgical sterilization of either type should be considered permanent. Individuals who think there is a chance that they might someday want more children are not good candidates for sterilization.

POSTCOITAL FAMILY PLANNING

A variety of methods, used after sexual intercourse occurs, exist for preventing unwanted births. With the exception of douching, which is largely ineffective, postcoital methods primarily interrupt the development of a fertilized egg rather than preventing conception.

Abortifacient: A substance or device that causes abortion.

Hysterectomy: Surgical removal of the uterus.

Ovariectomy: Surgical removal of the ovaries.

Tubal ligation: "Tying the tubes"; surgically cutting and tying the fallopian tubes to prevent the passage of an ovum from the ovary to the uterus.

Vasectomy: A surgical procedure designed to make the transmission of sperm through the *vas deferens* impossible.

Several "morning after" pills have been available, but it is generally advised that they be used only in emergencies such as rape. They must be taken within 72 hours of intercourse and have higher risks than most contraceptive methods (Hatcher et al., 1990).

RU-486, used for several years in Europe, was approved in 2000 for use in the United States. A synthetic steroid, RU-486 prevents the implantation of a fertilized egg or induces menstruation in the event that implantation has already occurred. As used in France, this "abortion pill" requires four separate visits to a medical facility: a preliminary evaluation, two separate supervised dosages of drugs, and a follow-up examination. Under these conditions, RU-486 is about 95% effective in inducing abortion (Klitsch, 1991). Similar procedures and results are expected in the United States.

THE ABORTION ISSUE

Abortion has been practiced throughout human history. Its acceptance has varied, but even in cultures that disapproved, termination of pregnancy has not generally been placed in the same category as murder. Much controversy, however, remains.

One major abortion issue centers on the question about the point at which a separate human life, entitled to rights under the law, begins. From some religious perspectives, the question is the precise time in the gradual fertilization and developmental process that the organism acquires a soul. Some anti-abortionists believe that life starts at the "moment of conception." This is currently the position of the Roman Catholic Church, although until 1869 the position was that life begins 40 days after conception (Ester-brook, 2000).

Many supporters of the "pro-life" position also hold that women who have sexual intercourse have a moral responsibility to carry a resultant fetus to term. By contrast, supporters of the "pro-choice" position, who believe that abortions should be a woman's legal choice, argue that the zygote and fetus are another part of the woman's body over which she should have control. These persons argue that a separate human life begins at the moment of birth.

One historical position has been that a unique human life begins, or the soul enters the organism, at the time of "quickening." This is the time, usually toward the end of the fifth month of pregnancy, that the pregnant woman begins to feel movement of the fetus.

In 1973, the abortion issue in the United States took a major turn when the Supreme Court handed down its famous Roe v. Wade decision. Based on the right to privacy between a woman and her physician, the Roe decision established that states could not interfere during the first trimester of pregnancy. In the second trimester, state interference could only be for purposes of protecting the woman's health. States were allowed to regulate or prohibit abortion during the third trimester.

A variety of court cases since that time have refined the original Roe decision, but the basic right to an abortion remains even if access to the procedure has been limited. In some states, teenagers must either notify their parents prior to having an abortion or get a judge's approval. As matters currently stand, the male progenitor has no legal rights in matters of abortion,

TABLE 3.3 PERCENTAGE OF AMERICAN WHO APPROVE OF LEGAL ABORTION UNDER CERTAIN CIRCUMSTANCES, BY GENDER, 2004

Percent Agreeing Abortion Should be Legal if . . .	Male	Female	Total
The woman's own health is seriously endangered by the pregnancy	86.9%	85.2%	86.0%
She became pregnant as a result of rape	79.1	73.8	76.2
There is a strong chance of serious defect in the baby	72.7	73.0	72.9
The family has a very low income and cannot afford any more children	43.4	39.0	41.0
She is married and does not want any more children	44.2	39.7	41.8
She is not married and does not want to marry the man.	44.3	38.0	40.9
The woman wants it for any reason	42.9	38.6	40.6

Source: Davis, James Allan, and Tom W. Smith: General Social Survey(s), 2004. (Machine-readable data file). Principal Investigator, James A. Davis; Director and Co-Principal Investigator, Tom W. Smith; Co-Principal Investigator, Peter V. Marsden, NORC ed. Chicago: National Opinion Research Center, producer, 1998; Storrs, CT: The Roper Center for Public Opinion Research, University of Connecticut, distributor. Micro- computer format and codebook prepared and distributed by MicroCase Corporation, Bellevue, Washington. Analysis by Gene H. Starbuck.

although a live birth can legally obligate him to provide financial support until the infant becomes an adult.

The abortion issue sometimes appears to be highly polarizing, with very strong opinions on both the "pro-choice" and "pro-life" sides. Most Americans, however, are ambivalent about the issue, approving of abortion in some situations but not others. A majority of Americans approve of abortion in cases of rape or incest and when carrying the fetus to term would result in major risk to the health of the mother or the likelihood of serious defect in the child. Fewer than half, however, approve of abortion in cases where the woman is having the abortion solely because she already has too many children, is unmarried, or would have financial problems (see Table 3.3).

HAVING ABORTIONS

Because it has been legal in the United States for three decades, abortion has become a relatively safe procedure. Although women who have abortions have somewhat more complications than women who do not get pregnant in the first place, legal abortions are safer than childbirth, using an IUD, or taking the pill. Major complications occur in less than 1% of abortions (*Facts in Brief,* 1992).

Although the decision to have an abortion is a difficult one for many women, Adler et al. (1990) found that most stress occurred before the abortion and that severe negative reactions occurred in only 5 to 10% of women. It is hard to measure the difficulties these women experienced compared to the stress and psychological trauma of having and raising an unwanted child. It would appear that negative postabortion psychological problems are less common than is postpartum depression in women who give birth,

The legal and political debate about abortion is not likely to end soon.

even including women who wanted the child. Little information exists about the psychological impact of abortion on the male progenitor.

In 1996, there were 1,366,000 abortions in the United States, or 351 abortions for every 1,000 live births (*Statistical Abstract,* 1999: Table 114). Both figures are down considerably from the peak years in the mid-1980s. In 1985, there were 1,589,000 abortions, or 422 abortions per 1,000 live births.

The decrease is partly because there are relatively fewer women in the age groups most likely to have abortions. Although more abortions are performed on women age 20 to 24, women who get pregnant are most likely to get abortions if they are younger than 15; more than half of the known pregnancies of girls in this young age group end in induced abortion (Henshaw & Van Vort, 1992).

Abortion ratio: Number of abortions for every 1,000 known pregnancies.

About 80% of reported induced abortions are performed on unmarried women. The **abortion ratio,** which is the number of abortions for every 1,000 known pregnancies, is only 94 for married women and 466 for those who are unmarried. Although 59% of abortions are performed on White women, their abortion ratio is 206 compared to 412 for women of color (*Statistical Abstract,* 1999: Table 124).

POSTNATAL OPTIONS

Abortion is only one option for an unmarried pregnant woman (see Figure 3.5). Single parenting is the most rapidly growing option and was chosen by about 21% of unwed pregnant American women in the late 1980s. The most common option cross-culturally and historically, marrying the father of the child-to-be, is sometimes not even mentioned today as an option for unmarried teens. Although it was once virtually the only viable option, in the 1980s only about 24% of never-married pregnant women got married before the birth of their child (Bachrach, Stolley, & London, 1992).

Relinquishment: A giving up or surrender of something; giving up legal rights to a child.
Adoption: Taking into one's own family and raising as one's own child.

A relatively rare choice for a pregnant woman to make is to give birth and then give up her rights of motherhood. Sometimes called the "adoption option," it is more correct to refer to it as **relinquishment,** since **adoption** refers to the relationship between the adoptive parents and the child (Strong & Devault, 1994).

Almost no married women relinquish their infants, and only about 2% of unmarried women do so (Strong & Devault, 1994). This figure is down from the unmarried mother relinquishment rate of about 14% in the early 1970s (Bachrach, Stolley, & London, 1992). In the late 1980s, there were about 33,000 infant relinquishments annually (Strong & Devault, 1994). At the same time, an estimated 200,000 women were seeking infants to adopt (Bachrach, London, & Maza, 1991).

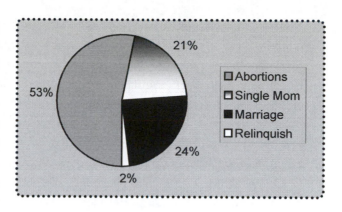

FIGURE 3.5.

Pregnancy Resolution, Single Women, 1985–1990

Source: Recalculated using data from Strong and Devault, 1994; U.S. Bureau of the Census, 1995; Bachrach, Stolley, and London, 1992.

Part of the reason for the declining popularity of relinquishment is the increased safety and availability of abortion. Also, there has been increasing social acceptance of single mothers, as well as accessibility of welfare benefits that make single motherhood more feasible (Daly, 1994). Perhaps reflecting the unpopularity of relinquishment and perhaps contributing to its unpopularity is the fact that it is not generally mentioned on a par with abortion in formal discussions of pregnancy resolution. As with other sources of information, marriage and family textbooks generally give considerably less coverage to relinquishment than to abortion (Stolley & Hall, 1994).

Although teenagers tend to have positive feelings about adoption and adopted children in general, they do not often consider it a viable option for themselves. They are much more likely to have talked with their friends, parents, and dating partners about single parenting and abortion than about relinquishment. Adolescents fear that choosing to relinquish would subject them to rejection from parents and peers, who might view their choice as "selfish, unloving and even incomprehensible" (Resnick et al., 1990:583).

While fear of peer rejection is important, other concerns are a stronger barrier to giving a child up for adoption. In one study, 80% of teenagers expressed concern about "feelings of abandoning the baby," and another 63% were concerned about "not knowing what is involved and what to expect with adoption" (Daly, 1994:339). Young persons know more about the proper use of birth control and how to get an abortion than they do about relinquishing parental rights.

Some recent research indicates that fear of negative consequences of relinquishment is partially unfounded. Placing for adoption does have some positive outcomes, especially as compared to single parenthood (Daly, 1994). The differences in outcome of parenting and relinquishment might partially be accounted for by social class variations, however. White unmarried pregnant teens are more likely to choose relinquishment than are minority youths (Kalmuss, Namerow, & Cushman, 1991). Women with higher socioeconomic status and higher academic ambitions are more likely to give up their parental rights (Resnick et al., 1990). Women who hold more traditional attitudes about family life are more likely to relinquish (Hayes, 1987). Religious fundamentalists, who face both the prohibition of abortion and the social stigma of illegitimate birth, are more likely to resolve an unintended pregnancy by giving the child up for adoption (Medoff, 1993).

To determine the influence that government policy might have, Medoff (1993) compared relinquishment rates of the various states. He found that the higher the Aid to Families with Dependent Children payment, the more likely women in poverty were to keep their child. Price and availability of abortions appeared to have no statistically significant effect on adoption decisions. Studies have not yet been done on the effect of recent changes in welfare laws on abortion decisions.

State regulations about relinquishment and adoption vary considerably. Medoff (1993) looked at four separate issues to see if they influenced relinquishment rates. First, while all states have social services departments and nonprofit, licensed adoption agencies, some allow private adoptions through intermediaries, and some do not. Second, states vary in terms of the extent to which they allow open adoptions, in which relinquishing mothers, adoptive parents, and adopted children know the identities of each other. Third, some states allow prospective adoptive parents to pay expenses of birth mothers, while other states forbid such practices. Finally, the length of time birth mothers are allowed to change their minds about relinquishment varies from state to state. While each of the four policy variations is important for other reasons, Medoff (1993) found that none had a statistically significant influence on relinquishment rates.

Contraception, abortion, and relinquishment are all methods of family planning designed to reduce the likelihood of unwanted parenthood. We turn now to family planning methods designed to do the opposite.

CHILDBIRTH AND FERTILITY ENHANCEMENT

Childbirth, in hunting-gathering societies, was often a truly family affair. Women of the clan, often collectively, assisted in childbirth and the immediate postpartum phase. Fathers, too, often had a part, if only in ceremony.

Couvade: The practice in which the husband of a woman in labor takes to his bed as though he were bearing the child.

The **couvade** provided participation for the men in the birthing process. The practice has been found among peoples in the Americas, Africa, Europe, India, and China (Wolf, 1996). When their wives are in labor, men appear to be going through the same process, including labor pains.

In some societies, the couvade is connected to a system of magic or religion; the man is drawing the attention of evil spirits away from his wife. It might allow the man to identify with the mother, thereby expressing his sympathy for the feminine role (Munroe & Munroe, 1989). It also appears to help establish the claim of the man to the legitimate fatherhood of the child (Broude, 1988).

The practice is more common in matrilocal societies and those in which motherhood is granted great importance (Broude, 1989). Even where the couvade was practiced, though, participation in the birth itself was primarily by women. Historically, this appears to be true almost universally (Rothman, 1993). In more specialized societies, a **midwife** presided over the birth. In most cases, the midwife got her expertise by having children herself, through folk knowledge, and by experience (Burtch, 1994).

Midwife: A person, usually a woman, who provides specialized care during childbirth.

Over time, midwifery became a more specialized position. During the Middle Ages in Europe, the Catholic Church appointed and licensed midwives, who were expected not only to provide care for women, but also to prevent abortions, infant substitutions, and infanticide (Bohme, 1984). Many midwives continued to operate independently, however, and their craft was not infrequently the target when witch hunts were fashionable (Donnison, 1988).

In the American colonies, midwives were more independent from the church than in Europe, but in both places, considerable friction developed between midwifery and the emerging field of medical science. By mid-20th century, licensed physicians had taken over the child-delivery business and midwives had all but disappeared. Feminist scholars have documented the process that not only moved childbirth from the home to the hospital, but also moved it from the care of women to the care of physicians, nearly all of whom were men (Donnison, 1988; Oakley, 1984; Rothman, 1993).

Modern medicine did contribute to a decline in fatalities among both mothers and infants. It also, however, removed control of the process not only from the mother but from all women. It also removed control of childbirth from the family and excluded the father from the process (Burtch, 1994).

In recent decades, a reaction to the impersonal "medicalization" of the birthing process resulted in several alternative methods. These include Lamaze's "natural" or "prepared" approach; the Dick-Read method; and Bradley's "husband-coached childbirth." The medical profession gradually responded by incorporating these methods into hospital delivery and in providing family birthing rooms and other innovations. There has also been a resurgence of interest in home births and midwifery (Rothman, 1993).

DEFINING INFERTILITY

Like childbirth, involuntary childlessness might sound like a primarily medical issue, but it has significant psychological, political, legal, and moral implications. Even defining the problem and looking at possible solutions is controversial.

While the term **infertility** is clear in its general meaning, like so many other terms, its exact meaning and measurement are fuzzy. A typical figure is that about 10 to 15% of married American couples are infertile, but this might be misleading. Some persons are clearly incapable of achieving pregnancy because of aging or such intentional procedures as hysterectomy or vasectomy. A woman taking the pill would not be called

Infertility: Inability to achieve pregnancy or to carry a fetus to live birth.

infertile, even though she is not likely immediately to become pregnant. Some individuals do not wish to have additional children, so they might not be defined as infertile even if they cannot achieve pregnancy. The desire to achieve pregnancy, along with unsuccessful attempts to do so, are components of most precise definitions of infertility.

Specifying a certain amount of time during which unsuccessful attempts to achieve pregnancy occur is somewhat arbitrary, since few couples achieve pregnancy each and every time they have intercourse. Couples who have intercourse regularly without the use of contraception take an average of 5.3 months for pregnancy to occur (Shane, Schiff, & Wilson, 1976). Only 25% of women conceive after one month of unprotected intercourse, 63% after six months, and about 80% after one year (Masters, Johnson, & Kolodny, 1992:96). The one-year rate has sometimes been used to report an infertility rate among American couples of 20%. Although it has long been known that infertility goes up as women get older, a 1982 study, using the one-year cutoff, reported an infertility rate of close to 40% for women ages 31–35 (Schwartz & Mayauz, 1982). At least in the popular press, the implication of this figure was that women who might wish to have children someday should think about doing so sooner rather than later, even at some sacrifice to career development.

To refute the 40% infertility figure, Faludi (1991) cited a British study of more than 17,000 women that found 91% of women of all ages were able to achieve pregnancy after 39 months (Bongaarts, 1982). In fact, the two studies are not necessarily contradictory since they deal with different ages of women and different definitions of infertility.

Perhaps the best summary of fertility incidence would be that about 10% of American couples are infertile, and another 10% are "underfertile," and that these rates begin to rise for women in over-30 age groups. Infertility is not the same as sterility, however, so even many of the over-30 infertility group might still achieve pregnancy.

CAUSES OF INFERTILITY

The Mayo Clinic reports that, in infertile couples, the man is infertile about 30% of the time, the woman about 50% of the time, and mutual problems exist the remaining 20% of the time (Larson, 1990). Other sources report that 40% of problems are attributed to women, 40% to men, and the remaining 20% to both (Derwinski-Robinson, 1990).

The two major causes of infertility in women are failure to ovulate and blockage of the fallopian tubes. Failure to ovulate can be treated with hormones that are popularly referred to as fertility drugs. This is a relatively successful approach, with reported pregnancy rates as high as 70% for women with failure to ovulate but who have otherwise healthy-appearing ovaries. The drugs do not increase the risk of spontaneous abortion nor birth defects, but they can over-stimulate the ovaries to the point of rupture. The most noticeable side effect of ovulation-stimulating drugs is the greatly increased incidence of multiple births. As many as 15% of resultant births are twins, and another 5% are triplets, quadruplets, quintuplets, or sextuplets (Masters, Johnson, & Kolodny, 1992).

> Women have the opportunity to pay their college expenses.

The problem of blocked fallopian tubes is often caused by endometriosis, sometimes by scarring from sexually transmitted diseases or other infections. In some cases, microsurgery or laser technology can repair the damaged tube. Where endometriosis is the cause, laser surgery yields pregnancy rates in the 40 to 65% range (Berger, Goldstein, & Fuerst, 1989).

The most common immediate cause of male infertility is low sperm count. Temporarily low sperm counts have been attributed to a number of causes, including long-distance bicycling, wearing tight underwear, spending too much time in hot baths or hot tubs, and ejaculating too frequently. Permanently low sperm counts can be the result of testicular injury, high fever, infection, radiation, and undescended testes. With the exception of behavior changes to reduce the short-term causes of low sperm counts, direct treatment of infertility in men has not been as successful as treatment for women (Masters, Johnson, & Kolodny, 1992).

ASSISTED REPRODUCTIVE TECHNIQUES

The last few decades have witnessed rapid changes in reproductive technology. Different techniques can now be used, alone or in combination with other procedures, depending on the type of infertility problem the couple has.

Artificial Insemination   When the fertility problem is one of low sperm count, **artificial insemination** with the husband's sperm (AIH) can be used. The advantage over sexual intercourse is that the fresh semen can be applied directly to the cervix, where sperm will have the best chance of reaching the fallopian tubes. Knowledgeable and willing couples can actually perform this procedure themselves. With professional assistance, several sperm samples can be quick-frozen and injected all at once, but this reduces the mobility of the sperm and might not actually increase the odds of conception.

> **Artificial insemination:** Placing semen in the vagina or uterus by means other than sexual intercourse.

If AIH does not work, or if the sperm count approaches zero, artificial insemination with a donor's sperm (AID) can be tried. The procedure is the same as for AIH except that the sperm does not come from the husband. Several sperm banks exist in North America, including one in Escondido, California, that accepts sperm only from men who have both IQs over 140 and significant intellectual accomplishments. Many medical schools have sperm banks and pay students for sperm samples.

In Vitro Fertilization   If a woman ovulates normally but has fallopian tubes that are blocked, *in vitro* fertilization can be used. The woman is usually given hormones to increase ovulation. The eggs are then surgically removed and placed in a container with a controlled culture and live sperm. One or more fertilized eggs can then be implanted directly into the woman's uterus. Sometimes extra fertilized eggs are frozen for possible use at a later time.

In vitro fertilization: Joining of sperm and egg outside the body.

Surrogate Mothers.   Surrogate parenthood is actually a very old practice. The Biblical practice of the Levirate essentially required that a man should serve as a surrogate progenitor for his dead brother's child. The Bible also reports that Sarah's maid Hagar gave birth to a child for Sarah and her husband, Abraham. These reports imply that the practice was not only considered acceptable at one time but also might have been an obligation.

Surrogate mother: A woman who is paid for the use of her uterus to produce a baby.

Today's **surrogate mothers** are usually paid to carry and give birth to a child who would then be given to someone else. The surrogate is typically impregnated, through artificial insemination, by the sperm of the husband of the couple who wants the child. Combinations of techniques, however, are possible. A woman who ovulates but has no uterus could have her egg fertilized *in vitro* by her husband's sperm, then implanted in the surrogate's womb. Alternately, a donor's sperm could be used.

A surrogate woman could also be artificially inseminated; the egg could then be flushed from the surrogate's uterus and placed in the womb of the woman who wished to have the child. Either her husband's or a donor's sperm could be used.

The more steps in the assisted reproduction process, the lower the success rate, and, generally, the more expensive the process. The cost of using artificial insemination and a surrogate mother can run well over $50,000, and some other technologies cost more and have relatively low success rates.

REPRODUCTIVE TECHNOLOGY AND CULTURE LAG

Culture lag: A time discrepancy between technological change and change in nonmaterial aspects of culture such as laws and values.

In 1950, William F. Ogburn introduced the term **culture lag.** He had noticed that social change such as that brought on by industrialization often resulted in the development of technologies with which the legal, moral, religious, and other elements of nonmaterial culture were not equipped to deal. Such appears to be the case with reproductive technology today, when few legal, ethical, and moral guidelines are available.

The Catholic Church has resolved the matter by firmly opposing any reproductive approach that directly involves anyone other than the husband and wife who wish to achieve pregnancy; this applies to surrogates and donors. The church also calls "morally unacceptable" such approaches as AIH because a third party is involved (*Catechism of the Catholic Church,* 1994). Although this is a very conservative approach, the Catholic Church has at least attempted to wrestle with the issues, something many other churches have not done.

In addition to religious concerns, reproductive technology has produced a good many unanswered legal questions. Where court cases and legislation exist, they are often contradictory and vary from one jurisdiction to another. Highlight 3.1 points to some of the issues involved.

ADOPTION

Assisted reproductive technology can provide a means of producing a child who is biologically parented by at least one member of the couple. Adoption can also provide a child for a couple, but that child is usually a genetic stranger. Because they are chosen, however, there are no accidental, unwanted adopted children.

We have seen that infant relinquishments in the United States fall far behind the demand for children to adopt. There are about 33,000 infant relinquishments and about 114,000 adoptions annually. This includes adoptions of older children and children from foreign countries (Strong & DeVault, 1994). About 2.1% of married couple households with children contain adopted children (U.S. Bureau of the Census, 1995: T. 77), but many more would adopt if more healthy infants were available.

Children who are more available are generally older ones who have been removed from highly abusive homes, or have physical, mental, or emotional disabilities. As many as 25% of children adopted in some states might have been prenatally exposed to drugs (Barth, 1991). Also, more Black children are available than White ones, and there is considerable controversy about the ethics of cross-racial adoption. These and other factors often make attempted adoption a difficult, expensive, and frustrating experience that is made more difficult by the high abortion rate.

Although difficult and not totally accepted in the United States, adoption is a common cross-cultural and historical event (Terrell & Modell, 1994). In many hunting-gathering societies, it was common for persons to be "adopted" by applying kinship terminology to nonrelatives or by applying terms of close kinship to more distant relatives.

In ancient Rome, heirs were often adopted, even by single men. Both formal and informal adoption continued in many agrarian societies. In most societies, it has been conduct and performance, care and reciprocity, which has defined kinship, not biological closeness. In the contemporary United States, however, there is an unusual bias against fictive kinship and relations other than those by marriage or blood (March & Miall, 2000; Wegar, 2000). Marshall (1977) refers to this as a "biogenic" bias in kinship characteristics, a bias also found in legal decisions involving child custody.

HIGHLIGHT 3.1 ISSUES IN REPRODUCTIVE TECHNOLOGY

Developments in reproductive technology have raised a number of questions in the United States in the last few decades. Read each case and try to answer each question. For even more fun, try to reach agreement on the issues with a group of friends.

1. In 1991, Arlette Schwartz served as a surrogate for her daughter, Christa, and gave birth to twins, who became Christa's legal children. What kinship term properly applies between the twins and Schwartz? Were the twins a product of incest?

2. In 1987, in the celebrated "Baby M" case, Mary Beth Whitehead was artificially inseminated with the sperm of William Stern. Although Whitehead signed a surrogate contract with William and his wife, Elizabeth, she later changed her mind. She turned down the $10,000 fee she had agreed to take from the intended parents and determined to keep the child. A judge upheld the surrogate contract, removed the child from Whitehead, and presided over Elizabeth Stern's adoption of the child. On an appeal, the New Jersey Supreme Court ruled that surrogacy for hire was like selling a baby and invalidated the contract. The court further ruled that Whitehead could have visitation rights as a parent but that Richard Stern, whose sperm was used, was the primary custodial parent.

   Which court's decision do you think was correct? Should states honor and enforce surrogacy contracts, or should the contracts be outlawed like slavery is?

3. In a 1991 case, similar to the Baby M situation, the surrogate mother, Elvie Jordon, decided she wanted 17–month-old Marissa back when she found out that Bob and Cindy Moschetta, the intended parents, were getting divorced. The California superior court ruled that the two biological parents, Jordon and Bob Moschetta, should share joint custody of the child and that Cindy Moschetta was to have no legal rights or visitation privileges.

   Do you agree with the judge's decision? Is the strong bias toward biological parents, found throughout North American law, appropriate?

4. Mary Sue Davis and Junior Davis had frozen embryos, the result of *in vitro* fertilization, in storage when they filed for divorce. They disagreed over the custody of the embryos. Junior Davis wanted to have them destroyed because he did not want to become a father, at least of Mary Davis's child. Mary Davis wanted the embryos because she might want to be impregnated with them. The judge ruled in favor of Mary Davis.

   Do you agree with the judge? If Mary Davis had become impregnated with the embryos and given birth, could she have successfully sued her ex-husband for financial support as the legal father of the child?

5. Suppose a couple uses donor sperm and donor eggs for *in vitro* fertilization. The fertilized egg is then implanted into an unrelated surrogate mother, who gives birth.

   If the intended parents both die in a car wreck before the baby is born, and the surrogate mother, egg donor, and sperm donor all want custody, who should get it?

   If the baby is born severely disabled and the parents change their mind about accepting the child, should they be able to? If none of the parties want the child, who should be liable for its support?

6. Researchers search for the most effective laboratory environment for *in vitro* fertilization. In the process, they often dispose of eggs that have been fertilized.

   If abortion became illegal, should the researchers be arrested? Would the sperm and egg donors also be guilty?

7. In January 2001, a University of Kentucky professor announced that he will work with a group of fertility researchers attempting to produce the first cloned human within two years.

   Should human cloning research be allowed? What might the legal and moral consequences of such research be?

The following issues will probably continue to be controversial for some time:

Should *in vitro* fertilization research be publicly funded? Should it be done at all?

Should the cost of assisted reproductive techniques be covered by insurance policies?

Should reproductive assistance such as donor sperm be provided for intended single parents?

Can sperm banks, or individual sperm donors, be held liable if their sperm infects a woman with AIDS?

Is it racist if intended parents shop for a sperm donor or surrogate of a particular race? Could a sperm bank be sued if the child turns out to be of a different race than that promised as a "match" for the parents?

Is it ethical to have sperm banks solely for certain kinds of donors, such as Nobel Prize winners or outstanding athletes? Is it ethical for "supermodels" or other exceptional women to auction their eggs to the highest bidder?

What other issues are likely to arise because of cultural lag in reproductive technology?

Perhaps most importantly, who should answer these question? Judges? Legislators? Presidents? Religious leaders?

SUMMARY AND CONCLUSION

Cultural practices affect fertility rates in both latent and manifest ways. The theory of demographic transition provides a framework for understanding historical population patterns. At a global level, fertility regulation historically produced a relatively sparse population, but the industrial revolution resulted to a worldwide population explosion. Societies that went through the revolution first saw not only gradual reductions in death rates but also subsequent reduction in birthrates. Many are now at or near zero population growth. Contemporary Third World countries still have rapidly growing populations.

At least in postindustrial countries, a wide range of methods is available for reducing the odds of pregnancy. Abstinence, historically the major option, is decreasingly effective because of user failure. Spermicides, barrier methods, the IUD, hormonal systems, and surgical sterilization are commonly used to prevent pregnancy.

Also available are methods of preventing unwanted births after sexual intercourse. These include "morning after" pills, RU-486, and various abortion procedures. Unplanned

---

FAMILIES IN THE NEWS *MISSING GIRLS IN INDIA*

Early tabulations from India's 2001 census are confirming what many demographers suspected—there are not as many girls as there should be. Ultrasound testing is increasingly widespread and is being used to determine the sex of the fetus. The widespread Indian preference for boys is resulting in many more abortions of female fetuses than male ones.

In 1982, prior to widespread availability of ultrasound, there were 962 female births for every 1,000 male births. This is about the number that would be expected naturally. But in 2001, that number had dropped to 927 female births for every 1,000 males.

In Punjab, the most prosperous farming state in India, the new figure is only 793 girls per 1,000 boys; in Gujarat, a major industrial state, 878 girls are born per 1,000 boys.

Amartya Sen, a Nobel Prize–winning economist at Cambridge University, says that India is catching up with China, South Korea, and other Asian nations in the decreasing sex ratio. Even though health care is improving and women are living longer, the cultural preference for sons has not changed. Boys carry the family name and inherit the property. In addition, boys have the responsibility for caring for aging parents. Couples fear that if they do not have sons, they will have no one to look after them when they get older.

Within the next 20 years, when today's babies are of marriage age, the sex imbalance is likely to affect traditional mate-selection practices. When there are not enough potential brides to go around, they will become more valuable. Grooms' families might have to pay dowries to brides' families, rather than the present arrangement in which brides' families provide the dowries.

Source: Summarized from Celia W. Dugger, www.nytimes.com, April 22, 2001.

pregnancies can also be carried to birth and either relinquished for adoption or raised by one or both biological parents.

Control of childbearing has been an important historical issue. Couples now have several choices of childbirth techniques. Many couples want to have children but are faced with fertility problems. Techniques are available for couples, with and without assistance from medical professionals, to increase the odds of achieving pregnancy. Some of the newer approaches are accompanied by legal, religious, moral, and ethical concerns. Although there is a shortage of available infants, some couples are able to solve their fertility problem by adopting a child.

In conclusion, this chapter once again demonstrates the inter-relationship between macrosociological forces and individual choices. The economy and religion, among other factors, structures choices about the number of children a people want to have. The technology affects how easy it is for couples to meet their reproductive goals. In turn, the number of children couples have affects the economy.

Today's family size is seen more as a choice than has been the case in the past. That is but one of the many issues couples must negotiate in their relationships.

Rethinking in Context Do you believe that there is an overpopulation problem in the world? If so, what should American foreign policy be with respect to the problem? How do personal, individual and family decisions influence national and international demographic variables?

INTERNET SITES

The United States Census Bureau http://www.census.gov

The Population Reference Bureau http://www.prb.org/

Geography perspective on the theory of demographic transition

http://geography.about.com/od/culturalgeography/a/demotransition.htm

Contraceptive technology, family planning, from Family Health International BIB:

http://www.fhi.org/

The Alan Guttmacher Institute, family planning advocate; online journal on family planning, research reports, etc.

http://www.agi-usa.org/

A pro-life site http://www.prolife.com/

Abortion rights http://www.naral.org/

QUESTIONS FOR REVIEW, REFLECTION, AND DISCUSSION

1. What were the lifetime fertility levels in preindustrial societies? Was that above or below the fecundity rate?
2. What is the difference between latent fertility regulation and manifest fertility regulation?
3. Who was Malthus?
4. What causes infertility?
5. How important is having children to you? Is it something that you feel is expected of you? Why or why not?
6. Do a little research and explore the terms "open adoption" and "closed adoption." What is the difference between the two?

ADDITIONAL READINGS

Bailey, M.J., Guldi, M.E., Hershbein, B.J. (2013). Is there a case for a "second demographic transition"? Three distinctive features of the post-1960 US fertility decline. National Bureau of Economic Research (NBER), NBER Working Paper No. 19599.

Berger, L.M., Cancian, M. and Meyer, D.R. 2012. Maternal re-partnering and new-partner fertility: Associations with nonresident father investments in children. *Children and Youth Services Review*, 32(4), 426–36.

Edin, K., & Nelson, T.J. (2013). *Doing the best I can: Fatherhood in the inner city*. Berkeley, CA: University of California Press, Ltd.

Meyer, D.R., & Cancian, M. 2012. I'm not supporting his kids: Nonresident fathers' contributions given mothers' new fertility. *Journal of Marriage and Family*, 74(1), 132–51.

Osiewalska, B. (2015). Couples' socioeconomic resources and completed fertility in Poland. *Studia Demograficzne*, 1(167), 31–60.

Tach, L., Edin, K., Harvey, H., & Bryan, A. (2014). The Family-go-round: Family complexity and father involvement from a father's perspective. *The Annals of the American Academy of Political and Social Science (AAPSS)*, 654, 169–184.

KEY TERMS

Courtly Love

Romanticism

Eros

Storge

Ludus

Pragma

Mania

Agape

Companionate Love

Sternberg's Triangle of Love

Symbolic Interactionism

Conflict Theory

Structure-Functionalism

Complementary Needs

Role Consensus

Wheel Theory of Love

Stimulus-Value-Role Model

4

FORMING INTIMATE RELATIONSHIPS

By Gene H. Starbuck and Karen Saucier Lundy

Gene H. Starbuck and Karen Saucier Lundy, "Forming Intimate Relationships," Families in Context: Sociological Perspectives, pp. 191-217, 466-526. Copyright © 2014 by Taylor & Francis Group. Reprinted with permission.

PRELUDE

Janeen and Armando each had three or four romances, each seeming more serious than the last, before they met each other their last year in high school. There was initial mutual attraction and rapport. They gradually came to talk to each other about their hopes, fears, and dreams. They began to depend on each other for companionship and going places together.

The couple began to develop their own shared private jokes and views of the world, based on their experiences together. They didn't talk much about the future, though; they weren't sure they would have a future together. Once in a while they talked about living together, but the question of marriage never came up.

Janeen and Armando became sociology majors. They learned both from their classes and from their professors' lives. Sociologists often pride themselves on their objective and rational view of society. But sociologists, too, are human products of that society.

Sociologists also fall in love, sometimes with the wrong person. We have good and bad relationships. We do heroic and silly things for the sake of those relationships.

Professional objectivity does not always lead to personal rationality, because romantic love has inherently irrational properties. Falling is love is gloriously risky business.

But who would want to give up on the possibilities?

The process of forming close personal relationships is complicated. Love is a major reason for two persons to form a relationship that is considered special to both partners. Only some of these relationships result in marriage. This chapter focuses on the development of close personal relationships, particularly those that have the potential to include sexual activity or a romantic commitment as part of the relationship.

Thinking Ahead Make a list of the characteristics that would attract you to a member of the opposite sex; make another list of those characteristics that you would find desirable in a close same-sex friendship. How do the lists compare? How do you think your lists would compare with the lists made by someone of the opposite sex?

This chapter is about that intimate phenomenon we call love, especially the type now associated with romance and marriage. It is only recently in history that romantic love has become the preferred mechanism for selecting mates, but that does not necessarily mean love was unknown in earlier times.

HISTORICAL IMAGES OF LOVE

Perceptions of love vary from one culture to another. Love has also changed over time and therefore has a history (Swidler, 1980, 1986; Barich & Bielby, 1996). This section will first present different viewpoints on the question, "Is love universal?" Then

Couple in love.

we will look at love in ancient Greece and Rome. Courtly love in Europe will be our next historical era, followed by the intertwined developments of romanticism and industrialization. This history contrasts with today's views of love but also helps us understand how today's views developed.

IS LOVE UNIVERSAL?

Strong feelings of attachment have probably always been characteristic of human groups. The relationships between mothers and their children, between brothers and sisters, and between adult men and women who have known each other for a long time, had characteristics that today could be defined as love. There is debate, however, about the universality of the type of love referred to as "romantic" or "passionate" love.

Hatfield and Rapson (1987) argued that passionate love could be found throughout all human eras. They found that children as young as 4 years of age have intense experiences of falling in love. Hatfield and Rapson (1987) also found no differences in the incidence of love for men and women or for different ethnic groups. This evidence would indicate that romantic love is indeed universal.

Jankowiak and Fischer (1992) undertook a cross-cultural study of romantic love, which they defined as "The idealization of the other, within an erotic context, with the expectation of enduring for some time into the future" (p. 150). Using the standard cross-cultural sample compiled by Mur-dock and White (1969), Jankowiak and Fisher found enough information about 166 cultures to determine whether romantic love, by their definition, existed or not. The concept of romantic love was known in 88.5% of cultures. Not all persons in these cultures experienced romantic love; in some, evidence of romantic love was found only in myths and in stories. Even where many individuals in the culture experienced romantic love, it was not necessarily associated with marriage. One's spouse and one's romantic lover were often different persons. Although it is not quite universal, Jankowiak and Fischer wrote, they believed romantic love to be characteristic of human groups even in early hunting-gathering societies.

Other researchers maintain that passionate love is a more recent arrival on the human scene. Solomon (1981) argued that romantic love can only exist in a society, such as the modern United States, that has a high emphasis on individuality, self-identity, independence, and social mobility. Perhaps the safest conclusion is that something like romantic love probably existed for at least some persons throughout history but that the meanings and uses of this form of intimacy have varied considerably. A short historical comparison, beginning with the ancient Greeks and Romans, illustrates this diversity of love in Western societies.

LOVE IN ANCIENT GREECE AND ROME

Along with other Greek philosophers, Plato spent a good deal of time discussing love. The purest kind of love, in his view, had little to do with interpersonal intimacy but involved a spiritual quest for truth and beauty. Less lofty love, involving sexual attraction and fulfillment, was also recognized, but even this form of love had little to do with marriage. Instead, it often involved a homosexual relationship, usually between an older man who served as political mentor and his younger apprentice. In his book *Symposium,* Plato had the character Aristophanes reserve passionate heterosexual love for the class of adulterers and promiscuous women. Passion between a husband and wife was not mentioned.

Female homosexual love was also recognized in ancient Greece, best exemplified by the teacher and poet named Sappho who wrote about her affection towards one of her students. Because she lived on the Greek island of Lesbos, female homosexuals came to be called lesbians.

Ancient religions and myths recognized the existence of passionate sexual love. In Greece, the goddess of love was Aphrodite, from which comes our word *aphrodisiac.* Her son was named Eros, the root of our word *erotic.* The Roman counterparts of this pair were Venus and her son Cupid, whose fateful arrows could transform men and women into helpless lovers.

Passionate love, however, was not expected to be part of marriage and family life. A couple could best hope to achieve the state of harmony and lack of disagreement known as *concordia.*

Even though Christianity began as a religion of love, its form of love was spiritual, not physical. Any kind of bodily manifestation of love, especially sexual activity, was believed to contaminate Godly love and was to be avoided if at all possible. Even marital love was not emphasized; the ideal person was one who denied all desires of the flesh. Some early Christian theologians said that intense love of one's spouse, because it conflicted with true love of God, was adultery (Hendrick & Hendrick, 1992).

Most early Christians, of course, continued to marry and have children; some had affairs, and some, presumably, were occasionally smitten by Cupid's arrows. Such occasions, however, were more often seen as tragedies than as models of appropriate behavior. Marriages continued to be arranged because they were seen as too important to be left to the glands of impetuous young lovers. The story of Romeo and Juliette was told in the Middle Ages as a reminder of what can happen when young lovers ignore their parents' wishes and marry for love. The story does indicate, in the telling, that marriage for love was possible and did occasionally occur. By about 1595, when Shakespeare told the tale, more sympathy was with the young lovers and less with their warring families (Benet, 1987).

COURTLY LOVE IN EUROPE

In the 12th century, in the context of feudal Europe, a new form of love arose. Pagan stories of passionate heterosexual love probably were still told, but the major form of human love referred to a relationship between an aristocratic lord and his follower. Kissing was a symbol of loyalty, as when a new knight knelt and kissed his master's ring. After a heroic action by a knight, his master might kiss him on both cheeks. Remnants of that custom remain in parts of Europe, in rituals that seem awkward to some Americans (Collins & Coltrane, 1995).

The new **courtly love** had elements of the three older forms: spiritual love for God, passionate heterosexual attraction, and loyalty of a servant to his master. Rather than a code of loyalty to a male master, however, the knight or other noble figure expressed love toward an exalted lady. She might recognize his attention by granting him a scarf or other garment as he went into battle. In most stories of courtly love, actual sexual contact occurred, if at all, only after a long period of trials and temptation during which each of the lovers would carry on their more mundane relationships with spouses and children. The essence of courtly love was a spiritual attraction that kept the woman on a pedestal, but there was enough hint of sexual temptation to keep the story interesting.

Embellished by traveling storytellers and poets known as troubadours, tales of courtly love spread. The stories were told in the courts of the aristocracy, and it was assumed that only in such courts could this noble type of love occur; hence the label "courtly love." Such stories are still told today. They are found in Arthurian legends about King Arthur and the Knights of the Round Table and in such accounts as "Tristan and Iseult" and "Brunhild and Siegfried."

Stories of adultery were probably based on some amount of fact, since marriages were not based on love and men were frequently away from their wives fighting wars. Ample opportunity existed for behavior that was not quite as spiritual as stories of courtly love might imply. Among commoners, however, the Church often harshly punished adultery and other nonmarital sex. Marriage remained an economic, not romantic, relationship, and those who could not afford a marriage were expected to remain chaste. Gradually, however, images of love changed throughout European societies.

Courtly love: A code of romantic behavior idealized among the aristocracy of medieval Europe.

One outgrowth of courtly love was an idealized form of etiquette that prescribed how a "lady" was to behave and be treated. The term *lady*, originally a title of nobility, came to mean any woman of high standard who deserved to be treated in a certain way by a *gentleman*. Such expectations later spread beyond the nobility and influenced behaviors of all women and men, especially in formal situations.

ROMANTICISM AND INDUSTRIALIZATION

Romanticism: An artistic and intellectual movement originating in Europe in the late 18th century.

A different form of love evolved in Europe in the late 1700s along with a broader movement known as **romanticism.** This movement in the artistic and intellectual life of Europe and North America was pervasive but difficult to categorize. Benet (1987:840) suggested several characteristics of romanticism:

> a belief in the innate goodness of man in his natural state; individualism; reverence for nature; primitivism; philosophic idealism; a paradoxical tendency toward both free thought and religious mysticism; revolt against political authority and social convention; exaltation of physical passion; the cultivation of emotion and sensation for their own sakes; and a persistent attraction to the supernatural, the morbid, the melancholy, and the cruel.

Although there are apparent contradictions in this list of characteristics, some of them were quite compatible with what came to be known as "romantic love." Individualism, revolt against authority, and cultivation of emotion all justify rebelling against one's family of orientation to cling to the new lover; exaltation of physical passion and sensation for its own sake justify unleashing the power of sexuality, whether fulfilled or not; and interest in mysticism and the supernatural justify the irrational nature of romantic love.

By the 19th century, the phenomenon of romantic love was well established, but its connection with mate selection was not firmly made. Although not all elements of romanticism are compatible with industrialization, individualism is. The power of extended families to choose mates for young persons waned as industrialization progressed. The power of romantic love increasingly became acceptable as a mechanism by which individuals could choose their own mates. In the United States, 20th-century leader of the industrial revolution, the triumph of romantic love over parental choice reached its peak. Today, a parent's suggestion that he or she might have a voice in their child's mate selection is treated as an unwarranted threat to the young person's "right" to choose to marry the partner chosen by love.

DEFINING LOVE

Trying to define and describe love has long been an interest of poets. Only recently have social scientists attempted to do so, but they have found that defining the concept remains elusive (Levine, 2005). Before love can be studied, it must be defined in a way that makes measurement possible. The first approach to clarifying the concept "love" is to compare several different definitions in use in American culture. Next, we will consider the word *love* as a symbol with consequences when used in certain contexts. This section ends with a mention of what three different sociological perspectives have to say about love.

DESCRIPTIVE VARIATIONS IN DEFINING LOVE

Some linguists argue that the importance of a concept to a particular culture can be determined by the number of words in the language that express shades of variation in that concept. Given the importance of love in American society, then, it is surprising that the English language lacks an extensive vocabulary for naming various types of love (Hendrick & Hendrick, 1992). Consider the many kinds of phenomena that can be referred to in the context of "love," as a fill-in-the-blank exercise can illustrate:

I love _____
- my parents.
- my lover.
- my spouse.
- my children.
- my grandparents.
- my dog.
- my shirt.
- my job.
- my sociology class.
- my car.
- colorful sunsets.
- God.
- rare prime rib.
- summer vacation.
- the Denver Broncos.
- a good laugh.
- a parade.
- rock music.

The list could go on extensively.

HIGHLIGHT 4.1 *SELECTED IMAGES OF LOVE*

When a couple of young people strongly devoted to each other commence to eat onions. James M. Bailey.

To endure for others. Henry Ward Beecher.

When another person's needs are as important as your own. Abe Burrows.

The word used to label the sexual excitement of the young, the habituation of the middle-aged, and the mutual dependence of the old. John Ciardi.

The drug which makes sexuality palatable in popular mythology. Germaine Greer.

The wisdom of the fool and the folly of the wise. Samuel Johnson.

To place our happiness in the happiness of another. Gottfried von Leibnitz.

A mutual admiration society consisting but of two members ... the one whose love is less intense will become president. Joseph Mayer.

Quicksilver in the hand. Leave the fingers open and it stays in the palm; clutch it and it darts away. Dorothy Parker

When a person's ... own boundary expands to include the other, that was previously outside himself. Frederick S. Perls.

A little haven of refuge from the world. Bertrand A. Russell.

A little foolishness and a lot of curiosity. George Bernard Shaw.

A mutual self-giving which ends in self-recovery. Fulton J. Sheen.

Friendship set on fire. Jeremy Taylor.

A mutual misunderstanding. Oscar Wilde.

Just another four-letter word. Tennessee Williams.

Source: Compact Disk Computer Search of the Software Toolworks Reference Library. 1990. Novato, CA: Software Toolworks.

Although the word *love* can be appropriately used to describe one's orientation toward each of these persons or things, that orientation is different in each case. One does not, hopefully, love one's spouse in the same way as loving one's shirt. Different emotions and different behavioral expectations are involved.

One way to clarify the meaning of a vague concept is to compare it to other concepts through the use of simile and metaphor. Kovecses (1991) found several metaphors used in our culture to make sense of love. Among these are love as unity, as in "we are one"; love as insanity, as in "I'm crazy about you"; and love as food, as in "I'm hungry for your love."

The Western world's intellectuals have differed on their images of love. Some of their insights are given in Highlight 4.1. The quotes reflect both negative and positive images of love, and both serious and whimsical ones.

LOVE AS A SYMBOL

Symbolic interactionist theory can provide one way of looking at love. Like every other word, *love* is a **symbol.** Understanding the characteristics of symbols can help in our search for what love means. Symbols have two major characteristics. First, symbols are arbitrary and learned. Second, symbols stand for types of **referents.**

To say that symbols are arbitrary means that any symbol can stand for any referent. With rare exceptions, there is no inherent connection between a spoken or written symbol and its referent. Whatever arbitrary symbol is used for a particular referent, people must learn to make the connection. Unless the group shares these meanings, communication will be impossible. A major part of the socialization process is learning the arbitrary symbols by which a group shares meanings.

A baby might first hear the word *love* when its mother is softly cuddling it. If that process is repeated, a connection begins to be made between the word *love* and a feeling of safety, warmth, and softness with another person. If a dad bounces his baby on his knee and says, "I love you," a sense of playfulness is added to the feeling of love. As the baby grows older, other family members, the religious institution, the media, friends, and others add more information to the concept of "love."

Our experiences associated with the symbol *love* are sufficiently similar that we can use the word in everyday language and believe that we share its meaning with others. We each learned the word in our own unique experiences, however, so no two persons have exactly the same referents for the symbol "love." There is room for honest disagreement between two lovers about exactly what their love means to each other.

The symbol "love" refers to a set of emotions and feelings, but we can never be sure that two people are referring to the same internal state when they use any "emotion" word. The feelings are subjective and nonempirical. The actions associated with feeling words, however, are more empirical. Although we might occasionally engage in the action of hugging someone we hate, it is a behavioral expectation more often associated with love.

The symbol "love" is associated with many behavioral expectations. When the word *love* is first used in a relationship, when one person first says, "I love you," the nature of the relationship changes. It is as if the person using the word is offering the other person a contract agreeing to certain expectations between the parties. If the other person accepts the offer, perhaps by saying "I love you too," the new relationship contract is in force. Exactly what the new expectations are is not usually clear, but generally a more committed and exclusive relationship now characterizes their mutual script.

Once two persons agree to a **love-appropriate relationship,** the word *love* occurs in certain predictable ways. It is likely to be used in almost ritual fashion on some occasions, especially when the two lovers are going to be apart from each other for a time. Use of the word in that context might refer to an emotional state, but it also is a

Symbol: A thing that stands for something else.

Referent: The something else for which a symbol stands.

Love-appropriate relationship: An affiliation in which the partners mutually accept the use of the word *love*.

Kissing is the traditional sign of affection concluding wedding ceremonies in many societies..

reminder of the committed and exclusive nature of the relationship. It is like saying, "While we are apart, I will behave myself and I expect you to do likewise."

Another common expectation in a love-appropriate relationship is that the expression be reciprocal. In such a relationship, an effective way for one partner to get the other to use the word *love* is to first say, "I love you." The partner is expected to reply, "I love you too." Once this script has been established, the failure of the partner to respond properly is sometimes an indication that something is wrong with the relationship.

While a particular couple might agree on most of the expectations about love, there are frequently differences of opinion that do not arise until one person's expectations have been violated. One partner, for example, might expect to receive flowers on his or her first common Valentine's Day because "that's what people in love do." If the other partner has not learned about that particular expectation of the **love contract,** hurt feelings and relationship disruption are possible. The exact meanings of the love contract, like many other aspects of a relationship, have to be negotiated over time. That negotiation process is more difficult in a society in which love contract expectations are not clearly defined.

The idea that there is a set of expectations associated with the use of the symbol *love* can help social scientists figure out what persons mean when they use the word. Once these expectations are isolated, they can be used as a measure of how much love exists in a particular relationship. Finding Out 4.1 illustrates an example of such

Love contract: Expectations partners in a love-appropriate relationship have for each other and themselves.

an approach. Although the meaning of love is difficult to pin down, Rubin found that it could be measured.

Although Rubin's scales provide both a definition and a measurement device, they do not cover the entire range of variation in the meanings associated with the symbol "love." There are several types of love, to which we now turn our attention.

TYPOLOGIES OF LOVE

The descriptions of love in Highlight 4.1 indicate that there are many different types of love, including some that might have negative consequences. Several researchers have attempted to organize this variation by developing **typologies** of love.

Typology: A systematic classification of related phenomena based on defined characteristics or traits.

LEE'S LOVE STYLES

Perhaps the most widely known typology of love was developed by Canadian researcher John Lee (1973, 1988). He visualized "colors of love" that were different styles adopted by individuals in their love relationships. We might think of them as components of a person's individual script that apply to love relationships with other persons.

Lee emphasized that these should not be seen as right or wrong kinds of love, but as individual variations. He also pointed out that the types were not mutually exclusive; most persons have styles that combine two or more major types. Lee sometimes portrayed the major types as being like colors on a wheel that, when spun, would combine to produce a distinctive style for each person. Lee's six "colors of love" are not associated with specific colors like red or green but rather constitute basic love styles.

Eros is intensely passionate. Physical and sexual attraction are important components of Eros, but the physical image is based on a sense of beauty rather than lust. The erotic lover is eager to get deeply involved quickly and is quite willing to self-disclose. Although intense, Eros is self-confident and not characterized by possessiveness or jealousy.

Eros (AIR-ohs): Love style with intense emotional and sexual attachment, but without possessiveness.

Storge develops much more slowly than does Eros and is less intense. It is the kind of friendship an adult might have for a favorite brother or sister. Storgic lovers typically have common attitudes, values, and interests. If sexual intimacy occurs, it grows out of a developing understanding of each other, rather than from the intense passion that is characteristic of Eros.

Storge (STOR-gay): Affectionate, companionate style of loving.

Ludus is love for mutual fun. The ludic lover often has several partners at the same time in order to avoid too serious a relationship with any one. Although approaching love as a game and entertainment, the ludic lover does not intend to deceive or hurt other persons; the "love contract" is often spelled out early in the game when the lover tells a partner that a long-term commitment is not wanted. Sexual activity is seen as good fun, rather than an outgrowth of a deep relationship or as an intensely passionate involvement.

Ludus (LEWD-us): Love as play and recreation.

FINDING OUT 4.1 *RUBIN'S MEASURES OF LIKING AND LOVING*

Zick Rubin (1970, 1973) was one of the first researchers to develop a quantitative measurement of romantic love. He began by constructing several statements that might be indicative of either loving or liking. He asked more than 200 undergraduate students whether they thought they would agree with each of the statements if applied to someone they loved and someone they liked. By process of elimination, he ended up with 13 statements associated with liking and 13 associated with loving. After further research, he narrowed it to 9 statements for each category, including:

Sample Love Scale items:
I feel that I can confide in _____ about virtually everything.
If I were lonely, my first thought would be to seek _____ out.
I would forgive _____ for practically anything.
I feel responsible for _____'s well-being.

Sample Liking Scale items:
I have great confidence in _____'s good judgment.
_____ is one of the most likable people I know.
_____ is the sort of person whom I myself would like to be.
It seems to me that it is very easy for _____ to gain admiration.

Once Rubin's scale was developed, he administered it to experimental subjects by having them indicate how strongly they agreed with each statement when different person's names were used in the blank statement. These degrees of agreement were then converted into numerical scores.

As Rubin predicted, when the person whose name was in the blank was identified as a friend, "liking scores" were considerably higher than "loving scores." When the other person was a dating partner, both scores were very high, with "loving scores" being somewhat higher.

Rubin tested his measuring scale in other ways also. By observing as couples interacted, in addition to administering the scale to them, he discovered that couples who scored high on the "loving scale" spent more time looking into each other's eyes when they engaged in conversation; mutual eye contact is another behavioral measure of love.

In addition, couples who scored high on the "loving scale" were more likely to say that there was a high probability they would get married. Follow-up studies found that couples with high love scores were more likely still to be dating each other six months later than were those who scored lower on the "loving scale." All of these tests indicate that Rubin's scales provide valid measurements of what most North Americans mean by the words *loving* and *liking*.

Pragma forms the root of the word *pragmatic*. It is practical love, based on a rational assessment of the partner's assets and liabilities. The pragmatic lover would choose a mate in somewhat the same way parents chose mates for their children when marriages were arranged. In looking for a mate, pragmatic lovers try to get the best deal they can in terms of the characteristics they define as important.

Mania is obsessive and compulsive love. It has the sexual attraction and emotional intensity of Eros, but it lacks confidence and is possessive and jealous. The manic lover has extreme emotional highs and lows, feeling especially anxious when his or her partner is not present. Manic lovers might be more prone to extreme jealousy and to violence to themselves and their partners when the relationship is threatened.

Agape is altruistic love, giving and nourishing without expecting anything in return. *Agape* is a Greek word meaning "love feast." In some Christian theologies, it is the kind of love God has for humankind and is celebrated as such in the Eucharist. Among human lovers, Agape is the rarest of Lee's types. Partners are chosen by agapic lovers because of what can be done for the chosen, not what can be done for the chooser. While sexuality might be a part of the relationship, Agape operates on a more spiritual plane.

RESEARCH WITH LEE'S TYPOLOGY

In a process similar to that used by Rubin in developing his Loving and Liking Scales, Hendrick and Hendrick (1992) used Lee's typology to develop their Love Attitudes Scale. This scale has been used to compare the love styles of different categories of persons.

Religiosity, a variable measuring how religious a person is, is related to love styles. The most religious persons most strongly endorsed Storge, Pragma, and Agape. They were least likely to endorse Ludus and Mania (Hendrick & Hendrick, 1987).

Ethnic differences in love styles have also been found. Contreras (in Hendrick and Hendrick, 1992) compared Mexican American couples with Anglo couples. The Mexican Americans were divided into a high-acculturation group, whose language and values were more like the dominant Anglo culture, and a low-acculturation group. No group differences were found on endorsement of Eros, Storge, or Agape. The Anglo group was less endorsing of Ludus than either Mexican American group. The high-acculturation group was most *manic*, followed by the low-acculturation group, with Anglos scoring the lowest. The low-acculturation group was higher in Pragma than either of the other groups.

Research using the Love Attitudes Scale has also been done on dating couples (Hendrick, Hendrick, & Adler, 1988). Partners in relationships tended to have love styles similar to each other. It is not known whether the similarity was negotiated as the relationship developed, or if persons with similar styles are attracted to each other. Couples who were still together a few months later were compared with those who

Pragma (PRAG-mah): Love style emphasizing practical elements in relationships and rationality in partner selection.

Mania (MAY-nee-ah): Love style with strong emotional intensity, sexual attraction, jealousy, and moodiness.

Agape (ah-GAH-pay): Love style characterized by nurturing concern and self-sacrifice.

had broken up. The major difference was that couples who scored high on Eros were likely to stay together, while those high on Ludus were more likely to break up. The latter finding is not surprising, since staying together is not necessarily a goal of the ludic lover.

Most of the studies utilizing the Love Attitudes Scale have been done on relatively small samples of American college students. Research that generally validates the value of the concept, however, has been carried out in other countries, including Japan (Kanemase et al., 2004; Masuda, 2003), Portugal (Goncalves & Castro, 2004; Neto & Conceicao, 2003); Spain, and Mexico (Rodriguez et al., 2003).

PASSION, COMPANIONSHIP, AND COMMITMENT

Whereas Lee's typology had six types of love, Hatfield and Walster (1978; Hatfield, 1988) proposed a two-type system composed of passionate and companionate love.

Passionate love, in Hatfield and Walster's system, is quite similar to Lee's Mania. If there is "love at first sight," it is probably passionate love. This type has a powerful physical component that might be associated with other forms of physical arousal. Dutton and Aron (1974) compared men who had just made a dangerous and frightening crossing of a wobbly suspension bridge with men who walked across a much safer, solid bridge. A female researcher handed all the men a questionnaire after they had crossed their bridge. The high-danger group of men exhibited more emotional and sexual arousal, and more attraction to the researcher, than did the low-danger group. Dutton and Aron concluded that the fear and anxiety was translated, in the minds of the men, into romantic interest.

Another study found that men who had just finished jogging found a woman to be more sexy and exciting than did men who had been sitting still (White, 1981). These studies suggest that, at least among men, a strong initial attraction to someone results partly from a coincidence of the presence of a socially approved love object combined with a generalized state of physical arousal. Whether that initial attraction results in "falling in love" depends on other factors such as perceived reciprocal interest (Aron et al., 1989).

Peele and Brodsky (1975) saw an analogy between romantic love and drug addiction. The person possessed by romantic love, like the drug addict, has tremendous emotional highs and lows; withdrawal symptoms; high dependency; inability to concentrate on anything else; and sometimes difficulty performing other role responsibilities to family, work, and school.

Romantic love is nearly always short lived, and sometimes destructive. It typically includes unrealistically positive illusions about the partner (Fowers, Veingrad, & Dominicis, 2002). John Money (1980) explained this characteristic of passionate romantic love by comparing it to a "love blot." He noted that clinical psychologists, in studying a patient, sometimes use a Rorschach inkblot test. Patients, shown a series of essentially random ink patterns, are asked what the patterns remind them of. The answers given are purported to reveal hidden aspects about the patient. The image seen is not found in the inkblot itself but is projected onto the inkblot by the observer. The pattern itself merely triggers what is in the mind of the observer, who then reveals a part of himself or herself.

Money (1980) concluded that individuals sometimes have images they carry around as part of their individual script. These images are triggered by, and projected onto, another person. The person doing the projecting falls in love not with the other person but with the "love blot" projected onto the other person. The other person cannot possibly live up to the idealized image thrust upon him or her. The initial lover becomes disillusioned, takes back the "love blot," and goes in search of a person who fits the ideal image. Whether Money's theory accurately describes what happens or not, it does provide an explanation of why romantic love rarely lasts long in the face of reality. The other type of love studied by Hatfield and Walster (1978), however, can last throughout a person's life.

Companionate love is most similar to Lee's Storge. Hatfield and Walster (1978:9) define it as "affection we feel for those with whom our lives are deeply entwined." Companionate love develops more slowly than does passionate love; it requires a sense of shared history that can develop only over time. While companionate lovers are first and foremost friends, they can also be sexual partners and have fun together, as erotic and ludic lovers might. Because the element of strong passionate attraction is absent, however, companionate love requires a greater level of intentional commitment.

Sternberg's triangle of love is an image of love made up of three components: passion, intimacy, and commitment. To Sternberg (1986, 1988), passion consists of psychological and physical arousal. Intimacy provides a sense of connectedness and closeness. As a cognitive rather than emotional component, commitment involves a decision to maintain the relationship over time (Lemieux & Hale, 2002).

Sternberg proposed a typology in which types of love were determined by varying degrees of the three major components. A love with large amounts of passion, intimacy, and commitment is called "consummate love." All other types would be low in at least one of the three components. If none of the components were present, there would be no love at all (see Table 4.1).

The more similar the love triangle for each partner, the higher the probability of each feeling happiness in the relationship (Sternberg, 1986; Hendrick & Hendrick, 1992). If both Mark and Mary are very high in passion and intimacy but only moderately high in commitment, they will have a compatible relationship. On the other hand, if Mark is very high in passion and intimacy and low in commitment, while Mary is very high in commitment but only moderate in passion and intimacy, they are mismatched.

Typologies by Rubin, Lee, Hatfield and Walster, and Sternberg derive from psychology and social psychology. The major sociological perspectives also have viewpoints about love, most of which look at its mate selection aspects.

SOCIOLOGICAL VIEWPOINTS ON LOVE

The three most important theoretical perspectives in sociology are symbolic interactionism, functionalism, and conflict theory. Each of these is applied throughout the text but can briefly be reviewed as they might look at love.

Symbolic Interactionism Symbolic interactionism has already been applied in this chapter to the discussion about how persons learn the meaning of the symbol "love." Even if love is associated with particular brain chemicals, persons must still learn what to label the feelings they associate with the presence of the chemicals. They must learn what actions are considered appropriate for persons with such feelings.

TABLE 4.1 STERNBERG'S TYPOLOGY OF LOVE

	Component of Love		
	Intimacy	Passion	Commitment
Nonlove	−	−	−
Liking	+	−	−
Infatuated Love	−	+	−
Empty Love	−	−	+
Romantic Love	+	+	−
Companionate Love	+	−	+
Fatuous Love	−	+	+
Consummate Love	+	+	+

Source: After Sternberg, R. J. (1986). "A triangular theory of love." *Psychological Review* 93:119–35.

In some societies, the feeling of passionate romantic love might be seen as something that, like stomach gas, is uncomfortable but will go away. In other societies, it might be seen as a tragedy. In still others, it might form the basis of marriage. If a person enters a relationship with a loved one, the love contract and other elements of the involvement must be negotiated to form a mutual script for that couple. How persons learn, label, negotiate, and act with others in a particular society is the business of symbolic interactionism.

Conflict Theory Conflict theory, in general, has not been extensively involved in the study of love, although feminism puts love in the context of other forms of exploitation of women (Collins & Coltrane, 1995). From this perspective, love is a social institution that tends to primarily benefit the "haves" of the society.

In the "battle of the sexes," Safilios-Rothschild (1977:3) argued, men are the "haves." Since men have more power, they are able to define love in such a way that women sacrifice their own best economic and emotional interests when they "love" their husbands and children. The assignment of women to the home and family "love" roles is used to encourage economic and social dependence (Kramarae & Treichler, 1985).

When analyzing love in this way, feminists are generally referring to the more passionate forms of heterosexual love. Safilios-Rothschild (1977:10–11) called for more "mature love" that would be an equal, genuine caring for the welfare and individualism of both partners. Similarly, Cancian (1987) called for an androgynous form of love in which there would be no difference in the way men and women feel and act. Dworkin (1976) argued that, in contemporary society, lesbianism is the only way for women to avoid sexist love.

Structure-Functionalism Structure-functionalism sees love as part of the glue that holds families and communities together. This approach generally refers to companionate and other kinds of love that help form attachments between brothers and sisters, aunts and uncles, close friends, and spouses. Even when mate selection is arranged, companionate love often develops as a foundation upon which couples build their lives together.

There are disagreements about whether passionate, romantic love is functional. It has the capacity, as cautionary tales such as Romeo and Juliette indicate, to be the enemy of the extended family and social stability (Jankowiak & Fisher, 1992). For reasons we have discussed above, it can be a temporary and unrealistic basis for a life-long partnership. For both of these reasons, romantic love could be seen as dysfunctional.

On the other hand, in a society where mate selection is by choice, romantic love serves as a cohesive force to help a couple through the difficult process of negotiating meanings in a new relationship. By the time romantic love wears off, companionate love has had time to develop. In this sense, romantic love can serve as a functional bridge between single status and stable marriage.

Although we have by now looked at several different perspectives on what love is and how it operates, we have not addressed the question of how love develops between two persons.

PROCESSES OF LOVE

Of all the persons one is likely to meet in a lifetime, only a few are potential romantic lovers. Questions about how persons fall in love, and with whom, have three basic kinds of theoretical answers: individualistic compatibility, value and role compatibility, and sequential stage models.

INDIVIDUALISTIC COMPATIBILITY THEORIES

This category of theories focuses on psychological or personality characteristics of individuals and how these characteristics might incline two individuals to be attracted to each other. The two types of individualistic compatibility theories most commonly discussed are parental image and complementary needs.

Parental Image Theories Parental image theories suggest that individuals, usually unconsciously, tend to select mates who are similar to their opposite-sex parent. Most variations on this theme stem from the psychoanalytic theories of Sigmund Freud. In his view, part of the developmental process involved boys and girls learning that love and sexual attachments are supposed to be toward members of the opposite sex. In the process, boys learn to identify with their father and desire their mother—or women like her. Girls learn to identify with their mother and see their father, or men like him, as proper love objects. Less Freudian versions of the theory more simply assume that parents are role models whose characteristics children come to see as desirable.

It is true that person's mates tend to have at least some characteristics in common with their parents (Jedlicka, 1984). Part of the problem with researching theories of this type is determining what similar characteristic between parents and love-objects to look for. Defined broadly enough, some common characteristics could be found between any two randomly selected persons on earth. It is not surprising, then, that one's spouse has some characteristics in common with one's opposite-sex parent, but that is not proof that the similarities were the cause of the attraction. Most characteristics that one's intimate partner and one's opposite-sex parent have in common are due to the fact that individuals tend to partner with those of the same social-class background, race, and religion. Both one's mate and one's parents are likely to share those characteristics.

Complementary Needs Complementary needs theories were first developed by Robert F. Winch (1958) to explain mate selection in societies, like the United States, where romantic love was the basis of choice. The theory assumes that individuals vary in the kind of psychological needs they have, and that they will be attracted to others who help meet those needs. If the other also has a need that the first person can meet, the two individuals have complementary needs and are likely to develop a mutual love.

This view finds popular support in the folk saying, "opposites attract," but it lacks empirical support from several studies that have attempted to test it (Booth, Carver, & Granger, 2000). It is difficult enough in research clearly to define "needs;" it is even more troublesome to define complementary ones. Most of the complementary needs that have been studied are variations of dominance and submission. Finding that one partner is generally dominant in a relationship, however, does not mean that the couple got together for that reason. The dominance might have developed after the couple fell in love. Also, the fact that one is dominant does not prove that he or she has an inherent need to be that way or that the partner has a need to be submissive. Like other theories relying on the measurement of needs or personality traits, complementary needs approaches lack empirical support and have been severely criticized (Cate & Lloyd, 1992; Eshleman, 1994).

VALUE AND ROLE COMPATIBILITY

These theories also have support from folk wisdom, this time in the sayings "birds of a feather flock together" and "water seeks its own level." Some of these perspectives focus on the importance of similarity in values, while others emphasize the compatibility of roles.

Value Theories Value theories suggest that individuals will be attracted to others who have similar ideas about what is good, right, and proper. Early studies using this approach found empirical evidence that premarital and marital partners do tend to have similar attitudes and values (Burgess & Wallin, 1953; Schellenberg, 1960). Value similarity can reduce the potential for conflict in relationships. Two lovers who both value either premarital chastity or premarital promiscuity, for example, are less likely to have problems about that issue than partners without such shared values. Conversations are freer among persons with shared values, as are decisions about mutual activities. When two persons share values, they are each reciprocally validated.

Although value similarity theories have common-sense support, they have also been criticized. Kerckhoff (1974) found that couples tend to have similar values but argued that the similarity resulted from homogamous variables and the fact that similar individuals are more likely to meet each other. Stephen (1985) also found that married couples held similar values, but he concluded that the similarities were more likely to have evolved along with the relationship rather than having been a cause of initial attraction.

Role Consensus Role consensus theories are similar to the value theories, except that roles are more specific behavioral expectations while values are more general. Role consensus theories propose that couples who have similar role expectations are more likely to become intimately involved (Berman & Miller, 1967; Lewis, 1973).

We have seen that persons have their own individual scripts, which provide expectations about the roles they and their partners should play. As a relationship develops, the partners need to negotiate a mutual script that will guide their interaction as a couple. If the young man and young woman both expect that the man will pay for the meals when they go out to eat, there is role compatibility in individual scripts, which will easily become their mutual dating script. If he expects to buy her meal, while she wants to buy her own, their individual scripts conflict and the mutual script must be negotiated. If the negotiation is successful, they have achieved script and role consensus even though it was lacking to begin with.

This example implies that becoming intimate is actually a process, rather than something that happens all at once. The next category of theories follows this assumption.

SEQUENTIAL STAGE THEORIES

Perhaps the most promising theories of developing intimacy are those that combine several of the elements discussed above but assume that different elements are important at different stages in a process. Two of the most widely accepted sequential approaches are Reiss's wheel theory and Murstein's stimulus-value-role model.

The Wheel Theory of Love The wheel theory of love, developed by Ira Reiss (1960; Reiss & Lee, 1988), was one of the first to combine several elements into a stage theory. Reiss imagined love as a wheel with four spokes (see Figure 8.1). While all four spokes are necessary for fully developed love, they turn in a particular order, creating a four-stage process. The wheel always turns in the context of cultural and value systems.

The first stage is the development of *rapport,* which encompasses a feeling of being at ease and able to communicate with each other. Similarity of social and cultural background increases the probability that two persons will develop rapport, as do value agreement and role consensus. If a couple develops rapport, the relationship is more likely to move to the next stage.

The second stage is *self-revelation,* or what is now generally referred to as self-disclosure. As partners trust each other more, they will each reveal more information about themselves. There is sharing of dreams for the future, sins of the past, political and religious beliefs, and other value orientations. The amount of self-revelation varies by gender and social class. Women are likely to reveal their feelings more than are men (Rubin et al., 1980), and middle-class persons tend to self-disclose more quickly than do those in the working class (Rubin, 1976).

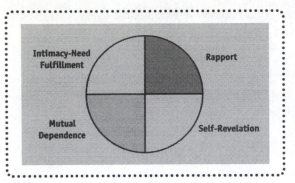

FIGURE 4.1

The Wheel Theory of Love

Source: Adapted from Reiss, Ira L. 1960. "Toward a Sociology of the Heterosexual Love Relationship." *Marriage and Family Living* 22:139–45.

As rapport and self-revelation increase, a couple builds up "interdependent habit systems" (Reiss & Lee, 1988:101). They each get used to doing things that require the other person. This *mutual dependence* is the third process in the development of love. Once the partners begin to work out ways of coordinating their time, money, and activities, they are much closer to a long-term commitment to each other (King & Christensen, 1983).

Couples who navigate the first three stages will then assess whether the relationship provides *intimacy-need fulfillment.* Reiss referred not to the notion of complementary needs but to the meeting of more universal human needs such as the need for someone to love, someone to confide in, and someone to provide sympathetic understanding. These are related to the need for intimacy. Again, needs vary depending on cultural and social conditions and definitions.

The Stimulus-Value-Role Model The stimulus-value-role (SVR) model was developed by Bernard Murstein (1970, 1976, 1987). He found that the process of developing an intimate relationship worked somewhat differently depending on whether it took place in a "closed" or "open" field situation (Cate & Lloyd, 1992). In the "closed" setting, persons are operating in relatively well-defined role situations such as boss-employee, worker–co-worker, or professor-student. "Open" field situations, on the other hand, allow either individual the choice to initiate interaction or not. They might be in the same college class together, meet at a party or other social event, or simply come across one another in the process of day-to-day living. The SVR theory was generally fashioned to explain the development of relationships in more "open" field situations.

The *stimulus* stage involves personal characteristics that might provoke an initial response in other individuals. Since little actual interaction is involved at this point, physical attractiveness is an important component of the stimulus stage. Social exchange theory, which would look at physical attractiveness as a resource, would predict that the best-looking persons would be the most desirable potential partners. Considerable research bears out the preference for attractive partners (Walster et al., 1966; Cate & Lloyd, 1992). A person's attractiveness can even affect the way others evaluate aspects of their personality. Both men and women perceive attractive persons to have more socially desirable personality traits than less attractive ones are thought to have (Saks & Krupat, 1988).

Although individuals express a preference for more attractive partners, the choices of partners might better be predicted by the "matching hypothesis." Perhaps because of fear of rejection, individuals seem to initiate relationship interaction more with others who are more nearly like themselves in levels of attractiveness. A person of average physical attractiveness is more likely to attempt a relationship with someone who is also average in looks than with one who is much more attractive (Berscheid & Walster, 1974).

Although physical attractiveness is very important at the stimulus stage, it is not the only factor. A person's reputation, behavior, sense of humor, apparent wealth and friendliness, and a number of other factors might also be considered.

If both persons are stimulated enough by the potential rewards of a relationship, they will move to the second stage.

Interaction leads to the *value comparison* stage. Increasing self-disclosure leads to an appraisal of the value compatibility of the couple. Views on such matters as politics, religion, gender roles, and leisure activities are revealed and evaluated. Self-disclosure of more personal matters will probably proceed more slowly as trust develops. If this stage is negotiated, the couple will move to the third stage.

The *role* stage involves an evaluation of each person's perception of how they and their partner would be likely to play various roles in their relationship. Compatibility is sought in such roles as companion, lover, housekeeper, breadwinner, and parent. If behavior or conversation reveal a potential role fit, the two are likely to be married or establish some other form of relationship that involves a long-term commitment.

Although Murstein portrayed the three stages as distinct processes that occurred in sequence, more recent formulations of SVR theory hold that all three processes can operate throughout the relationship (Murstein, 1987). Some processes will dominate, however, at different stages of the relationship. Physical attractiveness is very important at the stimulus stage but continues to operate throughout. At later stages, new forms of stimulus arise to maintain interest in continuing the relationship.

The process of establishing role and value agreement does not stop after the couple develops a relationship that they want to be permanent. They continue to communicate and negotiate meaning for the duration of their time together (Duck, 1994).

Both Reiss and Murstein developed their sequential theories to explain the process by which two persons progress from being strangers to being married. In this mate-selection context, the theories have received criticism. For one thing, many couples marry without ever establishing intimacy or role compatibility (Cuber & Harroff, 1968). On the other hand, some couples go through all the stages but never get married. Because of these criticisms, the sequential models have been presented in this chapter to explain the process of developing intimacy in relationships.

GENDER DIFFERENCES IN LOVE

Interest in studying gender differences has, in recent years, produced considerable discussion about the difference in love styles of men and women. We will first review one perspective on these differences, and then summarize specific research findings.

FEMINIZATION OF LOVE

Francesca Cancian (1986, 1987, 1989) wrote that there has been a "feminization of love" in American history. For purposes of her study, Cancian (1989:219) defined love as:

> a relatively enduring bond where a small number of people are affectionate and emotionally committed to each other, define their collective well-being as a major goal, and feel obliged to provide care and practical assistance for each other. People who love each other also usually share physical contact; they talk to each other frequently and cooperate in some routine tasks of daily life.

In Cancian's view, both men and women demonstrated this kind of love in families prior to the development of capitalism. As industrialization and capitalism proceeded, family life and work life were separated. This resulted in the public life of work and the private life of family; men were assigned roles in the public sphere while women were assigned roles in the private one (Ryan, 1979).

Cancian used the distinction, made earlier by Parsons and Bales (1956), between instrumental and expressive roles. As the "cult of domesticity" emerged, women were increasingly associated with the emotional work of expressive roles, while the men took care of instrumental tasks. Love became part of the emotional work assigned to women, so the definition of love was historically altered. The instrumental tasks of "doing things" for a loved one became separated from the former meaning of love.

Traits associated with emotion and feeling were assigned to the "feminine" role: warmth, expressiveness, revealing tender feelings, being gentle, and being aware of the feelings of others. Men were seen as independent and unemotional, with only their interest in sex having a connection to love (Rosencrantz et al., 1968; Cancian, 1986). Although working-class Americans are more likely than the middle class to see instrumental things such as giving money or washing someone's car as a possible sign of love, the general public still associates love primarily with emotion.

The belief developed that men are inherently less capable of love and intimacy than women. This view was supported by the psychoanalytic views of such writers as Chodorow (1978). Psychologists and others in the "helping professions," especially those who write for the popular press, still refer to the alleged inability of men to "share their feelings," to "commit to intimacy," and to truly love (Phillips, 1994).

Cancian argued that, if men appear not to love as much as women, it is because measurements of love are made with a feminine-biased ruler; they have tended to measure the expressive components of love, but not the instrumental and sexual ones. Even on the measures that show that women love more, Cancian maintains, the difference is generally very small. It is even possible that the stereotype that women love more than men is not borne out by available research.

MALE AND FEMALE LOVING STYLES

Some studies do find that women are more loving than men, especially when companionate types of love are involved. Women may invest themselves more deeply in intimate relationships (Sacher & Fine, 1996). Throughout their lives, women have more close friends than do men. Interactions among women are more likely to involve expressive discussions of family and relationships, while men are more likely to gather for an instrumental purpose such as playing or watching a sport (Dickens & Perlman, 1981).

Both men and women report closer relationships to their mothers than to their fathers (Komarovsky, 1976). If a father has to spend long hours away from his family to provide financial support, this is more commonly seen as an avoidance of love rather than as an instrumental expression of love.

Some research finds gender differences, but smaller ones than might first be guessed. Adams (1968:169) found that 58% of adult urban women said that their parents and relatives were very important to them, compared to 37% of men. Comparisons of actual contact, however, yielded different results. Of those who lived in the same city as their parents, 88% of women saw their parents weekly while 81% of men did so.

When Rubin (1973) compared scores of men and women on his "loving scale" and "liking scale" (review Finding Out 4.1), he found only small differences between men and women. When "love for partner" was measured, women scored 90.57 while men scored 90.44. In the category "liking for partner," women scored 89.10 while men scored 85.30. Only in the category of "love for friend" was there a significant difference; women scored 64.79, while men scored 54.47. Finally, in the category "liking for friend," women scored 80.21 compared to the men's 78.38.

Various studies about gender differences and Lee's "love styles" consistently find men to be more ludic (more playful) than women, and perhaps more erotic as well. Women usually score higher for Storge, Pragma, and Mania (Hendrick & Hendrick, 1992; Lacey et al., 2004). One's gender-role orientation appears to make more difference than one's actual sex. To study this issue, Baily, Hendrick, and Hendrick (1987) used the Sex Role Inventory developed by Bem (1974). Significant differences were found on all love scales except Storge. Subjects who scored high in masculinity also endorsed Ludic the most. Those labeled feminine most endorsed Mania and Agape. The androgynous subjects also endorsed Agape, along with Eros and Pragma.

By some measures, contrary to popular perception, men behave in more romantic ways in relationships than do women. Men are more likely than women to use the word *love* first in a relationship. Kanin et al. (1970) found that men fall in love earlier in the relationship, and report being surer that they are in love. Men average higher scores on the "romanticism scale" than do women (Barich & Bielby, 1996).

These findings are often explained by the supposition that women have more to risk in relationships than do men. The "status-borrowing" model implies that women are more dependent for economic support and social status on their husbands than the husbands are on their wives. Because more is riding on their choice of partners, the argument goes, women must move more slowly and carefully in making a choice. Men, with less to lose, can afford to give freer rein to their emotions.

Another explanation is that men are more likely to base their interest on physical attractiveness, which can be determined almost immediately. Women look for other qualities that take longer to assess, so they fall in love more slowly (Collins & Coltrane, 1991). Not only do men fall in love sooner, they also stay in love longer, and are more likely to resist the break-up of a relationship (Hill, Rubin, & Peplau, 1976). Greater love by men appears to continue into marriage, after the marital choice has been made. As perceived by both partners, there are twice as many marriages in which the man loves more than ones in which the woman loves more (Safilios-Rothschild, 1977:72).

Male-female differences in love are still not fully understood, but they can be exaggerated. An emphasis on the differences can obscure the significant similarities. Both women and men believe that love is very important in their lives and are capable of strong love of both the expressive and instrumental types (Cancian, 1989; Barich & Bielby, 1996).

SEXUAL STRATEGIES THEORY

As with every other major topic in this text, there are competing theories about human intimacy. Most of the theories we examine focus on social variables, but some approaches look at the development of human intimacy as a matter of biological strategies. Attempts to explain human and social behavior by referring to biological variables have been around a long time, but a specialized modern science with that goal began to be referred to as **sociobiology** in the 1970s, especially with the work of Edward O. Wilson (1975). The goal of this approach was to "expand the Darwinian . . . model of evolutionary dynamics to explain animal behavior as well as animal morphology" (Boulding, 1978:260).

Sociobiology: A scientific approach that attempts to use biological and evolutionary principles to explain the behavior of all social animals, including human beings.

The human behaviors of interest here are those related to selection of intimates that might have resulted from human evolution. Both genetics similarity theory and sexual strategies theory offer explanations about human selection of intimates. Such theories assume that individual behaviors that increase the chances of successfully passing on one's genes will be more likely than other behaviors to appear in the next generation. As long as the environment remains similar, then, humans will generally come to exhibit behaviors best adapted to that environment (Booth, Carver, & Granger, 2000).

These behavior patterns need not be consciously thought out, but they can take the form of predispositions to behave in a certain way. As a simple example, persons who hate sexual intercourse and avoid coitus are less likely to reproduce than those who enjoy sexual intercourse. If disliking or liking sexual intercourse is an inherited trait, then the species is likely to produce individuals who tend to like sexual intercourse.

One group of biologically based theories has been called "evolutionary psychology" (Wright, 1994; Schmitt, 2005). When applied specifically to human intimacy and attraction, the perspective has been called "sexual strategies theory" (Buss & Schmitt, 1993). This view attempts to explain both male and female selection of intimates, and why the two might differ.

Adult human intimacy is explained in terms of "sexual strategies" that increase the probability of reproducing one's own genetic material. In a sense, human beings are the sperm's and egg's way of producing more sperm and eggs, and the successful human being is one who best does its job in a particular environment. Sexual strategies, however, vary for men and women because their reproductive systems are different. The sex-irreducible difference (Money, 1980) limits reproductive possibilities for women to about one child per year during a relatively short reproductive life, while the reproductive possibilities for men are much less limited. Given the opportunity, a man conceivably could father thousands of children.

Buss and Schmitt (1993) contend that gender differences in intimate human behavior can best be explained in terms of male and female sexual strategies. Although the strategies are directed toward successful mating, not all are guided by the kind of long-term mating that is implied by life-long monogamy. There are short-term mating strategies, too, that can result in the possibility of reproduction. Whether they last one night, a few weeks, or a few months, they call for somewhat different approaches than long-term strategies. For both men and women, long-term and short-term strategies have both advantages and disadvantages. Under certain social conditions, long-term strategies benefit both men and women, but short-term strategies generally have more payoffs for men, who can maximize their reproductive potential by having a great many short-term sexual relationships (Buss & Schmitt, 1993; Schmitt, 2005; Buss, 2005; Tadinac, 2004).

Generally, sexual strategies theory concludes, women get greater payoffs from long-term mating. Since they can have only a limited number of genetic offspring during their lifetimes, they are best served by finding a mate who will provide long-term, quality material support and protection for themselves and their offspring. The mating strategies of women generally reflect these requirements.

Several studies support the contention that "short-term mating will represent a larger component of men's sexual strategies than of women's sexual strategies" (Buss & Schmitt, 1993:210). Surveys find that, while men and women are equally likely to be seeking a long-term mate, men are more likely to also be seeking a short-term mate. Men report desiring more sexual partners during any given time period, from six months to a lifetime, and are willing to have sexual intercourse after knowing the potential partner for a shorter period of time (McBurney et al., 2005; Schmitt, 2005).

One study on a college campus had attractive men and women ask strangers whether they would be willing to go on a date, go back to their apartment, or go to bed with them that evening. Of the women who were asked for a date, 50% accepted; only 6% agreed to go back to the man's apartment; and none agreed to have sex that night. Fifty percent of men who were asked to go on a date agreed, the same proportion as the women; 69% agreed to go back to her

apartment, and 75% agreed to go to bed with her that night (Clark & Hatfield, 1989; see Table 4.2).

While men and women both report high standards for long-term mates, men are more likely than women to apply less stringent standards for short-term mates (Kenrick et al., 1990).

Men also have fewer criteria by which they would refuse a partner as a short-term mate; only in the case of physical attractiveness did men maintain high standards (Buss & Schmitt, 1993).

TABLE 4.2 AGREEMENT WITH VARIOUS RELATIONSHIP PROPOSITIONS, BY GENDER, IN PERCENTAGE ACCEPTED

	Percentage Who Accepted	
The Proposition	Males	Females
Go on a date?	50%	50%
Go back to questioner's apartment?	69%	6%
Have sex that night?	75%	0%

Source: Clark, Roger D., and Hatfield, Elaine. 1989. "Gender Differences in Receptivity to Sexual Offers." *Journal of Psychology and Human Sexuality* 2:39–55.

While short-term mating has considerable reproductive advantage for men, according to sexual strategies theory, so does long-term mating. Under certain conditions, at least, long-term mating can provide a better quality mate and offspring, and provide mutual cooperation and division of labor. If women demand long-term mating patterns, it will be to men's advantage to go along (Buss & Schmitt, 1993).

Short-term mating does have some payoffs for women. Immediate material support, as in prostitution and dating, is one reward. Perhaps most importantly, short-term mating can provide criteria by which long-term mates can be selected. Only by knowing a man for a period of time can she judge his ability to meet her standards. Women see promiscuity on the part of a man, or the fact that the man is in a relationship with another person, as highly undesirable characteristics for short-term relationships. While men see these characteristics as undesirable in long-term mates, they are not as likely to see them as being undesirable for short-term mating (Buss & Schmitt, 1993). An international study in 53 countries found that, in all regions of the world, men were more likely to have a short-term sexual encounter with someone who already had a partner. Gender differences were smaller, however, in more gender-egalitarian regions (Schmitt, 2004).

That women are less likely to lower their standards for short-term mating implies they are judging all relationships on the basis of long-term standards (Shackelford, 2004). Men who are stingy early in a relationship are major turn-offs for women, while spending money and giving presents are highly valued. These are indicators that he has the capability and desire to support her later on.

Sociobiologists find that the interest women have in the potential of mates to support them is the result of evolutionary programming, not just the result of a social structure that prevents women from having access to material goods. In the United States, occupationally successful women still look for mates with superior supportive capacity, even though they could support a man who has fewer resources (Townsend, 1989). Cross-cultural studies have found that economic parity of men and women in society has no statistical association with the different stress women and men place on the material resources of prospective mates (Buss, 1989).

Today's college students still have somewhat traditional expectations with respect to their potential mates. Women generally expect their partners to be more intelligent, to be better able to solve problems, and to make more money than they themselves do; this fulfills the provider-protector role. Men expect their wives to do more of the parenting, a fulfillment of the nurturing role (Ganong et al., 1996). These findings applied to both Black and White students.

Studies of personal want ads in newspapers provide additional support for sexual strategies theory. Baize and Schroeder (1995) did a content analysis of want ads to find out what qualities men and women used to describe themselves, and which kinds of ads got the most responses. Younger women got more responses, while older men were better received. The woman's income and education had no influence on the number of responses, but better educated and wealthier men did get more. Descriptions of personality characteristics increased the number of responses for men's ads but not for women's. Finally, mention of physical attractiveness increased responses to both men's and women's ads, but significantly more so for women's. A similar study by Goode (1998) looked at ads that included photographs, as well as written information, of the men and women placing ads. Results confirmed that men were more influenced by physical attributes and women more by financial and occupational success.

Questionnaire data of students in junior high and senior high confirmed the well-documented finding that women prefer men older than themselves (Kenrick et al., 1996). The researchers also found, however, that the young men also preferred slightly older partners. They concluded that women in their 20s, the prime reproductive years, were most desirable for all ages of men, while women of all ages tend to prefer men somewhat older than themselves .

Keenan et al. (1997) surveyed college undergraduates to find out how men and women would behave on dating situations. The research was particularly interested in how much deception would be expected in the students' dates. Results showed that women expected deception in their dates, particularly with respect to the sexual interest of the men. Men, on the other hand, expected very little deception from their female dates. The researchers concluded that women are more cautious than men in dating situations because they bear the brunt of reproduction. This supports predictions made by sexual strategies theory.

The basic difference between men and women, and the sexual strategies those differences imply, can help explain some emotional differences between men and women. Members of both sexes get jealous, but do so in response to somewhat different things. A woman is always secure in the knowledge that her birth children carry her genetic material; she is not always secure in knowing that her mate will continue to provide material and emotional security. Men can never be absolutely certain that the child of their mate is actually carrying their genes. The kinds of things men and women become jealous about tend to reflect the areas of their greater insecurity.

To test this hypothesis, Buss et al. (1992) conducted a study of jealous responses to two different conditions. Men and women were asked how they would feel if the person with whom they were seriously involved was enjoying sexual intercourse with another person (sexual infidelity). They were also asked how they would feel if their current partner was developing a deep emotional attachment to another person (emotional infidelity). The result was that 60% of men said sexual infidelity was more distressing, while 85% of women thought emotional infidelity was worse. Differences in jealousy may reflect different emphases on short- and long-term strategies. For both men and women who were considering a short-term relationship, the sexual infidelity was worse. When considering long-term relationships, however, both men and women thought the emotional infidelity was more severe (Mathes, 2005).

If sexual strategies theory is accurate, men and women with the highest "mate value" should best be able to put their strategy into effect. The highest mate value for men is provided by the ability to provide material and physical security to women and their children, while the highest mate value among women is determined by their physical attractiveness and greater reproductive potential. Men and women who have high mate value should best be able to maximize their strategies (Buss & Schmitt, 1993).

Young and attractive women have a clear advantage in finding mates who can provide material support; their high mate value allows them to actualize their sexual strategies. High-value men also are able to act on their strategies. We have seen that polygyny is found in most cultures, but that within those cultures only the wealthy and powerful have more than one wife. It is these men who maximize their reproductive potential. Moulay Ismail, an emperor of Morocco who died in 1727, holds the record. He reportedly fathered more than 1,000 children (Wright, 1994).

In modern societies, however, polygyny is generally limited or banned outright, and contraception limits reproduction. Richer and more powerful men might no longer have significantly greater reproductive success. According to sociobiologists, however, human behavior is still influenced by reproductive strategies that evolved long ago. If this is true, dominant men should still get more sexual opportunities, whether they reproduce more or not. Mazur, Halpern, and Udry (1994) tested this hypothesis for teenage American males. The men were divided into categories based on how dominant they looked in pictures and asked about their sexual experiences. As was predicted, the dominant-looking men reported that they had been offered more sexual opportunities, although they had not had more offspring.

Sexual strategies theory would also predict that use of various sexual strategies would be influenced by the availability of potential mates. Barber (1999) conducted an historical analysis of women's dress styles and related them to the sex ratio, which indicates how many men are available for every 100 women. When sex ratios were low, there were fewer men available and marital opportunities were limited for women. In these periods, short skirts, which the researchers say signaled sexual availability perhaps even for short-term mating, were popular. When there were more men than there were women, the women had a better chance at long-term mating; the styles then featured narrow waists and low necklines, which signals reproductive value.

Factors other than a male's potential to provide and protect her and her offspring are important in women's selection of partners. One study found that such prosocial behavior as altruism in a man was more attractive than was dominance (Jensen-Campbell, Graziano, & West, 1995). This might imply that women are attracted to men who are dominant over others but altruistic to them.

Sociobiology and other gene-related theories have been controversial in the social sciences. Such theories do provide explanations for several findings about human intimacy, but the data do not necessarily prove the theory. A key theoretical assumption is that a wide variety of behaviors is passed on genetically from one generation to another. There is no definitive proof that such things as sexual interest and preferences are inherited characteristics.

Unconscious, genetically determined sexual strategies are only one possible explanation for such phenomena as age preferences in mate selection (Davis, 1998). It is quite likely, for example, that women have traditionally been interested in marrying older, more economically secure men because the opportunities for women to gain economic security on their own have been limited. As occupational opportunities for women have changed in the 20th century, the marital age gap between men and women has significantly declined.

Sexual strategies theory, like many gender-based perspectives, tends to exaggerate gender differences. Doosje et al. (1999) found some differences between men and women in mate preferences, but they also found that such differences account for only a small fraction of the variation in partner desirability. Mostly, men and women are looking for similar characteristics in mates. Personality types, compatible interests in hobbies, political views, and religious views, and several other factors are of equal importance to men and women but vary significantly from one individual to another.

Sociobiology, like structural-functionalism, has also been criticized on the grounds that it is a conservative justification for the status quo. It appears to justify less sexual responsibility on the part of the man, for example. Sociobiologists and evolutionary psychologists respond that the sexual strategies and genetic predispositions are not imperatives; cultures and individuals can, through institutions and values, organize themselves so that such things as long-term commitment and responsible parenthood become the best individual reproductive strategies. Because that would become the environment in which humans operated, evolutionists would argue, the strategies would adapt accordingly. Because human beings have evolved the capacity to communicate symbolically in large groups, any behaviors resulting from biological predispositions are highly flexible and subject to social forces.

BREAKDOWNS AND BREAKUPS

In the mate selection process, an individual typically has a series of relationships of various degrees of intensity. Before they marry, most persons face the end of at least one serious relationship. We will look at the major factors that result in premarital relationship breakup, briefly address the issue of jealousy, then address dating violence.

RELATIONSHIP RISKS AND STRENGTHS

One of the first studies of relationship breakups was done by Burgess and Wallin (1953). They followed 1,000 engaged couples to see which broke up and which did not. Those that broke up were more likely to have exhibited "parental disapproval of the engagement, differences in leisure-time preferences, differences in religious faith, lower levels of affectional expression and less confidence in the happiness of the future marriage" (Cate & Lloyd, 1992:84).

Twenty years later, a study of 231 college-aged premarital couples reached similar conclusions (Hill, Rubin, & Peplau, 1976). At the beginning of their relationships, couples that eventually broke up were more characterized by "lower level of love, unequal level of involvement between the partners, discrepant age and educational aspirations, differences in intelligence and physical attractiveness, a tendency to date less exclusively and shorter length of relationship" (in Cate & Lloyd, 1992:84).

Hill and colleagues (1976) also looked at gender differences in breakups. They reported that women initiated 51% of breakups, 42% were initiated by men, and 7% were by mutual agreement. Hill also found that two former partners were more likely to remain friends if the man initiated their breakup.

Hill (1976) conjectured that women end relationships more commonly because marriage is more important to them; they are more dependent on men for their money and status. Women, therefore, have to be more practical while the men can afford to be more romantic. It has also been suggested that relationships are more important to women, who are more attuned to relationship quality and are therefore more likely to end a relationship they see as low quality (Schwartz & Scott, 1994).

Relationships operate on what Waller (1951) referred to as the **principle of least interest.** The partner who demonstrates the least affection or love in the relationship is in a position of power because the end of the relationship would be less painful to her or him than to the partner.

More recent research on relationship breakup has generally confirmed the findings of Burgess and Wallin (1953) and Hill et al. (1976), but has found other factors as well. When interpersonal communication became a popular research topic in the 1980s, it was generally found that poor communication put a relationship at risk of breaking up.

Good communication does not always mean complete self-disclosure, however. Baxter and Wilmot (1985) found several "taboo topics" that dating couples avoided or were very careful about. Generally, couples avoided extensive talk about the relationship itself, about prior and other current relationships, about the norms they were developing for their own relationship, and negative things about themselves. While avoiding some of these can threaten a relationship, dwelling on them or discussing them too soon in a relationship can also be risky.

After a thorough review of studies about relationship termination, Cate and Lloyd (1992) classified relationship risks into three categories. The first is social incompatibility, which involves discrepancy in educational aspirations, social class, and other social characteristics. The second category is low relationship quality, including low levels of love and poor communication. The third category is social network influence. A supportive social network, including parental approval and a set of other people who approve and treat the pair as "a couple," is important to the success of a relationship. Sprecher and Femlee (1991) found that such support from the female partner's network was an especially important predictor of relationship stability.

JEALOUSY

While some jealousy might be inevitable in contemporary American relationships, and in small amounts might actually benefit partnerships, it can also be very destructive. That might not be the case, however, in all societies. Hupka (1991) reviewed anthropological studies and found that cultures ranged from very rare to very common. The Todas of southern India discouraged possessiveness of either material goods or of people. There were few restrictions on sexual gratification. The American Apache, by contrast, highly prized virginity and paternity; jealousy there was common. This supports the conflict-theory position that jealousy occurs when relationships are treated like property ownership (Collins & Coltrane, 1995).

Even in property-owning societies, however, the reasons for jealousy, and the typical strength of that jealousy, varies considerably. Buunk et al. (1987) compared jealousy in seven countries. Jealousy over a partner's sexual relationship was high in all countries, including the United States, but was much higher in the Soviet Union than in Mexico. In fact, in Mexico, flirting caused as much jealousy as a sexual relationship for both men and women. Kissing caused considerable jealousy in Hungary, but it did not cause nearly as much concern in the Netherlands.

It is reasonable to conclude that jealousy occurs in all modern societies, but its origins vary. The behavioral reaction to jealousy, too, can vary. Relationship jealousy is a major cause of dating violence.

DATING VIOLENCE

Concern about family violence has led to the discovery that there is a considerable amount of violence among dating couples. Exactly how much there is depends on how violence is defined and measured. A national survey of high school students (Centers for Disease Control and Prevention, 2000) asked, "Have you during the past twelve months been physically hurt by a boyfriend or girlfriend on purpose?" Nearly 9% said yes, including 9.3% of the females and 8.3% of the males. In addition, 12.5% of the females and 5.2% of the males reported being "forced to have sexual intercourse."

Sugarman and Hotaling (1989) looked at 20 studies and calculated the average percentage of persons involved in dating violence over their lifetimes. They estimated that 33% of males and 39% of females would be perpetrators of violence at some time during dating, while 33% of males and 36% of females would be victims. Today's figures might be lower than that. Billingham et al. (1999) found declining rates of dating aggression and violence from 1976 to 1996.

Exposure to violence in one's family of orientation appears to increase the probability of being involved in courtship violence. Most studies find that either witnessing parents engaged in abuse or being a victim of child abuse increased the chances for both men and women of being victims and perpetrators of courtship abuse (Cate & Lloyd, 1992; Foshee, Bauman, & Linder, 1999). Of course, not all young people who witness or are victims of abuse in their families of orientation will become abusive in their own relationships. If they have little exposure to violence in their schools and communities, and if they believe that dating violence is unacceptable, young men and women will be less likely to become abusers (O'Keefe, 1998).

Evidence suggests that some peer groups are more prone to violence than are others. Victims of abuse are more likely to report having peers who were also abused than do nonabused persons; perpetrators report having more friends who were also aggressive in dating (Gwartney-Gibbs, Stockard, & Bohmer, 1987).

Individuals' love styles are related to courtship aggression. Coercive perpetrators are more likely to have a ludic love style and least likely to demonstrate Agape. Those with Storge or Pragma are most likely to be victims (Russell & Oswald, 2002).

FAMILIES IN THE NEWS *TRADITIONAL SWAZILAND NOW HAS MODERN DATING SERVICE*

Swaziland has one of Africa's few remaining monarchies. It has a very traditional culture. It has a king, referred to as "The Mouth That Tells No Lies," who has seven wives. Swaziland has much talk of witches and magic. But it also has Internet cafes, and now it has a dating agency.

Badeli Mamba, 26, says the Swazi language has no word for "romance." There is no custom of giving roses and chocolates, of reading poetry, or of sharing candlelit dinners. Mamba could hardly believe it when she saw a newspaper ad promising to help find husbands or wives.

Pholile Hlatshwayo, a man who embroiders clothes for a living, placed the ad after helping a friend find a husband. Hlatshwayo was surprised when he was deluged with calls and decided he had a good business going. Although the police investigated, they could find nothing illegal about the operation.

His customers are about evenly divided between men and women. One man wanted help finding a second wife, but most are only looking for monogamous relationships. Some men want a new professional woman, while others use the service to find a more traditional wife.

Mamba was not impressed with the first man she was arranged to meet. She dumped the second when he confessed that he was HIV-positive. She was smitten, though, with the third. He even agreed to pay her family the traditional bride price of 17 cows. But when he failed to return from a business trip to Johannesburg, she was heartbroken.

Within a few weeks she had sufficiently recovered to call Hlatshwayo's dating service again. She still believes she can find love there.

Source: Rachel L. Swarns, www.nytimes.com, April 14, 2001.

One study asked about the respondent's exposure to parental violence, exposure to peers who had been involved in violence, and their own experiences with violence. The best predictor as to whether individuals had been victims of violence was whether they had inflicted violence, and the best predictor of whether they had inflicted violence was whether they had been a victim. This "reciprocal influence" of aggression and victimization applied to both men and women (Gwartney-Gibbs, Stockard, & Bohmer, 1987).

The research indicates that, in violent courtships, partners tend to be both aggressors and victims (Frieze, 2005; Sinclair & Frieze, 2002). The forms and consequences of violence are different for men and women, however. Men are more likely to use the more severe forms of violence, and women are more likely to be injured (Sugarman & Hotaling, 1989). For both men and women, those who are verbally abusive and threatening are more likely to be physically aggressive, and those who are physically aggressive are more likely to also be sexually aggressive (Ryan, 1998).

Most observers would see violence as a sign of serious problems in a relationship, but partners involved in courtship violence do not report that its impact is as negative as might be expected. Cate and Lloyd (1992) found that in only a few cases did an act of violence cause a relationship to break up. One fourth to one third of partners in their sample reported that violence made the relationship worse, at least for a time. In the remainder of cases, either the violence had no effect or was even reported to have resulted in improvements in the relationship. Partners who are in relationships in which abuse has occurred report no less love for each other than do those in nonabusive ones, nor do they report high dissatisfaction with their relationship (Gryl, Stith, & Bird, 1991; O'Leary et al., 1989). This finding results partly from the fact that most of the courtship violence was of a relatively minor type like pushing, grabbing, or shoving (Schwartz et al., 1997).

Rape is a form of violence that has historically been thought to occur primarily among strangers. In recent years, however, "date rape" has received considerable attention in both the popular press and research journals.

SUMMARY AND CONCLUSION

Love of some kind has probably always been part of human interaction, but it has taken many forms. In ancient Greece and Rome, love for the truth, homosexual love, and romantic love were all recognized, but they were not necessarily related to mate selection or married life.

A form of distant but interpersonal intimacy, called courtly love, developed in the late medieval times. Romanticism as a literary, artistic, and philosophical movement, made romantic love acceptable. As industrialization made mate selection an individual matter, romantic love became the mechanism of choice.

A good many definitions of love are available. One way to investigate the meaning of love is to see how it operates as a symbol. Such an approach has resulted in the development of ways to measure love.

The typology of love developed by Lee includes six types of love: Eros, Storge, Ludis, Pragma, Mania, and Agape. Other approaches distinguish between passionate love, companionate love, and commitment. Sternberg includes passion, intimacy, and commitment in his three components of love.

The major sociological perspectives each have a different way of looking at love. Symbolic interactionism looks at the way love is learned and how it operates in the lives of individuals and families. Functionalism generally finds that love provides a mechanism to hold human groups together, although it recognizes that some forms of love might be dysfunctional. Conflict-feminism sees love as another mechanism that helps keep wealth and power out of the hands of women.

Various theories look at the way love between two persons develops. Some views are that two persons are inherently compatible because of genetic similarity, similarity to parents, or because they possess complementary needs. Other perspectives look at similarity of values and role consensus. Several variables are combined in the sequential stage theories of Reiss and Murstein.

Our society's images of love might have been "feminized" by capitalism and other forces. Research finds that women might demonstrate more companionate love, but men might be more romantic. Such differences, however, are small.

Sociobiology and related approaches explain attraction in terms of its reproductive consequences. Sexual strategies theory suggests that men benefit more than do women from short-term mating strategies, while both men and women can benefit from long-term strategies.

Most people go through more than one close, intimate relationship before they make a long-term commitment. The end of those relationships can cause great pain and unusual behavior. Dating violence can be a cause of breakup, or a response to a threatened breakup.

In conclusion, this chapter has drawn from historical, psychological, and sociological sources to discuss love and the formation of intimate relationships.

Rethinking in Context Reconsider the list of attractive characteristics you made before reading the chapter. Did your list correspond with the gender expectation suggested in the chapter? Were the characteristics you desired more compatible with short-term or long-term mating selection? What process of developing intimacy does your list imply?

INTERNET SITES

Links to several sources on spirituality and love
http://home.sandiego.edu/~lnelson/love.shtml
Links to several "do it yourself" love quizzes
http://www.links2love.com/quizzes_love.htm
Center for evolutionary psychology
http://www.psych.ucsb.edu/research/cep/index.html
Online matchmaking
http://www.matchmaker.com/
http://www.match.com/
A somewhat unusual history of love
http://www.neo-tech.com/pleasures/history.html
Dating violence
http://www.4woman.gov/violence/dating.cfm

REFERENCES

Abbey, Antonia, Frank M. Andrews, & L. Jill Halman. 1992. "Infertility and Subjective Well-Being: The Mediating Roles of Self-Esteem, Internal Control, and Interpersonal Conflict." *Journal of Marriage and the Family* 54:408–17.

Abernathy, Virginia. 1993. *Population Politics: The Choices That Shape Our Future.* New York: Plenum Press.

Acock, Alan, & David H. Demo. 1994. *Family Diversity and Well-Being.* Thousand Oaks, CA: Sage. Adams, Bert N. 1968. *Kinship in an Urban Setting.* Chicago: Markham.

Adler, Nancy E., Henry P. David, & Brenda Major. 1990. "Psychological Responses After Abortion." *Science* 248:41–44.

Ahrons, Constance R. 2004. *We're Still Family: What Grown Children Have to Say About Their Parents' Divorce.* New York: Harper Collins.

Aldous, Joan, & Rodney F. Ganey. 1999. "Family Life and the Pursuit of Happiness: The Influence of Gender and Race. *Journal of Family Issues* 20:155–80.

Amato, Paul R. 1987. "Family Processes in One-Parent, Stepparent, and Intact Families: The Child's Point of View." *Journal of Marriage and the Family* 49:327–37.

Amato, Paul R. 1999. "The Postdivorce Society: How Divorce Is Shaping the Family and Other Forms of Social Organization." In *The Postdivorce Family: Children, Parenting, and Society,* edited by Ross A. Thompson and Paul Amato. Thousand Oaks, CA: Sage.

Amato, Paul R. 2000. "The Consequences of Divorce for Adults and Children." *Journal of Marriage and the Family* 62:1269–87.

Amato, Paul R. 2003. "Reconciling Divergent Perspectives: Judith Wallerstein, Quantitative Family Research, and Children of Divorce." *Family Relations* 52:332–39.

Amato, Paul R., & Alan Booth. 1991. "The Consequences of Divorce for Attitudes Toward Divorce and Gender Roles." *Journal of Family Issues* 12:306–22.

Amato, Paul R., & Jacob Cheadle. 2005. "The Long Reach of Divorce: Divorce and Child Well-Being Across Three Generations." *Journal of Marriage and the Family* 67:191–206.

Amato, Paul R., & Joan G. Gilbreth. 1999. "Nonresident Fathers and Children's Well-Being: A Meta-Analysis. *Journal of Marriage and the Family* 61:557–73.

Amato, Paul R., & Bruce Keith. 1991. "Parental Divorce and Adult Well-being: A Meta-analysis." *Journal of Marriage and the Family* 53:43–58.

Amato, Paul R., & Denise Previti. 2003. "People's Reasons for Divorcing: Gender, Social Class, the Life Course, and Adjustment." *Journal of Family Issues* 24:602–26.

Amato, Paul R., & Stacey J. Rogers. 1997. "Do Attitudes Toward Divorce Affect Marital Quality?" Paper presented at the meeting of the American Sociological Association, Toronto.

Aquilino, William S. 1994. "Later-Life Parental Divorce and Widowhood: Impact on Young Adults' Assessment of Parent-Child Relations." *Journal of Marriage and the Family* 56:908–22.

Aquilino, William S. 2005. "Impact of Family Structure on Parental Attitudes Toward the Economic Support of Adult Children over the Transition to Adulthood." *Journal of Family Issues* 26:143–67.

Arditti, Joyce. 1992. "Differences Between Fathers with Joint Custody and Noncustodial Fathers." *American Journal of Orthopsychiatry* 62:186–95.

Arendell, Terry. 1986. *Mothers and Divorce: Legal, Economic, and Social Dilemmas.* Berkeley: University of California Press.

Aron, A., D. G. Dutton, E. N. Aron, & A. Iverson. 1989. "Experiences of Falling in Love." *Journal of Social and Personal Relationships* 6:243–57.

Aulette, Judy Root. 1994. *Changing Families.* Belmont, CA: Wadsworth Publishing.

Ayoub, Catherine C., Robin M. Deutsch, & Andronicki Maraganore. 1999. "Emotional Distress in Children of High-Conflict Divorce: The Impact of Marital Conflict and Violence." *Family and Conciliation Courts Review* 37(3):297–314.

Bachrach, Christine A., Kathryn A. London, & Penelope L. Maza. 1991. "On the Path to Adoption: Adoption Seeking in the United States, 1998." *Journal of Marriage and the Family* 53:705–18.

Bachrach, Christina A., Kathy Shepherd Stolley, & Kathryn A. London. 1992. "Relinquishment of Premarital Births: Evidence from National Survey Data." *Family Planning Perspectives* 24:27–32.

Baize, Harold R., Jr., & Jonathan E. Schroeder. 1995. "Personality and Mate Selection in Personal Ads: Evolutionary Preferences in a Public Mate Selection Process." *Journal of Social Behavior and Personality* 10:3:517–36.

Baker, Angela K., Kimberly J. Barthelemy, & Lawrence A. Kurdek. 1993. "The Relation Between Fifth and Sixth Graders' Peer-Related Classroom Social Status and Their Perceptions of Family and Neighborhood Factors." *Journal of Applied Developmental Psychology* 14:547–56.

Barber, Jennifer S., William G. Axinn, & Arland Thornton. 1999. "Unwanted Childbearing, Health, and Mother-Child Relationships." *Journal of Health and Social Behavior* 40(3):231–57.

Barich, Rachel Roseman, & Denise D. Bielby. 1996. "Rethinking Marriage: Change and Stability in Expectations, 1967–1994." *Journal of Family Issues* 17:139–69.

Barth, Richard P. 1991. "Adoption of Drug-Exposed Children." *Children and Youth Services Review* 13:323–42.

Baxter, L. A., & W. W. Wilmot. 1985. Taboo Topics in Close Relationships. *Journal of Social and Personal Relationships* 2:253–269.

Beardsley, Richard K., John W. Hall, & Robert E. Ward. 1939. *Village Japan.* Chicago: University of Chicago Press.

Beeghley, Leonard, & Jeffrey W. Dwyer. 1989. "Social Structure and the Divorce Rate," *Perspectives on Social Problems* 1:147–70.

Beer, William R. 1992. *American Stepfamilies.* New Brunswick, NJ: Transaction.

Bem, Sandra L. 1974. "The Measurement of Psychological Androgyny." *Journal of Consulting and Clinical Psychology* 42:155–62.

Benet, William Rose, ed. 1987. *Benet's Reader's Encyclopedia,* 3rd ed. New York: Harper & Row.

Benokraitis, Nijole B. 1993. *Marriages and Families: Changes, Choices, and Constraints.* Englewood Cliffs, NJ: Prentice Hall.

Berger, Peter L., & Hansfried Kellner. 1964. "Marriage and the Construction of Reality." *Diogenes* 45:1–25. Berger, G., M. Goldstein, & M. Fuerst. 1989. *The Couple's Guide to Fertility.* New York: Doubleday.

Berman, E., & D. R. Miller. 1967. "The Matching of Mates." In *Cognition, Personality and Clinical Psychology,* edited by R. Jesser and S. Fenschback. San Francisco: Jossey-Bass.

Berscheid, Ellen, & Elaine Walster. 1974. "Physical Attractiveness." Pp. 158–216 in *Advances in Experimental Social Psychology,* Vol. 7, edited by L. Berkowitz. New York: Academic Press.

Blake, Nelson M. 1962. *The Road to Reno: A History of Divorce in the United States.* New York: Macmillan.

Bohannan, Paul. 1970. "The Six Stations of Divorce." Pp. 29–55 in *Divorce and After,* edited by Paul Bohannan. New York: Doubleday.

Bohme, Gernot. 1984. "Midwifery as Science: An Essay on the Relations between Scientific and Everyday Knowledge." In *Society and Knowledge: Contemporary Perspectives in the Sociology of Knowledge,* edited by N. Stehr and V. Meja. New Brunswick, NJ: Transaction Books.

Bongaarts, John. 1992. "Infertility After Age 30: A False Alarm." *Family Planning Perspectives* 14:75.

Booth, Alan, ed. 1991. *Contemporary Families: Looking Forward, Looking Back.* Minneapolis, MN: National Council on Family Relations.

Booth, Alan. 1999. "Causes and Consequences of Divorce." Pp. 29–48 in *The Postdivorce Family: Children, Parenting, and Society,* edited by Ross A. Thompson and Paul R. Amato. Thousand Oaks, CA: Sage Publications.

Booth, Alan, & Paul R. Amato. 2001. "Parental Predivorce Relations and Offspring Postdivorce Well-Being. *Journal of Marriage and the Family* 63:197–212.

Booth, Alan, & John Edwards. 1992. "Starting Over: Why Remarriages Are More Unstable." *Journal of Family Issues* 13:179–94.

Boulding, Kenneth. 1978. "Sociobiology or Biosociology?" Pp. 260–76 in *Sociobiology and Human Nature,* edited by Michael S. Gregory, Anita Silvers, and Diane Sutch. San Francisco: Jossey-Bass.

Bramlett, M. D., & W. D. Mosher. 2002. *Cohabitation, Marriage, Divorce, and Remarriage in the United States.* National Center for Health Statistics. *Vital Health Statistics* 23(22). Online at http://www.cdc.gov/nchs/data/series/sr_23/sr23_022.pdf. Accessed December 2, 2005.

Bray, James H. 1988. "Children's Development during Early Remarriage." Pp. 279–98 in *Impact of Divorce, Single Parenting and Stepparenting on Children,* edited by E. Mavis Hetherington and Josephine D. Arasteh. Hillsdale, NJ: Erlbaum.

Brinig, Margaret F. 1998. "Economics, Law, and Covenant Marriage." *Gender Issues* 16(1–2):4–33.

Bromwich, P., & T. Parsons. 1990. *Contraception: The Facts.* Oxford: Oxford University Press.

Bronstein, Phyllis, Miriam Frankel Stoll, & JoAnn Clauson. 1994. "Fathering after Separation or Divorce: Factors Predicting Children's Adjustment." *Family Relations* 43:469–79.

Buchanan, Christy, Eleanor E. Maccoby, & Sanford M. Dornbush. *Adolescents After Divorce.* Cambridge, MA: Harvard University Press.

Burch, Ernest S. 1970. "Marriage and Divorce among North American Eskimos." Pp. 152–81 in *Divorce and After,* edited by Paul Bohannon. New York: Doubleday.

Burgess, Ernest W., & Harvey J. Lock. [1945] 1953. *The Family: From Institution to Companionship.* New York: American Book.

Burgess, Ernest W. & Paul Wallin. 1953. *Engagement and Marriage.* Philadelphia: Lippincott.

Burtch, Brian E. 1994. *Trials of Labour: The Re-emergence of Midwifery.* Buffalo: McGill-Queen's University Press.

Buss, David M. 1989. "Sex Differences in Human Mate Preferences: Evolutionary Hypotheses Tested in 37 Cultures." *Behavior and Brain Sciences* 12:1–49.

Buss, David M., R. J. Larsen, D. Westen, & J. Semmelroth. 1992. "Sex Differences in Jealousy: Evolution, Physiology, and Psychology." *Psychological Science* 3:251–55.

Buss, David M., & David P. Schmitt. 1993. "Sexual Strategies Theory: An Evolutionary Perspective on Human Mating." *Psychological Review* 100:204–32.

Buunk, Bram, & Ralph B. Hupka. 1987. "The Elicitation of Sexual Jealousy." *The Journal of Sex Research* 23(1).

Cancian, Francesca M. 1986. The Feminization of Love. *Signs: Journal of Women in Culture and Society* 11:692–709.

Cancian, Francesca M. 1987. *Love in America: Gender and Self-Development.* New York: Cambridge University Press.

Cancian, Francesca M. 1989. "Gender Politics: Love and Power in the Private and Public Spheres." Pp. 219–35 in *Family in Transition,* 6th ed., edited by Arlene S. Skolnick and Jerome H. Skolnick. Glenview, Il: Scott, Foresman.

Cate, Rodney M., & Sally A. Lloyd. 1992. *Courtship.* Newbury Park, CA: Sage.

Catechism of the Catholic Church. 1994. Mahwah, NJ: Paulist Press (Libreria Editrice Vaticana).

Centers for Disease Control and Prevention. 2000. "Youth Risk Behavior Surveillance—United States, 1999." *Morbidity and Mortality Weekly Report 49:*SS-5. U.S. Department of Health and Human Services. Atlanta, GA. Centers for Disease Control and Prevention, 2000. *Surveillance Report* Vol. 11 # 2, Table 5. Online at http://www.cdc.gov/hiv/stats/hasr1102/table5.htm. Accessed May 4, 2001.

Chambers, David L. 1990. "Stepparents, Biologic Parents, and the Law's Perceptions of 'Family' after Divorce." Pp. 102–29 in *Divorce Reform at the Crossroads,* edited by Stephen D. Sugarman and Herma Hill Kay. New Haven, CT: Yale University Press.

Cherlin, Andrew J. 1978. "Remarriage as an Incomplete Institution." *American Journal of Sociology* 84:634–50.

Cherlin, Andrew J. 1992. *Marriage, Divorce, Remarriage,* revised and enlarged edition. Cambridge, MA: Harvard University Press.

Clark, Roger D. 1992. "Family Structure, Liberty and Equality, and Divorce: A Cross-National Examination." Pp. 175–96 in *Fertility Transition, Family Structure, and Population Policy,* edited by Calvin Goldscheider. Boulder, CO: Westview Press.

Clark, Roger D., & Elaine Hatfield. 1989. "Gender Differences in Receptivity to Sexual Offers." *Journal of Psychology and Human Sexuality* 2:39–55.

Coberly, Frank Sheldon. "Marital Adjustment in Blended Families: The Effects of Stepchidren in the Home on Married Couples." *Dissertation Abstracts International: Section B: The Sciences and Engineering* 56(10–b):5831.

Cole, H. M. 1989. "Intrauterine Devices." *Journal of the American Medical Association* 261:2127–30.

Coleman, Marilyn, & Lawrence H. Ganong. 1990. "Remarriage and Stepfamily Research in the 1980s: Increased Interest in an Old Family Form." *Journal of Marriage and the Family* 52:925–40.

Coleman, Marilyn, and Lawrence H. Ganong. 1997. "Stepfamilies from the Stepfamily's Perspective." *Marriage and Family Review* 26(1–2):107–21

Collins, Randall, & Scott Coltrane. 1991, 1995. *Sociology of Marriage and the Family: Gender, Love, and Property.* Chicago: Nelson-Hall.

Coltrane, Scott, & Michele Adams. 2003. "The Social Construction of the Divorce 'Problem': Morality, Child Victims, and the Politics of Gender." *Family Relations* 52:363–72.

Cooney, Teresa M., & Peter Uhlenberg. 1989. "Family-building Patterns of Professional Women: A Comparison of Lawyers, Physicians, and Postsecondary Teachers." *Journal of Marriage and the Family* 51:749–58.

Cowan, Ruth Schwartz. 1983. *More Work for Mother: The Ironies of Household Technology from the Open Hearth to the Microwave.* New York: Basic Books.

Crosbie-Burnett, Margaret, & Jean Giles-Sims. 1994. "Adolescent Adjustment and Stepparenting Styles." *Family Relations* 43:394–99.

Crosby, John. 1980. "A Critique of Divorce Statistics and Their Interpretations." *Family Relations* 29:51–68.

Cuber, John H., & Peggy B. Harroff. 1968. *The Significant Americans: A Study of Sexual Behavior among the Affluent.* Baltimore: Penguin Books.

Daly, Kerri J. 1999. "Crisis of Genealogy: Facing the Challenges of Infertility." Pp. 1–40 in *The Dynamics of Resilient Families,* edited by Hamilton I. McCubbin, Elizabeth A. Thompson, Anne I. Thompson, and Jo A. Futrell. Thousand Oaks, CA: Sage Publications.

Daly, Kerri. 1994. "Adolescent Perception of Adoption: Implications for Resolving an Unplanned Pregnancy." *Youth and Society* 25:330–50.

Daly, Martin, & Margo Wilson. 1984. "Sociobiological Analysis of Human Infanticide." Pp. 487–502 in *Infanticide: Comparative and Evolutionary Perspectives,* edited by Glenn Hausfater and Sarah Blaffer Hrdy. New York: Aldine.

Davies, Lorraine, William R. Avison, & Donna D. McAlpine. 1997. "Significant Life Experiences and Depression among Single and Married Mothers." *Journal of Marriage and the Family* 59:294–308.

Davis, Anthony. 1998. "Age Differences in Dating and Marriage: Reproductive Strategies or Social Preferences?" *Current Anthropology* 39(3):374–80.

Davis, James Allan, & Tom W. Smith: General Social Survey(s), year(s). (Machine-readable data file). Principal investigator, James A. Davis; director and co-principal investigator, Tom W. Smith; co-principal investigator, Peter V. Marsden, NORC ed. Chicago: National Opinion Research Center, producer, 1998; Storrs, CT: The Roper Center for Public Opinion Research, University of Connecticut, distributor. Micro computer format and codebook prepared and distributed by MicroCase Corporation, Bellevue, WA. Analysis by Gene H. Starbuck.

Davis, Kingsley. 1971. "Sexual Behavior." Pp. 313–60 in *Contemporary Social Problems,* edited by Robert Merton and Robert Nisbet. New York: Harcourt Brace Jovanovich.

Davis, Shannon N., & Theodore N. Greenstein. 2004. "Interactive Effects of Gender Ideology and Age at First Marriage on Women's Marital Disruption." *Journal of Family Issues* 25:658–82.

Dawson, Deborah. 1991. "Family Structure and Children's Health and Well-Being: Data from the 1988 National Health Interview Survey on Child Health." *Journal of Marriage and the Family* 53:573–84.

De Barbieri, M. Teresita. 1994. "Gender and Population Policy." Pp. 257–66 in *Beyond the Numbers: A Reader on Population, Consumption, and the Environment,* edited by Laurie Ann Mazur. Washington, DC: Island Press.

Demo, David, & Alan Acock. 1988. "The Impact of Divorce on Children." *Journal of Marriage and the Family* 50:619–48.

Demo, David, & Alan Acock. 1996. "Singlehood, Marriage, and Remarriage: The Effects of Family Structure and Family Relationships on Mothers' Well-Being." *Journal of Family Issues* 17:388–407.

Derwinski-Robinson, B. 1990. "Infertility and Sexuality." Pp. 291–304 in *Sexual Health Promotion,* edited by C. I. Fogel and D. Lauver. Philadelphia: W. B. Saunders.

Dickens, Wenda, & Daniel Perlmen. 1981. "Friendship over the Life Cycle." Pp. 91–122 in *Personal Relationships Vol. 2,* edited by Steve Duck and Robin Gilmour. London: Academic Press.

Donnison, Jean. 1988. *Midwives and Medical Men: A History of the Struggle for the Control of Childbirth.* London: Historical Publications.

Duck, Steve. 1994. *Meaningful Relationships: Talking, Sense, and Relating.* Newbury Park, CA: Sage.

Duncan, Greg J., Jeanne Brooks-Gunn, & Pamela Kato Klebanov. 1994. "Economic Deprivation and Early Childhood Development." *Child Development* 65:296–318.

Dutton, Donald, & Arthur Aron. 1974. "Some Evidence for Heightened Sexual Attraction under Conditions of High Anxiety." *Journal of Personality and Social Psychology* 4:510–17.

Dworkin, Andrea. 1976. *Our Blood: Prophecies and Discourses on Sexual Politics.* New York: Harper & Row.

Edin, Kathryn, & Laura Lein. 1997. "Work, Welfare, and Single Mothers' Economic Survival Strategies." *American Sociological Review* 62:253–66.

Ehrlich, Paul. 1997. *The Population Explosion.* New York: Buccaneer Books.

Elwell, Frank. 1999. *Malthus' Home Page.* Online at http://www.faculty.rsu.edu/~felwell/Theorists/Malthus/Index.htm.

Emery, Robert E. 1999. "Postdivorce Family Life for Children: An Overview of Research and Some Implications for Policy." Pp. 3–28 in *The Postdivorce Family: Children, Parenting, and Society.* Thousand Oaks, CA: Sage Publications.

Emery, Robert E., & Peter Dillon. 1994. "Conceptualizing the Divorce Process: Renegotiating Boundaries of Intimacy and Power in the Divorced Family System." *Family Relations* 43:374–79.

Eshleman, J. Ross. 1994. *The Family: An Introduction,* 7th ed. Boston: Allyn and Bacon. Esterbrook, Gregg. 2000. "Abortion and Brain Waves." *The New Republic,* January 1.

Faludi, Susan. 1991. *Backlash: The Undeclared War Against American Women.* New York: Crown Publishers.

Fathalla, Mahmoud F. 1994. "From Family Planning to Reproductive Health." Pp. 144–49 in *Beyond the Numbers: A Reader on Population, Consumption, and the Environment,* edited by Laurie Ann Mazur. Washington, DC: Island Press.

Fergusson, David M., L. John Horwood, & Michael T. Lynsky. 1994. "Parental Separation, Adolescent Psychopathology, and Problem Behaviors." *Journal of the American Academy of Child and Adolescent Psychiatry* 33:1122–31.

Fine, Mark A., Marilyn Coleman, & Lawrence H. Ganong. 1998. "Consistency in Perceptions of the Step-Parent Role Among Step-Parents, Parents and Stepchildren." *Journal of Social and Personal Relationships* 15(6):810–28.

Fine, Mark A., Brenda W. Donnelly, & Patricia Voydanoff. 1991. "The Relationhsip between Adolescents' Perception of their Family Lives and the Adjustment in Stepfather Families. *Journal of Adolescent Research* 6:423–36.

Fine, Mark A., & Lawrence A. Kurdek. 1992. "The Adjustment of Adolescents in Stepfather and Stepmother Families." *Journal of Marriage and the Family* 54:725–36.

Fine, Mark A., Patricia Voydanoff, & Brenda W. Donnelly. 1993. "Relations between Parental Control and Warmth and Child Well-being in Stepfamilies." *Journal of Family Psychology* 7:222–32.

Fineman, Martha. 1989. "Societal Factors Affecting the Creation of Legal Rules for Distribution of Property and Divorce." *Family Law Quarterly* 23:279–99.

Fishman, Barbara. 1983. "The Economic Behavior of Stepfamilies." *Family Relations* 32:359–66.

Foshee, Vangie A., Karl I. Bauman, & G. Fletcher Linder. 1999. "Family Violence and the Perpetration of Adolescent Dating Violence: Examining Social Learning and Social Control Processes." *Journal of Marriage and the Family* 61:331–42.

Fowers, Blaine J., Marla Reis Veingrad, & Carmentxu Dominicis. 2002. "The Unbearable Lightness of Positive Illusions: Engaged Individuals' Explanations of Unrealistically Positive Relationship Perceptions. *Journal of Marriage and the Family* 64:450–60.

Frieze, Irene Hanson. 2005. *Hurting the One You Love: Violence in Relationships.* Belmont, CA: Wadsworth/Thom-son.

Funder, K., M. Harrison, & R. Weston. 1993. *Settling Down: Pathways of Parents After Divorce.* Melbourne, Australia: Australian Institute of Family Studies.

Furstenberg, Frank F., Jr. 1980. "Reflections on Remarriage: Introduction to *Journal of Family Issues* Special Issue on Remarriage." *Journal of Family Issues* 1:443–53.

Furstenberg, Frank F., Jr. 1987. "The New Extended Family: The Experience of Parents and Children after Remarriage." Pp. 42–61 in *Remarriage and Stepparenting,* edited by Kay Pasley and Marilyn Ihinger-Tallman. New York: Guilford.

Furstenberg, Frank F., Jr. 1990. "Divorce and the American Family." *Annual Review of Sociology* 16:379–403.

Furstenberg, Frank E., & Graham B. Spanier. 1984. *Recycling the Family: Remarriage After Divorce.* Beverly Hills, CA: Sage.

Gander, Anita Moore. 1991. "After the Divorce: Familial Factors That Predict Well-Being for Older and Younger Persons." *Journal of Divorce and Remarriage* 15:175–92.

Ganong, Lawrence H., Marilyn Coleman, & Deborah Mistrina. 1995. "Home Is Where They Have to Let You In: Beliefs Regarding Physical Custody Changes of Children Following Divorce." *Journal of Family Issues* 16:466–87.

Ganong, Lawrence H., Marilyn Colemen, Aaron Thompson, & Chanel Goodwin-Watkins. 1996. "African American and European American College Students' Expectations for Self and for Future Partners."*Journal of Family Issues* 17(6):758–75.

Giddens, Anthony. 1992. *The Transformation of Intimacy: Sexuality, Love & Eroticism in Modern Societies.* Cam-bridge, UK: Polity Press.

Glenn, Norval D. 1996. "Values, Attitudes, and the State of American Marriage." Pp. 15–34 in *Promises to Keep: Decline and Renewal of Marriage in America,* edited by David Popenoe, Jean Bethke Elshtain, and David Blankenhorn. Lanham, MD: Rowman and Littlefield.

Glenn, Norval D., & Michael Supancic. 1984. "The Social and Demographic Correlates of Divorce and Separation in the United States: An Update and Reconsideration." *Journal of Marriage and the Family* 46:563–75.

Goldschieder, Calvin. 1992. *Fertility Transition, Family Structure, and Population Policy.* Boulder, CO: Westview Press.

Goncalves, Luis, & Helena Castro. 2004. "The Love Style Among Young Portuguese Students: Gender Differentiation." *Psicologia Educacao Cultura* 8:249–62.

Goode, Erich. 1996. "Gender and Courtship Entitlement: Responses to Personal Ads." *Sex Roles* 343(3–4):141–69. Goode, Erich. 1998. "Photographs as Sexual Advertisements: Responses to Personal Ads." *Sociological Focus* 31(4):373–89.

Goode, William J. 1963, 1970. *World Revolution and Family Patterns,* New York: Free Press. Goode, William J. 1964. *The Family.* Englewood Cliffs, NJ: Prentice-Hall.

Goode, William J. 1993. *World Changes in Divorce Patterns.* New Haven: Yale University Press.

Greenstein, Theodore N. 1990. "Marital Disruption and the Employment of Married Women." *Journal of Marriage and the Family* 52:657–76.

Greenstein, Theodore N. 1995. "Gender Ideology, Marital Disruption, and the Employment of Married Women." *Journal of Marriage and the Family* 57:31–42.

Grizzle, Gary L. 1999. "Institutionalization and Family Unity: An Exploratory Study of Cherlin's (1978) Views." *Journal of Divorce and Remarriage* 30(3–4):125–37.

Gryl, Frances E., Sandra M. Stith, & Gloria W. Bird. 1991. "Close Dating Relationships among College Students: Differences by Use of Violence and Gender." *Journal of Social and Personal Relationships* 8:243–64.

Gutmann, Joseph, & Amnon Lazar. 1998. "Mother's or Father's Custody: Does It Matter for Social Adjustment?" *Educational Psychology* 18(2):225–34.

Gwartney-Gibbs, Patricia A., Jean Stockard, & Susanne Bohmer. 1987. "Learning Courtship Aggression: The Influence of Parents, Peers, and Personal Experiences." *Family Relations* 36:276–82.

Handwerker, W. Penn. 1986. "Culture and Reproduction: Exploring Micro/Macro Linkages." Pp. 1–29 in *Culture and Reproduction: An Anthropological Critique of Demographic Transition Theory,* edited by W. Penn Handwerker. Boulder, CO: Westview Press.

Hans, Jason D. 2002. "Stepparenting After Divorce: Stepparents' Legal Position Regarding Custody, Access, and Support." *Family Relations* 51:301–07.

Hatcher, Richard, et al. 1998. *Contraceptive Technology,* 17th ed. Decatur, GA: Ardent Media.

Hatfield, Elaine. 1988. "Passionate and Companionate Love." Pp. 191–217 in *The Psychology of Love,* edited by Robert J. Sternberg and Michael L. Barnes. New Haven, CT: Yale University Press.

Hatfield, Elaine, & Richard L. Rapson. 1987. "Passionate Love: New Directions in Research." Pp. 109–39 in *Advances in Personal Relationships, Vol. 1,* edited by Warren H. Jones and Daniel Perlman. Greenwich, CT: JAI.

Hatfield, Elaine, & G. William Walster. 1978. *A New Look at Love.* Lantham, MA: University Press of America.

Haub, Carl, & Martha Farnsworth Riche. 1994. "Population by the Numbers: Trends in Population Growth and Structure." Pp. 95–108 in *Beyond the Numbers: A Reader on Population, Consumption, and the Environment,* edited by Laurie Ann Mazur. Washington, DC: Island Press.

Haub, Carl, & Machiko Yanagishita. 1996. *World Population Data Sheet.* Washington, DC: Population Reference Bureau, Inc.

Hauser, St., M. A. B. Vieyra, A. M. Jacobson, & D. Wertlieb. 1989. "Family Aspects of Vulnerability and Resilience in Adolescence: A Theoretical Perspective. Pp. 103–33 in *The Child in Our Times: Studies in the Development of Resiliency,* edited by Timothy F. Dugan and Robert Coles. New York: Brunner/Mazel

Hayes, Cheryl D., ed. 1987. *Risking the Future: Adolescent Sexuality, Pregnancy, and Childbearing, Vol. 1.* Washing ton, DC: National Academy Press.

Heaton, Tim B., Cardell K. Jacobson, & Kimberlee Holland. 1999. "Persistence and Change in Decisions to Remain Childless." *Journal of Marriage and the Family* 61:531–39.

Hendrick, Susan S., & Clyde Hendrick. 1987. "Love and Sex Attitudes and Religious Beliefs." *Journal of Social and Clinical Psychology* 5:391–98.

Hendrick, Susan S., and Clyde Hendrick.. 1992. *Romantic Love.* Newbury Park, CA: Sage.

Hendrick, Susan S., Clyde Hendrick, & N. L. Adler. 1988. "Romantic Relationships: Love, Satisfaction, and Staying Together." *Journal of Personality and Social Psychology* 54:980–88.

Henshaw, S. K., & J. Van Vort, eds. 1992. *Abortion Factbook, 1992 Edition: Readings, Trends, and State and Local Data to 1988.* New York: The Alan Guttmacher Institute.

Hern, Warren. 1991. "Effects of Cultural Change on Fertility in Amazonian Indian Societies: Recent Research and Projections." *Population and Environment* 13:23–44.

Hill, Charles T., Zick Rubin, & Letitia A. Peplau. 1976. "Breakups Before Marriage: The End of 103 Affairs." *Journal of Marriage and the Family* 32:147–68.

Hope, Steven, Chris Power, & Bryan Rodgers. 1999. "Does Financial Hardship Account for Elevated Psychological Distress in Lone Mothers?" *Social Science and Medicine* 29:381–89.

Houseknecht, Sharon K., Suzanne Vaughn, & Anne S. Macke. 1984. "Marital Disruption among Professional Women: The Timing of Career and Family Events." *Social Problems* 31:273–84.

Hupka, R. B. 1991. "The Motive for the Arousal of Romantic Jealousy: Its Cultural Origin." Pp. 252–70 in *The Psychology of Jealousy and Envy,* edited by R. E. Zambrana. Thousand Oaks, CA: Sage.

Jankowiak, William R., & Edward F. Fisher. 1992. "A Cross-Cultural Perspective on Romantic Love." *Ethnology* 31:149–55.

Jedlicka, Davor. 1984. "Indirect Parental Influence on Mate Choice." *Journal of Marriage and the Family* 46:65–70.

Joung, I. M. A., K. Stronks, H. van de Mheen, F. W. A. van Poppel, J. B. W. van der Meer, & J. P. Mackenbach. 1997. "The Contribution of Intermediary Factors to Marital Status Differences in Self-Reported Health." *Journal of Marriage and the Family* 59:476–90.

Julien, Danielle, Howard J. Markman, & Sophie Léveillé. 1994. "Networks' Support and Interference with Regard to Marriage: Disclosures of Marital Problems to Confidants. *Journal of Family Psychology* 8:16–31.

Kalmuss, Debra, Pearila Brickner Namerow, & L. Cushman, 1991. "Adoption Versus Parenting Among Young Pregnant Women." *Family Planning Perspectives* 23:17–23.

Kanemase, Yuji, Junichi Taniguchi, Ikuo Daibo, & Mawanori Ishimori. 2004. "Love Styles and Romantic Love Experiences in Japan. 2004." *Social Behavior and Personality* 32:265–82.

Kanin, Eugene J., Karen D. Davidson, & Sonia R. Scheck. 1970. "A Research Note on Male-Female Differentials in the Experience of Heterosexual Love." *Journal of Sex Research* 6:64–72.

Kay, Herma Hill. 1990. "Beyond No-Fault: New Directions in Divorce Reform." Pp. 6–36 in *Divorce Reform at the Crossroads,* edited by Stephen D. Sugarman and Herma Hill Kay. New Haven: Yale University Press.

Keenan, Julian Paul, Gordon G. Gallup Jr., Nicole Goulet, & Mrinmoyi Kulkarni. 1997. "Attributions of Deception in Human Mating Strategies. *Journal of Social Behavior and Personality.* 12(1):45–52.

Kenrick, Douglas T., & R. C. Keefe. 1992. "Age Preferences in Mates Reflect Sex Differences in Reproductive Strategies." *Behavioral and Brain Sciences* 15:75–133.

Kenrick, Douglas T., Richard C. Keefe, Cristina Gabrielidis, & Jeffery Cornelius. 1996. "Adolescents' Age Preferences for Dating Partners: Support for an Evolutionary Model of Life-History Strategies." *Child Development* 67(4):1499–1511.

Kerckhoff, Alan C. 1974. "The Social Context of Interpersonal Attraction." Pp. 61–78 in *Foundations of Interpersonal Attraction,* edited by L. Huston. New York: Academic Press.

King, Charles E., & Andrew Christensen. 1983. "The Relationship Events Scale: A Guttman Scaling of Progress in Courtship." *Journal of Marriage and the Family* 45:671–78.

Kissling, Frances. 1994. "Theo-Politics: The Roman Catholic Church and Population Policy." Pp. 320–29 in *Beyond the Numbers: A Reader on Population, Consumption, and the Environment,* edited by Laurie Mazur. Washington, DC: Island Press.

Kitson, Gay C. 1985. "Marital Discord and Marital Separation: A County Survey." *Journal of Marriage and the Family* 47:693–700.

Kitson, Gay C. 1992. *Portrait of Divorce: Adjustment to Marital Breakdown.* New York: Guilford Press.

Klitsch, M. 1991. "Antiprogestins and the Abortion Controversy: A Progress Report." *Family Planning Perspectives* 23:275–82.

Knox, David, & Caroline Schacht. 1994. *Choices in Relationships: An Introduction to Marriage and the Family.* Minneapolis, MN: West.

Komarovsky, Mirra. 1976. *Dilemma of Masculinity.* New York: W. W. Norton & Co.

Kovecses, Z. 1991. "A Linguist's Quest for Love." *Journal of Social and Personal Relationships* 8:77–97.

Kramarae, Cheris, & Paula A. Treichler. 1985. *A Feminist Dictionary.* Boston: Pandora Press.

Krull, Catherine, & Frank Trovato. 1994. "The Quiet Revolution and the Sex Differential in Quebec's Suicide Rate: 1931–1986." *Social Forces* 74:1121–47.

Kumagai, Fumie. 1983. "Changing Divorce Rates in Japan." *Family History* Spring:85–108.

Kurdek, Lawrence A., & Mark A. Fine. 1993. "Parent and Nonparent Residential Family Members as Providers of Warmth and Supervision to Young Adolescents." *Journal of Family Psychology* 7:245–49.

Kurtz, Linda. 1994. "Psychosocial Coping Resources in Elementary School-age Children of Divorce." *American Journal of Orthopsychiatry* 64:554–62.

Lacey, Rachel Saul, Alan Reifman, Jean Pearson Scott, Steven M. Harris, & Jacki Fitzpatrick. 2004. "Sexual-Moral Attitudes, Love Styles, and Mate Selection." *Journal of Sex Research* 41:121–28.

Larson, David E., ed. 1990. *Mayo Clinic Family Health Book.* New York: William Morrow.

Laumann, Edward O., John H. Gagnon, Robert T. Michael, & Stuart Michaels. 1994. *The Social Organization of Sexuality: Sexual Practices in the United States.* Chicago: University of Chicago Press.

Laumann-Billings, L., & R. E. Emery. 1998. *Young Adults' Painful Feelings about Parental Divorce.* Unpublished manuscript University of Virginia. Reported in Emery, 1999.

Lee, John A. 1973. *The Colors of Love: An Exploration of the Ways of Loving.* Don Mills, Ontario: New Press.

Lemieux, Robert, & Jerold L. Hale. 2002. "Cross-Sectional Analysis of Intimacy, Passion, and Commitment: Testing the Assumptions of the Triangular Theory of Love." *Psychological Reports* 90:1009–14.

Leon, Kim, & Erin Angst. 2005. "Portrayals of Stepfamilies in Film: Using Media Images in Remarriage Education." *Family Relations* 54:3–23.

Lester, David, & Kazuhiko Abe. 1993. "The Regional Variation of Divorce Rates in Japan and the United States." *Journal of Divorce and Remarriage* 1/2:227–20.

Levine, Stephen B. 2005. "What Is Love Anyway?" *Journal of Sex and Marital Therapy* 31:143–51.

Levinger, George. 1965. "Marital Cohesiveness and Dissolution: An Integrative Review." *Journal of Marriage and the Family* 27:19–28.

Lewis, Robert A. 1973. "A Longitudinal Test of a Developmental Framework for Premarital Dyadic Formation." *Journal of Marriage and the Family* 35:16–27.

Liss, Lora. 1987. "Families and the Law." Pp. 767–93 in *Handbook of Marriage and the Family,* edited by Marvin B. Sussman and Suzanne K. Steinmetz. New York: Plenum Press.

Lorenz, Frederick O., Ronald L. Simon, Rand D. Conger, Glen H. Elder, Jr., Christine Johnson, and Wei Chao. 1997. "Married and Recently Divorced Mothers' Stressful Events and Distress: Tracing Change Across Time." *Journal of Marriage and the Family* 59:219–32.

Lyman, Stanford M., & Marvin B. Scott. 1970. *A Sociology of the Absurd.* New York: Appleton-Century-Crofts.

Lynam, Donald R., Richard Milich, & Rick Zimmerman. 1999. "Project DARE: No Effects at 10–Year Follow-Up." *Journal of Consulting and Clinical Psychology* 67(4):590–93.

Maccoby, Eleanor E., & Robert H. Mnookin. 1992. *Dividing the Child: Social and Legal Dilemmas of Custody.* Cambridge, MA: Harvard University Press.

Madden-Derdich, Debra A., & Joyce A. Arditti. 1999. "The Ties that Bind: Attachment between Former Spouses." *Family Relations* 48(3):243–49.

Malia, Sarah E. C. 2005. "Balancing Family Members' Interest Regarding Stepparent Rights and Obligations: A Social Policy Challenge." *Family Relations* 54:298–319.

Manning, Wendy D., & Pamela J. Smock. 1999. "New Families and Nonresident Father-Child Visitation." *Social Forces* 78(1):87–116.

Manning, Wendy D., Susan D. Stewart, & Pamela J. Smock. 2003. "The Complexity of Fathers' Parenting Responsibilities and Involvement with Nonresident Children." *Journal of Family Issues* 24:645–67.

March, Karen, & Charlene Miall. "Adoption as a Family Form." *Family Relations* 49:359–62.

Martin, Teresa Castro, & Larry Bumpass. 1989. "Recent Trends in Marital Disruption." *Demography* 26:37–51.

Masheter, Carol. 1991. "Postdivorce Relationships between Ex-Spouses: The Roles of Attachment and Interpersonal Conflict." *Journal of Marriage and the Family* 53:103–10.

Mastekaasa, Arne. 1997. "Marital Dissolution as a Stressor: Some Evidence on Psychological, Physical, and Behavioral Changes During the Preseparation Period." *Journal of Divorce and Remarriage* 26:155–83.

Masters, William H., Virginia E. Johnson, & Robert C. Kolodny. 1992. *Human Sexuality,* 4th ed. New York: HarperCollins.

Mathes, Eugene W. 2005. "Relationship Between Short-term Sexual Strategies and Sexual Jealousy." *Psychological Reports* 96:29–35.

Matlock, M. Eileen, et al. 1994. "Family Correlates of Social Skill Deficits in Incarcerated and Nonincarcerated Adolescents." *Adolescence* 29:119–30.

Mazur, Allan, Carolyn Halpern, & J. Richard Udry. 1994. "Dominant Looking Male Teenagers Copulate Earlier." *Ethology and Sociobiology* 15:87–94.

McCall, Patricia L., & Kenneth C. Land. 1994. "Trends in White Male Adolescent, Young-Adult, and Elderly Suicide: Are There Common Underlying Structural Factors?" *Social Science Research* 23:57–81.

McCubbin, Hamilton I. 1979. "Integrating Coping Behavior in Family Stress Theory." *Journal of Marriage and the Family* 41:237–44.

McLanahan, Sara, & Larry Bumpass. 1988. "Intergenerational Consequences of Family Disruption." *American Journal of Sociology* 94:130–52.

McLanahan, Sara, & Gary Sandefur. 1994. *Growing Up with a Single Parent: What Hurts, What Helps.* Cambridge, MA: Harvard University Press.

McLaren, Angus. 1992. *A History of Contraception: From Antiquity to the Present Day.* Cambridge, MA: Blackwell Publishers.

McNeal, Ralph B., Jr. 1995. "Extracurricular Activities and High School Dropouts." *Sociology of Education* 68:62–81.

Medoff, Marshall H. 1993. "An Empirical Analysis of Adoption." *Economic Inquiry* 31:59–70.

Meyer, Daniel. 1999. "Compliance with Child Support Orders in Paternity and Divorce Cases." Pp. 127–57 in *The Postdivorce Family: Children, Parenting, and Society.* Thousand Oaks, CA: Sage.

Meyer, Daniel R., & Judi Bartfeld. 1996. "Compliance with Child Support Orders in Divorce Cases." *Journal of Marriage and the Family* 58:201–12.

Money, John. 1980. *Love and Love Sickness: The Science of Sex, Gender Difference, and Pair-Bonding.* Baltimore: Johns Hopkins University Press.

Murdock, George P., & D. White. 1969. "Standard Cross-Cultural Sample." *Ethnology* 8:329–69.

Murstein, Bernard I. 1970. "Stimulus-Value-Role: A Theory of Marital Choice." *Journal of Marriage and the Family* 32:465–81.

Murstein, Bernard I. 1987. "A Clarification and Extension of the SVR Theory of Dyadic Pairing." *Journal of Marriage and the Family* 49:929–47.

Neto, Felix, & Maria da Conceicao. 2003. "The Roles of Loneliness, Gender, and Love Status in Adolescents' Love Styles." *International Journal of Adolescence and Youth* 11:181–91.

Nielsen, Linda. 1999. "Demeaning, Demoralizing, and Disenfranchising Divorced Dads: A Review of the Literature." *Journal of Divorce and Remarriage* 31(3–4):139–77.

Nock, Steven L., James D. Wright, & Laura Sanchez. 1999. "America's Divorce Problem." *Society* 36(4):43–52.

Norton, Arthur J., & Jeanne H. Moorman. 1987. "Current Trends in Marriage and Divorce Among American Women." *Journal of Marriage and the Family* 49:3–14.

Oakley, Ann. 1984. *The Captured Womb: A History of Medical Care of Women.* London: Basil Blackwell.

O'Keefe, Maura. 1998. "Factors Mediating the Link between Witnessing Interparental Violence and Dating Violence." *Journal of Family Violence* 13:1:39–57.

O'Leary, K. Daniel, Julian Barling, Ileana Arias, Alan Rosenbaum, June Malone, & Andrea Tyree. 1989. "Prevalence and Stability of Physical Aggression between Spouses: A Longitudinal Analysis." *Journal of Consulting and Clinical Psychology* 57:263–68.

Parsons, Talcott, & Robert F. Bales. 1956. *Family Socialization and Interaction Process.* London: Routledge & Kegan Paul.

Pasley, Kay, Marilyn Ihinger-Tallman, & Amy Lofquist. 1994. "Remarriage and Stepfamilies: Making Progress in Understanding." Pp. 1–14 in *Stepparenting: Issues in Theory, Research, and Practice,* edited by Kay Pasley and Marilyn Ihinger-Tallman. Westport, CT: Greenwood Press.

Pavalko, Eliza, & Glen H. Elder Jr. 1990. "World War II and Divorce: A Life-Course Perspective." *American Journal of Sociology* 95:1213–34.

Peele, Stanton, & Archie Brodsky. 1975. *Love and Addiction.* New York: Taplinger.

Pett, Marjorie A., Bruce E. Wampold, Charles W. Turner, & Beth Vaughan-Cole. 1999. "Paths of Influence of Divorce on Preshool Children's Psychosocial Adjustment." *Journal of Family Psychology* 13(2):145–64.

Phillips, Angela. 1994. *The Trouble with Boys.* New York: Basic Books.

Piotrow, P. T., W. Rinehart, & J. C. Schmidt. 1979. "IUDs: An Update on Safety, Effectiveness, and Research." *Population Reprts,* Series B(3).

Pirog-Good, Maureen A., & Patricia R. Brown. 1996. "Accuracy and Ambiguity in the Application of State Child Support Guidelines." *Family Relations* 45:3–10.

Polenko, Karen A., John Scanzoni, & Jay D. Teachman. 1982. "Childlessness and Marital Satisfaction." *Journal of Family Issues* 3:545–73.

Popenoe, David. 1988. *Disturbing the Nest: Family Change and Decline in Modern Societies.* New York: Aldine de Gruyter.

Rankin, Robert M., & Jerry S. Maneker. 1985. "The Duration of Marriage in a Divorcing Population: The Impact on Children." *Journal of Marriage and the Family* 47:43–52.

Reiss, Ira L. 1960. "Toward a Sociology of the Heterosexual Love Relationship." *Marriage and Family Living* 22:139–45.

Reiss, Ira L., & Gary R. Lee. 1988. *Family Systems in America,* 4th ed. New York: Holt, Rinehart and Winston.

Reissman, Catherine. 1991. *Divorce Talk: Women and Men Make Sense of Personal Relationships.* New Brunswick, NJ: Rutgers University Press.

Resnick, Michael D., Robert Wm. Blum, Jane Bose, M. Smith, & R. Toogood. 1990. "Characteristics of Unmarried Adolescent Mothers: Determinants of Child Rearing Versus Adoption." *American Journal of Orthopsychiatry* 60:577–84.

Rhode, Deborah L., & Martha Minow. 1990. "Reforming the Questions; Questioning the Reforms: Feminist Perspectives on Divorce Law." Pp. 191–210 in *Divorce Reform at the Crossroads,* edited by Stephen D. Sugar-man and Herma Hill Kay. New Haven, CT: Yale University Press.

Riley, Glenda. 1991. *Divorce: An American Tradition.* New York: Oxford University Press.

Roberts, Keith A. 1995. *Religion in Sociological Perspective.* 2nd ed. Belmont, California: Wadsworth.

Rodgers, Bryan. 1994. "Pathways Between Parental Divorce and Adult Depression." *Journal of Child Psychology and Psychiatry* 35:1289–1308.

Rodgers, Roy H., & Linda M. Conrad. 1986. "Courtship for Remarriage: Influences on Family Reorganization after Divorce." *Journal of Marriage and the Family* 48:767–75.

Rodriguez, Isabel A., Marilyn Montgomery, Martha Pelaez, & Wilfredo Salas Martinez. 2003. "Love Attitudes and Experiences in Courtship in Young Adults of Three Different Cultures." *Revista Mexicana de Psicologia* 22:177–88.

Rosencrantz, Helen Bee, Susan Voge, Inge Broverman, & Donald Broverman. 1968. "Sex Role Stereotypes and Self-Concepts in College Students." *Journal of Consulting and Clinical Psychology* 32:287–95.

Rothman, Barbara. 1993. *Encyclopedia of Childbearing: Critical Perspectives.* Phoenix: The Oryx Press.

Rubin, Lillian. 1976. *World of Pain: Life in the Working-Class Family.* New York: Basic Books.

Rubin, Zick 1973. *Liking and Loving: An Introduction to Social Psychology.* New York: Holt, Rinehart and Winston.

Rubin, Zick, Charles T. Hill, Letitia Ann Peplau, & Christine Dunkel-Schetter. 1980. "Self-Disclosure in Dating Couples: Sex Roles and the Ethic of Openness." *Journal of Marriage and the Family* 42:305–17.

Russell, Brenda, and Debra L. Oswald. 2002. "Sexual Coercion and Victimization of College Men: The Role of Love Styles. *Journal of Interpersonal Violence* 17:273–85.

Russell, Stephen T. 1994. "Life Course Antecedents of Premarital Conception in Great Britain." *Journal of Marriage and the Family* 56:480–92.

Ryan, Kathryn M. 1998. "The Relationship between Courtship Violence and Sexual Aggression in College Students." *Journal of Family Violence* 13(4):377–94.

Ryan, Mary. 1979. *Womanhood in America,* 2nd ed. New York: New Viewpoint.

Sacher, Jennifer A., & Mark A. Fine. 1996. "Predicting Relationship Status and Satisfaction after Six Months among Dating Couples." *Journal of Marriage and the Family* 58:21–32.

Sadik, Nafis. 1994. "Investing in Women: The Focus of the '90s." Pp. 209–26 in *Beyond Numbers: A Reader on Population, Consumption, and the Environment*, edited by Laurie Ann Mazur. Washington DC: Island Press.

Safilios-Rothschild, Constantina. 1977. *Love, Sex, and Sex Roles*. Englewood Cliffs, NJ: Prentice-Hall.

Saks, Michael J., & Edward Krupat. 1988. *Social Psychology and Its Applications*. New York: Harper & Row.

Schellenberg, James A. 1960. Homogamy in Personal Values and the 'Field of Eligibles.'" *Social Forces* 39:157–62.

Schmidt, David P. 2004. "Patterns and Universals of Mate Poaching Across 53 Nations: The Effects of Sex, Culture, and Personality on Romantically Attracting Another Person's Partner." *Journal of Personality and Social Psychology* 86:560–84.

Schmitt, David P. 2005. "Fundamentals of Evolutionary Psychology." Pp. 258–91 in *The Handbook of Evolutionary Psychology,* edited by David Buss. Hoboken, NJ: John Wiley.

Schwartz, Daniel, & M. J. Mayauz. 1982. "Female Fecundity as a Function of Age." *The New England Journal of Medicine* 306:424–26.

Schwartz, Mary Ann, & Barbara Marliene Scott. 1994. *Marriages and Families: Diversity and Change.* Englewood Cliffs, NJ: Prentice Hall.

Schwartz, Miguel, Susan G. O'Leary, & Kimberly Kendziora. 1997. "Dating Aggression among High School Students." *Violence and Victims* 12(4):295–305.

Shackelford, Todd K., Aaron T. Goetz, Craig W. LaMunyon, Brian J. Quintus, and Viviana A. Weekes-Shackel-ford. 2004. "Sex Differences in Sexual Psychology Produce Sex-Similar Preferences for a Short-Term Mate. *Archives of Sexual Behavior* 33:405–12.

Shane, J. M., I. Schiff, & E. A. Wilson. 1976. "The Infertile Couple: Evaluation and Treatment." *Clinical Symposia* 28:5.

Sinclair, H. Colleen, & Irene Hanson Frieze. 2002. "Stalking: Perspectives on Victims and Perpetrators." Pp. 186–211 in *Stalking: Perspectives on Victims and Perpetrators,* edited by Keith Davis, Irene Frieze, and Roland Maiuro. New York: Springer.

Smith, Donna. 1990. *Stepmothering.* New York: St. Martin's Press.

Smith, Robert J., & Ella L. Wiswell. 1982. *The Women of Suye Mura.* Chicago: University of Chicago Press.

Solomon, Robert. C. 1981. *Love: Emotion, Myth, and Metaphor.* New York: Anchor.

South, Scott J. 1985. "Economic Conditions and the Divorce rate: A Time-Series Analysis of the Postwar United States." *Journal of Marriage and the Family* 47:31–41.

South, Scott J., Kyle D. Crowder, & Katherine Trent. 1998. "Children's Residential Mobility and Neighborhood Environment Following Parental Divorce and Remarriage." *Social Forces* 77(2):667–93.

Spain, D., & S. M. Bianchi. 1996. *Balancing Act: Motherhood, Marriage, and Employment among American Women.* New York: Russell Sage.

Spitze, Glenna, John R. Logan, Glenn Deane, & Suzanne Zerger. 1994. "Adult Children's Divorce and Intergenerational Relationships." *Journal of Marriage and the Family* 56:279–93.

Sprecher, Susan, & Diane Femlee. 1991. "Effects of Parents and Friends on Romantic Relationships: A Longitudinal Investigation." Paper presented at the American Sociological Association annual convention, Cincinnati, OH.

Statistical Abstract. *Statistical Abstract of the United States.* Washington, DC: U.S. Government Printing Office.

Steinmetz, Suzanne K. 1977–78. "The Battered Husband Syndrome." *Victimology: An International Journal* 2:499–509.

Stephen, Timothy D. 1985. "Fixed-Sequence and Circular-Casual Models of Relationship Development: Divergent Views on the Role of Communication in Intimacy." *Journal of Marriage and the Family* 47:955–63.

Sternberg, Robert J. 1986. "A Triangular Theory of Love." *Psychological Review* 93:119–35.

Sternberg, Robert J. 1988 "Triangulating Love." Pp. 119–38 in *The Psychology of Love*, edited by Robert J. Stern-berg and Michael L. Barnes. New Haven, CT: Yale University Press

Stolley, Kathy Shepherd, & Elaine J. Hall. 1994. "The Presentation of Abortion and Adoption in Marriage and Family Textbooks." *Family Relations* 43:267–73.

Strong, Bryan, & Christine DeVault. 1994. "Response to Stolley and Hall." *Family Relations* 43:274–76.

Sugarman, David B., & Gerald T. Hotaling. 1989. "Dating Violence: Prevalence, Context and Risk Markers." Pp. 3–32 in *Violence in Dating Relationships,* edited by Maureen Pirog-Good and Jan Stets. New York: Praeger.

Sweet, James, & Larry Bumpass. 1987. *American Families and Households.* New York: Russell Sage.

Swidler, Ann. 1980. "Love and Adulthood in American Culture." Pp. 120–47 in *Themes of Work and Love in Adulthood,* edited by Neil Smelser and Erik Erikson. Cambridge, MA: Harvard University Press.

Tadinac, Meri, and Ivan Hromatko. 2004. "Sex Differences in Mate Preferences: Testing Some Predictions from Evolutionary Theory." *Review of Psychology* 11:45–51.

Tannahill, Reay. 1980. *Sex in History.* New York: Stein and Day.

Teachman, Jay D., & Karen Polonko. 1990. "Negotiating Divorce Outcomes: Can We Identify Patterns in Divorce Settlements?" *Journal of Marriage and the Family* 52:129–39.

Terrell, John, & Judith Modell. 1994. "Anthropology and Adoption." *American Anthropologist* 96:155–61.

Townsend, John Marshall. 1989. "Mate Selection Criteria: A Pilot Study." *Ethology and Sociobiology* 10:241–53.

Tschann, Jeanne M., Janet R. Johnston, & Judith S. Wallerstein. 1989. "Resources, Stressors, and Attachments as Predictors of Adult Adjustment after Divorce." *Journal of Marriage and the Family* 51:1033–46.

U.S. Bureau of the Census. 1995. "Who Receives Child Support?" Online at http://www.census.gov/ftp/pub/socdemo/www/chldsupp.html.

U.S. Bureau of the Census, 2003. "Table UC3. Opposite Sex Unmarried Partner Households by Presence of Own Children/1 Under 18, and Age, Earnings, Education, and Race and Hispanic Origin/2 of Both Partners: 2003. Online at *http://www.census.gov/population/socdemo/hh-fam/cps2003/tabUC3–all.xls*. Accessed November 6, 2005.

U.S. National Center for Health Statistics. 1990. "Advanced Report of Final Marriage Satistics, 1987." *Monthly Vital Statistics Report* 38(12)Suppl., April 3.

Vandervalk, Inge, Ed Spruijt, Martijn De Goede, Wim Meeus, & Cora Maas. 2004. "Marital Status, Marital Process, and Parental Resources in Predicting Adolescents' Emotional Adjustment: A Multilevel Analysis. *Journal of Family Issues* 25:291–317.

Vaughan, Diane. 1988. "Uncoupling: The Social Construction of Divorce." Pp 384–403 in *Social Interactions: Readings in Sociology,* 3rd ed., edited by Candace Clark and Howard Robbey. New York: St Martin's.

Visher, Emily B., & John S. Visher. 1988. *Old Loyalists, New Ties: Therapeutic Strategies with Stepfamilies.* New York: Brunner/Mazel.

Waite, Linda J., & Maggie Gallagher. 2000. *The Case for Marriage: Why Married People are Happier, Healthier, and Better Off Financially.* New York: Doubleday.

Waller, Willard. 1951. *The Family: A Dynamic Interpretation.* New York: Dryden.

Wallerstein, Judith S., & Sandra Blakeslee. 1989. *Second Chances: Men, Women, and Children a Decade After Divorce.* New York: Ticknor & Fields.

Wallerstein, Judith S., & Joan B. Kelly. 1976. "The Effects of Parental Divorce: The Experiences of the Child in Later Latency." *American Journal of Orthopsychiatry* 46:256–69.

Wallerstein, Judith S., & Joan B. Kelly. 1980. *Surviving the Breakup: How Children and Parents Cope with Divorce.* New York: Basic Books.

Wallerstein, Judith S., & Julia Lewis. 1998. "The Long-Term Impact of Divorce on Children: A First Report from a 15–Year Study." *Family and Concilliation Courts Review* 36(3):368–83.

Walster, Elaine, Vera Aronson, Darcy Abrahams, & Leon Rottman. 1966. "Importance of Physical Attractiveness in Dating Behavior." *Journal of Personality and Social Psychology* 4:508–16.

Weber, Max. [1904] 1958. *The Protestant Ethic and the Spirit of Capitalism.* Translated by Talcott Parsons. New York: Scribner's.

Wegar, Katarina. 2000. "Adoption, Family Ideology, and Social Stigma: Bias in Community Attitudes, Adoption Research, and Practice. *Family Relations* 49:363–70.

Weiss, Robert S. 1975. *Marital Separation: Managing after a Marriage Ends.* New York: Basic Books. Weitzman, Lenore. 1985. *The Divorce Revolution.* New York: Free Press.

White, Gregory. 1981. "Physical Attractiveness and Courtship Progress." *Journal of Personality and Social Psychology* 39:360–68.

White, Lynn K. 1990. "Determinants of Divorce: A Review of Research in the Eighties." *Journal of Marriage and the Family* 52:904–12.

White, Lynn K. 1994. "Growing up with Single Parents and Stepparents: Long-Term Effects on Family Solidarity." *Journal of Marriage and the Family* 56:935–48.

White, Lynn K., & Alan Booth. 1985. "The Quality and Stability of Remarriages: The Role of Stepchildren." *American Sociological Review* 50:189–98.

White, Lynn K., & Alan Booth. 1985. "The Transition to Parenthood and Marital Quality." *Journal of Family Issues* 6:435–49.

White, Lynn, & Bruce Keith. 1990. "The Effect of Shift Work on the Quality and Stability of Marital Relations." *Journal of Marriage and the Family* 52:453–62.

Wilson, Barbara Foley, & Sally Cunningham Clarke. 1992. "Remarriages: A Demographic Profile." *Journal of Family Issues* 13:123–41.

Winch, Robert F. 1958. *Mate Selection.* New York: Harper.

Wolf, Arthur P., & Chieh-Shan Huang. 1980. *Marriage and Adoption in China, 1845–1945.* Stanford, CA: Stanford University Press.

Wolf, Robin. 1996. *Marriages and Families in a Diverse Society.* New York: HarperCollins.

Wright, Robert. 1994. *The Moral Animal: Evolutionary Psychology and Everyday Life.* New York: Pantheon.

Wu, Zheng. 1995. "Premarital Cohabitation and Postmarital Cohabiting Union Formation." *Journal of Family Issues* 16:212–32.

Yanagida, Kunio. 1957. *Japanese Manners and Customs in the Meiji Era.* Translated by Charles S. Terry. Tokyo: Obunsha.

Ziaxiang, A., L. Xinlian, & G. Zhahua. 1987. "The Causes of Divorce." Pp. 162–77 in *New Trends in Chinese Marriage and the Family,* edited by L. Jieqiong. Beijing: China International Book Trading.

QUESTIONS FOR REVIEW, REFLECTION, AND DISCUSSION

1. Does love exist in all cultures?
2. What was Zick Rubin's contribution to social science? Describe his work.
3. What was Bernard Murstein's contribution to social science? Describe his work.
4. Compare the following love styles (Lee's love styles) to each other: eros, storge, ludus, pragma, mania, and agape. How do the styles differ?
5. How is companionate love similar to storge?
6. How is symbolic interactionism used to explain love?
7. What are the stages in the Wheel Theory of Love?
8. What is meant by the feminization of love?
9. What does love mean to you? Have you even been in love? How did you know that you were in love?
10. How does romantic love differ from courtly love? How are they similar?

ADDITIONAL READINGS

Baumeister, R. F., & Leary, M. R. (1995). The need to belong: Desire for interpersonal attachments as a fundamental human motivation. *Psychological Bulletin, 117*(3), 497–529.

Butler, E. A. (2015). Interpersonal affect dynamics: It takes two (and time) to tango. *Emotion Review, 7*, 336–341.

Debrot, A., Schoebi, D., Perrez, M., & Horn, A. B. (2013). Touch as an interpersonal emotion regulation process in couples' daily lives: The mediating role of psychological intimacy. *Personality and Social Psychology Bulletin, 39*, 1373–1385. doi:10.1177/0146167213497592

Schoebi, D., & Randall, A.K. (2015). Emotional dynamics in intimate relationships. *Emotion Review, 7*(4), 342–348.

Toma, C.L., & Choi, M. (2015). The couple who Facebooks together, stays together: Facebook self-presentation and relationship longevity among college-aged dating couples. *Cyberpsychology, Behavior, and Social Networking*, 18(7), 367–372.

Viejo, C., Ortega-Ruiz, R. & Sánchez, V. (2015). Adolescent love and well-being: The role of dating relationships for psychological adjustment. *Journal of Youth Studies, 18*(9), 1219–1236.

KEY TERMS

Defense of Marriage Act (DOMA)

Gay

Lesbian

Same-Sex

5

JILTED AT THE ALTAR

The Debate Over Same-Sex Marriage

By Craig A. Rimmerman

This article is included in the reader because it contains a great deal of information regarding landmark legal cases; however, keep in mind that laws have changed since this article was published. The Supreme Court of the United States ruled (on June 26, 2015) that the Constitution guarantees the right of same-sex couples to marry in all 50 states.

Craig A. Rimmerman, "Jilted at the Alter: The Debate Over Same-Sex Marriage," The Lesbian and Gay Movements: Assimilation or Liberation?, 2nd ed., pp. 111-116, 118-122, 130-136, 205-218. Copyright © 2014 by Perseus Books Group. Reprinted with permission.

Equality is a good start, but it is not sufficient. Equality for queers inevitably means equal rights on straight terms, since they are the ones who determine the existing legal framework. We conform—albeit equally—with their screwed-up system. That is not liberation. It is capitulation.

—Peter Tatchell

Certainly nobody expected that an arrest that night of two gay men for a minor criminal offense would reverberate in American constitutional law, challenging not only the traditional understanding of what makes a family but also the proper role of government in maintaining that understanding. Nobody foresaw the cultural storm that would gather from the events that transpired in a modest second-floor apartment. Nor could anyone have foreseen how a single arrest might expose the deep malignity in a law that was superficially directed at a certain conduct, but that in practice was used to brand an entire group of people as strangers to moral tradition.

—Dale Carpenter on the background to
Lawrence v. Texas

We won and got everything we hoped for. If I had to survive Thea, what a glorious way to do it.

—Edith Windsor, the lead plaintiff in the Defense of Marriage Act case, *United States v. Windsor*

The fight over same-sex marriage has become a central issue in the ongoing cultural wars in the United States. Some analysts have argued that gay marriage has replaced abortion as *the* focal issue of cultural conflict. In recent years, we have seen considerable political and organizing activity on all sides of the same-sex-marriage debate. Conservative activists have marched in Washington and throughout the United States and have flooded the US Senate with letters, telegrams, and e-mails supporting a constitutional ban limiting marriage to heterosexual couples. Lesbian and gay rights activists have also marched, lobbied, and accessed the legal system to challenge state and local laws that prevent them from marrying. For political scientist Gary Mucciaroni, "same-sex marriage is the culmination of the long march toward gender and sexual equality rooted in the feminist movement" (2008, 24). The conflict over same-sex marriage has engulfed all branches and levels of government, has been the focus of many state referenda, and has come before the Supreme Court of the United States. The tremendous publicity that the issue has received has also forced presidential and congressional candidates to take positions on same-sex marriage. Candidates over time have chosen to use the subject as a wedge issue in their electoral strategies. But there are signs that this is now changing as "polls show that about fifty-five per cent of the American people now support same-sex marriage" (Toobin 2013a, 28). And among younger people support is even stronger. Indeed, a June 2013 Field poll indicated that "78 percent of voters under 39 favor making gay marriage legal" (Medina 2013). A November 2012 Gallup poll reported that "73 percent of people between 18 and 29 years old said they favored it, while only 39 percent of people older than 65 did" (Connelly 2012).

SAME-SEX MARRIAGE IN HISTORICAL CONTEXT

The same-sex marriage debate exploded on the national scene in the early 1990s, despite the fact that lesbians and gay men had been challenging their exclusion from the rights of marriage since the early 1970s. Early legal challenges were pursued without the support of organized lesbian and gay interests, though somewhat surprisingly, "from the earliest days of gay liberation, some activists demanded the right to marry," even as others who identified with the gay liberationist agenda denounced marriage "as a discredited patriarchal institution." Indeed, many liberationists coming out of the 1969 Stonewall Rebellion "rejected everything they associated with heterosexuality, including sex roles, marriage, and the family" (Chauncey 2004, 89). But others claimed that they should have the right to do anything and everything that heterosexuals could do, including holding hands with a partner in public or getting married. Given the repressive context of the times, either of these activities was viewed by many as a radical challenge to straight society. In the end, though, support for marriage was a minority position within the larger lesbian and gay movements' agenda. As Chauncey points out, lesbian feminist activists were understandably hostile to pursuing marriage rights as a key component of the movements' agenda. To most lesbian feminists, "marriage was an inherently patriarchal institution, which played a central role in structuring the domination of women. As they sought to build a new women's culture shorn of patriarchal influence, many questioned monogamy and worked to construct new kinds of relationships and living patterns" (93).

National organizations that were established in the 1970s, including the Gay Rights National Lobby (which later became the Human Rights Campaign), the Lambda Legal Defense and Education Fund, the Lesbian Rights Project, and the National Gay Task Force, and a growing number of local organizations largely ignored the issue, "either because they were critical of marriage, saw it as a hopeless cause, or most commonly, simply had other priorities. Instead of focusing on the rights of same-sex *couples*, gay politics at the time focused on securing the rights of *individuals* against discrimination in employment and on building *community* institutions and a collective culture" (Chauncey 2004, 94).

Lone couples who filed legal challenges did so within this broad movement context and without the support of experienced legal advocates (Pinello 2006, 23). In May 1970, Jack Baker and J. Michael McConnell became the first gay couple to apply for a marriage license. Their application was denied by the Hennepin County, Minnesota, clerk, and in *Baker v. Nelson* (1971), the Minnesota Supreme Court ruled that "the men had no federal due process or equal protection rights to marry. The first marriage case involving a lesbian couple arose in Kentucky and met a similarly unsuccessful fate" in the 1973 decision *Jones v. Hallahan* (22).

Over the course of the next two decades there were "at least four more failed attempts to seek judicial recognition of same-sex marriage (*Singer v. Hara* 1974; *Adams v. Howerton* 1980; *DeSanto v. Barnsley* 1984; and *Dean v. District of Columbia* 1992)." These developments prompted Yale law professor William Eskridge to conclude that "legal agitation for gay marriage in the 1970s [and 1980s and 1990s] was a complete flop" (Pinello 2006, 22). But a number of important factors came to the fore by the early 1990s that allowed same-sex marriage to emerge as an issue for national debate: "The stage for the national marriage debate was set by the changing character of marriage, the changing circumstances of gay life, and the changing place of gay people in American society. ... But it was the vision of a few key legal strategists and the decisions of a few state courts that took the issue to the next level" (Chauncey 2004, 123).

One of the most important developments in the lesbian and gay movements' organizing strategy was the emphasis on family issues by the early 1990s. These family issues included parenting by same-sex couples, partnership recognition, spousal benefits in the workplace, gay-supportive public school policies, and policies to support lesbian, gay, bisexual, and transgender youth. Several factors contributed to the changing historical circumstances, with consequences for the larger lesbian and gay movements and for the human beings that were the basis for the movements. One key development was the case of Sharon Kowalski:

> In 1983 Kowalski was involved in an automobile accident that left her ability to communicate seriously impaired. The courts awarded guardianship to Kowalski's father rather than to her partner, Karen Thompson, who for years was denied access to Kowalski. Across the United States, lesbian communities hosted forums, organized fundraisers, and worked to raise public awareness about the case. After an eight-year battle the courts eventually made Thompson the legal guardian, but in the meantime "Free Sharon Kowalski" became a rallying cry among lesbians concerned about the lack of legal recognition for their relationships. (D'Emilio 2007, 49)

The *Kowalski* case received considerable coverage in the gay press, heightening attention of the broader policy issues involved. Some gay pride marches opened with an empty wheelchair to dramatize the injustices associated with the case (Chauncey 2004, 113).

The AIDS crisis that emerged in the 1980s also inspired a call for full legal recognition of gay marriage by some movement activists. The reality of AIDS "suddenly forced tens of thousands of committed gay couples to deal with powerful institutions—hospitals, funeral homes, state agencies—that did not recognize their commitments. Even if AIDS patients were on their deathbeds, their life-partners were often excluded from visiting because they were not officially 'spouses' or next of kin" (Eisenbach 2006, 307). Indeed, "AIDS patients and their partners discovered that they weren't covered by each other's medical insurance, weren't entitled to enter the doctors' offices and hospital rooms of their loved ones, weren't authorized to claim remains or plan funerals or inherit estates. Grieving survivors were barred from collecting Social Security and pension benefits" (Von Drehle 2013, 22). What made matters even worse is that hospitals were under no obligation to inform partners or loved ones about the medical-care process. This situation was devastating; those personally enveloped in these untenable circumstances and their supporters in the larger lesbian and gay movements looked for meaningful policy change in the form of same-sex marriage.

Another important factor contributing to the emphasis on family issues and the attention to same-sex marriage was the lesbian and gay baby boom. More people were choosing to become parents, thus challenging traditional notions of "family." The process varied considerably, as babies were "conceived through the cooperation of gay men with the procreative desires of lesbian friends to the use of sperm banks, adoption agencies, surrogacy, and sex among friends" (D'Emilio 2007, 50). These developments all meant that children and families became a more visible face of the lesbian and gay movements, thus challenging traditional notions of heteronormativity while at the same time reinforcing the assimilationist approach to political, social, and cultural change. In the end, the *Kowalski* case, the AIDS crisis, and the lesbian and gay baby boom all helped to catapult same-sex marriage onto the movements' policy agenda by the late 1980s and early 1990s.

...

THE 1996 DEFENSE OF MARRIAGE ACT

The conservative backlash also manifested itself in politics at the national level. During the 1996 campaign, conservative activists and politicians organized a rally condemning the practice three days prior to the Iowa caucuses. Three of the announced Republican presidential candidates attended, addressed the rally, and "signed a pledge to 'defend' heterosexual marriage against the threat posed by three lesbian and gay couples in Hawaii who had sued the state for the right to marry" (Cahill 2004, 81). This pledge, the Marriage Protection Resolution, was introduced by a coalition of eight conservative religious groups (Rimmerman 2002, 75). The *Los Angeles Times* observed in April 1996 that "homosexual marriage has abruptly emerged as an emotional flashpoint in the debate about America's social mores"

(Cahill 2004, 81). It was no surprise, then, that Republican presidential nominee, Bob Dole, introduced the federal Defense of Marriage Act (DOMA) in the Senate, though it was surprising to some that President Clinton ultimately signed it into law on September 21, 1996. The Senate had voted 85–14 in September 1996 in favor of the act, which the House had passed by a vote of 342–67 that summer. Congressional hearings about the legislation had turned ugly, as members of Congress and witnesses warned that if men were allowed to marry other men, "they would soon be permitted to marry children and other animals" (Chambers 2000, 295). Others worried that same-sex marriage would lead to the collapse of Western civilization. The official Republican Party position was a conservative one: "Let the people of each state decide whether or not to allow homosexuals to marry in their state. If a state decides to permit such unions, so be it" (Whitman 2005, 97). Proposed by Republicans with the enthusiastic support of their Christian Right supporters, the legislation was timed perfectly to coincide with the 1996 election season. The law was designed to accomplish two goals: "(1) prevent states from being forced by the Full Faith and Credit Clause to recognize same-sex marriages validly celebrated in other states, and (2) define marriages for federal purposes as the union of one man and one woman" (Strasser 1997, 127). What the law meant in practice is that gay couples, even once they can actually legally be married, would be excluded "from all federal protections, responsibilities, and benefits that ordinarily accompany any other marriage in America" (Wolfson 2004, 42).

What prompted Clinton to sign DOMA into law? He was clearly worried that the same-sex-marriage issue could achieve heightened saliency as a potential wedge issue during the 1996 general election. Having endured the unpleasantness of the debate about gays in the military during the first six months of his presidency, he wanted to avoid a similar controversy about marriage. With this in mind, he signed it into law after midnight, eschewing the Rose Garden ceremony that often accompanies White House bill signings. Understandably, Clinton received strong criticism from some members of the lesbian and gay movements. But, whereas he had reversed his position regarding the military ban, he at least was consistent with regard to lesbian and gay marriage: he had announced his opposition in the 1992 campaign. But those who were most critical of the president argued that DOMA was both unnecessary and highly discriminatory and that Clinton was forced to sign the law to avoid attacks by the Christian Right during the 1996 presidential campaign. Indeed, the Dole campaign had run a radio ad that criticized Clinton for supporting an end to the military ban. The Clinton forces responded by releasing their own ad celebrating the president's signing of DOMA. This ad was run on Christian radio stations across the country, despite the fact that the president criticized the authors of the act for attempting to inject such a difficult issue into presidential politics during an election year.

Lesbian and gay rights groups protested the radio ad loudly. In response, the Clinton campaign pulled it after two days (Rimmerman 2002, 76). Ever the politician, Clinton recognized the potency of same-sex marriage as a potential wedge issue during the 1996 campaign. In stopping the ad, he helped remind other candidates of how they might balance their desire for electoral victory with the interests of their lesbian and gay supporters.

Could the lesbian and gay movements have done more to force the Clinton administration to support same-sex marriage? Note that it was not a crucial issue for many movement members at that time. Those who think it should be a key goal—individuals such as Jonathan Rauch, Andrew Sullivan, and Bruce Bawer—generally represent the movements' more moderate to conservative element.

...

Clinton endorsed overturning DOMA in March 2013 when it was politically safe for him to do so and when he understandably thought that his endorsement could help. In a March 2013 editorial in the *Washington Post,* Clinton wrote, "I join with the Obama administration, the petitioner Edith Windsor, and the many dedicated men and women who have engaged in this struggle for decades in urging the Supreme Court to overturn the Defense of Marriage Act" (2013).

Clinton's position would have been inconceivable as president of the United States in the fall of 1996. But fortunately for advocates of same-sex marriage, the issue moved out of the national arena and back to the states with the historic December 1999 decision by Vermont's chief justice, Jeffrey Amestoy, that Vermont's legislature must grant lesbian and gay couples the "common benefits and protections" that heterosexuals receive. Not surprisingly, a conservative backlash soon followed. Vermont legislators who supported the civil union legislation were targeted for defeat by Christian Right organizers, and some lost their re-election bids in 2000.

Conservative forces throughout the United States immediately moved to pre-empt recognition of same-sex marriages in their own states. The publicity surrounding the *Baehr* case appears to have done much more for opponents of lesbian and gay marriage than for its proponents. Further, the marriage issue vaulted to the forefront of the movements' agenda without a full and frank discussion of what this rights-based strategy would mean for the movements' organizing and educational efforts and for the direction of both short-term and long-term political and cultural change. Same-sex marriage would not manifest itself in the national political scene again until the June 16, 2003, US Supreme Court decision in *Lawrence v. Texas,* a ruling that political scientist H. N. Hirsch has called "a stunning federal Supreme Court decision" (2005, ix).

...

THE UNITED STATES V. WINDSOR AND HOLLINGSWORTH V. PERRY 2013 SUPREME COURT DECISIONS

On June 26, 2013, the United States Supreme Court issued two landmark decisions that brought some legal and policy clarity to the debate over same-sex marriage. Justice Anthony Kennedy issued an opinion in the *Windsor* case that vindicated the rights of lesbian and gay Americans as he and the court had done previously in *Romer v. Evans* (1996) and *Lawrence v. Texas* (2003). In writing for the 5–4 majority that struck down DOMA, Kennedy claimed that "'DOMA instructs all federal officials, and indeed all persons with whom same-sex couples interact, including their own children, that their marriage is less worthy than the marriages of others. The principal purpose and the necessary effect of this law are to demean those persons who are in a lawful same-sex marriage'" (Toobin 2013a, 27). In making this decision, the Court ruled that married-same sex couples are entitled to federal benefits, which is a major policy advance. As commentator Adam Liptak pointed out, "the decision on federal benefits will immediately extend many benefits to couples in the states where same-sex marriage is legal, and it will give the Obama administration the ability to broaden other benefits through executive actions" (Liptak 2013). More specifically, "the ruling makes clear that gay couples living in states that recognize their unions will immediately gain access to more than 1,000 federal benefits, like Social Security and family leave rights. Less certain is how couples in the remaining 37 states will fare" (Bernard 2013). Indeed, "Kennedy's decision was carefully limited to the question of Congress's authority to restrict marriage to opposite-sex couples; he insisted that he was not deciding the much larger question of whether states can restrict marriage along those lines" (Cole 2013, 28). And by declining to decide on the case from California, *Hollingsworth v. Perry,* the court essentially permitted same-sex marriages there. Writing for the 5–4 majority, Chief Justice John Roberts announced that the court would not intervene in the controversy over California's Proposition 8, which lower courts had invalidated previously. But what the court did not say in both of these rulings is perhaps just as important as what it did say: "the rulings leave in place laws banning same-sex marriage around the nation, and the court declined to say whether there was a constitutional right to same-sex marriage" (Liptak 2013). In the end, the court essentially said that it is not yet ready "to cut off the unfolding state-by-state legislative debate on gay marriage." Harvard Law professor Richard Fallon reflected on the implications of both court decisions for the future of same-sex marriage: "the five-justice coalition favoring gay rights was willing to go only so far at this point." And the court's decisions in June 2013 obviously have consequences for the future of same-sex marriage, as Fallon points out: "although a majority thought it was important to resolve the DOMA issue, a majority did not believe it was not similarly desirable to resolve the larger equal protection issue" that is posed by laws on the books against marriage ("Analysis" 2013). Legal commentator David Cole offered this trenchant assessment of the two Court decisions:

> Together, these decisions are a consummate act of judicial statesmanship. They extend federal benefits to all same-sex married couples in states that recognize gay marriage, expand the number of states recognizing gay marriage to thirteen, yet leave open for the time being the ultimate issue of state power to limit marriage to the union of a man and woman. The Court took a significant step toward recognition of the equality rights of gays and lesbians. But by not imposing same-sex marriage on the three quarters of the states whose laws still forbid it, the Court has allowed the issue to develop further through the political process—where its trajectory is all but inevitable. (2013, 28)

Andrew Rosenthal pointed out that "the rulings leave a lot unsettled." Why do they do so? Because the "surviving part of DOMA frees states from having to recognize marriages legally performed in other states—which seems clearly unconstitutional . . . but was not part of this case. So, if you're a same-sex couple married in New York and you're driving west through the Lincoln Tunnel, when you see that yellow line marking the border of New Jersey, you're no longer married. How ridiculous" (2013).

···

REFERENCES

"Analysis: Supreme Court in No Rush to Grant National Gay-Marriage Right." 2013. *New York Times,* June 26.

Bernard, Tara Siegel. 2013. "How the Court's Ruling Will Affect Same-Sex Spouses." *New York Times,* June 26.

Cahill, Sean. 2003. "Public Policy Issues Affecting Gay, Lesbian, Bisexual, and Transgender People: Envisioning a GLBT-Inclusive Introductory American Political Science Textbook." Prepared for delivery at the 2003 annual meeting of the American Political Science Association, August 28–31.

_____. 2004. *Same-Sex Marriage in the United States: Focus on the Facts.* New York: Lexington.

Chambers, David L. 2000. "Couples: Marriage, Civil Union, and Domestic Partnership." In *Creating Change: Sexuality, Public Policy, and Civil Rights,* edited by John D'Emilio, William B. Turner, and Urvashi Vaid. New York: St. Martin's Press.

Chauncey, George. 1994. *Gay New York.* New York: Basic Books.

_____. 2004. *Why Marriage? The History Shaping Today's Debate over Gay Equality.* New York: Basic Books.

Clinton, Bill. 2013. "It's Time to Overturn DOMA." *Washington Post,* March 7.

Cole, David. 2013. "Equality and the Roberts Court: Four Decisions." *New York Review of Books,* August 15, 28–30.

Connelly, Marjorie. 2012. "Support for Gay Marriage Growing, but U.S. Remains Divided." *New York Times,* December 7.

D'Emilio, John. 1983. *Sexual Politics, Sexual Communities: The Making of a Homosexual Minority in the United States, 1940–1970.* Chicago: University of Chicago Press.

_____. 2007. "Will the Courts Set Us Free? Reflections on the Campaign for Same-Sex Marriage." In *The Politics of Same-Sex Marriage,* edited by Craig A. Rimmerman and Clyde Wilcox, 39–64. Chicago: University of Chicago Press.

Eisenbach, David. 2006. *Gay Power: An American Revolution.* New York: Carroll and Graf.

Joann McAllister, Mary Lou Finley, and Steven Soifer. Vancouver: New Society.

Liptak, Adam. 2013. "Supreme Court Bolsters Gay Marriage with Two Major Rulings." *New York Times,* June 26.

Medina, Jennifer. 2013. "Anticipation Turns to Acceptance as California Awaits Marriage Ruling." *New York Times,* June 23.

Mucciaroni, Gary. 2008. *Same-Sex, Different Politics: Success and Failure in the Struggles over Gay Rights.* Chicago: University of Chicago Press.

Pinello, Daniel R. 2006. *America's Struggle for Same-Sex Marriage.* New York: Cambridge University Press.

_____. 2002. *From Identity to Politics: The Lesbian and Gay Movements in the United States.* Philadelphia: Temple University Press.

Rosenthal, Andrew. 2013. "The Court's Same-Sex Marriage Rulings." *New York Times,* June 26.

Strasser, Mark. 1997. *Legally Wed: Same-Sex Marriage and the Constitution.* Ithaca, NY: Cornell University Press.

Toobin, Jeffrey. 2013a. "Adieu, DOMA!" *New Yorker,* July 8 and 15, 27–28.

Von Drehle, David. 2013. "How Gay Marriage Was Won." *Time,* April 8, 16–24.

Whitman, Christine Todd. 2005. *It's My Party Too: The Battle for the Heart of the GOP and the Future of America.* New York: Penguin Press.

Wolfson, Evan. 2004. *Why Marriage Matters: American Equality and Gay People's Right to Marry.* New York: Simon and Schuster.

QUESTIONS FOR REVIEW, REFLECTION, AND DISCUSSION

1. What was the purpose of the Defense of Marriage Act (DOMA)?
2. Who were the supporters of DOMA? Who were the opponents of DOMA?
3. Who signed DOMA into law? Why did he sign it? What year did he sign it?
4. What was the United States v. Windsor case about and who was involved?

ADDITIONAL READINGS

Gates, G.J. (2015) Marriage and family: LGBT individuals and same-sex couples, *Future of Children, 25*(2), 67–87.

Hermann, D. H. J. (2016). Extending the fundamental right of marriage to same-sex couples: The United States Supreme Court decision in Obergefell v. Hodges, *Indiana Law Review, 49*(2), 367–396.

Pinsof, D., & Haselton, M. (2016). The political divide over same-sex marriage, *Psychological Science, 27(4),* 435–442.

Vecho, O., Paul P. V., & Schneider, B. Adolescents' attitudes toward same-sex marriage and adoption in France. *Journal of GLBT Family Studies. 12*(1), 24–45.

UNIT 2

FAMILY
COMMUNICATION

KEY TERMS

Theory

Family Systems Theory

Equifinality

Symbolic Interaction Theory

Social Learning Theory

Attachment Theory

Dialectical Perspective

6

THEORETICAL PERSPECTIVES ON FAMILY COMMUNICATION

By Chris Segrin and Jeanne Flora

In this selection we review a number of influential theories of family communication and relationships. Although not all of the theories discussed in this selection were explicitly developed as theories of family interaction per se, each has been widely and fruitfully applied in the scientific study of families.

What is a theory, and why do social scientists develop theories? Simply put, a theory is an explanation of a fact pattern. Social scientists generally do not develop theories to explain individual cases or incidents. Rather, theories are developed to explain how and why certain things happen, particularly when those things happen repeatedly. For example, scientists and therapists realized that a lot of couples who get divorced exhibit certain patterns of destructive conflict. For that reason, they attempted to develop a theory that explains how and why conflict can harm a marriage. If only a handful of divorced couples had problems with conflict, scientists probably would not have been motivated to develop an explanation for why conflict harms marriage. Scientific theories serve a number of useful functions. Perhaps the most basic function of a theory is to *explain* how and why a phenomenon occurs or operates. A related function of theories is to *predict* when a phenomenon might or might not happen. For example, in recent years there has been great interest in developing theories of divorce that allow for prediction of who will divorce and who will stay married. In addition, theories sometimes allow scientists and therapists to *control* a phenomenon. If a valid theory of divorce explains the phenomenon as caused by dysfunctional communication patterns, instituting training seminars or therapy techniques that address those communication problems might be a useful way to lower the divorce rate.

In this selection, we present an analysis of family systems theory, symbolic interaction theory, social learning theory, attachment theory, and the dialectic perspective. Notice how each theory offers different explanations of how and why family interactions function as they do. It is important to keep in mind that no theory offers the one and only explanation for a fact pattern. There are often multiple explanations for why family interactions function as they do. The utility of a theory is therefore determined, at least in part, by how well it holds up under empirical scrutiny. In other words, are the available data consistent with the propositions of the theory? All of the theories discussed in this selection have been associated with numerous studies that support the essential components and elements of the theory.

FAMILY SYSTEMS THEORY

HISTORICAL BACKGROUND

As social scientific theories go, family systems theory has unique beginnings. In fact, family systems theory emerged from a line of work that was more closely related to engineering and biology than to families or human relationships. Family systems theory was derived from general systems theory (GST), which is a theoretical perspective developed for explaining how elements of a system work together to produce outputs from the various inputs they are given. A "*system*" is nothing more than a "set of elements standing in interrelation among themselves and with the environment" (Bertalanffy, 1975, p. 159). Two key figures in the development of GST were biologist Ludwig von Bertalanffy and mathematician and engineer Norbert Wiener (e.g., Bertalanffy, 1968; Wiener, 1948). Wiener is most noted for his work on *cybernetics*, which is the science of self-correcting systems. An early application of GST came from work on antiaircraft gunnery during World War II. An essential realization of this work was the necessity to constantly compare the aim of the weapon, and the resultant course of its munitions delivery, to the position of the target. When the ammunition was being delivered too far ahead of the plane or too far behind, the operator of the weapon had to take this into consideration and adjust the aim of the antiaircraft gun. In the abstract, this concept is known as *cybernetic feedback* and would be an essential component of GST.

Whitchurch and Constantine (1993) identified three basic assumptions of GST. First, systems theories can unify science. The principles of GST are thought by many to cut across traditional academic boundaries. That is to say, they apply to systems in the natural as well as in the social sciences. For this reason, concepts and processes that describe the functioning of an automobile engine (mechanical engineering) could be equally applicable to a description of the functioning of a family (family science), or the functioning of a particular ecosystem (biology). A second assumption of GST is that a system must be understood as a whole. This concept, known as *holism*, is fundamental to all systems approaches. A system cannot be understood by merely studying each of its components in isolation from each other. There is little to be learned about the functions and outputs of an automobile engine by carefully examining the alternator and oil filter. That would not be much more useful than trying to learn about a family by carefully studying their cat and their daughter. The concept of holism implies that "the whole is greater than the sum of its parts." To understand the system, one must look at it holistically, considering all elements and how they relate to each other. A third assumption of GST is that human systems are self-reflexive. *Self-reflexivity* means that we can develop our own goals and monitor our own behavior. This is inherent in the fact that human systems are cybernetic systems that can process feedback, which is what allows for adjustments in behaviors in order to reach a goal.

THE FAMILY AS A SYSTEM

At first glance, the connection between "family" and such concepts as engines, antiaircraft artillery, and ecosystems may not be obvious. However, the family is a system that operates in accord with many of the same principles as these other systems. At the same time, the family is a special type of system with some characteristics that set it apart from some other types of systems. The family is often characterized as an open and ongoing system (Broderick, 1993). Systems that are *open* take input from the environment and produce output back to the environment. The input that families take from the environment includes things as simple as food bought at the grocery store to more complex matters such as information on the best colleges to send their children to. Output also includes a vast range of things from garbage to professional work to children who become members of society. Although no family is truly a closed system, families vary in the extent to which they are open. Families that are extremely open are said to have permeable *boundaries*. Boundaries are simply dividing lines that determine who is in and who is out of the system (Yerby, Buerkel-Rothfuss, & Bochner, 1995). The permeable boundaries of the very open family suggest that people can come and go with ease, into and out of the family system, Such a family, for example, may allow a distant cousin to move in for an extended period of time. At the same time, a teenage child might move out of the home to study in Europe as an exchange student. Families that are less open are more inclined to keep to themselves and send clear messages about the limited extent to which they will tolerate "outsiders" entering into the system.

Any system that is *ongoing* has a past, present, and future. If one considers the extended family, most families could be viewed as perpetual. Obviously, we all have ancestors, and barring some catastrophe, our families will all continue long after we are gone. In the grand scheme of things, when people think about their families (e.g., parents, siblings, grandparents, aunts, and uncles) they are really considering a mere snapshot in time. The greater ongoing system has a very long history and is sure to have a very long future.

The fact that families are open and ongoing systems means that they have a number of qualities that distinguish them from other types of systems (Broderick, 1993). For instance, all open and ongoing systems are *dynamic.* The relationships among their elements and the environment are not static; rather, they change over time. The way that a mother relates to her child at age 1 is very different from the way she relates to her child at age 15. The qualities of open and ongoing systems are *emergent.* The elements of the family interact to produce something that is more than just a collection of individuals. Systems theorists often make an analogy to baking a cake. Combining eggs, flour, sugar, and milk and baking it results in something very different from a mere collection of the individual ingredients. Families have a similar quality of emergent properties. Families also exhibit regular patterns from which we can deduce *rules*. For example, observing a family over a long period of time might reveal that whenever a member has a birthday, he or she is excused from any household chores. To the extent that this pattern is evident, one could say that this is a "rule" in the family It is also the case that these patterns of interaction, or rules, are *hierarchically structured*. This means that rules exist at different levels of abstraction, and some take precedence over others (see chap. 4). Open and ongoing systems also *regulate relationships among their components*. In order to maintain the integrity of the system, it is essential to have some rules or patterns that hold the elements together and allow for the smooth functioning of the overall system. Parents who scold their children for fighting with each other are, in the abstract, attempting to regulate their relationships. Constant and intense fighting among family members could otherwise threaten the family's well-being and ability to realize their goals. Finally, open and ongoing systems *regulate relationships between the system and the environment.* All families exist in a greater society ecosystem or suprasystem. Because they are open, interaction with elements outside of the immediate family system is essential. For this reason, families develop rules and patterns of conduct for these interactions, with the goal of protecting the integrity of the family system. A family rule that children cannot go out on dates until they are 15 is an example of a rule designed to regulate relationships between the family and the external environment.

The family's distinction as an open and ongoing system helps to delineate it from a variety of other systems. However, the family is not the only open and ongoing system. Many animal societies and environmental ecosystems could also be characterized as open and ongoing systems. To more fully appreciate the concept of family systems it is necessary to look closer at some of the family processes that are inherent in family systems theory.

MAJOR PROCESSES IN FAMILY SYSTEMS THEORY

System processes are the characteristics that describe how the family system functions as a whole unit (Bochner & Eisenberg, 1987). One way to understand family systems theory is to examine the family processes that are assumed to play an important role in the family's day to day functioning.

MUTUAL INFLUENCE

According to family systems theory, all family components are interdependent. That is to say, what happens to one member affects all other members of the family. The actions of every family member will influence the actions of other family members. Family systems theorists feel that families are constantly in the processes of influencing each other, and that this process never ends. So, for example, a child graduating from college is not just an individual achievement; it is a family event. For parents, it may represent the culmination of years of child rearing, a reduced financial burden, and the possibility of a more distant relationship with the child as he or she moves away to start a new job. To a sibling, this event may represent more freedom to use the family car, no longer having to share a bedroom, and the absence of a reliable tennis partner. Either way, the graduation of one member of the family impacts all other members of the family. Keep in mind, however, that there is no linear cause (child graduates) and effect (more distant relationship with the child) relationship in this hypothetical family. The act of going to college, graduating, and moving away to take a job is also influenced by the family. For example, a child without a close relationship to his or her parents might be more likely to move out of state after graduation. The concept of mutual influence suggests that all family members influence each other.

STABILITY

All families seek some level of regularity in their lives. Regularity brings predictability, and at least some degree of predictability allows for smooth functioning of the family. The tendency to seek stability is called *morphostasis*. Patterns, routines, and rules all allow families to function with some level of stability. A total lack of stability, or chaos, could easily destroy a family system. In a state a chaos, family roles are unclear, the behavior of family members is unpredictable, and important tasks may go undone because everyone thought that someone else would do them. Alternatively, family members may waste energy duplicating one another's efforts. It is easy to see how such a scenario would make the family such an inhospitable place as to motivate most of its members to leave the system. Although some degree of flexibility and change is healthy for the family (see section on family functioning in chap. 1) all families need and seek some stability.

CHANGE

Just as families need some stability, healthy families must experience some change. In fact, families are also driven to seek change. This tendency is known as *morphogenesis*. Morphogenesis is the tendency to reorganize and evolve over time. As family members marry, have children, age, and die, the family evolves. This is a natural and unavoidable evolution. Families also exist is a larger society, and as society itself changes, so do most families. Fifty years ago family members may have looked down on a mother who took a full-time job while her children were still young. Given the changing economic and social conditions of society, families today may be more inclined to not only accept but also honor someone who takes on so many tasks.

FEEDBACK AND CALIBRATION

Families are information processors. They perform the cybernetic function of examining their own behavior and trying to correct it so as to achieve goals. In a feedback loop, the family examines its output, and if that output is not meeting the goal or reaching some standard, they send a message (which becomes new input) to correct the behavior that led to the deviant outcome. An obvious example of this would be rearing children. Families will often correct or punish deviant behavior of their children in hopes that the children will ultimately grow up in accord with some standard defined by the family. The goal of feedback and control is to reach some level of *homeostosis*, or equilibrium. A married couple with full-time jobs that often keep them apart from each other may plan a vacation together to allow them to re-establish some balance between separateness and connection in their relationship. *Negative feedback*, also know as error-actuated feedback, occurs when the family initiates corrective action upon awareness of a deviation from some standard. This is the way that most thermostats operate. Once the temperature deviates from a set point, the thermostat sends a signal to the furnace or air conditioner to produce more heating or cooling. Parents who punish their children for bad behavior operate on negative feedback. *Positive feedback*, or deviation-amplifying feedback, works to enhance changes from a set point. For example, if a young adult child who lives with his parents and works a part-time job suddenly starts looking into colleges to attend, the parents might respond by verbally encouraging him, offering financial assistance with tuition, and relieving him of household chores so that he can pursue his studies. In this way, the parents use feedback to actually encourage change in their son's behavior, once they realize that he is contemplating a change from the norm of his part-time job.

EQUIFINALITY

The concept of equifinality refers to the fact that the same end state may be reached in many different ways. Different families can achieve the same goals by traveling down very different paths. Consider, for example, the goal of providing for the family. Some may do this through the father's employment. In other families, both the mother and the father work. In still other families, teenage children may work and contribute some of their wages to the family. In all cases, the family system generates income to provide for their needs, but in very different ways. The family systems concept of equifinality is useful and important because it is a reminder that there is no single version of family well-being and functionality. Instead, there are many different ways that families can pursue the same goal. A related systems concept, *multifinality*, indicates that the same set of inputs may lead to different outputs. Two middle-class, suburban families with similar incomes and resources may end up raising very different children. This is because different families will process the same inputs differently.

These, and additional concepts and processes in family systems theory, are assembled in Table 6.1.

EVALUATION OF FAMILY SYSTEMS THEORY

Family systems theory is the dominant paradigm in family science. It has been noted that "Many, if not most, family communication specialists have a systems theory worldview" (Whitchurch & Dickson, 1999). Nevertheless, family systems theory has been criticized on several grounds (see Klein & White, 1996, and Whitchurch & Constantine, 1993, for reviews). One position is that family systems theory is not really a true theory, but rather a philosophical perspective. There is some ambiguity and generality in family systems theory that makes it hard to generate concrete, testable hypotheses. Also, some people feel that family systems theory goes too far in emphasizing the role of all family members in influencing the phenomena that the family experiences. If a father loses his job, more often than not he is more responsible for that outcome than the family's 1-year old child is. On a related point, family systems theory has also been criticized by feminist scholars who argue that systems conceptualizations do not recognize the fact that women and children often have less power and resources than do men. For that reason, it may be unwise to view the contribution of women and children to family matters as equal to that of men. This criticism has become particularly heated when topics such as family violence and sexual abuse are discussed. Although systems theorists would not "blame" the victim,

TABLE 6.1 (CONTINUED): KEY CONCEPTS IN FAMILY SYSTEMS THEORY	
Family Systems Concept	**Definition**
• Boundaries	The border between the system and its external environment
• Enmeshment	A lack of differentiation between family members so as to minimize the development of individual identities
• Equifinality	The idea that the same end state can be reached by many different paths
• Feedback	The family's response to a behavior or process that is observed
• Goals	The family's desired outcomes or end states
• Holism	The family can only be understood by examining it in its entirety; the whole is more than the sum of its parts; also known as nonsummativity
• Homeostasis	Maintaining a state of equilibrium through feedback and calibration
• Interdependence	The idea that all components of the system are interrelated; what happens to one happens to all; the actions of one element affect the actions of the others
• Morphogenesis	The family's tendency to evolve and change with time
• Morphostasis	The tendency to seek stability or equilibrium
• Multifinality	The idea that the same set of inputs can lead to different outputs in different families
• Mutual Influence	Family members influence each other
• Negative Feedback	Error-actuated feedback that is engaged when actions deviate from a family standard; this feedback attempts to suppress the deviation

Continued

Continued from page 121

TABLE 6.1 (CONTINUED): KEY CONCEPTS IN FAMILY SYSTEMS THEORY

Family Systems Concept	Definition
• Positive Feedback	Deviation-amplifying feedback that is designed to stimulate and enhance deviation for a norm
• Requisite Variety	Having the necessary range of resources and responses to adequately address the demands encountered in the environment
• Rules	Prescribed patterns of behavior in the family; they contribute to the family's stability
• Subsystem	A smaller system within the family system such as husband–wife or parent–child
• Suprasystem	The larger system in which the family is embedded such as the extended family or society more generally

they would try to understand family problems as a function of the relationships among family members, instead of the behavior of an individual perpetrator. Whitchurch and Constantine argue that this later critique is based on a misunderstanding of GST, and that recent developments in family systems theory actually recognize different levels of power in the family through the concept of hierarchy.

SYMBOLIC INTERACTION THEORY

HISTORICAL BACKGROUND

Even before the development of symbolic interaction theory, 20th-century pragmatists, such as John Dewey and William James, began to argue that reality is not objectively "set in stone"; rather, it is constantly changing. This way of thinking about reality was somewhat novel for the early 20th century. Furthermore, this new notion of reality advocated that participants constantly co-create a subjective social reality as they interact. Inspired by the ideas of these earlier thinkers, George Herbert Mead is credited with articulating the foundations of the theory later named symbolic interaction (SI) theory. Along with Mead, Manford Kuhn is recognized for contributing to and affirming the unique ideas of SI.Mead was a very popular and respected teacher at the University of Chicago, and, after his death, his students compiled lecture notes from his classes to produce a book they titled *Mind, Self, and Society* (1934). One of Mead's students, Herbert Blumer (1969), termed Mead's theoretical tenets "symbolic interaction theory."

Mead and others were interested in the way humans create, react to, and redefine the shared, symbolic meanings in their social environment. Mead began with the premise that words and nonverbal behaviors are the primary symbols to which humans assign meaning. He stressed the idea that meaning only occurs when people share common symbols and interpretations in a state of intersubjectivity. He also elaborated on the idea that symbolic meanings are heavily influenced by perceptions, including people's own perceptions and other people's perceptions of them and the social structure around them, For example, imagine a college student who comes home over a break from school with baskets full of dirty laundry. Her mother washes and folds the clothes for her. What does this behavior symbolize? Because SI sees meaning as occurring between people, we cannot know the meaning until we study the mother and daughter's interaction and perceptions. Perhaps (a) the daughter perceives herself as mature and self-sufficient; (b) based on prior interaction, the mother views and accepts the daughter as self-sufficient; and (c) the two come to a common interpretation that the mother is not obligated to do the laundry, but chooses to do so as a symbol of care for her busy daughter. In another mother–daughter relationship, this very same behavior could symbolize an obligatory caretaking duty full of resent, guilt, and the perception of a lazy daughter.

Mead (1934) and Blumer (1969) felt that the study of human beings required methods different from those of the study of physical objects or laws of nature. This is because human behavior can only be understood by knowing what it means to the person who is actually performing the behavior. Because SI emphasizes individuals' perceptions and the intersubjectivity shared by participants, it is difficult to observe and understand communication from the outside. Not until researchers know the perspective of the individual, can they understand him or her. Mead and Blumer advocated the use of case studies and examination of stories and personal histories in order to understand people's behaviors from the perspective of the people themselves.

Today, SI can be thought of as a diverse collection of theories rather than as a particular theory (Klein & White, 1996). Over time, many branches of the theory developed (e.g., social construction theory, role theory, and self-theory), emphasizing slightly different aspects of symbolic, human interaction. For instance, social construction theory spun off SI to explain co-constructed meaning rather than shared meaning. That is, social construction theory builds on the ideas of SI to further emphasize that "meaning does not reside inside one person's head, waiting to be shared with another. Rather, meaning exists in the practice of communication between people" (Turner & West, 2002, p. 61; see also Chen & Pearce, 1995). To illustrate the social construction of meaning, consider what happens when people become grandparents for the first time. They are often assigned a new title (i.e., grandma, nana, grammy, etc.), which is already loaded with basic cultural meaning. However, the title takes on further meaning as the grandparent–grandchild relationship develops. Through family interaction, the family co-constructs what they mean by the term *grandma*. In some families, grandma is a distant relative who sends gifts on holidays. For others, Grandma is a primary caretaker, acting more like some "moms." In sum, society's expectations for grandparents influence the meaning assigned to the role, but an additional layer of meaning is generated through the family's own interaction.

CENTRAL THEMES, ASSUMPTIONS, AND CONCEPTS IN SI

There are at least three central themes of SI and several underlying assumptions associated with these themes (Klein & White, 1996; LaRossa & Reitzes, 1993; West & Turner, 2000). Each theme relates to one of the three concepts that title Mead's (1934) book, *Mind, Self, and Society*. The first theme involves the importance of meanings for human behavior and relates to Mead's concept of *mind*. Three assumptions reveal this theme (Blumer, 1969; West & Turner, 2000, p. 76):

1. Humans act toward others on the basis of the meaning those others have for them.
2. Meaning is created in interaction between people.
3. Meaning is modified through an interpretive process.

This collection of assumptions acknowledges that human minds have the capacity to use symbols to represent thought. In particular, people rely on common, significant symbols that have shared, social meaning. As a symbol system, language works because people act in accordance with shared meanings. Even though people have many shared symbols, symbolic meaning is always being modified in interaction. Through perspective taking and other interpretive processes, people come to understand others' views. For instance, in symbolic role-taking, people try to take another person's perspective, or step inside his or her mind, in order to see how another person sorts out meaning. Very young children have a difficult time perspective taking. In a game of hide and seek, young children may think that if their own eyes are closed, then no one else can see them. They soon learn that what they see is not what other people see.

The second theme addresses how humans develop self-concepts and relates to Mead's (1934) concept of *self*. Two assumptions reveal this theme (LaRossa & Reitzes, 1993; West & Turner, 2000, p. 78):

1. Individuals develop self-concepts through interaction with others.
2. Self-concepts provide an important motive for behavior.

Mead (1934) describes the *self* as an *I* and a *Me*. During interaction, the *I* simply acts, impulsively and spontaneously. The *Me* is more reflective, concerned with how people come across to their social world. The Me employs social comparisons and considers the way other people view the self. More specifically, the Me attends to reflected self-appraisals. *Reflected self-appraisals* refer to the appraisals or evaluations other people make of the self. The extent to which another person's view affects one's self-concept depends on how much one values the other person's opinion. Young children often take the comments of their primary caretakers very seriously, because they have few other referents in their lives. Some college students, on the other hand, only take their parents' opinions with a "grain of salt" because they are receiving a great deal of reflected self-appraisal from other important sources including friends, romantic partners, professors, and so forth. As SI indicates, the way people view their *self* motivates their future behavior. For example, people who have been told they are bad at math and who view themselves as bad at math have little reason to be motivated to major in math. Their self-concept may even set forth a self-fulfilling prophecy, whereby they see little reason to try hard at math because they already perceive they are bad. Putting forth little effort at math helps them meet their already low expectations.

Finally, the third theme describes the relationship between individuals and society and relates to Mead's (1934) concept of *society* (West & Turner, 2000, p. 79):

1. People and groups are influenced by cultural and social processes.
2. Social structure is worked out through social interaction.

Mead (1934) states that *society* is comprised of particular others and generalized others, *Particular others* refer to dose significant others, such as family and friends, and *generalized others* refer to the larger community or society. According to SI, people act in the context of societal norms and values, whether they be the norms and values of their particular others or generalized others. For example, family members know what is normal behavior for their family culture (i.e., their particularized others), and they act with those norms in mind. Some families have a ritual of eating dinner together around a table every night. Other families do not expect members to eat at the same time or in the same place. Just as the interaction in one's family creates a set of norms and values, society (i.e., generalized others) influences what is viewed as normal family interaction. The media, for instance, is one societal force that shapes standards for family interaction.

EVALUATION AND APPLICATION TO FAMILY COMMUNICATION

Sociologist and symbolic interaction theorist Ernest W. Burgess was "the first to define family in terms of its interaction: 'a unity of interacting personalities,' by which he meant a family as a living, changing, growing thing, 'a unity of interacting persons,' rather than 'a mere collection of individuals'" (as cited in Whitchurch & Dickson, 1999, p. 691). Burgess' pioneering approach viewed interaction as the defining feature of families. His work became a theoretical cornerstone of family research. SI inspired a new way of studying families, by examining family interaction and the creation and maintenance of family symbols and themes.

In particular, SI has guided research on topics such as the socialization of family members, symbolic interpretations of family events, and family identities and narratives. As Steinmetz (1999) states: "We are not born with a sense of who we are, but must develop a sense of 'self' through symbolization with other people" (p. 375). Symbolic interaction draws attention to the critical role that parents, siblings, and other outside forces play as socializing agents for children (Bohannon & White, 1999; Cheng & Kuo, 2000). Children observe appropriate behavior for certain roles, and they receive reflected self-appraisal from the significant others in their family. Second, SI explains how families symbolize both routine and extraordinary events, though a great deal of attention has been given to extraordinary events, such as marriage, death, or major family illnesses (Book, 1996; Rehm & Franck, 2000; see also chap. 3). Informed by the society around them, families develop rituals for family events, such as weddings or funerals, or rituals for routine events, such as bedtime rituals to put a child to sleep. Finally, families generate stories to symbolize one family member's identity or the whole family identity (Hequembourg & Farrell, 1999; Stone, 1988).

There are a number of obvious strengths and weaknesses of SI. As a strength, SI highlights that meaning is dynamic and subjective, and understandings are worked out as family members interact with one another and with society. The problem is that researchers sometimes have a difficult time studying family meanings and symbols because they are often so subjective. Apart from actually living with a family, the only way researchers can learn about these subjective understandings is by asking family members to report their perceptions and tell their own story. Some family members may not even be aware of their own subjective meanings, and, if they are, they may be unwilling to report or may adjust their story for someone outside the family. Nonetheless, SI and its theoretical offshoots continue to inspire a great deal of research in family studies.

SOCIAL LEARNING THEORY

BACKGROUND

Social learning theory was developed by Stanford University psychologist Albert Bandura (Bandura, 1977). Bandura developed social learning theory, not as a theory of family communication per se, rather as a more general theory of behavioral acquisition. More recently, Bandura has expanded social learning theory into the more general social cognitive theory (e.g., Bandura, 1986, 1994). However, for purposes of the present discussion we will contain our presentation largely to explanation of the basic principles of social learning theory.

In the premier study of what was later to become social learning theory, Bandura, Ross, and Ross (1963) documented that children will imitate a model who is reinforced for performing certain behaviors. To explore this issue, they randomly assigned nursery school students to watch a filmed portrayal of a child model. Under one condition, the model behaved aggressively and was rewarded for doing so. Under the second condition the model behaved aggressively and was punished for doing so. In the control group the model did not behave aggressively at all. Shortly thereafter, the children were allowed to play, and researchers measured their aggressive behavior during the play session. They found that children who observed the aggressive model get rewarded exhibited significantly more aggressive behavior themselves than either those under the aggression-punished condition or those in the control group. Also, those who saw the model get punished for aggressive behavior behaved much less aggressively than those under the other conditions. Bandura and his colleagues theorized that the children learned the consequences of behaving aggressively by observing what happened when the model behaved aggressively. When the model was rewarded, the nursery school children imitated or enacted the same behavior that produced the reward for the model. When the model was punished, the children seemed to avoid performing the behavior that resulted in punishment for the model. This idea of observational learning through modeling would become a central element of Bandura's social learning theory.

One can think of the process of social learning as a search for "if-then" relationships (Smith, 1982). Consistent with the more general principles of behavioral theory, according to social learning theory, people seek rewards and try to avoid punishments. Bandura notes that, fortunately, people are able to learn what brings rewards and what brings punishments at least some of the time through observing what happens to other people. Imagine what life would be like if the only way we could learn about the consequences of driving without a seatbelt, playing with a loaded gun, picking up rattlesnakes, and drinking household chemicals was through direct experience. Most people would not live to see their 20th birthday. Fortunately, we are able to learn about the consequences of these behaviors by observing other people's misfortunes. Similarly, we are able to learn about behaviors that bring more positive consequences by also observing others. Once the "if-then" rule (e.g., "If I touch a hot stove, then I will burn my hand" or "If I scream and cry, then my mother will give me candy") is learned, most people act accordingly to secure the reward or avoid the punishment.

LEARNING ABOUT THE CONSEQUENCES OF BEHAVIOR

In social learning theory, people are assumed to gain most of their knowledge about the consequences of performing various behaviors through two possible sources. The first, and the most obvious, is through *direct experience*. In this rudimentary mode of learning, people acquire knowledge of behavioral consequences by actually experiencing them. For example, if a child eats a chili pepper and it burns his or her mouth, that experience teaches the child to avoid eating chili peppers in the future. If the child eats a chocolate candy bar, and it tastes good, the child would learn the reinforcing value of eating chocolate and would presumably perform the behavior frequently in the future. The idea of learning through direct experience and the rewards and punishments that are associated with our behaviors is a basic element of behavior theory, and is a mode by which even the simplest of animals can and will learn. However, because of their ability to form mental representations and their ability to abstract rules from observations of actions and their consequences, humans (and some other animals) are also able to learn through observation and the vicarious experience that it presents. Learning by vicarious experience happens when we take note of the effects of other people's behaviors. For example, if John observed his parents reward his sister with $20 for bringing home a report card with straight As, he is likely to abstract the following if-then rule: "If you get straight As in school, then mom and dad will give you money" So long as receiving money is seen by John as a positive outcome, he is likely to try to enact that behavior (i.e., working hard in school to get good grades) himself. Note that John did not learn the if-then rule by directly experiencing the effects of getting good grades. Rather, he learned the rule vicariously, through observing what happened when his sister got good grades.

THE PROCESS OF SOCIAL LEARNING

Let us dissect the process of observational learning, or learning by modeling, a bit further. Learning through vicarious experience is dependent on several interrelated processes. To start, there must be some *attention* paid to the model. Each day people are exposed to dozens, hundreds, and in some cases, thousands of other people. Each of these people is a potential model from whom others can learn about the consequences of enacting various behaviors. However, social learning can only happen if we pay attention to both the model's behavior and its associated consequences. Without attention to the model, there can be no observational learning. Second, there must be *retention* of the if-then rule that is learned by observing the model. That is to say, we have to form a mental representation of what was learned, and store that in memory, perhaps as a more abstract rule. Bandura (1986) notes that retention can be enhanced by rehearsal. The more people rehearse the socially learned rule (e.g., if I apologize for doing something wrong, people will forgive me) the more likely they are to have access to it at critical times, and therefore to perform the appropriate behavior for either securing rewards or avoiding punishing responses from the social environment. Next, there are a number of *behavioral production processes* that are vital to performing the observed behavior. People must have the ability to produce or enact the behavior that they observed. This often requires organization of constituent subskills into a new response pattern. Sometimes people are able to enhance their ability to perform observed behaviors by receiving informative feedback from others on troublesome aspects of their behavior. For example, a father might teach his daughter how to kick a soccer ball by modeling the behavior. If the daughter does not perform the behavior with the same competence as the father's, he might give her feedback on what she has done incorrectly in order to help her perform the behavior in the best way possible. Finally, there has to be *motivation* to perform the modeled behavior. In the previous example, the father might model the proper way to kick a soccer ball 100 times in the presence of his daughter. However, even if she pays attention to him, remembers how to do it, and has the competence to perform the modeled behavior, she will not do so unless she has sufficient motivation.

Where does the motivation to perform behavior come from? Social learning theory recognizes that incentives can be inherent in the behavior, vicariously produced, or selfproduced (Bandura, 1986). Some behaviors are inherently satisfying to most people. For example, people generally like to eat ice cream. The motivation to eat ice cream comes from consequences that are inherent in the behavior itself, not from some abstract or complex rule that is learned (e.g., "eating ice cream will keep the dairy farmers in business and will therefore be good for the state economy."). Bandura refers to the effects of such behaviors as eating ice cream or drinking water when thirsty as "direct incentive." Sometimes the incentive for performing a behavior is *self-produced*. With self-produced incentives, people essentially reward themselves for a job well done. There is nothing inherently satisfying about bowling a strike. However, bowling enthusiasts will mentally congratulate themselves upon bowling a strike because they have come to value this sort of performance. To people who do not care about or understand bowling, knocking down 10 pins with a heavy ball may seem like a meaningless behavior. Most important to social learning theory, people are sometimes motivated to perform behaviors because of vicarious incentives. People often acquire and perform behaviors because they see other people do so and get rewarded. The fashion and clothing industry—an industry that relies heavily on modeling—is constantly trying to impart vicarious knowledge of the consequences of performing various behaviors (e.g., wear this brand of shoes and you will be a good athlete; wear this style of pants and you will look great and gain the admiration of your peers, etc.).

APPLICATION TO FAMILY COMMUNICATION

Even though social learning processes operate throughout the life span, and through observation of virtually any person, their applicability to child learning in the family context is undeniable. Smith (1982) noted that "we acquire most of our basic values and personal habits by initially observing our parents' behavior and later the behavior of admired friends and reference groups" (p. 201). Children often grow up to hold political and religious values similar to those of their parents, pursue many of the same hobbies and occupations that their parents do, and sometimes even drive the same brand of car that their parents drive. Social learning theory provides a compelling account for how and why this happens. The theory is a reminder that anything that parents do in the presence of their children can and often will communicate abstract if-then rules to the children. If the surrounding circumstances are right, these rules may then become prompts for behavior, or inhibitors of behavior, depending on the content of the mental representation.

Smith (1982) described a number of conditions that affect the success of modeling, several of which have obvious applicability in the family setting. One such factor is the similarity between the model and the observer. The more similar the model is to the observer, the more likely the observer is to enact the modeled behavior. Similarity between the model and the self contributes to self-efficacy in the observer. When people experience self-efficacy, they feel that they are able to adequately perform the behavior. Supposedly the thinking with models similar to the self is that "if they can do it, then I can do it." It is obvious that there is considerable perceived similarity within family groups. For this reason, family members can be ideal models of behavior. Smith also notes that modeling is more successful when models have high status. Certainly parents and older siblings have very high status in the eyes of young children. Because most children start out in life looking up to their parents, they naturally use their parents as a benchmark for appropriate behavior. Also, modeling is most successful when there are multiple models. In the family context, it is often the case that more than one person performs a particular behavior. So, for example, if two or three members of the family are avid golfers, children raised in that family will have multiple models to observe, and are consequently very likely to adopt the same behaviors (i.e., take up golfing) themselves.

Family science researchers have continued to apply social learning theory to the explanation of many functional and dysfunctional aspects of family interaction. For example, there are many who feel that people learn how to be spouses and how to be parents by observing their own parents in these roles. In the area of family dysfunction, there is compelling evidence for social learning processes in family or partner violence, substance abuse, and even divorce (e.g., Andrews, Hops, & Duncan, 1997; Mihalic & Elliot, 1997; Swinford, DeMaris, Cernkovich, & Giordano, 2000; see chaps. 11, 13, and 15 for more in-depth analysis of these family issues). When parents engage in physical violence or substance use in the presence of their children, they inadvertently communicate that this is an acceptable form of behavior. This is because young children lack the reasoning skills to independently determine what is right and what is wrong. Therefore, they use their parents as a benchmark for appropriate conduct. The idea is that, if the parents do it, it must be the correct thing to do. So if the mother and father resort to physical violence when engaged in conflict or consume large amounts of alcohol when stressed, children who observe that behavior are likely to enact it themselves later in life. Similarly, when children observe their parents' divorce, they are likely to learn the if-then rule that goes "if you have problems in your marriage, then you get divorced." This is one of several hypotheses for the intergenerational transmission of divorce. It is apparent that social learning processes are so powerful that the if-then rules learned in family contexts and the behaviors that they prompt will often hold up in the face of intense challenges. For example, most people know that divorce and domestic violence are not positive experiences. Yet, the template for behavior that is learned in the family of origin through social learning can be nearly impossible for some people to modify or escape. Despite "knowing" that family violence is wrong, when confronted with intense conflict, that becomes the default response. As disturbing as these family patterns are, they are a testimony to the power of social learning.

ATTACHMENT THEORY

BACKGROUND

Attachment theory was originally developed by John Bowlby and was based on his observational studies of children who experienced separation from their parents during World War II (Bowlby, 1969, 1973, 1980). Bowlby was also influenced by ethological theories that explore similarities and differences in behavior across species. Ultimately he argued that attachment processes outlined in the theory are evident in nonhuman as well as human primates and serve an adaptive function for the survival of the species. Although Bowlby developed his theory as something of an alternative to the orthodox psychodynamic view of child development that was articulated by Sigmund Freud, Bowlby's thinking still preserves many of the trappings of psychodynamic ideology.

Bowlby (1973) observed that human infants are innately driven to seek out and remain in close proximity to their primary caregivers. Indeed, this pattern of behavior is typical of most primates. Bowlby characterized attachment behavior as "any form of behavior that results in a person attaining or retaining proximity to some other differentiated and preferred individual"

(p. 292). This type of behavior is viewed as "hardwired" into the brain. That is to say, people do not need to learn proximity seeking to the caregiver, Rather, this tendency is already present at birth. Bowlby felt that this pattern of behavior was the result of natural selection. Because it is adaptive to the survival of the species, those who did not seek the proximity of a caregiver as an infant were less likely to survive and pass on their genes.

FUNCTIONS OF ATTACHMENT

As noted earlier, attachment processes between the infant and primary caregiver are assumed to be functional. Bowlby argued that attachment is adaptive to the survival of the species. His writings highlight four distinct functions that are served by attachment, all of which appear to be beneficial to the infant's survival and development. Perhaps the most basic function of attachment is *proximity seeking*. Infants have an innate tendency to seek out their primary caregiver. Given that this person is the source of protection and nourishment, it is obvious how this tendency serves the infant's best interests. *Separation protest* is a second function of attachment. This simply implies that the infant will resist separation from his or her primary caregiver. Behaviorally, it is evident in crying and screaming when the infant is separated from the caregiver. The *safe haven* function refers to the tendency to seek out the caregiver in times of stress or danger. Eventually children will explore their environment apart from their parents. However, attachment will readily send the child back to the presence of the parent for protection during times of stress. Finally, the *secure base* function indicates that an attachment that is felt as secure will motivate or allow the child to explore his or her environment, beyond immediate contact with the caregiver. The idea is that the secure attachment with the caregiver provides a sort of psychological foundation on which the child can mount an exploration into the unknown elements of his or her environment. If the child knows in the back of his or her mind that the caregiver is available for protection, exploration of the environment is not felt to be as risky. All of these functions of attachment should keep the infant out of harm's way and in the presence of the individual who can shelter, protect, and nourish. There can be little doubt about the adaptive nature of such processes. Infants (or animals) who enact attachment behaviors are most likely to survive the perils of early development and grow into functional adults.

WORKING MODELS AND ATTACHMENT STYLES

In attachment theory, interactions between the infant and his or her primary caregiver (usually the mother) become the basis for internal *working models*. These are mental representations that summarize and organize interactions between the self and the caregiver. Early attachment experiences contribute to both internal working models of the self and internal working models of others. In the self model, the child views him-or herself as either worthy or unworthy of love and support. Experiences with a parent who is warm and responsive would obviously lead to an internal working model of the self as worthy of love. However, if early childhood experiences with the caregiver are marked by coldness and unavailability, the child will come to view the self as unworthy of love and support. As Reis and Patrick (1996) wisely observed, "just how this internalization occurs remains one of the most important and unresolved issues in attachment research" (p. 526). Internal working models of others are a mental representation of the benevolence of other people. Other models are something of a prototype of other human beings and how they can be expected to treat the child. These representations are summarized along themes of availability, responsiveness, and trustworthiness. Essentially, the child will generalize from experiences with the primary caregiver and assume that this is how most people will treat him or her. According to attachment theory, once these internal working models are established, which may happen as early as age 1 or 2, they are relatively stable throughout the remainder of the life span.

Obviously, different children have different internal working models of the self and others. These various internal working models become the foundation for attachment styles. Bowlby (1973) felt that the nature of the caregiver's response to the child was the dominant factor that determined the infant's attachment style. Originally, attachment theorists suggested that there were three distinct attachment styles. People with a secure attachment style had caregivers who were responsive to their needs, available, and affectionate. Those with an *anxious—avoidant* attachment style had early interactions with caregivers who were cold, not nurturing, and unavailable. If the primary caregiver was inconsistent or unpredictable in his or her responsiveness to the child, the child was thought to develop an *anxious—ambivalent* attachment style. Research on attachment theory has shown that infants with different attachment styles will behave differently around their mothers (Ainsworth, Blehar, Waters, & Wall, 1978). For example, infants with a secure attachment will gladly explore their environment when in the presence of their mothers. Upon separation they become distressed but then readily settle back down when reunited with their mothers. Infants with an anxious— avoidant attachment style tend to avoid close contact with their mothers and keep to themselves. Finally, the anxious-ambivalent infants will exhibit extreme distress upon separation from their mothers. However, when reunited, these children show signs of anger and ambivalence.

	Model of self	
	Positive	Negative
Positive	Secure Comfortable with intimacy and autonomy	Preoccupied Preoccupied with relationships
Negative	Dismissing Dismissing of intimacy Counter-dependency	Fearful Fearful of intimacy Socially avoidant

Note. From "Attachment Styles Among Young Adults: A Test of a Four Category Model;" by K.Bartholomew & L.M.Horowitz, 1991 Journal of Personality and Social Psychology, 61,pp. 226–244. Copyright 1991 by the American Psychological Association. Adapted with permission.

FIGURE 6.1.

The Bartholomew and Horowitz (1991) Model of Attachment Styles

More recently, a four-category scheme of attachment styles has been proposed, based on positive and negative models of the self and others (Bartholomew & Horowitz, 1991). In this model, early experiences with caregivers are thought to produce internal working models of the self that are generally positive (worthy of love and acceptable to others) or negative (unworthy of love, unacceptable to others). At the same time, children are assumed to develop internal working models of others that are either positive (others are trustworthy and available) or negative (others are unreliable and rejecting), When the internal working models of the self and others are crossed, there are four possible attachment styles: *secure, preoccupied, dismissing,* and *fearful.* These are depicted in Figure 6.1.

As evident in Figure 6.1, the four-category scheme preserves the secure attachment style of the original three-category scheme. However, it divides the avoidant styles into two substyles: the dismissing and the fearful. In each case, the internal working model of others is negative, but in the dismissing style the internal working model of the self is positive, whereas it is negative in the fearful style. It should be noted that this scheme was developed and validated largely on young adults. One might wonder how, for example, a person develops a positive internal working model of the self but a negative model of others. Infants appear much more readily willing to internalize the negative behavior of others as a negative reflection on the self. However, people who start out in life with a positive view of the self, but then have a string of bad experiences with others, could plausibly maintain their positive view of the self while holding a more negative view of other people. Note that this explanation hinges on the person's ability to *not* always internalize the negative actions of others as a poor reflection on the self. This undoubtedly entails a more adult way of thinking about the social world and its relation to the self.

EVALUATION AND APPLICATION TO FAMILY COMMUNICATION

Embedded within attachment theory are some very powerful ideas and statements about family communication early in life. According to Bowlby (1969, 1973, 1980) the nature of the parent–infant interaction sets a template for social relationships that the child will carry with him or her for life. Notably, much of this early parent–child communication is nonverbal. As children grow older, their attachment figures shift from parents to romantic partners and spouses (Hazan & Shaver, 1987; Reis & Patrick, 1996). This implies that communication patterns in the family of origin may be revisited in some way in the family of orientation. For example, people with secure attachment styles have a tendency to end up in traditional or independent marriages, whereas those with dismissing or preoccupied styles are more likely to be in separate style marriages (Fitzpatrick, Fey, Segrin, & Schiff, 1993) (see chap. 6 for a discussion of the different martial types). Those with a secure attachment style are also more likely to report high marital satisfaction compared to those with other styles of attachment (Feeney, 2002; Feeney, Noller, & Callan, 1994; Meyers & Landsberger, 2002). A positive view of the self (i.e., secure or dismissive attachment style) is positively associated with family outcomes such as perceived rewards from marriage and parenting (Vasquez, Durik, & Hyde, 2002). Finally, secure attachment has been linked with less destructive marital conflict patterns and more positive attitudes toward parenting (Cohn, Silver, Cowan, Cowan, & Pearson, 1992; Feeney, Noller, & Roberts, 2000). Findings such as these are useful for employing attachment theory as an explanation for the effects of family of origin experiences on later family of orientation experiences. They also draw attention to the critical role of parent–child communication in the early years of life. Even preverbal children appear very attuned and attentive to their parents' style of relating to them. This early parental communication evidently leads to self-concept development and views of the trustworthiness of others that impacts later communication patterns and relationships.

Attachment theory has been very useful for explaining why people with a history of childhood abuse often find themselves in abusive relationships as adults. This noxious form of parent-child communication has been linked with a host of negative social and psychological outcomes later in life (see chaps. 13 and 15 for a more in-depth analysis). An abused child would be expected to develop a negative internal working model of the self and therefore not feel worthy of love from others. Perhaps the child even feels that abusive conduct from others is somehow deserved or warranted. This sets up a mental representation of close relationships as normatively including abusive behavior. When such a child grows older and begins seeking romantic partners, attachment theorists speculate that this mental model of close relationships causes the person to, perhaps unknowingly, seek out others who will be abusive. In so doing, they recreate their childhood experiences and settle into a social life that is at once painful but familiar.

It would not be an exaggeration to state that attachment theory has been subject to hundreds of studies in the past 25 years. Researchers have used attachment styles to explain so many different phenomena that it begins to strain the imagination of the reader and credibility of the theory. The eagerness with which researchers have studied attachment styles in the past 15 years appears to be fueled by a variable—analytic mentality in which the search is on for any phenomenon, concept, or experience that varies as a function of attachment styles. Regardless of the utility of this approach, it obviously indicates the current mass appeal of attachment theory in the social and behavioral sciences.

One assumption of attachment theory that has been hotly debated is the stability of attachment styles. Bowlby (1969, 1973, 1980) argued that the attachment styles formed in childhood are enduring throughout the life span. However, some scientists disagree with this assumption. For example, Coyne (1999) has been critical of theories that characterize early childhood experiences as frozen in time, like the Wooly Mammoth, unable to be changed. Rather, Coyne argues that we have experiences throughout the life span that are influential in developing and changing our interpersonal perspectives. Further, he argues that early childhood experiences have only modest associations with later adult experiences such as depression. In the research literature there is at least suggestive support for the stability of internal working models and attachment styles over time (e.g., Bram, Gallant, & Segrin, 1999; Feeney et al., 2000). However, when attachment style is measured categorically (e.g., secure and dismissive), about 25% of respondents appear to change their attachment style over periods of 1 to 4 years (Feeney & Noller, 1996). Further, people may experience a different attachment style depending on the relationship. When considering their 10 "most important" relationships, 88% of respondents reported that these relationships corresponded with at least two attachment styles, and 47% reported correspondence with three attachment styles (Baldwin, Keelan, Fehr, Enns, & Koh-Rangarajoo, 1996). If attachment styles change over time and by relationship, the fundamental importance of parent–child interaction that is postulated by attachment theory could be seriously questioned.

THE DIALECTICAL PERSPECTIVE

Every year, millions of Americans travel home to their family of origin during the holiday season. In most cases people seem eager to reunite with family members and spend time with them. Often, after a week or so, people return back to their homes, jobs, and school, and seem as eager to get back to their life away from the family of origin as they were to see the family members in the first place. Why does it happen that at one moment people want to be united with their family members, and at the next they want to leave family members behind and get back to school or work? The dialectical perspective (Baxter & Montgomery, 1996, 1997) explains that these seeming contradictions are an inherent part of our relationships with other people. Even though the dialectical approach describes forces that operate in virtually all relationships, family theorists have found its principles and ideas to be very useful for explaining the form and function of family relationships.

CONTRADICTION IN FAMILY RELATIONSHIPS

In the dialectical perspective, contradictions are seen as an inherent aspect of any relationship. Contradictions cause change in our relationships and they keep relationships growing instead of static. They are relational forces that are unified opposites. By "unified" Baxter and Montgomery (1997) suggest that the opposing relational forces are interdependent. In other words, the meaning or experience of one force is dependent on the other. For example, if one lived in a tropical climate where the outdoor temperature was consistently between 70 and 90° F is there any such thing as it being "hot" or "cold" outside? For people who live in the Midwestern United States where the weather can range from 0 to 100°F "hot" and "cold" have obvious and clear meanings. The point is that the experience of "hot" takes on meaning relative to its alternative: "cold." If there were no such thing as "cold," "hot" would not be very meaningful.

What are some contradictions, or unified opposites, that play a part in family life? One example cited by Baxter and Montgomery (1996) is *autonomy versus connectedness*. Reconsider the previous example about the family reunion over the holidays. In all close relationships, there is an obvious desire for a sense of "connectedness" among the members of the relationship. This might be established and maintained though sharing time and space, engaging in conversation, and engaging in joint activities. Without any of these, it would be hard to say that there is much of a relationship at all. However, there are very few people who want to spend 24 hours a day together. Even the closest married couples and the most attached parent–child dyads seem to desire some time on their own. Consequently, family members must strike a balance in their relationships, over time, between connectedness and separateness. These opposing forces that impinge on the relationship are known as dialectic tensions. Other dialectic tensions that must be managed in family relationships include novelty versus predictability, disclosure versus privacy, stability versus change, and conventionality versus uniqueness (Baxter & Montgomery; Bochner & Eisenberg, 1987). According to the dialectical approach, these oppositional forces are balanced by different families in different ways. Rarely are they handled with an "either-or" approach.

Before leaving the topic of contradictions, it is important to note that the opposing forces described in the dialectical approach are not located in the struggle between one person and another. Rather, Baxter and Montgomery (1996, 1997) note that these oppositional forces are part of the *relationship*. In other words, they are relational, not individual, forces. In a mother–daughter relationship, the disclosure–privacy dialectic is not an issue of the mother expecting and offering full disclosure while the daughter expects and maintains full privacy. That would be an antagonism between two individuals. Rather, this is a relational force that each must manage. There are surely some things that the mother wants to disclose to the daughter and some things that she would like to keep private. Similarly, the daughter would also want to disclose some things to her mother and keep some matters to herself. This dialectical tension calls on the mother and daughter to balance their desires for disclosure and privacy in a way that is comfortable for their relationship. Most people who have been in such a family relationship can attest to the difficulty of negotiating this dialectic tension.

PRAXIS AND PRAXIS PATTERNS

According to the dialectical perspective, "people are at once both actors and objects of their own action" (Baxter & Montgomery, 1997, p. 329). This concept is called praxis. People consciously and often freely make choices about how they choose to treat their family members. This is abundantly evident in messages that are sent from one family member to another. At the same time, sent messages and communication patterns have a way of influencing the relationship in such as a way as to impact the original message sender. Consider, for example, a parent with an anger-management problem. If the parent expresses anger with his child through enacting physical violence, he could be seen as a sender of dysfunctional verbal and nonverbal communication, but at the same time, he will be *acted on* by his own communication. Assume, for example, that the Child Protective Services were made aware of the abuse, took the child from the family home, and had the father arrested. Suddenly, his act of communication has massive consequences that come back and act on him and his relationship with the child.

Different relationships use different mechanisms for managing the dialectical tensions that they experience. These mechanisms or tactics are called *praxis patterns*. Baxter and Montgomery (1996, 1997) divide these tactics into those that are dysfunctional and those that are functional. One of the common but dysfunctional praxis patterns is *denial*. Here, members of the relationship simply deny the presence of the contradiction by only honoring one of the poles while excluding the other. In a family that felt the opposing forces of conventionality and uniqueness, family members would be using denial if they simply ignored the pull for uniqueness and honored only the drive for conventionality Another dysfunctional praxis pattern is *disorientation*. This happens when there is no real "management" of the oppositional forces in the relationship. Rather, members of the relationship resign themselves to the fact that these contradictory motives are inevitable and negative. Consequently, they are likely to find themselves in double-bind situations where any behavior or communication will feel like it clashes with one of the opposing relational forces.

Baxter and Montgomery (1996, 1997) have also identified a series of more functional praxis patterns. These are more effective means for managing the dialectical tensions in such a way as to minimize negative relational outcomes. One functional praxis pattern called *spiraling alternation* involves alternating between the opposite poles of a dialectic at different points in time. For example, every Sunday family members may get together for dinner, honoring connectedness, but it may be understood that every Saturday night everyone is free to do their own thing or go out with their friends, honoring the desire for autonomy. In *segmentation*, members of the relationship honor opposing poles of the dialectic, not over time, but over topic or activity domain. For example, a family might be very open when it comes to discussing spiritual beliefs and finances, but very private when it comes to discussing sexuality By having open communication on some topics and treating others with a "hands-off" attitude the family alternates between the two poles of the disclosure-privacy dialectic. *Balance* is a praxis pattern in which members of the relationship try to respond to both ends of the opposition by seeking a compromise. One problem with balance is that neither polarity is fully satisfied at any point in time. *Integration* is something of an ideal in conflict resolution and management of dialectical tensions. When members of a relationship integrate, they find a way of simultaneously satisfying both polarities of a dialectical tension. Baxter and Montgomery (1996) suggest that in some cases family dinnertime can be seen as an integration praxis pattern in which the family bond is established and maintained, and yet individual actions and accomplishments are recognized and embraced though the input of individual members into the interaction. With *recalibration* members of the relationship create "a transformation in the expressed form of the contradiction such that the opposing forces are no longer regarded as oppositional to one another" (Baxter & Montgomery, p. 65). With this praxis pattern, members of the relationship find a way to reframe the contradiction "such that the polarities are encompassed in one another" (p. 65). The phrase "if you love something, set it free" may be a reflection of this mentality. By freeing one's partner to behave as he or she will, members of a relationship can experience security through that freedom. Finally, the praxis pattern of *reaffirmation* "celebrates the richness afforded by each polarity and tolerates the tension posed by their unity" (Baxter & Montgomery p. 66). In some ways, the "for better or worse" part of a marriage vow may represent reaffirmation for some married couples. If the couple accepts both the good times and the bad, and realizes that they will have a better and stronger relationship as a result of working through each, they may be enacting a reaffirmation praxis pattern.

EVALUATION AND APPLICATION TO FAMILY COMMUNICATION

The dialectical approach has proven to be very useful to family theorists and researchers who are interested in explaining various family processes and tasks. For example, the work of Bochner and Eisenberg (1987), which predated the formal development of the dialectical approach, argued that there are two dialectical tensions that are central to family functioning. They characterize the first as *integration versus differentiation*. All families are made up of individuals with their own unique identities. At the same time, families as a collective unit have an identity. One task that faces all families is honoring the desire for a collective identity as a family unit versus allowing individuals within the family to develop their own unique identities as individuals, or their own unique relationships with other family member (e.g., mother–daughter and between two siblings). Another dialectic that has a substantial impact on family functioning according to Bochner and Eisenberg is *stability versus change*. Most families have predictable patterns of interaction. These might be reflected in activities such as the family dinner, picking up children from school, or watching television together in the evening. Some degree of predictability is desirable for most families. On the other hand, too much stability in the family can lead to stagnation. As families evolve through time, they experience changes that are internal to the system (e.g., birth of a child) and changes that are external to the system (e.g., societal changes). There is some need to adapt to these changes, but without entirely abandoning the family's traditions and destroying any sense of predictability in family interaction. According to Bochner and Eisenberg, managing these two important dialects is a significant task that families must address in order to maintain their integrity.

The work of Bochner and Eisenberg (1987) shows how the assumptions and ideas of the dialectical approach can be fruitfully employed for describing certain family processes. At the same time, the dialectical approach does not have all of the elements of a formal theory such as social learning theory. For this reason it more difficult to use the dialectical approach for prediction or intervention to change or improve family functioning. Its major utility is in *explaining* the nature of family relationships. Also, some of the concepts in the dialectical perspective can be difficult to grasp, much less identify, in a practical setting. For example, the praxis patterns of integration, recalibration, and reaffirmation are somewhat vaguely conceptualized and therefore difficult to observe or identify in an actual family setting. Further, these praxis patterns may not be as common as other praxis patterns such as denial, segmentation, or balance.

CONCLUSION

In this selection we explore several theories that are and have been very influential in the field of family science. These general theories have inspired hundreds of research studies and numerous more specific theories that draw on many of the postulates of the theories presented here. We start by examining family systems theory. According to this perspective, family processes can only be understood by examining the family in its totality. All family processes and events are thought to be connected to the larger family system and social suprasystem in which the family itself resides. Families are assumed to have emergent qualities that make them more than just the sum of their individual parts. Symbolic interaction theory highlights the vital role of the family in creating self-concepts and understandings of the world. Symbolic interaction theorists feel that meaning is at least to some extent negotiated through our interactions with other people. Because the family is the primary source of social interactions and relationships, it has a monumental role in shaping people's self-concepts and what it means to be a father, sister, grandmother, and so forth. Although meanings are negotiated through social interactions over the entire life span, the process starts in the family. Social learning theory explains how people acquire behaviors through observing other people perform behaviors, along with the consequences that they experience subsequent to the behavior. Learning by modeling is a fundamental process in social leaning theory. When people observe a model perform a behavior and get rewarded for doing so, they are likely to start performing the behavior themselves. Like symbolic interaction theory, social learning theory has obvious applications to family interaction because the family provides a multitude of compelling models for children to observe. Attachment theory focuses on early infant–caregiver interactions as the basis for forming enduring internal working models of interpersonal relationships. An internal working model is a mental representation of the self as worthy or unworthy of love and attention and others as reliable and trustworthy or rejecting and uncaring. Attachment theorists feel that the nature of early interactions with a caregiver will inform young children's internal working models which then influence the nature of their interpersonal relationships well into adulthood. Finally, we examine the *dialectical perspective*. This approach to understanding family processes is built around dialectical tensions or functional contradictions that are an inherent part of any family relationship. In the dialectical perspective, family members are seen as having to balance or manage tensions such as connectedness—separateness, stability—change, and novelty—predictability. The dialectical perspective also explains how families manage dialectical tensions through a variety of techniques known as praxis patterns.

Of all the theories that we discuss in this selection, only *family systems theory* was explicitly developed as an explanation of family dynamics (although it was derived from the more general version of systems theory). All of the other theories were developed as explanations of more general interpersonal processes. However, the family either plays a prominent role in the reasoning of the theory (as in attachment theory) or the theory has obvious and immediate applicability to the family. In either case, scholars have seized on these theories as some of their primary tools for explaining and understanding family interactions and relationships. Their continued application to the understanding of issues such as child abuse, alcoholism in the family, marital satisfaction, divorce, and parent–child interaction is a testimony to the utility of these family interaction theories.

QUESTIONS FOR REVIEW, REFLECTION, AND DISCUSSION

1. Define theory. What are the functions of theories?
2. Who are Ludwig von Bertalanffy and Norbert Wiener?
3. Who has criticized family systems theory and why?
4. List four major theories. Who developed those theories?
5. What happens when securely attached infants are separated from their primary caregivers?

ADDITIONAL READINGS

De Los Reyes, A., Ohannessian, C., & Laird, R. (2016). Developmental changes in discrepancies between adolescents' and their mothers' views of family communication, *Journal of Child & Family Studies*, 25(3), 790–797.

Galvin, K.M., & Braithwaite, D.O. (2014). Theory and research from the communication field: Discourses that constitute and reflect families, *Journal of Family Theory & Review*, 6(1), 97–111.

Jackl, J. A. (2016). "Love doesn't just happen...": Parent-child communication about marriage, *Communication Quarterly*, 64(2), 193–209.

Koerner, A. F., & Schrodt, P. (2014). An introduction to the special issue on family communication patterns theory. *Journal of Family Communication*, 14(1), 1–15.

Schrodt, P. (2016). Coparental communication with nonresidential parents as a predictor of children's feelings about being caught in stepfamilies, *Communication Reports*, 29(2), 63–74.

SHORT ANSWER QUIZ ITEMS

1. Explain attachment theory? What are the attachment categories? How do those categories differ from each other?
2. Explain family systems theory? Why have feminist scholars criticized family systems theory?

UNIT 3

SEX AND
GENDER

KEY TERMS

Gender

Social Constructionism

Discourse Analysis

7

SEX DIFFERENCES VERSUS SOCIAL PROCESSES IN THE CONSTRUCTION OF GENDER

By Mary Crawford and
Michelle R. Kaufman

Wanna get rowdy
Gonna get a little unruly
Get it fired up in a hurry
Wanna get dirrty
It's about time that I came to start the party
Sweat drippin' over my body
Dancing getting just a little naughty
Wanna get dirrty
It's about time for my arrival.

When artist Christina Aguilera released this song with her album *Stripped* (2002), she connected her femininity with sexuality, describing it as "dirty" and "sweaty." Coming from the girl-next-door pop star, this song caused much controversy in the pop music world. Aguilera quickly adopted the image of being slutty and risqué. Aguilera's changing image, driven by the words of her song, illustrates the importance of language in gender representation. How an individual presents herself (or himself) as female or male, feminine or masculine, is in large part an accomplishment of language.

Starting in the early 1970s, social scientists' interest in gender grew exponentially, and with it their interest in the communication styles of women and men. Over time, the field has developed and changed. Today, "there is less emphasis on cataloguing differences in the speech of women and men and more interest in analyzing what people accomplish with talk" (Crawford, 2001, p. 244).

In this selection, we attempt to develop a dynamic approach to both gender and language, one that is grounded in the theories and methods of our subdiscipline, feminist social psychology. We conceptualize gender as a social system and language as a social process, and we situate our discussion at the intersection of the two. We discuss ways in which gender is constructed through language and how this creates and maintains a hierarchy of power. We argue for the use of a social constructionist perspective and discourse analytic methods as a potentially fruitful direction for future research.

GENDER AS A SYSTEM

Gender has been described as a system of social classification and hierarchy based on social power, whereby control over resources and opportunities are held by a given group (Molm & Hedley, 1992). The possession of social power increases one's status, which is a person's ability to influence or control others (Crawford, 2006).

What does it mean to conceptualize gender as a system? Gender distinctions occur at many levels of society. Gender-related processes influence behavior, thoughts, and feelings in individuals; they affect interactions among individuals; and they help determine the structure of social institutions. How can researchers analyze the workings of this pervasive system of social classification that shapes the relations between women and men? For analytical purposes, it is useful to think of the gender system as operating at three levels: sociocultural, interactional, and individual (Crawford, 2006). These levels are linked and mutually reinforcing. Societal structures create limits within which people must act; interactions between and among individuals reinforce larger structural inequities; and individuals often internalize aspects of their gendered position in society, coming to accept their society's definition of masculinity or femininity as part of the self and identity. In this selection we focus primarily on the first two of these three levels of gender, looking first at societal structures and then at interactional processes.

SOCIETAL STRUCTURES CREATE GENDER

Societies can organize hierarchies and allocate resources on the basis of a wide variety of arbitrary distinctions—tribe, religion, caste, skin color, age—distinctions that vary in importance from one society to another. On the basis of these arbitrary distinctions, the dominant group(s) in a society have access to more of what that society values as a scarce resource, be it land, livestock, leisure time, education, or political office. Gender is perhaps the only one of these hierarchical classification schemes that is universal. Every known society makes social distinctions based on gender (Sidanius & Pratto, 1999). "To a greater or lesser degree, most modern societies are patriarchal, a word that literally means 'ruled by the fathers'" (Crawford, 2006).

The sociocultural structuring of gender as a system of relative advantage for men and disadvantage for women can be seen in many areas of contemporary societies. In the political sphere, for example, women account for only about 14% of national parliaments and other governing bodies worldwide (Galliano, 2003). There is no modern society in which women have equal or near-equal control of political decision making, the use of the military or law enforcement, or the technology of warfare (Sidanius & Pratto, 1999).

The gender hierarchy can also be seen in access to education, leisure, and wealth. Worldwide, literacy rates are lower for women than for men (Galliano, 2003). Men control more wealth and have more leisure time in virtually every society in which data are collected by the United Nations (Pratto & Walker, 2004). When women work for pay, they are paid less than men are for similar or comparable tasks. Moreover, women do a great deal more unpaid work than men do in child and elder care, subsistence farming, and housework. Overall, women work longer hours for smaller rewards (Crawford, 2006).

There has been much debate about the origins of male dominance; contemporary theories include psychodynamic, cognitive, evolutionary, social constructionist, and social role approaches (Eagly, Beall, & Sternberg, 2004; Unger, 2001). Although the origins of patriarchy may be unresolved, much is known about how gender-based power imbalances are perpetuated. The power of dominant groups is not static. Rather, power is actively maintained through a variety of social processes. For example, societies create legitimizing myths that justify prejudice and discrimination against subordinated groups (Sidanius & Pratto, 1999). Many of the legitimizing myths of gender come from patriarchal traditions emphasizing that women are different from men. Some of these beliefs are hostile, such as the archetype of women as evil, sexually polluting, and dangerous—the whore stereotype. Others are seemingly benevolent, such as the belief in women as more pure, noble, and self-sacrificing than men—the Madonna stereotype (Glick & Fiske, 2001). Both hostile and benevolent forms of sexism serve as justifications for the social control of the subordinated gender. Whether women are seen as evil (in need of control) or pure (relegated to a pedestal), they are still defined in terms set by the dominant group.

Though larger political and social structures are important in creating and maintaining gender distinctions and inequalities, they are not the only sites where gender is played out. We turn now to interpersonal interactions, examining the salience of gender as a cue and the use of gender in self-representation.

SOCIAL INTERACTIONS CREATE GENDER

Gender is an important cognitive category used to classify others in social interactions, and many studies have shown that it is highly salient in social perception. For example, in a study in which participants watched a video of a discussion group and later were asked to remember who said what, they were more likely to confuse two people of the same gender than two of the same age, the same race, or even the same name (Fiske, Haslam, & Fiske, 1991). These participants had spontaneously classified the people in the discussion group on the basis of gender. Although they sometimes could not remember which speaker had made a particular statement, they were likely to remember whether the speaker was a woman or a man.

The cognitive salience of gender is problematic because it opens the way for intergroup bias and outgroup homogeneity effects. In other words, people tend to favor their own group and see members of other groups as different from them and "all alike." These biases were demonstrated in a study in which pairs of male or female college students were asked to discuss "American women" or "American men" for 5 minutes (Harasty, 1997). Analyses of the open-ended discussions showed that participants made more generalizations about the gender outgroup than about their own gender group. In other words, female pairs made more global "men are ..." statements and male pairs more global "women are ..." statements. When talking about others of their own gender, dyadic members were more specific and less likely to make sweeping generalizations. The more general comments also tended to be more negative. Overall, outgroup members were spoken of as more alike and less worthy than ingroup members.

Not only do individuals classify others on the basis of gender in everyday interaction, they strive to present themselves socially as good examples of their gender. Gender tends to be accompanied by an ascribed status that is created by cultural norms. "Maleness" is associated with greater power, prestige, and social value than "femaleness" (Cohen, Berger, & Zelditch, 1972; Unger, 1976, 1978).

The gender system requires that men "do" being men and women "do" being women (Zimmerman & West, 1975). "Doing gender" is not just a display of the stereotypical differences between the sexes; it is linked to power. When women and men do gender, they are also doing status, and women, in particular, are "doing subordination" (Crawford, 2006). Doing gender is often an unconscious process, and the production of a gendered self seems natural and spontaneous. Nevertheless, this process constitutes the social representation of gender: "There is no such thing as 'being a woman' outside the various practices that define womanhood for my culture—practices ranging from the sort of work I do to my sexual preferences to the clothes I wear to the way I use language" (Cameron, 1996, p. 46).

LANGUAGE AS A SOCIAL PROCESS

Much of research in language, a majority of which has been conducted under the umbrella of linguistics, treats language as an asocial phenomenon (Holtgraves, 2002). The use of language can also be viewed as a social system, whereby word choice, conversational dominance, or tone of voice can be used to express and create a speaker's power and social status in relation to the perceiver. Most psycholinguists focus on an individualist perspective in the analysis of language, in which the production and comprehension of language is assumed to occur in a vacuum outside of the social context. Only recently has cognitive psychology recognized the communicative side of language as it occurs in dyads.

COGNITIVE VIEWS OF LANGUAGE AND COMMUNICATION

Clark (1996) conceptualized language use as the secondary aim in a joint activity, whereby two people carry out a task. According to Clark, the joint activity is the primary focus of social interaction, and language use is secondary. All joint activities rely on communicative acts, verbal or nonverbal, and discourse is a joint activity in which language plays an important role. Clark has extensively studied language in joint activities and actions. For example, he has investigated the ways in which dyads must establish a "common ground," or what others have called common knowledge (Lewis, 1969), joint knowledge (McCarthy, 1990), or mutual knowledge or belief (Schiffer, 1972), in order to carry out a joint activity successfully.

According to Fillmore (1981), the primary place for language use is in dyadic conversation, and all other uses of language are secondary and derivative to this primary function. Clark built on this position, developing a cognitive psychology of dyadic interaction. He separated a conversation into a hierarchy of parts, including conversation (the introduction, body, and exit of a topic); section (transitions or digressions from the main conversation topic); adjacency pairs (two ordered utterances, such as "thank you," and then "you're welcome"); and turn (who speaks when). Clark described conversation as purposeful but unplanned and therefore analyzed it as a series of utterances between two individuals whose goals are primarily action oriented.

Clark has forcefully argued that language is a distinctively human activity and that the prototype for language is dyadic conversation. Although Clark has looked at language and communication as it occurs within dyads, he and others in the cognitive tradition have not fully conceptualized language as a social production. In cognitively focused research on conversation, speakers are often represented outside their social contexts or in socially trivial settings. As far as the researchers are concerned, the participants' task is to make themselves understood so that they can accomplish a joint venture (e.g., setting a lunch date) as efficiently as possible. Although establishing joint understanding of semantic meaning and joint enactment of an action are important, they are not the only purposes of dyadic communication. Instead, we argue that language use should be thought of as fundamentally social from the beginning. It is in conversation that individuals present themselves to others as members of a social group and seek to establish and maintain social status.

LANGUAGE AND GROUP MEMBERSHIP

Although the utterances created and the ideas constructed in language come from the individual, the process of conversation and communication is certainly a social behavior and should be evaluated as such. Only recently has social psychology contributed significantly to research on language (Holtgraves, 2002), particularly its role in stereotyping and prejudice (e.g., Maass, Salvi, Arcuri, & Semin, 1989), social reasoning (e.g., Hilton, 1995), and person perception (e.g., Berry, Pennebaker, Mueller, & Hiller, 1997). Group membership may function to activate a particular stereotype, which, in turn, influences evaluations of a target and perceptions of the target's speech style. For example, in an early line of research, Thakerar and Giles (1981) found that when participants were led to believe a speaker was high in status, they perceived the speaker's speech to be more standard than if they believed the speaker was of low status. Similarly, Williams, Whitehead, and Miller (1972) found that participants rated the speech of African American children to be below standard and less confident than that of Caucasian children, even though the same (Caucasian) voices were used in both instances.

More recently, in a study by Popp, Donovan, Crawford, Marsh, and Peele (2003), participants were asked to generate dialogue for a fictional college student whose race and gender were varied. Participants then rated the character on a series of adjective pairs that comprised five factors: social appropriateness, dominance, directness, emotionality, and playfulness. Results showed a consistency of stereotyping patterns for Caucasian and African American targets, such that Caucasians were rated significantly more socially appropriate, less direct, lower in emotionality, and more playful in their speech than were African Americans. Stereotyping patterns were also found for the gender of the targets; female targets were rated as less direct in their speech and as possessing higher emotionality than male targets.

In sum, group membership does matter in evaluating the speech style and communication of others. Relationships have been shown in terms of race, status, and other categories. Because gender is one of the most salient cognitive categories in person perception, we can expect that gender stereotypes often affect perceptions of speech and communication. Women and men who show identical behavior in a given situation may be functioning in different social spheres because of others' social reactions to them as women or men, reactions that include how others speak to them and evaluate their speech (Crawford, 1995; Weatherall, 2002).

THE INTERSECTION OF GENDER AND LANGUAGE

Although social psychologists have begun to examine language as a form of social power, and gender researchers have been discussing the construction of gender as a power system, the two fields have not consistently collaborated on how gender and language interact to create a social power structure for men and women. Despite pioneering feminist research on gender, language, and power (Henley, 1977; Thorne & Henley, 1975; Thorne, Kramarae, & Henley, 1983; see also Crawford & Popp, 2003), much research on gender and language has continued to focus on differences between men and women's speech styles. There has been less attention to how these differences are co-constructed in social interaction, and what the consequences are for differences when they are so closely tied to social power.

GENDERED INTERACTION AS A POWER PROCESS

To begin an examination of the interaction of gender and language as they relate to power structures, one must first evaluate how gender is constructed through language. As mentioned previously, the gender system requires that men "do" being men and women "do" being women. In the context of language, men generally "do" being men by showing dominance in a conversation, and women "do" being women by more commonly assuming the role of a subordinate listener.

The interaction of gender and language, and the subsequent power structure created, has been acknowledged in some previous research. For example, Ruscher (2001) has written about the ways in which people tend to "talk down" to outgroup members. Social categorizations such as gender, race, or age indicate status in social interactions (Berger, Wagner, &

Zelditch, 1985). If the speaker in an interaction views the listener to be of lower social status on the basis of these categorizations, the speaker tends to conclude (sometimes unconsciously) that the listener is incompetent. The presumption of incompetence often leads to speech that is patronizing or controlling.

Language addressed to infants, elderly people, mentally retarded people, foreigners, and pets shares certain syntactical and lexical characteristics that linguistically create the effect of patronizing control (Ruscher, 2001). These include lexical simplification, exaggerated pitch changes, and increased repetition. Because speech addressed to elders or babies may have a caring function, it is likely to be more patronizing than controlling. However, speech addressed to other categories of lower status people may have a higher rate of direct imperative (command) forms and efforts to control the conversation, such as ignoring the target's attempts to make a contribution. The controlling aspect of talking down "explicitly functions to keep low-status individuals 'in their place'" (Ruscher, 2001, p. 88).

Talking down was demonstrated with respect to gender in a study by Duval and Ruscher (1994) that began with teaching the Heimlich maneuver to college student participants. (This task was chosen because it was not gender stereotyped and was equally unfamiliar to female and male college students.) The slides showed a male and a female actor demonstrating the maneuver on each other, with male and female voices alternating descriptions of the steps involved in the task. Following the presentation of the slides, the participants were asked to teach the Heimlich maneuver to another student, and they were videotaped while they explained the steps of the maneuver to an opposite-sex or same-sex partner. Results showed that men used more imperative verbs when teaching the maneuver to women than in any of the other teacher–learner combinations, suggesting that the gender difference in status prompted talk that was both patronizing and controlling.

Another example of the use of power in language is to not allow another person to be heard at all by interrupting, controlling the topic discussed, or taking up a majority of the talk time (Crawford, 1995). Many studies show that men use these tactics frequently when engaging in conversation with women more than they do when speaking with other men and more than women do when speaking to each other. For example, in a now-classic study in which researchers listened in on same- and mixed-gender conversations in public places, 96% of the interruptions in conversations between males and females were made by male speakers. In same-gender dyads, the number of interruptions was the same for each speaker (Zimmerman & West, 1975). Not all interruptions are intended to assert conversational dominance. However, in a recent meta-analysis, it was found that men commit more intrusive interruptions, in which an active attempt is made to end a conversation or take over the discussion. This has been found to be more common in naturalistic settings where conversations resemble everyday interaction than in laboratory settings (Anderson & Leaper, 1998).

Despite the stereotype that women are more talkative than men, studies have shown men to take up a majority of the talk time in a variety of settings, including classrooms, business meetings, and informal conversations (Crawford, 1995). In a review of 63 studies conducted over a 40-year span, 34 of the studies showed that men talk more than women, whereas only

2 displayed the opposite finding (the others showed no gender differences in talk time or mixed results; see James & Drakich, 1993). These differences were most robust in formal, task-oriented settings such as committee meetings, classrooms, and problem-solving groups. However, even in less formal social settings, over 37% of the studies showed men talking more than women, whereas only 6% showed women talking more than men. These studies suggest that men dominate conversations, especially in more formal settings where one's status and control over the situation may be more tied to material or social gain.

SUBVERSIONS OF GENDERED POWER

The classification of women's language as "powerless" and men's language as "powerful" originated in Robin Lakoff's *Language and Woman's Place* (1975). Lakoff suggested that the association of indirect speech with the language of women and direct speech with that of men is a reflection of the power imbalance between men and women in society. Lakoff proposed that a cluster of features characteristic of women's talk (hesitation, tag questions, euphemisms, etc.) constituted a unique speech style. However, Lakoff may have underestimated the flexibility of speech styles, mistakenly equating form with function (Crawford, 1995). In some instances, the use of stereotypically feminine language may function quite differently.

Kira Hall (1995) conducted a series of interviews with phone sex workers, many of whom reported that they used so called women's language—sexy, inviting, and supportive—as a commodity to attract customers. The phone sex workers knew how to create stereotypical female sex objects—such as the nymphomaniac and the lesbian— through the deliberate adoption of a particular speech style. Because phone sex is easily marketable, the study of mixed-gender linguistic exchanges should acknowledge the more seditious aspects of conversational consent. One operator, who was a male posing as a female on the phone service, talked about the importance of a "soft and quiet voice" in order to convince his callers of his womanhood. "It's better to sound soft and quiet than loud and noisy … if you're a woman … [It's] better to sound soft, you know, softer. You know, like whispering, rather than OH HO HO HO, really *loud,* you know, and *screaming*" (p. 202).

Although phone sex lines may be viewed as offensive or degrading to women, several women Hall interviewed saw the use of their language to gain callers as empowering and their position in the conversation as dominant. They reported being in complete control of every conversation. In fact, many of the phone sex workers felt they were so superior linguistically and socially to the average male caller that they did not view male power as an issue when on the phone lines (Hall, 1995).

In the more mundane realm of communication between relationship partners, there has been much discussion about the ways in which women and men differ in their communication styles. Pop psychologist John Gray (1992) has made a lucrative career out of examining supposed gender differences in communication in his self-help books and television appearances (see Dindia, chap. 1, this volume). Gray preaches the existence of fixed gender differences and instructs his audience to embrace and attempt to understand these supposed differences so that they can enhance their marital relationships. The Mars–Venus therapy omits a discussion as to how women and men could become so different, and instead it relies on gender stereotypes about social roles to reinforce the thought that difference is natural and normal. For example, Gray metaphorically describes how men tend to retreat to their "caves" rather than deal with an issue with their spouse. Gray tells his clients that women should recognize men's entitlement to not become involved in domestic life until they are ready to return from that cave. In this excerpt from a televised couples' discussion group (as cited in Crawford, 2004,[1] p. 70), Gray stands in a family room set next to a large recliner:

JG: See, *whenever a Martian has stress,* on MARS, *we go to our cave.*
        This is our cave.
        This is our territory.
        ((Sits in Recliner))
        Nobody can tell me what to do. The problem is, women don't understand it's healthy and normal for men to do this, and this is what they need to do. Then you PUNISH *them for going to the cave.* ((Stands. Using exaggerated gestures, points to the family room set)) Let him have his space. Don't take it personally. And if you don't go in, he'll come out. He gets lonely in there.

The Mars–Venus media present a seemingly perfect discourse of essential gender difference. The function of this self-help series is to reproduce and make natural the stereotypical language and communication between men and women, which is usually oppressive to women (Crawford, 2004). Because the women who use this guide seem content in their marriage upon following these steps, the popularity of Mars–Venus is somewhat puzzling and problematic from a feminist perspective. Although some critical responses were made by women during the discussions analyzed by Crawford (2004), the participants are still urged to "accept the fact" that men need their caves. In this excerpt (Crawford, p. 72), a group of women debate the fairness of men's entitlement to caves:

MM: You know (.) *all this* is asking women once again (.) to take the *high road* (.) And that *bothers me* (.) Now I have to *suppress* (.) *I have to sacrifice* (.) Got to *keep it in* (.) And when *he's* ready, *I have to* be ready too.

.

.

SC: But that-that's what *marriage* IS. I mean =
DT: =But it still seems rude to me (.) *I don't get a cave.*

.

.

SC: *He* wants to be in his *cave* ((gestures with hand on table)) and not be bothered by you (.) and *you're* not *doing* that.
DT: Whether it's turning on the TV or running away ((on the part of the husband)) (.) we can *use* this ((the M/V ideology)) so we can *deal* with it so I don't get so RESENTFUL.

But the reality I (.) I *still* think it's WRONG ((gestures with hand on table)), and it's not very nice.

Crawford (2004) has speculated that at least some women in unsatisfying heterosexual relationships may use the Mars–Venus discourse to open up areas for discussion and contestation in their marital arrangements. Rather than accepting notions of deep-seated gender differences, they subvert the simplistic metaphors of Mars and Venus in order to voice their own marital agenda. This agenda may include renegotiating an inequitable division of domestic work and childcare. Like the phone sex workers studied by Hall (1995), these women may use beliefs about difference toward their own ends.

MODELS FOR A SOCIAL PSYCHOLOGY OF GENDER AND LANGUAGE

We have argued that the study of gender and language should prioritize the social aspects of language, particularly the social psychology of power and status. Many theoretical models and research programs have aimed to do this. Others have discussed the strengths and weaknesses of well-established models such as speech act theory (Crawford, 1995; Schiffrin, 1994; Turnbull, 2003), ethnomethodology (Crawford, Schiffrin, & Weatherall, 2002), and conversation analysis (Kitzinger, 2000; Kitzinger & Frith, 1999; Turnbull, 2003; Weatherall, 2002), and we will not review those discussions here. All these methods are, broadly speaking, empirical; that is, their data come from people using language, not from hypothetical examples devised by linguists. All conceive of meaning and action in language use as jointly achieved in interaction. All endorse the importance of the immediate social context and the broader cultural framework in shaping language use and speech style (Schiffrin, 1994). However, they vary in the degree to which they view social reality itself as constructed through language. In what follows, we argue for a social constructionist perspective as a fruitful approach to further research in this area.

SOCIAL CONSTRUCTIONISM

A social constructionist view of language theorizes that language use and communication is the base of and socially constructs power. Social constructionists question several aspects of the conventional sex-gender model: (a) the view of gender as a property of individuals; (b) that gender is a static and enduring set of traits; (c) the separation of sex and gender into a dichotomy; and (d) the claim that biological sex is a foundation that stands apart untouched by culture and language (Marecek, Crawford, & Popp, 2004).

In a social constructionist view, power is possessed by an individual or a group as an effect of discourse (Weatherall, 2002), and relations of power are negotiated through the medium of language (Crawford, 1995; Potter & Wetherell, 1987). For example, the social control of female sexuality may be expressed in religious teachings, moral discourses, and media representations. It is also evident in everyday language, such as slang ("player" vs. "ho"; see Crawford & Popp, 2003). From a social constructionist perspective, these meanings are not fixed, but they are always evident in human interactions. Furthermore, people do not passively perceive cultural messages without awareness. The ongoing flow of meanings about gender is part of the flow of social life.

From a social constructionist perspective, power is a central dimension of social life. However, power is conceptualized not as a fixed property or characteristic of individuals, but rather as a network of social forces that is continually produced, enacted, resisted, and subverted. Therefore, social constructionists prefer research methods that allow close examination and analysis of mundane, naturally occurring social interactions. By analyzing such interactions, they hope to "document the micropolitics of subordination, dominance, and resistance" (Marecek et al., 2004, p. 195).

Social constructionists view language as an extremely flexible tool for creating social reality; they have studied not only the use of rhetorical devices for legitimizing the speaker's claims (Potter & Wetherell, 1987) but also the use of subversive conversational devices such as humor (Crawford, 1995, 2003). Often, social constructionists focus on how people shift strategically among different accounts of themselves, their attitudes, and their behavior in the context of differing settings and relationships. For example, in a naturalistic study of conversation among friends, a woman talked about gender stereotypes in subtly different ways when she was with her female peers than when she was with a mixed-gender group. With women, she spoke directly of the disadvantages that stereotypes create for women; with men, she talked more generally of the disadvantages stereotypes cause for "society" (Stapleton, 2001). Which behaviors reflect her "real" attitudes? A social constructionist would argue that the reality is constructed by—and changes with—the social context (Marecek et al., 2004; Crawford, 2006).

Because social constructionists believe that power relations are negotiated through the medium of language, they view mundane conversational interaction, as well as more formal and public types of speech, as important activities with practical material consequences (Marecek et al., 2004). For this reason, they often prefer qualitative and interpretive methods that permit close analysis of the meaning and function of talk. The term *discourse analysis* refers both to a rapidly evolving field of study and an eclectic group of methods for studying language use and the ideological assumptions underlying it (Schiffrin, Tannen, & Hamilton, 2003). Not all discourse analysis is social constructionist. One of the most distinctive aspects of a discourse analytic approach grounded in social constructionism is that it conceives of gender (including gender identity) not as existing prior to and separate from language, but as being discursively constituted through language (Weatherall, 2002).

Discourse analytic approaches currently are generating a great deal of research; space permits mention of only a few examples to illustrate the range and utility of the methods. Edwards (1998) used interaction from a couples' counseling session to examine how the language deployed by the wife and husband served to justify particular constructions of reality. Is an extramarital sexual encounter an "affair" or a "fling"? Did the encounter take place with a "girl" or "another woman"? The categories used by the couple in counseling did not reflect a preexisting consensual reality. Instead, Edwards argued, they were locally constructed and managed to do particular things—to justify one's own behavior and criticize the partner's behavior, for example. In another recent study, discussed earlier in this selection, Crawford (2004) used the method of critical feminist discourse analysis to examine the text of *Men are From Mars, Women are From Venus,* as well as couples' strategic use of its faux-psychological rhetoric in negotiating and resisting change in their marriages. In an example from a different domain, Nichter (2000) analyzed the "fat talk" of adolescent girls about their bodies. Regardless of their actual weight or body size, these girls frequently complained of being too fat or having ugly body parts. Nichter analyzed the functions of this talk in creating rapport with others and eliciting support and reassurance about one's body. At the same time as it fulfilled these relatively benign functions, the "fat talk" also reaffirmed the cultural norm that body size is a critical feature on which females should be judged and ranked.

Other researchers have examined the construction and presentation of masculinity in interaction. For example, Wetherell and Edley (1999) used critical discourse analysis to identify three social positions taken by men in talk about what it means to be a man. The "heroic" position aligned itself with hegemonic masculinity: being tough, courageous, emotionally in control, and competitive. In contrast, some men characterized themselves as being normal, average, nonmacho men or as rebelliously flouting conventions of masculinity (e.g., by cooking or knitting). In other words, they positioned themselves in contrast to the heroic ideal. However, Wetherell and Edley argued that the contrary positions nevertheless functioned to reproduce male power much like the heroic position, because the men who characterized themselves as such said that they were different from normal or rebellious other men in being more independent and autonomous—aspects of the heroic ideal.

Because masculinity is so closely linked with social power, studies of masculinity often focus on how men position themselves with respect to less powerful groups (Crawford, 2001). For example, Mulkay (1988) did extensive discursive research on men's humor about women and sexuality. Mulkay argued that such humor objectified women, represented them as sexually available at all times, and contained themes of silencing women's agency and voice. Cameron (1997) analyzed the talk of male college students and described the derogation of other men whom the students characterized as "gay." Within this group of friends, naming others as part of a gay outgroup (regardless of the accuracy of the label) provided a means of generating group solidarity and displaying group members' own heterosexual and dominant masculinity. (For a fuller description of these and other studies using discourse analysis to examine the production of gendered selves, see Crawford, 2001 and Weatherall, 2002.)

ON THE SEARCH FOR SEX DIFFERENCES

Although research on the relationship between gender and language is abundant, much of it has focused on decontextualized sex differences. This focus has been the subject of criticism and debate almost since its inception. Barrie Thorne and Nancy Henley, pioneers in the feminist study of gender and language, argued as early as 1975 that this area of research should not be given a high priority. Thorne, Kramarae, and Henley, in their influential 1983 book, contrasted the focus on difference to a (more fruitful, in their view) focus on dominance.

More broadly, some feminists have argued that the study of sex differences in any area of psychology is likely to be a waste of research time and energy, prompting others to defend the utility of such research (Canary & Dindia, 1998; Hare-Mustin & Marecek, 1994; Hyde, 1994; Kitzinger, 1994; Unger, 1979, 1989, 1992). One recurrent viewpoint is that a focus on difference encourages social scientists and laypeople alike to think of women and men as polar opposites; distracts attention from the linkage of gender with power and status; treats gender as a fixed, static attribute of individuals rather than a complex social categorization system; and disregards the diversity of women and men (Crawford, 1995, 2001; Canary & Emmers-Sommer, 1997; Pratto & Walker, 2004).

We have argued for the utility of a social constructionist perspective and described studies that relied on various versions of constructionist-grounded discourse analysis. To devote still more time to researching static and decontextualized gender differences in language use would, in our view, be a mistake. Gender is more fruitfully construed as a process enacted in a cluster of activities such as the division of labor, sexual intimacy, and children's play (Canary & Emmers-Sommer, 1997).

Social constructionism offers rich new prospects for a better understanding of how gender is socially produced and maintained. We propose spending more time focusing on the intersection of gender and language use as it relates to the creation of social power. The most fruitful research path for the future may involve turning the question of sex differences on its head—not asking, How do men and women use language differently? but rather, How are femininity and masculinity produced and maintained through language?

REFERENCES

Anderson, K. J., & Leaper, C. (1998). Meta-analysis of gender effects on conversational interruptions: Who, what, when, where, and how. *Sex Roles, 39,* 225–252.

Berger, J., Wagner, D. G., & Zelditch, M., Jr. (1985). Introduction: Expectation states theory—Review and assessment. In J. Berger, & M. Zelditch, Jr. (Eds.), *Status, rewards, and influence: How expectations organize behavior* (pp. 1–72). San Francisco: Jossey-Bass.

Berry, D. S., Pennebaker, J. W., Mueller, J. S., & Hiller, W. S. (1997). Linguistic bases of social perception. *Personality and Social Psychology Bulletin, 23,* 526–537.

Cameron, D. (1996). Performing gender identity: Young men's talk and the construction of heterosexual masculinity. In S. Johnson, & U. H. Meinhof (Eds.), *Language and masculinity* (pp. 47–64). Oxford, England: Blackwell.

Canary, D. J., & Dindia, K. (Eds.). (1998). *Sex differences and similarities in communication.* Mahwah, NJ: Lawrence Erlbaum Associates.

Canary, D. K., & Emmers-Sommer, T. M. (1997). *Sex and gender differences in personal relationships.* New York: Guilford.

Clark, H. H. (1996). *Using language.* New York: Cambridge University Press.

Cohen, B. P., Berger, J., & Zelditch, M. (1972). Status conceptions and interactions: A case study of developing cumulative knowledge. In C. McClintock (Ed.), *Experimental social psychology.* (pp. 408–11). New York: Holt, Rinehart & Winston.

Crawford, M. (1995). *Talking difference: On gender and language.* London Sage.

Crawford, M. (2001). Gender and language. In R. K. Unger (Ed.), *Handbook of the psychology of women and gender* (pp. 228–244). Hoboken, NJ: Wiley.

Crawford, M. (2003). Gender and humor in social context. *Journal of Pragmatics, 35,* 1413–1430.

Crawford, M. (2004). Mars and Venus collide: A discursive analysis of marital self-help psychology. *Feminism & Psychology, 14,* 63–79.

Crawford, M. (2006). *Transformations: Women, gender, and psychology.* New York: McGraw-Hill. Crawford, M., & Popp, D. (2003). Sexual double standards: A review and methodological critique of two decades of research. *The Journal of Sex Research, 40,* 13–26.

Crawford, M., & Unger, R. (2004). *Women and gender: A feminist psychology.* Boston: McGraw-Hill.

Duval, L. L., & Ruscher, J. B. (1994, July). *Men use more detail to explain a gender-neutral task to women,* Poster presented at the annual meeting of the American Psychological Society, Washington, DC.

Eagly, A. H., Beall, A. E., & Sternberg, R. J. (Eds.). (2004). *The psychology of gender* (2nd ed.). New York: Guilford.

Edwards, D. (1998). The relevant thing about her: Social identity categories in use. In C. Antaki, & S. Widdicombe (Eds.), *Identities in talk* (pp. 15–34). London: Sage.

Fillmore, C. (1981). Pragmatics and the description of discourse. In P. Cole (Ed.), *Radical pragmatics* (pp. 143–166). New York: Academic Press.

Fiske, A. P., Haslam, N., & Fiske, S. T. (1991). Confusing one person with another: What errors reveal about the elementary forms of social relations. *Journal of Personality and Social Psychology, 60,* 656–674.

Galliano, G. (2003). *Gender: Crossing boundaries.* Belmont, CA: Wadsworth.

Gray, J. (1992). *Men are from Mars, Women are from Venus. A practical guide to improving communication and getting what you want in your relationships.* New York: HarperCollins.

Glick, P., & Fiske, S. T. (2001). An ambivalent alliance: Hostile and benevolent sexism as complementary justifications for gender inequality. *American Psychologist, 56,* 109–118.

Hall, K. (1995). Lip service on the fantasy lines. In K. Hall, & M. Bucholtz (Eds.), *Gender articulated* (pp. 183–216). New York: Routledge.

Harasty, A. S. (1997). The interpersonal nature of social stereotypes: Differential discussion patterns about in-groups and out-groups. *Personality and Social Psychology Bulletin, 23,* 270–284.

Hare-Mustin, R. T., & Marecek, J. (1994). Asking the right questions: Feminist psychology and sex differences. *Feminism & Psychology, 4,* 531–537.

Henley, N. M. (1977). *Body politics.* Englewood Cliffs, NJ: Prentice-Hall.

Hilton, D. J. (1995). The social context of reasoning: Conversational inference and rational judgment. *Psychological Bulletin, 118,* 248–271.

Holtgraves, T. M. (2002). *Language as social action: Social psychology and language use.* Mahwah, NJ: Lawrence Erlbaum Associates.

Hyde, J. S. (1994). Should psychologists study gender differences? Yes, with some guidelines. *Feminism & Psychology, 4,* 507–512.

James, D., & Drakich, J. (1993) Understanding gender differences in amount of talk: A critical review of research. In D. Tannen (Ed.), *Gender and conversational interaction* (pp. 281–312). New York: Oxford.

Kitzinger, C. (1994). Sex difference: Feminist perspectives. *Feminism & Psychology, 4,* 501–596.

Kitzinger, C. (2000). Doing feminist conversation analysis. *Feminism & Psychology, 10,* 163–193.

Kitzinger, C, & Frith, H. (1999). Just say no? The use of conversation analysis in developing a feminist perspective on sexual refusal. *Discourse and Society, 10,* 293–316.

Lakoff, R. (1975). *Language and woman's place.* New York: Harper & Row.

Lewis, D. K. (1969). *Convention: A philosophical study.* Cambridge, MA: Harvard University Press.

Marecek, J., Crawford, M., & Popp, D. (2004). On the construction of gender, sex, and sexualities. In A. H. Eagly, A. E. Beall, & R. J. Sternberg (Eds.), *The psychology of gender* (2nd ed.), (pp. 192–216). New York: Guilford.

Maass, A., Salvi, D., Arcuri, L., & Semin, G. (1989). Language use in intergroup contexts: The linguistic intergroup bias. *Journal of Personality and Social Psychology, 68,* 116–126.

McCarthy, J. (1990). Formalization of two puzzles involving knowledge. In V. Lifschitz (Ed.), *Formal-izing common sense: Papers by John McCarthy* (pp. 158–166). Norwood, NJ: Ablex.

Molm, L. D., & Hedley, M. (1992). Gender, power, and social exchange. In C. L. Ridgeway (Ed.), *Gender, interaction, and inequality* (pp. 1–28). New York: Springer-Verlag.

Mulkay, M. (1988). *On humor.* New York: Basil Blackwell.

Nichter, M. (2000). *Fat talk.* Cambridge, MA: Harvard University Press.

Popp. D., Donovan, R. A., Crawford, M., Marsh, K. L., & Peele, M. (2003). Gender, race, and speech style stereotypes. *Sex Roles, 48,* 317–325.

Potter, J., & Wetherell, M. (1987). *Discourse and social psychology.* London: Sage.

Pratto, F., & Walker, A. (2004). The bases of gendered power. In A. H. Eagly, A. E. Beall, & R. J. Stern-berg (Eds.), *The psychology of gender* (2nd ed.), (pp. 242–268). New York: Guilford.

Ruscher, J. B. (2001). *Prejudiced communication: A social psychological perspective.* New York: Guilford.

Schiffer, S. R. (1972). *Meaning.* Oxford University Press.

Schiffrin, D. (1994). *Approaches to discourse.* Maiden, MA: Blackwell.

Schiffrin, D., Tannen, D., & Hamilton, H. E. (2003). *The handbook of discourse analysis.* Maiden, MA: Blackwell.

Sidanius, J., & Pratto, F. (1999). *Social dominance: An intergroup theory of social hierarchy and oppression.* New York: Cambridge University Press.

Stapleton, K. (2001). Constructing a feminist identity: Discourse and the community of practice. *Feminism & Psychology, 11,* 459–491.

Thakerar, J. M., & Giles, H. (1981). They are—so to speak: Noncontent speech stereotypes. *Language and Communication, 1,* 251–256.

Thorne, B., & Henley, N. (Eds.). (1975). An overview of language, gender and society. In B. Thorne, & N. Henley (Eds.), *Language and sex: Difference and dominance* (pp. 5–42). Rowley, MA: Newbury House.

Thorne, B., Kramarae, C, & Henley, N. (Eds.). (1983). *Language, gender, and society.* Rowley, MA: Newbury House.

Turnbull, W. (2003). *Language in action: Psychological models of conversation.* New York: Psychology Press.

Unger, R. K. (1976). Male is greater than female: The socialization of status inequality. *The Counseling Psychologist, 6,* 2–9.

Unger, R. K. (1978). The politics of gender: A review of relevant literature. In J. Sherman, & R. Den-mark (Eds.), *Psychology of women: Future directions of research* (pp. 463–517). New York: Psychological Dimensions.

Unger, R. K. (1979). *Female and male: Psychological perspectives.* New York: Harper & Row.

Unger, R. K. (1989). Explorations in feminist ideology: Surprising consistencies and unexamined conflicts. In R. Unger (Ed.), *Representations: Social constructions of gender* (pp. 203–211). New York: Baywood.

Unger, R. K. (1992). Will the real sex differences please stand up? *Feminism & Psychology, 2,* 231–238.

Unger, R. K. (2001). *Handbook of the psychology of women and gender.* Hoboken, NJ: Wiley.

Weatherall, A. (2002). *Gender, language, and discourse.* New York: Routledge.

Wetherell, M., & Edley, N. (1999). Negotiating hegemonic masculinity: Imaginary positions and psych-discursive practices. *Feminism & Psychology, 9,* 335–356.

Williams, E, Whitehead, J. L., & Miller, L. (1972). Relations between attitudes and teacher expectancy. *American Educational Research Journal, 9,* 263–277.

Zimmerman, D. H., & West, C. (1975). Sex roles, interruptions, and silences in conversation. In B. Thorne, & N. Henley (Eds.), *Language and sex: Differences and dominance* (pp. 105–129). Rowley, MA: Newbury House.

QUESTIONS FOR REVIEW, REFLECTION, AND DISCUSSION

1. What is gender? What is the difference between gender and sex?
2. How can the use of language be viewed as a social system?
3. How are gender and language interconnected?
4. What is discourse analysis? How is it used?

ADDITIONAL READINGS

Bem, S. L. (1983). Gender schema theory and its implications for child development: Raising gender-aschematic children in a gender-schematic society. *Signs, 8,* 598–616.

De Reus, L., Few, A. L., & Blume, L. B. (2005). Multicultural and critical race feminisms: Theorizing families in the third wave. In V. L. Bengtson, A. C. Acock, K. R. Allen, P. Dilworth-Anderson, & D. M. Klein (Eds.), *Sourcebook of family theory & research* (pp. 447–468). Thousand Oaks, CA: Sage.

de Vries, A. L. C., Doreleijers, T. A., & Cohen-Kettenis, P. T. (2007). Disorders of sex development and gender identity outcome in adolescence and adulthood: Understanding gender identity development and its clinical implications. *Pediatric Endocrinology Reviews, 4,* 343–351.

Hengstebeck, N.D., Helms, H. M., & Rodriguez, Y. (2015). Spouses' gender role attitudes, wives' employment status, and Mexican-origin husbands' marital satisfaction, *Journal of Family Issues, 36*(1), 111–132.

Suar, D., & Gochhayat, J. (2016). Influence of biological sex and gender roles on ethicality, *Journal of Business Ethics*, 134(2), 199–208.

ENDNOTE

1. For a description of this annotation, see Crawford, 2004.

KEY TERMS

Lesbian

Gay

Bisexual

Transgender

Transexual

Queer

Intersexed

Homophobia

Heterosexism

Heteronormativity

8

NARRATIVES OF SEXUALITY, ADOLESCENCE, AND EDUCATION

By Richard A. Quantz

From the point of view of adults, adolescence is understood as a problem to be managed, and the center of that problem is the adolescent body with its awakening desires and lack of discipline. Of course, that awkward age of early puberty in which the body begins to develop sexual desire and the brain moves toward abstract thinking has existed throughout human history, but not until the twentieth century did this period become identified as a unique stage in human development. Before then, puberty was indicative of change in status between childhood and adulthood. Romeo and Juliet may have been young lovers, but by the standards of the seventeenth century, they were also adult lovers.

The recognition of adolescence as a unique and individual stage in human growth and development accompanied the broad progressive ideas of the early twentieth century, but it was Sigmund Freud who did the most to turn the sexuality of this stage into a problem. Freud's theories are often misrepresented in contemporary popular culture, but one thing it gets right is Freud's belief that psychologically healthy adults maintained a careful balance between suppression and expression of their sexuality. Suddenly, following Freud, getting that balance right in adolescence became one central and essential key to developing into happy, mature adults.

This felt need to help adolescents find the right balance became a central theme of education in the 1950s. Perhaps it was the increased freedom made possible by the automobile or the independence made possible by the prosperous postwar American economy that led American adults to call on schools to help. Or, perhaps it was the fear promoted by the popular characterization of youth found in pop culture.

Richard A. Quantz, "Narratives of Sexuality, Adolescence, and Education," Sociocultural Studies in Education: Critical Thinking for Democracy, pp. 249-254. Copyright © 2014 by Taylor & Francis Group. Reprinted with permission.

Consider the 1955 movie *Blackboard Jungle,* where the Vic Morrow and Sidney Poitier characters promote the idea of youth out of control. Or consider the media promotion of James Dean as a visual ideograph of the brooding and dangerous adolescent male, and all of this topped off with Elvis Presley's "blatant sexuality" found in his swinging hips (which was reinforced when television banned showing Elvis from the waist down[1]). Whatever the cause, the 1950s saw an increased focus on addressing the "problems of adolescence" in schools.

In *The Education of Eros: A History of Education and the Problem of Adolescent Sexuality,* Dennis Carlson argues that four major "problems" became central concerns of American high schools: the problem of becoming adjusted to normal family life and gender roles, the problem of the unwed teen mother, the problem of sexually transmitted diseases, and the problem of homosexuality.[2] Each of these "problems" generated its own narratives that worked to organize and pattern the conversation around sexuality and education during the 1950s and, in fact, every decade since. Later in this chapter, I will explore these narratives as they are told and retold in today's world, but before moving to these narratives, I would like to present some basic understandings assumed in this chapter.

TERMINOLOGY AND SEXUALITY

As in all topics of social identity and cultural politics, the representation of sexuality in our language has become an important site for care and reflection. In recent years, there has been a dramatic increase in the insertion of sexuality into public conversation. Once a topic relegated only to backrooms and psychologists' offices, sexuality is now openly discussed on television and in the newspapers. As a sign of the growing acceptability of public discussions of sexuality, on January 21st of 2012, President Obama used the word *gay* in his inaugural address, becoming the first president to do so. In this section, I am going to clarify some of the terms that we find in these conversations, but keep in mind that the use of these terms is rapidly evolving, and I make no claim that the usage presented in this chapter is the correct or final word on terminology.

LGBTQ is a collective acronym referring to those who identify as lesbian, gay, bisexual, transgender (or transsexual), or queer (or questioning). Sometimes the letter "I" is included to refer to those who identify as intersexed. According to Eli R. Green, Eric N. Peterson, and Josh Fletcher, these terms can be defined as follows:[3]

Lesbian: Term used to describe female-identified people attracted romantically, erotically, and/or emotionally to other female-identified people. (Many lesbians, though not all, object to being called "gay.")

Gay: 1. Term used in some cultural settings to represent males who are attracted to males in a romantic, erotic, and/or emotional sense. Not all men who engage in "homosexual behavior" identify as gay, and as such, this label should be used with caution. **2.** Term used to refer to the LGBTQI community as a whole, or as an individual identity label for anyone who does not identify as heterosexual.

Bisexual: A person emotionally, physically, and/or sexually attracted to both males/men and females/women. This attraction does not have to be equally split between genders, and there may be a preference for one gender over others.

Transgender: A person who lives as a member of a gender other than that expected based on anatomical sex. Sexual orientation varies and is not dependent on gender identity.

Transsexual: A person who identifies psychologically as a gender/sex other than the one to which he or she was assigned at birth. Transsexuals often wish to transform their bodies hormonally and surgically to match their inner sense of gender/sex.

Queer: 1. An umbrella term that embraces a matrix of sexual preferences, orientations, and habits of the not-exclusively-heterosexual-and-monogamous majority. *Queer* includes lesbians, gay men, bisexuals, transpeople, and intersex persons. **2.** This term is sometimes used as a sexual orientation label instead of *bisexual* as a way of acknowledging that there are more than two genders to be attracted to, or as a way of stating a non-heterosexual orientation without having to state whom they are attracted to.

Intersexed: Someone whose sex a doctor has a difficult time categorizing as either male or female. A person whose combination of chromosomes, gonads, hormones, internal sex organs, and/or genitals differs from one of the two expected patterns.

Sam Killerman[4] defines *questioning* as the process of exploring one's own sexual orientation, investigating influences that may come from their family, religious upbringing, and internal motivations.

RETHINKING GENDER

While it used to be thought that one's gendered performances "naturally" matched one's assignment to a sex, by now, most Americans have come to understand that a person's assignment to a biological category of sex and one's gendered identity are two different things. One can be assigned the category "male," for example, but perform in ways that a culture thinks are "feminine." In recent years, many people have tried to break down these things we call "sex" and "gender" in order to develop a way to think about them that more closely matches human experience. One of the more recent approaches suggests that our sex/gender identity can best be described as some combination of four different dimensions: gender identity, gender expression, biological sex, and sexual orientation (or to whom you are attracted). One particular version of the four dimensions approach suggests that each dimension is itself made up of two subdimensions, which themselves can be recognized as strong or weak influences, creating an enormous variety of ways in which individuals can construct their gender. So, for example, under the dimension gender identity, any individual might score high or low or in between on either or both of the "Woman-ness" and "Manness" scales. Or under the dimension of gender expression, any person might score high or low or in between on either or both of the "masculine" or "feminine" scales. Whether we use the four dimension approach or a two dimension approach or some other number of dimensions, most people today do seem to agree that gender, sex, and sexuality are somehow entwined in our socially constructed sense of self and others. Gone are the days when we think we can know a person by merely looking at them. Unfortunately, most schools have not yet begun to catch on to this complexity and continue to assume that all students are *cisgendered*—that is, the individual students all feel a clear alignment among gender identity, gender expression, biological sex, and sexual attraction.

Some universities have begun to recognize that sex and gender are no longer to be considered straightforward and have adopted policies such as the availability of gender-neutral bathrooms and asking students to identify whether they wish to be addressed with gendered or gender-neutral pronouns such as ze or hir. Ze and hir are "alternate pronouns that are gender neutral and pre-ferred by some gender diverse persons. Pronounced /zee/ and /here/, they replace 'he'/'she' and 'his'/'hers.'"[5] But while a few universities have responded to the recognized complexity of gender and sexuality, the number of high schools that do are few and far between.

Some junior high and high schools have been specifically created as a safe haven to gender diverse students. Careful to clarify that these schools are open to and enroll straight/ cisgendered students, they nonetheless have a very high percentage of LGBTQ students. Perhaps the best known of these alternative high schools is the Harvey Milk High School, a New York City public high school located in the East Village that enrolls about 100 LGBTQ and straight/cisgendered students. The Alliance Charter School in Milwaukee, funded by the state of Wisconsin and designed to be LGBTQ friendly and that enrolls a little more than 150 students—about half of which identify as LGBTQ—gained much attention following a 2011 *Time* magazine article.[6] The Alliance School is one of the few gender diverse–friendly schools that enrolls students starting in the sixth grade. Some attempts to create such schools have not been able to survive the opposition from social conservatives who complain that public money should not be spent on protecting children just because of their sexuality when many other children are also bullied and harassed, as well as opposition from gay rights groups who argue that children should not have to be segregated to be safe and instead advocate for the creation of safe environments for LGBTQ children wherever they attend school.[7]

Some districts have encouraged the development of student support groups, such as Gay, Lesbian, and Straight Education Network (GLSEN) and such formal programs as SafeZone, to attempt to create a safer and more equitable environment for LGBTQ students. GLSEN was founded in 1990 to create a national alliance, as its name suggests, of LGBTQ and straight/ cisgendered students, parents, and teachers interested in promoting safe environments for every member of a school community "regardless of sexual orientation or gender/ identity expression."[8] GLSEN sponsors several well-known programs and projects, such as ThinkB4YouSpeak.com (a website designed to fight anti-LGBT language through advertising); gay-straight alliances (GSAs are student clubs located in schools); Ally Week ("a week for students to identify, support and celebrate Allies against anti-LGBT language, bullying, and harassment in America's schools"[9]); Day of Silence (a day in April in which students around the world take a vow of silence to ritually show the silencing of LGBT students); Changing the Game: The GLSEN Sports Project (which focuses specifically on elementary and secondary sports programs to promote respect for all athletes regardless of sexual orientation or gender identity/expression[10]); and Safe Space (a diversity training program to help educators develop a place where anti-LGBT language and action are not tolerated). All of these projects are designed to create a safe and respectful environment for all members of a school community.

HOMOPHOBIA, HETEROSEXISM, AND HETERONORMATIVITY

There is a clear distinction between prejudice, prejudicial racism, and institutional racism. The terms homophobia, heterosexism, and heteronormativity are parallel terms applied to gender.

Homophobia refers to the fear or the hatred of homosexuals and homosexual behavior or of any gender-diverse identity or expression. Typically, the concept of homophobia implies that the hatred derives from an irrational fear. As such, homophobia, like racial prejudice, is a psychological concept and is often mistakenly used as a concept to explain social events. While there is little question that much too much anti-gay bullying and violence derive from individuals who suffer from an irrational fear of homosexuality, this book is more concerned with sociocultural causes for anti-gender-diverse behavior.

Heterosexism is a term that is used by some as another parallel term to racial prejudice, which, therefore, focuses on individuals' attitudes to gender-diverse people and action. This book, however, will use heterosexism as a parallel term for prejudicial racism. In this book, *heterosexism* refers to any act based on prejudice that results in the creation or maintenance of inequality or dominance of a people based on sexual orientation or gender identity/expression. In other words, in this book, I will reserve the term heterosexism for actions or programs based on homophobia, but not as a synonym for homophobia itself. As such, heterosexism is located in the sociocultural and not the psychological realm.

Heteronormativity refers to actions or programs that follow the rules or codes, either explicit or covert, that are institutionalized within the organizations and the structures of society when those codes lead to the creation or maintenance of inequality or domination of people based on sexual orientation or gender identity/expression. Heteronormativity assumes that heterosexuality is "normal," and all other forms of sexual orientation or gender identity/ expression are not. Heteronormativity is built right into the institutions of our society so that one need not be homophobic to engage in practices that lead to the domination of gender-diverse people.

Obvious examples of heteronormativity can be found in the still-common practice of forbidding same-sex couples at proms, enforcing gender-aligned dress codes that deny transgendered individuals the right to self-expression, and the requirement of each student to identify him- or herself as a "him" or "her." But heteronormativity enters into schools in more formal ways, as when sex education teaches about "normal" sexual activity as located only between males and females. As is true with race—when we try to be race-blind, we actually end up treating everyone as if she or he were white—ignoring gender diversity results in treating all people as if they were straight or cisgendered. The fear that arises over sexuality of any kind in schools, whether heterosexual or homosexual or other, leads most school people to try to eradicate references to sexuality from their classrooms. The attempt to do so, however, is of course futile because the refusal to recognize sexuality in the classroom merely imposes heteronormativity, which is clearly the recognition and privileging of one sexuality over all others.

QUESTIONS FOR REVIEW, REFLECTION, AND DISCUSSION

1. At what point in history was puberty identified as a unique stage in human development?
2. What is the difference between gay, transgender, and intersexed?
3. What are some examples of heteronormativity provided in the chapter? Provide three examples that are not listed in the chapter.
4. Have you ever witnessed instances of homophobia? What happened? How do you think the individuals involved felt? What do you think was the root of the fear?

ADDITIONAL READINGS

Bockting, W. O. (2014). Transgender identity development. In D. L. Tolman, & L. Diamond (Eds.), *Handbook of sexuality and psychology* (pp.739–758). Washington, DC: American Psychological Association.

Brill, S., & Pepper, R. (2008). *The transgender child: A handbook for families and profession-als*. San Francisco, CA: Cleis Press.

Diamond, L. M., Pardo, S. T., & Butterworth, M. R. (2011). Transgender experience and identity. *Handbook of identity theory and research* (pp. 629–647). New York, NY: Springer.

McGuire, J.K., Kuvalanka, K. A., Catalpa, J.M., & Toomey, R. B. (2016). Transfamily theory: How the presence of trans family members informs gender developmental in families. *Journal of Family Theory & Review*, 8(1), 60–73.

Stacey, J., & Biblarz, T. J. (2001). (How) does the sexual orientation of parents matter? *American Sociological Review, 66*, 159–183.

ENDNOTES

1. See Alan Hanson, "As Seen on TV in the Fifties . . . Elvis on the Living Room Screen," Elvis History Blog, September 2011, www.elvis-history-blog.com/karal-ann-marling.html.
2. Dennis Carlson, *The Education of Eros: A History of Education and the Problem of Adolescent Sexuality,* Studies in Curriculum Theory (New York: Routledge, 2012).
3. This list was constructed by Josh Fletcher (Miami University, 2011–2012) and Richard Quantz (2013) from the following: Eli Green and Eric N. Peterson, "LGBTTSQI Terminology," LGBT Resource Center at UC Riverside, 2006, www.trans-academics.org/lgbttsqiterminology.pdf.
4. Sam Killerman, "Comprehensive List of LGBTQ+ Term Definitions," It's Pronounced Metrosexual, 2011–2013, http://itspronouncedmetrosexual.com/2013/01/a-comprehensive-list-of-lgbtq-term-definitions/. This list also includes many of the terms on the Green and Peterson list with some different wording.
5. Green and Peterson, "LGBTTSQI Terminology."
6. Kayla Webley, "A Separate Peace?" *Time,* October 13, 2011, www.time.com/time/specials/packages /article/0,28804,2095385_2096859_2096805-1,00.html.

7. Karen Hawkins, "Plans for Gay-Friendly Chicago High School Nixed," *USA Today,* November 20, 2008, http://usatoday30.usatoday.com/news/education/2008-11-20-gay-high-school_N.htm.

8. "Our Mission," Gay, Lesbian, & Straight Education Network, www.glsen.org/values.

9. "Ally Week," Gay, Lesbian, & Straight Education Network, www.allyweek.org/about/.

10. See "Changing the Game," Gay, Lesbian, & Straight Education Network, 2010–2013, http://sports .glsen.org/.

11. While Mrs. Reagan's campaign started as an anti-drug advertising promotion, it was expanded to include premarital sex.

12. Carla Shoff, "Teenage Fertility: Does Place, Race, or Poverty Matter?" master's thesis, The Pennsylvania State University, 2009.

13. Vito Russo and Gene Woodling, *The Celluloid Closet: Homosexuality in the Movies,* Triangle Classics, rev. ed. (New York: Quality Paperback Book Club, 1995); Vito Russo, *The Celluloid Closet,* Sony Pictures Classics, Culver City, CA: Columbia TriStar Home Video, 2001.

14. Christine Sparta, "Emergence from the Closet," *USA Today,* March 11, 2002, http://usatoday30 .usatoday.com/life/television/2002/2002-03-11-coming-out-timeline.htm.

15. "Where We Are on TV Report: 2012–2013 Season," GLAAD, 2012, www.glaad.org/publications /whereweareontv12.

16. Tim Appelo, "THR Poll: 'Glee' and 'Modern Family' Drive Voters to Favor Gay Marriage—Even Many Romney Voters," *The Hollywood Reporter,* November 3, 2012, www.hollywoodreporter. com/news /thr-poll-glee-modern-family-386225.

17. For a full list of Focus on the Family's activities see www.focusonthefamily.com/.

18. Justin Richardson, Peter Parnell, and Henry Cole, *And Tango Makes Three* (New York: Simon & Schuster Books for Young Readers, 2005).

19. See Exodus Global Alliance at www.exodusglobalalliance.org/.

20. See JONAH International: Institute for Gender Affirmation at http://jonahweb.org/index.php.

21. Southern Poverty Law Center, "Conversion Therapy," www.splcenter.org/conversion-therapy.

UNIT 4

MARITAL DISSOLUTION AND REMARRIAGE

KEY TERMS

Dissolution of Marriage

Legal Separation

Informal Separation

Alimony

Divorce Mediation

Crude Divorce Rate

Refined Divorce Rate

Joint Custody

9

DIVORCE AND RESCRIPTED FAMILIES

By Gene H. Starbuck and
Karen Saucier Lundy

PRELUDE

Jose and Julie started their marriage as a happy couple very much in love. They both adored their three children. But over time, they grew apart. They increasingly got into fights and didn't make up the way they used to.

Jose began spending more and more time after work with his pals at the bar. Julie developed a close friendship with a man at work; one night, after a few drinks, that friendship became a one-time sexual relationship. Jose suspected she had been unfaithful, but she never admitted it. Their marriage continued to disintegrate.

Finally Jose and Julie got a divorce. Their dreams of lifelong love and joy were shattered. Their children now lived with a single mother and saw their father less and less frequently. Jose remarried in a few years; Julie never did.

Thousands of couples, and their children, go through similar experiences every year. Over time, most go on to live happy, normal lives. Some never fully recover.

Under the circumstances, did Jose and Julie do the right thing in getting a divorce?

This chapter will put the topic of divorce in its social and historical context. Some of the causes of divorce will be examined. We will also look at what happens in the lives of couples and children who are involved in divorce, remarriage, and the construction of stepfamilies.

Thinking Ahead What do you think has happened to the divorce rate in the United States in the last 30 years? Why? How does this compare to other countries? What kinds of social changes would be likely to lower the divorce rate? Would these changes be desirable? In what ways do stepfamilies differ from intact families? How would family systems theorists answer these questions? Feminist theorists? Scripting theorists?

For most societies and times, marriages were more likely to end by death than by divorce. Today's American marriages are more likely to end in divorce than death (Whitehead, 1996).

The process of divorce, long and complicated, significantly affects adults and children who go through it. After divorce, individuals must re-script their personal lives and redefine their family systems and subsystems. For most who remarry, another major rescripting process is required. This often results in stepfamilies that have their own unique problems and opportunities.

DIVORCE IN COMPARATIVE CONTEXT

This section begins with definitions of terms, followed by discussion of divorce as affected by modes of production, especially the industrial revolution. A review of the history of divorce in the United States follows. The section also includes a comparison of ways to calculate divorce rates.

ENDING THE MARITAL UNION

Not all people believe that death completely ends a marriage. Mormons believe that marriage can be for "time and eternity," surviving the death of both partners. The "ghost father," a practice common in many African groups, and the case of the Biblical Levirate in which a dead man was able to "impregnate" his wife with a little help from his living brother, are other cases in which, socially, a marriage did not really end at death.

For most purposes, however, it is assumed in Western societies that marriages end when one partner dies. Provisions are made, either legally or by custom, for the transfer of property. After a "suitable" time, the surviving partner is free to remarry.

A divorce enables the former partners to carry on separate lives legally although the former partners might continue to interact if they had children. Considerable rescripting of roles is often necessary for couples to change from spouses to nonintimate coparents.

Partly to reduce the stigma attached to the term *divorce,* it is now sometimes called **dissolution of marriage**. In some societies that do not allow absolute divorce, and in others as an alternative to divorce, there is the possibility of a "divorce from board and bed," or **legal separation**. This is the same as an absolute divorce, except that remarriage cannot legally occur and sometimes certain inheritance rights are maintained.

Today, it is more common for couples to have an **informal separation**. Like the legal separation, this is typically used as either a prelude to divorce or a "time out" during which marital problems will be worked on. As many as one in six American marriages undergo a temporary informal separation of 48 hours or more because of discord at some time (Kitson, 1985).

Legal annulments, relatively rare today, are generally included with divorces when divorce rates are calculated. Where divorces are not legally possible, annulments are more common. The Catholic Church, which does not approve of absolute divorces, does recognize annulments. Some Catholics get a divorce through the civil process and then pursue an annulment via the formal church process.

Although an annulment legally means that a marriage "never happened," the participants and the community know that something occurred. A child from the marriage is considered legitimate, and the "nonhusband" can be ordered to provide child support (Eshleman, 1994).

With both formal and informal separations, the married partners generally know where each other can be found. In the case of **desertion**, however, one partner leaves without saying where he or she will be living. The marriage is still intact in that neither partner can legally remarry, but marital interaction ends. For many, especially the poor, desertion has historically served as the functional equivalent of divorce. For those who want a more formal end of the relationship, desertion has been one of the most widely accepted grounds for divorce (Riley, 1991).

MODES OF PRODUCTION AND DIVORCE

The process of divorce has changed as modes of production have changed. Industrialization seems to have had a homogenizing effect on divorce rates and processes in many of the world's countries.

Hunting-Gathering Divorce Something like divorce has been available in most societies as a way of ending unsatisfactory marriages. Although divorces were difficult to get in some hunting-gathering societies, they were generally easier than in horticultural and agrarian societies. One example is provided by the Inuit, often called Eskimos, in what is now northern Alaska.

Burch (1970) found that both marriage and divorce traditionally occurred among the Inuit with little or no ceremony. Either partner could accomplish a divorce simply by ceasing to live with and having sexual intercourse with the spouse. The spouse desiring the divorce could simply depart or put the partner's belongings outside the door of their

Dissolution of marriage: Divorce.
Legal separation: A condition in which a married couple separates, has a legally recognized property and custody settlement, lives apart, but may not remarry.
Informal separation: A condition in which married couples maintain separate residences because of problems living together.

Desertion: Legally or culturally unjustified abandonment of a spouse, children, or both.

Traditional Eskimos had a stable high-divorce, high-remarriage system. This a Siberian Eskimo family in about 1910.

dwelling. Divorced couples frequently remarried by moving back in with each other, but they were free to form other marriages.

Such arrangements characterize what Goode (1993) referred to as "stable high-divorce-rate" systems. These societies have consistently high divorce rates; Burch (1970) estimated an almost 100% divorce rate among the Inuit. Rather than being considered a problem, however, the high rate is institutionalized as part of the marriage and family system. Such matters as child custody and division of property have normative and fairly clearly defined solutions.

Stable high-rate divorce systems typically have high remarriage rates. Individuals quickly either remarry their old partner or find a new one. The household division of labor and economic organization of the group, thus, is relatively unaffected by the high divorce rate.

Divorce in Agrarian Societies Ancient Rome had relatively high divorce and remarriage rates. Although the *pater familias* had considerable control, at least in later Roman times, divorce could be realized by mutual consent of the married partners (Goode, 1993).

As Catholicism spread throughout the Roman Empire and all of Europe, divorce rates gradually declined. Just before the industrial revolution, divorce was nearly impossible to get anywhere in Europe. Although King Henry the Eighth (1509–1547) of England broke with the Roman Catholic Church in order to get a divorce, the new Anglican Church was almost as strict as the Catholic Church. In all of England. there were only 375 recorded divorces in the years 1670–1857. Only recently have Italy (1970), Portugal (1974), Spain (1981), and Ireland (1995) allowed divorce, and even now there is a waiting period of up to seven years in some cases (Goode, 1993).

Divorce was rare in advanced-agrarian China, although the rates varied depending on which of the three types of marriage was involved (Wolf & Huang, 1980). In the "standard" or "major" type, the bride was essentially absorbed into the extended family of the groom. This was the most common form of marriage in most of China and had an extremely low divorce rate (Wolf & Huang, 1980).

A stable-high-rate system was found in Japan before its major industrialization. As in China, the traditional Japanese marriage form was patrilineal and patrilocal, but the Japanese bride had more independence than did her Chinese counterpart. After the wedding, she moved into her husband's family for what, in effect, was a trial period. If divorce occurred, it was usually because the groom's parents sent the bride back to her own parents. The marriages that ended in this way usually did so within the first year or two. Remarriage rates were close to total, however, and later marriages lasted longer than did first marriages (Beardsley, Hall, & Ward, 1939; Goode, 1963, 1993; Smith & Wiswell, 1982; Yanagida, 1957).

Much of the Arab world has also had relatively high divorce rates. Islamic law allowed a husband to get a divorce simply by repeating, "Go, I divorce you" three times ("Talak. Talak. Talak"). It was rare and much more difficult for a woman to initiate a divorce (Goode, 1993). Young children went to their mother's family home with her, but they were considered to be part of their father's lineage and were returned to his home at a certain age. The woman's father was responsible for her support until she could be remarried (Goode, 1993).

Industrialization and Divorce William J. Goode (1963, 1970, 1993) proposed that the industrial revolution resulted in higher divorce rates. A person's status is defined more by achievement than by ascription in industrial systems. Individuals increasingly rely on their own educational achievements and work experiences, and they become less dependent upon their families of orientation for adult status and livelihood.

As individual freedom increases in the economic sphere, there is pressure to increase it in the personal and family spheres as well. Persons begin to believe they have the "right" to seek their own happiness, rather than follow the script laid out by tradition and by their families. Marriage begins to be seen more as a matter of individual development than as a lifelong spiritual or family commitment. The result is the "desacralization" of the social institution of marriage (Goode, 1993).

Industrialization and individualism have led to a steady increase in divorce rates. In North America, after a long-term increase, divorce rates peaked in the United States in about 1980. In other countries, rates have continued to climb.

The industrialized world shares other divorce-related characteristics. Wives file for divorce in two thirds to three fourths of the cases, and custody of minor children goes to the mothers in 80% to 90% of cases. Although fathers are expected to provide child support after divorce, all countries have difficulty enforcing this expectation (Goode, 1993).

With the possible exception of Russia, the United States retains the highest divorce rates in the modern world, but other countries are catching up. Popenoe (1988) argued that Sweden has surpassed the United States in the effective, if not the reported, divorce rate. Cohabitation before marriage is almost universal in Sweden, and cohabiting relationships have a considerably higher break-up rate than do marriages.

Goode (1964, 1993) intended his model not only as a description about what has happened in countries that have already gone through the industrial revolution, but also as a prediction about what will happen as other countries industrialize. Central and South America, which always had very low rates, have recently begun to see their divorce rates climb. Similar patterns can be found in Africa, although less is known about patterns in the sub-Saharan region (Goode, 1993).

Societies that had stable-high-rate systems just before industrialization provide apparent exceptions to Goode's hypothesis that industrialization increases divorce rates. This was the case in Taiwan, Japan, Malaysia, and Indonesia (Wolf & Huang, 1980; Yanagida, 1957; Kumagai, 1983; Goode, 1993). In virtually all of the societies with initial high-rate systems, however, divorce rates reached some low point, and then began to creep back up in the pattern previously seen in European societies.

In the Muslim Arab countries, there seems to be no clear association between industrialization and divorce. Part of the reason, Goode (1993) argued, is that industrialization has not yet fully affected these countries. While the petroleum industry has become highly industrialized, the Arab societies are still largely organized around preindustrial patterns.

DIVORCE IN THE UNITED STATES

Glenda Riley (1991) found that the United States has always had a fairly high divorce rate, at least compared to Europe. Immigrants usually left their extended families behind, so older relatives had less influence on their marital selection and behavior. The continual westward movement of earlier European-Americans had the same effect.

Early Protestant teachings that emphasized individualism ultimately influenced divorce. Martin Luther argued that marriage should not be a sacrament of the church and that religion should be a matter between an individual and God, not to be regulated by church or state. This individualism took root in the American colonies more strongly than in Europe, and it contributed to the development of capitalism and the industrial revolution, along with higher divorce rates (Weber, 1958; Goode, 1963).

In the New England colonies, divorce was rare. The Massachusetts Bay Colony granted the first divorce in 1630. In the Plymouth colony, a total of nine absolute divorces and several "divorces from bed and board" were granted in the first 72 years (Riley, 1991).

New England initially followed the English pattern requiring an act of parliament or legislature for a bill of divorce. As colonial and state legislatures became busier, however, authority to grant divorces was transferred to the courts. The last state to have legislative divorces was Delaware, where the practice ended in 1897 (Blake, 1962).

From the beginning, divorce in the colonies took on the adversarial nature of legal proceedings used in civil suits. One partner sued to prove that the other was "at fault" for breaking the marriage contract. The plaintiff attempted to prove that the defendant had done something that was a ground for divorce.

The first formal list of grounds for divorce in colonial America was in a statute passed by the Court of Magistrates in New Haven in the 1650s: adultery, desertion, and male impotence (Cohn, 1970; in Riley, 1991). Grounds for divorce varied considerably from one jurisdiction to another. In South Carolina, there were no grounds for absolute divorce; only divorce from bed and board was allowed until 1949. In New York, divorce was allowed only on the Biblically acceptable ground of adultery until 1968 (Riley, 1991).

In early America, the "guilty" party in a divorce suit could be punished by fines, whipping, the stocks, or banishment. The guilty party was often forbidden from remarriage. If a wife was the successful plaintiff, she could receive **alimony**. This term was first applied to the money paid by the husband to the wife during a legal separation or divorce from bed and board, and was later applied to divorce. In early Massachusetts, a woman could receive her dower rights, or one third of her husband's property, only if she were the "innocent" party (Riley, 1991).

Alimony: Support paid to a spouse by the former spouse after divorce or separation.

Early Americans followed the patrilineal European tradition that generally left the children with their father after divorce. In the 19th century, this custom gave way to the **tender years rule**, which states that children, especially if they were young, were better off staying with their mother. From 1887 to 1906, mothers got custody by a 3 to 1 ratio over fathers (Riley, 1991).

Tender years rule: The legal guideline that young children are better off living with their mothers.

Throughout American history, women have filed for divorce more than have men. In the 19th century, women were the plaintiffs in about two thirds of the divorces. Part of the reason for this might be that, as mothers increasing got custody, some fathers were reluctant to ruin the reputation of the woman who would be raising their children (Riley, 1991; Steinmetz, 1987).

Another possibility is that husbands' behavior was more likely to be defined as grounds for divorce. Men were probably more likely to commit adultery and to be alcoholics. Only men could be impotent, although either could be infertile, and only men were required to provide support to their spouse and children. Men were more likely to commit the kind of injurious physical abuse that would provide grounds under the cruelty statutes.

Although it could be defined as desertion if a wife refused to move to a new location with her husband (Liss, 1987), this was seldom actually used as grounds for divorce. It was established in law that if a husband's actions drove his wife from their home, he was considered the deserter (Riley, 1991).

The wife's role in marriage was primarily to perform the labor in and near the home, to be a sexual partner, and to bear and care for children. Unlike the case in some other cultures, failure to fulfill these traditional expectations has typically not been formal grounds for divorce in the United States.

The federal government has generally stayed out of marriage and divorce regulation, leaving each state to define its own divorce laws. The U.S. Constitution contains a "full faith and credit" clause (Article IV, section 1) that obligates each state to accept acts of the other states, so a divorce in any state is considered legal in all other states.

As the country expanded, divorce laws were often more liberal in the newer western states. Because of the different laws, a number of major cities in the newer states developed the reputation of being "divorce mills," including Indianapolis, Indiana; Fargo, North Dakota; Guthrie, Oklahoma; and Salt Lake City, Utah. The most recent and famous "divorce mill" was Reno, Nevada. Some local citizens lobbied to increase business by maintaining the laws that made divorce easier (Riley, 1991).

Although many "divorce mills" later changed their laws to make divorce more difficult, the general direction of change was toward more liberal laws. In some cases, the law itself did not change, but the interpretations of the law did. One example is the change in the meaning of *cruelty*. Initially, the term referred only to the most serious physical abuse. Less serious physical abuses and "mental abuses" gradually were included. In some jurisdictions, the cruelty ground was so broadly defined that it included almost anything.

These changes, perhaps driven by the forces of industrialization mentioned by Goode, resulted in a gradual increase in the divorce rate. The American divorce rate grew steadily from the colonial period until 1980, after which it leveled off and even declined slightly.

The general upward trend saw numerous peaks and valleys. Divorce rates increased briefly after every major war. The rate almost doubled after the Civil War ended (1865). There was a small peak in about 1920, just after World War I. The most noticeable peak

At one time, being a "divorce mill" was good business for Reno.

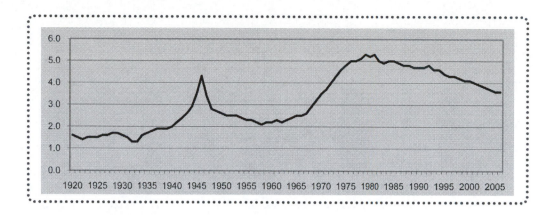

FIGURE 9.1.

U. S. Divorce Rate,
per 1,000 Population,
1920–2006

Source: 1920–1995 from
*Historical Statistics of the
United States,* Cambridge
University Press, Table Ae
507–513; 1996–2006, U.S.
Bureau of the Census,
Statistical Abstract, 2009,
Table 77.

occurred around 1945, at the end of World War II. Wars resulted in hasty marriages, social disorganization, and separation of young spouses for long periods (Cherlin, 1992; Pavalko & Elder, 1990). Figure 9.1 measures the divorce rate as the number of divorces per 1,000 married women and graphically depicts the changes that occurred in this rate between 1920 and 1997.

A significant decline in divorce occurred during the Great Depression of the 1930s. Jobs and housing became scarce, and many couples who might otherwise have gotten divorced could not afford to do so (Cherlin, 1992). In addition, many men were forced to leave their families in search of work, rendering a divorce unnecessary since there was an informal separation anyway.

A clear reversal of the general upward trend occurred in the 1950s and early 1960s, a period sometimes referred to as the "Golden Age of the American Nuclear Family." The Baby Boom had begun, America was at the zenith of world power, suburbs were proliferating, and economic times were generally good.

Then, beginning in the mid-1960s, the divorce rate began a rapid increase that lasted until about 1980. Much of this rise was accounted for by the demographic variable of the baby boom. In 1964, the first of the "boomers" reached age 18, the high-risk time for early marriage and divorce. In 1980, the last of the boomers was growing out of the high-risk age group. Because a relatively large share of the population was in the high-risk age group between 1964 and 1980, the divorce rate for the country as a whole increased

Related to the baby boom, the 1960s and 1970s was a time in which all social institutions, including marriage and the family, were being questioned and challenged. A number of other structural and economic factors, including rapidly changing gender roles, also contributed to the increase in divorce rates (Beeghley & Dwyer, 1989; South, 1985). Since 1980, the divorce rate has trended slightly downward. Among the reasons for this decline are the continued aging of the baby boomers and the smaller percentage of the population that is in the age group at greatest risk for divorce. The increased average age at first marriage might also be important.

FIGURE 9.2.

Percent of Adults Who
Have Ever Divorced, by
Race/Ethnicity

Source: U. S. Census
Bureau, "Survey of Income
and Program Participants.
http://www.census.gov/
population/soc-demo/
marital-hist/2004, Table 3.

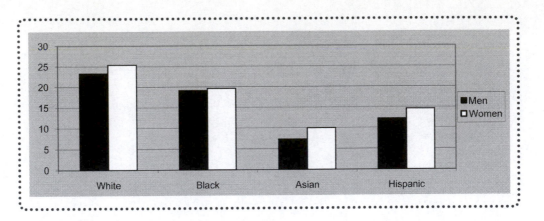

The general trends discussed here show up regardless of the way the divorce rate is measured. The exact amount of increase and decrease depends on how the rate is calculated (see Finding Out 9.1).

Figure 9.2 compares the percent of adults who have ever divorced. Whites are most likely to divorce; Asians are least likely.

THE DIVORCE REVOLUTION

As Riley (1991) noticed, divorce has always been controversial in the United States; some advocates wanted to make divorce more difficult to get, others wanted it to be easier. The easy-divorce faction argued that the whole process of finding one spouse "guilty" of something, and the antagonism that often resulted from the adversarial process, ultimately harmed the children involved in the divorce. Reformers looked for a way to allow couples to divorce with as little rancor as possible.

"No fault" divorce laws were an attempt to solve this problem. The idea of divorce by "mutual consent" had been around for many years; the idea that either partner could initiate a divorce simply by declaring the irremediable breakdown of a marriage was a more recent innovation. Divorce would become more an administrative matter than an issue battled out in the courts.

The first "no-fault" divorce law became effective in California in 1970. The idea spread quickly; by 1977, all but three states had either replaced all their divorce grounds with the no-fault rule or had added a no-fault clause to the traditional fault-based grounds. The last holdout, South Dakota, accepted a no-fault clause in 1985 (Blosky & Monroe, 2002). There is now discussion in some states about rescinding the no-fault laws.

Divorce mediation:
A conflict-resolution
process in which
a third party helps
a couple resolve
divorce issues.

In some jurisdictions, a couple may, if there are no children or other major issues involved, get divorced by mail. In other places, there is a provision for **divorce mediation.** Although such processes might reduce conflict, the results tend to follow the traditional outcome, in which the mother has custody and the father is expected to pay child support and get visitation rights (Teach-man & Polonko, 1990).

FINDING OUT 9.1 CALCULATING THE DIVORCE RATE

There are at least five ways to calculate and report divorce rates, each with advantages and disadvantages (Crosby, 1980). These methods lead to slightly different conclusions about recent U.S. trends in divorce, as Table 9.1 reveals.

TABLE 9.1. VARIOUS DIVORCE CALCULATIONS FOR SELECTED YEARS, UNITED STATES

Year	Absolute Number of Divorces	Current Divorces Divided by Current Marriages	Crude Divorce Rate	Refined Divorce Rate
1970	708,000	div./2,159,000 = .328	3.5	14.9
1980	1,189,000	div./2,390,000 = .497	5.2	22.6
1981	1,213,000	div./2,422,000 = .500	5.3	22.6
1988	1,167,000	div./2,396,000 = .487	4.7	20.7
1994	1,182,000	div./2,329,000 = .508	4.6	21.8
1997	1,163,000	div./2,384,000 = .488	4.3	N.A.
1998	1,135,000	div./2,256,000 = .503	4.2	N.A.

Sources: 1994 data from National Center for Health Statistics, in Famighetti, 1995. 1970–1988 from *Statistical Abstract 1999.* 1998 divorces from *http://www.cdc.gov/nchs/fastats/divorce.htm* 1988 marriages from *http://www.cdc.gov/nchs/fastats/marriage.htm* accessed February 14, 2001.

1. One way to report divorces is simply to provide the *absolute number of divorces* for a particular jurisdiction for a given time period. A one-year period is used for most purposes. The figures are initially gathered at the county level and then aggregated to provide totals for states, regions, or the entire country. For many purposes, a sample of counties is selected rather than collecting data from all counties in the country.

   The absolute number of divorces, although easier to calculate, does not reveal information about the actual risk of divorce because it does not consider the population base. The absolute number might go up simply because there are more persons in the population.

   In the United States, the year with the largest absolute number of divorces was 1981, when there were 1,213,000 (see Table 9.1). Even by 1998, that number had not yet been surpassed.

2. Another way to report divorce is to use some *comparisons of number of divorces with number of marriages* in a given jurisdiction and time period. Both numbers can fairly easily be obtained from official records.

   In 1970, there were 2,159,000 marriages and 708,000 divorces. If we divide the former by the latter we get a marriage-to-divorce ratio of 3.05 to 1. More commonly, the number of divorces is divided by the number of marriages; in 1970, this resulted in a divorce-to-marriage ratio of .328 to 1.

Continued

Continued from previous page

As Table 9.1 indicates, the divorce-to-marriage ratio peaked in 1981 at .500 to 1, dropped back down, and then peaked again in 1994 at .508 to 1. Although there were considerably fewer divorces in 1994 than 1981, the ratio was higher in 1994 because there were considerably fewer marriages in that year. The number of divorces and the number of marriages continued to fall in 1998.

Many persons read these figures as saying that .50, or 50%, of all marriages will end in divorce. This is not necessarily the case because the divorces in any given year are from marriages from many previous years and are being compared to the marriages from only one year.

A divorce figure such as this can be especially misleading if applied to smaller jurisdictions. A rapidly growing area, for example, attracts persons who have gotten married somewhere else. The divorce counts in the growing area, the marriage in the other region. Over time, the divorce-to-marriage ratio will be artificially higher in regions to which families are moving and artificially lower in areas from which they come.

3. Perhaps the most common way that divorce is reported in statistical sources is the **crude divorce rate.** This is the number of divorces per year for a jurisdiction, per each 1,000 persons in that same jurisdiction. In 1970, there were 708,000 divorces and 203,302,031 individuals in the United States. The former figure divided by the latter yields 0.00348; multiplied by 1,000, this rounds to 3.5, the figure reported in Table 9.1.

The highest crude divorce rate was reached in 1981, at 5.3 per 1,000 population. Since 1981, the figure has gradually been going down. The crude divorce rate stood at 4.2 in 1998.

Although it is sometimes difficult to know exactly how many persons live in a particular area at a certain time, this measure provides at least some indication of the actual risk of divorce in a population. However, not all persons in a population are married; the population includes infants and single adults, who are not at risk for divorce.

4. A more precise approach is to use the **refined divorce rate,** which is the number of divorces per 1,000 married women who are 15 years of age and older. In 1970 there were 708,000 divorces and 47,516,778 married women. Dividing the former by the latter yields 0.0149; multiplied by 1,000 that yields 14.9, the figure reported in Table 9.1. The highest refined divorce rate in U.S. history was 22.6, reported in both 1980 and 1981. The rate for 1994 was 21.8.

This is a more accurate figure because only those at risk for divorce are included in the base figure. It is very difficult in many populations, however, to find out how many married women there are at any given time.

Crude divorce rate: Number of divorces per year per 1,000 persons in the population.

Refined divorce rate: Number of divorces per year per 1,000 married women aged 15 and older.

Current national and international comparisons, therefore, more often use the crude divorce rate.

5. The rate that many persons wish to know is *average marital risk*. This would be some figure that would indicate what percentage of marriage begun in a given year would eventually end in divorce. Although that would be nice to know, it involves seeing into the future or relying on very old information.

To calculate this rate correctly would require a longitudinal study. All marriages registered in 1996, for example, would be followed until they ended either in divorce or death. After all marriages had ended, the percentage ending in divorce could be calculated. This would take at least until 2076, however, because a few marriages from 1996 will last 80 or more years. Alternatively, we could go back to 1916 and see how many marriages of that year ended in divorce. However, since the divorce rate has gone up since then, that figure would not be very useful for predicting the stability of today's marriages.

Calculations not using one of the two methods suggested above are estimated by demographers. The National Center for Health Statistics (1980) estimated that marriages begun in 1952 would have a lifetime dissolution rate of 32.1%; those begun in 1962 would be about 40%; and those begun in 1972 would be about 50%. Norton and Moorman (1987) estimated that about 56% of current first marriages would end in divorce. Perhaps the most extreme of the estimates came from Martin and Bumpass (1989), who estimated that as many as two thirds of today's marriages will end in divorce. This figure, however, included remarriages. The most widely accepted estimate today is that about 50% of first marriages initiated in recent years will end in divorce (Amato, 2000; Cherlin, 1992).

Other changes in divorce law have happened in the postindustrial era, although considerable differences remain from state to state. One change has been the removal of the tender-years rule in child custody in favor of "gender neutral" criteria such as "the best interests of the child." In spite of the legal changes, mothers retain custody in about 90% of cases. Most of these are ones in which the father does not fight the mother's desire for custody, but even when their desires clash, mothers get custody twice as often as do fathers. Most of these decisions are made during divorce mediation or other negotiation processes. In California, a judge settles the matter in fewer than 2% of cases. In these, mothers and fathers are about equally likely to get custody (Maccoby & Mnookin, 1992).

Rather than award sole custody to one or the other parent after divorce, many states now allow, or even encourage, **joint custody.** This has two separate types, legal and residential. With joint legal custody, each parent retains the right to make legal

Joint custody: The awarding of shared residential or legal custody to both parents after divorce.

decisions about such things as medical care, to be informed by schools about the child's progress, and other matters. Joint legal custody might be accompanied by joint residential custody, in which the child is expected to spend roughly equal time living with each parent. Joint custody appears to be associated with better father-child relationships and better child outcomes (Arditti, 1992; Buchanan, Maccoby, & Dornbush, 1996), but it is unclear whether the joint custody itself makes the difference or if the kinds of couples who can make joint custody work are the kinds who would maintain good postdivorce relationships anyway (Amato, 2000).

Changes have also occurred in the division of marital property. The traditional, or common law, procedure was to assume that the property belonged to the husband, but that, in certain cases, some of it could be given to the divorcing wife. Some states have adopted community-property laws, in which property acquired during marriage, with such exceptions as inheritance and gifts, belonged equally to both partners. In practice, the two approaches now have similar results; common-law states now prescribe "equitable" division, while community-property states adhere to an "equal" division of property standard (Goode, 1993; Fineman, 1989).

A major dispute today concerns what is counted as property. Weitzman (1985) and others argued that such things as pensions and insurance should be considered property; in some cases, that view has prevailed. The status of educational and occupational licenses and degrees is also disputed. Suppose one partner sacrifices his or her own education to support the other partner, who earns an M.D. degree. Some argue that the degree should be considered an asset, marital property that partly belongs to the supporting partner. Others argue that it cannot be treated as an asset because it has no direct market value. Since women are typically in the supporter role in this situation, many feminists argue for the "shared asset" position (Rhode & Minow, 1990).

Alimony, now usually referred to as "spousal support awards," was never common; it is even less common now. Rather than a continual obligation, spousal support now more often takes the form of a short-term obligation or payment for a certain period of training (Kay, 1990).

Whether child support was ordered, and the amount of the award, historically has varied widely among jurisdictions and even among judges within a jurisdiction. To combat this problem, the federal government began, in 1984, to require the states to use more consistent guidelines. All states now have formulas that include such variables as the predivorce income of the couple, the percentage of that income made by each partner, and the estimated monetary needs of the children at certain income levels. Although some ambiguity and variability in the application of guidelines still exists, consistency has improved significantly (Pirog-Good & Brown, 1996).

In 90% of cases, it is the father who is ordered to pay child support to the custodial mother. Of those ordered to pay, fathers are more likely to comply than mothers. About 45% of custodial mothers receive all or part of the amount they were owed in the past year, compared to about 39% of men. By contrast, 33% of custodial fathers received none of the support ordered, compared with 25% of custodial mothers who received nothing. The average amount received by fathers was 51% of what mothers received, but the total income of custodial mothers was about 78% of that for custodial fathers (Bureau of the Census, 2003).

The problem of "deadbeat dads" rivals that of "welfare moms" in much of the popular press, but only recently has there been research explaining the lack of payment. Virtually no research has been done on "deadbeat moms" or "welfare dads."

Some men decline to pay because they do not take their obligation seriously and can get away without paying (Aulette, 1994; Weitzman, 1985). Other researchers have pointed out that some men cannot afford to pay the amount ordered (Meyer & Bartfeld, 1996). Meyer (1999) found that the total income of the father, along with his total financial burden, were the strongest factors in whether a father paid child support or not. Remarried men virtually always contribute to the support of their new wife and any children she might bring into the marriage, or children they have together, leaving less money for his children in his previous marriage (Manning, Stewart, & Smock, 2003). Custodial mothers can get Temporary Assistance to Needy Families (TANF) and other funds if they are poor, but there is no comparable program to help poor custodial fathers meet their obligation of support.

If their former wives are on welfare, some men argue, their payment will not help their children; the child-support payment is deducted from the mother's welfare amount without improving the child's standard of living (Krouse, 1990). Some fathers object to paying support when they cannot be personally involved in their children's lives. A common complaint is that their former wives will not follow the court's visitation order, so they will not follow the court's payment order. In some cases, fathers believe their remarried ex-wives are living better than they themselves are and see no need to provide additional money. Finally, some men doubt that the support they do provide actually is spent on the children (Krouse, 1990).

Whatever the reason, recent legal changes have made it possible to garnish the wages of fathers who do not meet their obligations and to withhold income tax refunds and licenses. These programs do increase the amount of child support paid, but if a man feels too burdened by the collection, he can quit his job, making him even less able to pay (Meyer, 1999).

Some legal analysts have argued that there should be more shared community support for all children, including those of divorce (Krause, 1990). Sweden, for example, provides day care and medical care to all children and pays a child-support stipend to all parents, whether divorced or not (Popenoe, 1988). These procedures help Sweden remain a stable-high-divorce society. Although the United States is a high-divorce society, the institutional arrangements remain those of a low-divorce system.

The impact on society of continuing high divorce rates is significant. High rates become a self-perpetuating cycle. As more couples divorce, it becomes more acceptable, and as it becomes more acceptable, more divorce occurs. In addition, high rates of divorce reduce the marriage rate. One of the traditional advantages of marriage was the near-certainty that one could count on having a permanent relationship. High rates of divorce significantly reduce that certainty, reducing the potential reward of marriage and increasing the potential pain. Consequently, fewer people choose to get married (Waite & Gallagher, 2000).

THE POSTDIVORCE SOCIETY

A high divorce rate affects individuals, but it also has significant social implications as well. Amato (1999) describes these new conditions as a "postdivorce society." He found three major areas in which society has changed along with high divorce rates.

Family Bonds First, family bonding has changed in a variety of ways. Intimate relationships have different meanings than they once did. Fewer relationships are seen as potentially permanent. More couples cohabit before, or instead of, marrying. People have more sexual partners, both in and out of marriage, than was previously true.

Intergenerational ties have weakened. Children of divorce and their parents generally have weaker ties with one another, and grandparents of those children often end up with very weak relationships, especially on the father's side. Elderly divorced fathers are less likely to get support from their children than never-divorced fathers.

The number of stepfamilies has grown significantly, along with the percentage of children who will live in a stepfamily at some time in their lives. This creates a family structure that is more complex and often less stable.

Inequality The nature of social inequality has changed with the emergence of a high-divorce-rate society. The number of children living in single-mother homes has increased poverty for both women and children. This, in turn, has generated more gender inequity than would be the case if more of the working women were married rather than single. In spite of increasing equality in the workplace, there has been a net decline in the standard of living of women compared to men in recent decades (Spain & Bianchi, 1996).

Structural and Cultural Factors Increased divorce has led to the necessity for more women to enter the labor force. Some find themselves needing to work after the divorce; others want to work to be prepared in case of a divorce. In addition, increased numbers of women in the labor force increases the number of divorces. With increasing numbers of working wives, both married men and married women have an increased opportunity to meet alternative partners. This increases the perceived benefit of a divorce.

A high divorce rate is both a cause and an effect of changes in American values. Americans have become increasingly individualistic and decreasingly familistic. The norm of lifelong marriage sometimes conflicts with the norm of increased personal and economic development, in spite of the fact that individuals with the strongest commitment to lifelong marriage have the happiest lives and the most successful marriages (Glenn, 1996; Amato & Rogers, 1997).

In addition, high divorce rates bring an increased number of people into contact with the legal system. This creates a greater demand for lawyers. Other professionals, such as marriage counselors and mediators, are also needed in greater numbers. Finally, politicians and other policy makers have had to develop a new set of rules and procedures for dealing with issues raised in a postdivorce society (Amato, 1999).

In response to concern about the high rate of divorce, some states have considered enacting "covenant marriage" laws. Louisiana did so in 1997. There are several versions of such laws, but they basically allow couples the option of choosing a form of marriage that is both more difficult to get into and to get out of. Premarital counseling is required. More proof of fault, and more counseling, is required before a divorce is allowed. While such a law indicates a societal concern about divorce, its effectiveness is not yet established. Very few couples are choosing the covenant marriage in Louisiana. Some observers suggest that it is attacking only the symptoms, not the causes, of high divorce rates (Brinig, 1998; Nock et al., 1999).

DIVORCE "WHYS"

The question "What causes divorce?" can be addressed at various levels of analysis. At each level, a set of "causes" or "reasons" can be constructed in response to relevant questions. At the macrosociological level, the question is about rates of behavior. At the microsociological level, the "whys" for divorce are constructed from the set of reasons considered acceptable in a particular society at a particular time.

MACROSOCIOLOGICAL AND DEMOGRAPHIC VARIABLES

At the most macrosociological level, the question becomes "What causes some societies to have different divorce rates than others?" or "What causes divorce rates to change over time?" We have mentioned Goode's macro-level studies of the effect of industrialization on divorce. At this level, the divorce rate is not a measure of how miserable marriages are; marital stability is not the same as marital satisfaction or happiness. The fact that divorce rates in the United States were higher in 1996 than in 1956 does not necessarily mean that marriages were "better" or "happier" in 1956. It could mean that couples were more likely to remain in miserable marriages in 1956. Of course, the possibility remains that marriages were happier in the past.

At a somewhat less abstract level of analysis than Goode's, discussion about "causes" of divorce are often given in terms of correlations between various social variables and the divorce rate. While it is sometimes assumed that these variables represent causes, it is safer to call them "correlates," since causality is so difficult to prove. Among these correlates are ethnicity, socioeconomic status, type of employment, age at marriage, duration of marriage, geographic residence, religion, and presence of children.

Race and Ethnicity African-Americans have a much higher divorce rate than Whites. The rate for Latinos is close to that for Anglos. Asians have the lowest divorce rate (Martin & Bumpass, 1989; Sweet & Bumpass, 1987; White, 1990; Bramlett & Mosher, 2002). This association is affected by many other variables, including income levels, educational levels, and urban residence. When these variables are controlled for, differences between Blacks and Whites decrease substantially.

Socioeconomic Status   In general, socioeconomic status is inversely proportional to divorce rates. The highest rates are found among couples with low incomes, low educational levels, and low-status jobs. Conversely, those with higher and more stable incomes have lower divorce rates (Cherlin, 1978; Bramlett & Mosher, 2002). Regardless of a couple's own socioeconomic status, living in a community with high rates of poverty, unemployment, and welfare use increases that couple's probability of divorce (South, 2001; Bramlett & Mosher, 2002).

In general, the higher the educational level the lower the divorce rate (Furstenberg, 1990). For men, each additional level of education has a correspondingly lower divorce rate, but the same is not quite true for women. High school dropouts have relatively high rates. Lower rates are found for high school graduates, and rates are even lower for college-educated women. For women with five or more years of college, however, divorce rates go back up. Professional women, with degrees beyond the bachelors level, are more likely to get divorced and less likely to remarry than women with only a bachelors degree. This relationship is especially strong for women who started graduate school after they were married (Houseknecht, Vaughn, & Macke, 1984; Cooney & Uhlenberg, 1989).

Employment Type   Steadily employed husbands have lower divorce rates than those who are unemployed or have unstable employment histories (Martin & Bumpass, 1989; Bramlett & Mosher, 2002). Couples in which one or both partners are employed in shift work have increased probabilities of divorce (White & Keith, 1990).

Women employed more than 35 hours per week have more than twice the risk of marital disruption compared with women employed 20–35 hours weekly, although the negative effect is at least partly offset by the positive effect of the added family income (Greenstein, 1990). The relationship between hours worked and divorce is strong for women with nontraditional gender ideology; there is no relationship for women with traditional gender views (Greenstein, 1995).

Age at Marriage   The age of a person when he or she gets married is strongly associated with the probability of divorce, at least until about age 25 (Bramlett & Mosher, 2002). Martin and Bumpass (1989) concluded that age at marriage was the strongest predictor of divorce during the first five years of a marriage and remained a strong predictor even in marriages of longer duration. Women who marry at ages 14 to 17 are three times as likely to divorce as those who wait until their 20s. Eighteen- and 19-year-old brides are twice as likely to divorce as their 20-something counterparts. Teenage grooms are twice as likely to divorce than those who marry in their 20s (Spanier & Glick, 1981). The age difference between husband and wife does not appear to affect the probability of divorce (Bramlett & Mosher, 2002). Young marriages are especially likely to end for women who have a traditional gender ideology (Davis & Greenstein, 2004).

Duration of Marriage   Partly because of the waiting period required by most states, few couples (less than 4% of all couples) get divorced in their first year of marriage. Rates climb sharply through the second, third, and fourth years, which are the modal, or most common, times to get divorced. After that, each year of marriage reduces the risk of divorce. After 10 years, 33% of first marriages have ended in divorce; after 15 years, 43% have done so (Bramlett & Mosher, 2002).

Religion   Of the three most commonly compared American religions, homogamous Jewish marriages have the lowest divorce rates, followed by Catholics and then Protestants. The highest rates are found among those with no religious affiliation and those who consider their religion unimportant to them. Mixed-faith marriages have higher rates than do homogamous ones (Glenn & Supancic, 1984; Bramlett & Mosher, 2002).

Among Protestants, the most conservative and fundamentalist groups such as Nazarenes, Pentecostals, and Baptists, have higher rates than do more mainstream Protestant groups like Methodists, Episcopalians, and Presbyterians (Glenn & Supancic, 1984). This might be the result of nonreligious factors. Members of conservative Protestant groups have lower average socioeconomic status, which contributes to higher divorce rates (Roberts, 1995).

Children   Although having children is generally associated with lower levels of marital satisfaction, the presence of children does not necessarily increase the divorce rate. The birth of the first child reduces the divorce rate almost to zero in the year following the birth (White, 1990), although over the long term the divorce rate goes up if the child is born within seven months of the wedding (Bramlett & Mosher, 2002). Couples with preschool children have considerably lower rates of marital dissolution than couples with no children (Fergusson, Horwood, & Lloyd, 1990; Waite, Haggstrom, & Kanouse, 1985).

Older children have the opposite effect. The presence of adolescent children in both first marriages and remarriages increases the possibility of divorce (Waite & Lillard, 1991; White & Booth, 1985). Having young children in the home would appear to postpone divorces, not prevent them (Rankin & Maneker, 1985). White and Booth (1985) referred to this as the "Braking Hypothesis."

Other Factors   A large number of other factors have been found to be associated with higher divorce rates:

- Couples who cohabit before marriage are more likely to divorce than those who do not (Amato, 2000; Bramlett & Mosher, 2002).
- Divorce rates are lowest in the northeast, led by Massachusetts, Connecticut, New York, and New Jersey. The highest rates are in the south and west, led by Nevada. The latter has a divorce rate considerably higher than the United States as a whole, largely because people go there with the specific purpose of getting a divorce (*Statistical Abstract,* 2004–2005: t.113).
- Urban couples have higher divorce rates than rural ones (Bramlett & Mosher, 2002).
- Lower divorce rates are found among couples whose friends and family approve of the marriage and share attitudes about marriage (Goode, 1956).

- Adults whose parents divorced, or who grew up with a never-married parent, are more likely to end their own marriage by divorce (McLanahan & Bumpass, 1988; Bramlett & Mosher, 2002). One explanation for this "intergenerational transmission" of divorce is that children of divorce marry earlier and are somewhat more likely to be struggling financially. It is also possible that children of divorce lacked good role models for marriage but did have role models for divorce. Whatever the reason, the impacts of divorce can continue for years, affecting even the lives of children not yet born at the time of the original divorce (Amato & Cheadle, 2005).

PERSONAL "WHYS"

Individuals are called upon to give accounts for their behaviors, especially when those behaviors are considered deviant (Lyman & Scott, 1970). The reasons tend to be given in terms intended to make the behavior more socially acceptable. Whether these are the "real" reasons for the actions is difficult to ascertain, but sociologists can report what individuals say about their behavior.

The grounds given by plaintiffs in divorce actions provide one source of information about the "whys" that have historically been given for divorce. In systems requiring fault, plaintiffs in each state had a short list of statutory grounds from which to choose.

In the period 1887–1906, the most common grounds offered when women filed were desertion (33.6%), cruelty (27.5%), and adultery (10.0%). The same three grounds were most popular for men but with a different distribution: desertion (49.4%), adultery (28.7%), and cruelty (10.5%) (Riley, 1991:124).

As the definition of cruelty expanded and became easier to demonstrate, it became the grounds of choice for most plaintiffs. In a typical jurisdiction in the period 1928–1944, 88% of women and 78% of men used "cruel and inhuman treatment" as the grounds for their divorces. Desertion, second most common at that time, was used by 8% of women and 19% of men (Riley, 1991:149).

While stated grounds provided "official whys" of divorce, individuals also have reasons they tell to friends, to themselves, to other family members, and to researchers. The "whys" might vary, depending on the audience to whom the individual is providing his or her account, and depending upon the questions asked.

A study conducted in the late 1980s found that "communication problems" were the number-one reported reason for divorce. Infidelity was second, followed by constant fighting and emotional abuse. "Falling out of love" was fifth (Patterson & Kim, 1991). More recently, Amato and Previti (2003) found that sexual infidelity was the most common "why," followed by "incompatibility," drinking or drug use, and "growing apart."

This list provides a reminder that accounts, or explanations about the reasons for divorce, come from a temporal and cultural context. In the year 1900, men were not expected to contribute significantly to housework. Although wives might have complained about lack of their husband's help in the home, it certainly would not have provided socially or legally acceptable grounds for divorce. Personality differences, communication problems, falling out of love, and growing apart are additional modern "whys" for marital problems and divorces that would not have been offered in earlier times.

Some accounts are more acceptable today than are others in reducing the stigma felt by divorced persons. Few blame the woman who has been the victim of severe physical abuse if she gets a divorce; in fact, she is likely to be stigmatized if she does not leave.

Reasons given for divorce vary somewhat from one society to the next. Although the divorce rate in China is small today compared to that of the United States, their large population means there are many divorces. As elsewhere, women file the majority (82%) of petitions (Ziaxiang, Xinlian, & Zhahua, 1987).

The most common general reason for divorce in China, cited by 21% of respondents in one study, was a hasty marriage. This category included marrying quickly for love at first sight and premarital pregnancy. An overconcern for materialism, noted by 15%, was the second leading "why." This included a preoccupation with money and pleasure, a reason constructed in the context of China's communist ideology (Ziaxiang, Xinlian, & Zhahua, 1987; in Beno-kraitis, 1993).

THE DIVORCE PROCESS AND OUTCOMES

The decision to divorce is not an easy one; it involves the end of a set of hopes and dreams, and often a sense of failure. Deciding just how bad a marriage has to get before a divorce is considered the appropriate remedy is a personal choice made in a community and society. How easy the divorce will be to get, what one's friends and family will think, and whether there is a socially and legally acceptable "why" are among the many factors a person or couple considers.

How life might be after the divorce is also a consideration, including the probability of remarriage or surviving as a single person and the effect on children and others (Amato, 2000; South, Trent, & Shen, 2001). Levinger (1965), following an exchange theory approach, argued that persons consider both their pushes and pulls in favor of divorce, balanced against the pushes and pulls in favor of remaining in the marriage. Sometimes a person will elect to remain in a poor marriage because the alternatives are thought to be even worse. The divorce decision, usually arrived at slowly, involves detaching from several role involvements.

At the beginning of a relationship, two persons, whose realities previously did not include each other, redefine themselves and construct a mutual identity (Berger & Kellner, 1964). If the relationship does not work out, each person must once again redefine himself or herself. Diane Vaughan (1988) referred to this process as "uncoupling." The end of a marriage is not only painful, it is a long, difficult, and complicated process.

THE STATIONS OF DIVORCE

Anthropologist Paul Bohannon (1970) conceptualized divorce as a process involving six "stations": emotional, legal, economic, coparental, and psychic. These are not to be seen as rigid

FIGURE 9.3.

Six Stations of Divorce

Source: Concept from Bohannan, Paul. 1970. "The Six Stations of Divorce." Pp. 29–55 in *Divorce and After,* edited by Paul Bohannan. New York: Doubleday.

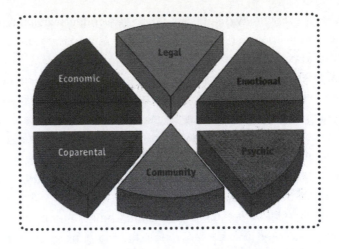

stages in a clearly defined series of events; not all stations apply to every case, nor is there an empirically established amount of time for each station. The two partners involved might not proceed at the same pace. Still, Bohannan provides a useful framework for looking at the divorce process (see Figure 9.3).

The Emotional Divorce   At least one marital partner typically withdraws emotionally from the marriage long before there is legal action. Love is gradually replaced by indifference or by more negative emotions like anger, rejection, depression, or unhappiness.

Ups and downs occur in nearly all marriages. It is difficult for partners to know for sure whether the current condition is a low point in an otherwise good relationship or part of a long-term downward trend. Some marriages continue for a lifetime after an emotional divorce if a legal divorce is not obtained.

The Legal Divorce   Although a legal divorce does occur at a specific time, after which the partners are free to remarry, the legal process can be a long and difficult one. States require a waiting period between the initial filing and final decree, and practical delays often slow the process even more. Negotiation over details of the settlement occurs, often with the involvement of attorneys. Under the no-fault system, divorces themselves are not contested, but property and custody settlements can be complicated, especially when the negotiations occur in the context of the emotional wounds associated with divorce. A couple may be separated, legally or informally, for a long period before the divorce is final.

The Economic Divorce   This station of divorce involves resolving matters such as division of property and debt, alimony, and child support. While there is an agreement at the time of the legal divorce, many couples continue to negotiate long after the divorce is final. This is especially true for child support; changing circumstances or a failure to abide by the divorce decree can bring matters of the economic divorce back into court.

The economic divorce affects men and women differently, with women generally getting the worst of the deal. Married men and women with complementary role divisions of labor share the benefits and costs of a woman who devotes time to her family rather than to her career. Because she shares her husband's income, insurance, and other marketplace benefits, the wife is shielded from the disadvantages of not fully participating in the paid labor force. Once she is divorced, however, those disadvantages are fully felt (Rhode & Minow, 1990).

Stroup and Pollock (1994) concluded that, among White divorcees, women experienced an average income loss of 22% while men's income dropped an average of 10%. Peterson (1996) used Weitzman's (1996) raw data to estimate a 27% decline in women's standard of living and a 10% increase in men's standard of living following divorce. More extreme differences were found by Bianchi et al. (1999). By their estimate, custodial mothers experienced a 36% decline in standard of living, while noncustodial fathers had a 28% increase. Whatever the exact figure, divorce is a major cause of poverty among women and their custodial children (Amato, 2000). The end of a cohabiting relationship has similar effects (Avellar & Smock, 2005).

The Coparental Divorce For couples with children, the divorce changes the interaction between the former spouses. The inability to clearly define the former partner as a coparent but not a spouse is a major source of coparental conflict after divorce (Madden-Derdich et al., 1999). At the same time, continued attachment between the former partners may be a natural outcome of shared parenting (Madden-Derdich & Arditti, 1999).

New boundaries of intimacy and power must be established between the former spouses and among former spouses and their children (Emery & Dillon, 1994.) Negotiation occurs directly between the adults, and, if children are in contact with both, they often become agents of negotiation for their parents. The custodial mother has a powerful influence on how the children perceive the father and on the father's relationship with the children. He has less influence on the child's relationship with the mother (Nielsen, 1999).

Although custody issues are technically resolved by the final divorce decree, considerable negotiation goes into that decision. Further, both formal and informal changes in children-related arrangements often continue long after the legal divorce is granted (Ganong, Coleman, & Mistrina, 1995). Physical mobility, remarriage, and the preferences of children themselves are among the variables that change coparental arrangements.

Couples who divorce later in life or after long marriages often find that their adult children provide social and emotional support (Gander, 1991). Divorced mothers are more likely to receive such support than are divorced fathers (Wright & Maxwell, 1991).

The Community Divorce When two people marry, they undergo a rite of passage that informs the community that their roles have changed and that they are now to be treated as husband and wife. They develop mutual friends and community ties.

When they divorce, no formal rite of passage clearly defines their new roles with respect to the community. The more the couple interacted as a dyad in the community, the more difficult is the process of the community divorce. Couples who have been active together in a religious organization must redefine their religious roles. Recreation, too, is often affected.

Dyadic friends of the divorcing couple often feel as though they have to "choose sides" or they wish not to become involved at all (Weiss, 1975). One study found that more than three fourths of divorced women reported losing friends as a result of the divorce (Arendell, 1986); presumably, divorced men lose friends also.

As part of the community in which a couple is located, kin networks are affected. Generally, each former partner retains ties to the kin network of his or her family of orientation; this affects the intergenerational relationships. Divorced women with custody of minor children have more contact with their own parents than do married women with children, and they get more help from their parents. Divorced men, on the other hand, get less help, and their children see the paternal grandparents less often (Spitze et al., 1994).

The Psychic Divorce   The psychic divorce, which can be a lifetime effort for some persons, involves complete psychological recovery from the divorce and the development of a self completely apart from the previous mutual script. For many, this involves a grieving process similar to that felt after the death of a spouse.

Some counselors say that the psychic process is complete only when the individual forgives both the former mate and himself or herself and when there is no longer anger or bitterness (Masheter, 1991). Although counselors sometimes say that persons cannot remarry successfully until the psychic divorce is complete, this expectation may be too high for many persons, and the suggestion lacks empirical support.

As Bohannon's six-station conceptualization of divorce implies, divorce is typically a long, difficult process. Extreme moods, from depression to euphoria, are common. Those who see themselves as the ones who initiated the divorce fare better emotionally than do those who believe the marriage should not be ended (Weiss, 1975). Contrary to their expectations, Sheets and Braver (1996) found that women were more satisfied with the divorce process than were men. Women reported greater satisfaction with custody and visitation outcomes, as well as all economic arrangements except child support. Women were more likely to believe the divorce process was fair.

OUTCOMES OF DIVORCE

Several studies have found that, compared with married individuals, divorced men and women have lower levels of psychological well-being. This includes lower happiness, more symptoms of psychological distress, and poorer self-concepts (Amato, 2000; Demo & Acock, 1996; Simon & Marcussen, 1999). Divorced adults have more health problems and higher death rates (Aldous & Ganey, 1999; Waite & Gallagher, 2000). Divorced individuals report more social isolation, less satisfying sex lives, and more negative life events than their married counterparts (Joung et al., 1997; Laumann et al., 1994; Lorenz et al., 1997; Mastekaasa, 1997).

There is some question whether the divorce causes the negative outcomes or whether people with negative outcomes are more likely to be divorced. Longitudinal studies do find that unhappiness and stress do increase over time for people who get divorced. However, the decreases in well-being actually begin before the divorce occurs (Booth & Amato, 1991; Mastekaasa, 1997).

These studies would support the idea that divorce itself, and the immediately preceding period of time, cause much of the distress.

The "selection effect" suggests that people with various indicators of poor well-being are more likely to get divorced. This has been found true for problems with alcohol (Mastekaasa, 1997). Depression in women, as much as ten years earlier, increases the probability of divorce (Davies et al., 1997; Hope et al., 1999). The safest conclusion is that both explanations are true; divorce does generate negative well-being, but there is some selection effect also (Amato, 2000).

In spite of the generally negative findings, some individuals are better off after divorce. As with most crises, divorce can also provide opportunities. Divorce allows persons to end a poor and even destructive marriage (Lund, 1990). Higher levels of autonomy and personal growth characterize divorced compared to married individuals (Amato, 2000; Marks, 1996).

Recently divorced women speak of personal growth in management of daily life, in social relationships, and in developing an individual identity (Reissman, 1991). Many divorced women experience improvements in their careers and report higher levels of life happiness than before the divorce (Acock & Demo, 1994). Most studies of positive outcomes of divorce focus on women. If more such studies were done on both men and women, more positive outcomes would probably be found (Amato, 2000).

Several factors moderate the impact of divorce for adults. Individuals fare better if they have higher educational levels, more money, better job security, and a large support network of family and friends (Amato, 2000; Booth & Amato, 1991; Demo & Acock, 1996). Getting support from a new intimate partner or spouse appears to be especially beneficial (Funder et al., 1993; Demo & Acock, 1996). The individual who initiates the divorce has better postdivorce adjustment (Kitson, 1992). Finally, individuals who report a large number of problems during the marriage have better postdivorce adjustment than those who saw few marital problems (Booth & Amato, 1991).

CHILDREN OF DIVORCE

From the children's perspective, it might be more correct to say that their parents' divorce significantly reorganized their family than that the divorce destroyed it (Ahrons, 2004). That reorganization, however, can have several consequences, in both the short and long term.

DIVORCE-RELATED STRESSORS

Emory's (1999) review of studies done on the impact of divorce on children reached five conclusions. First, divorce creates a number of stressors on families and children. Relationship with parents change, and there is exposure to conflict of several kinds. Children of divorce are more likely than other children to change residences, and the move is usually to a poorer neighborhood (South et al., 1998). Moving to a new home and other factors often results in changes in friendship patterns. Financial insecurity is often one of the stressors. As Figure 9.4 demonstrates, while children with single divorced parents are less likely to be in poverty than children in never-married homes, they are much more likely to be poor than

FIGURE 9.4.

Percent of Children
in Poverty, by Race/
Ethnicity and Family
Status

Source: U.S. Census Bureau,
*Current Population Survey,
2008.* http://www.pubdb3.
census.gov/macro/032008/
pov/new03_100.htm.

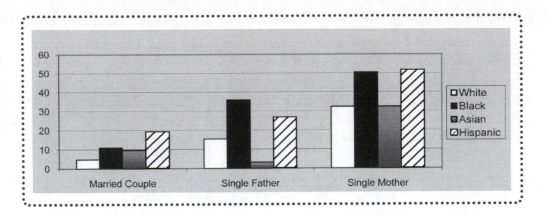

children in two-parent homes. This holds true with all racial/ethnic groups. Again, causality is an issue in the data; poor people are more likely to divorce, so the divorce does not cause all the poverty. There is no doubt, though, that the financial standing of children drops when their parents divorce.

As McCubbin's (1979) ABC-X model reminds us, existence of stressors does not necessarily lead to a problem. The kinds of stressors precipitated by divorce, however, are quite likely to lead to "pileup" of stressors that can lead to a crisis.

CHILDREN AT RISK

Emery's (1999) second point about the impact of divorce on children is that the stressors associated with divorce can lead to adjustment problems of various kinds. Children are at risk for social, psychological, educational, and vocational problems.

Judith Wallerstein and Joan Kelly began a longitudinal study of divorce in 1971. They published results of 5-year and 10-year followup studies on children of divorce (Wallerstein & Kelly, 1976, 1980; Kelley & Wallerstein, 1976; Wallerstein & Blakeslee, 1989.)

Wallerstein found that children reacted to the news of divorce with shock, shame, anger, disbelief, and grief. Rather than blame themselves for the divorce, as popular literature often reports, children tended to blame one parent or the other. Five years later, nearly 40% of the children remained moderately or severely depressed; the majority still hoped that their parents would get back together. Even 10 years later, the children of divorce continued to have difficulties forming intimate relationships.

The children in the study have now been interviewed 25 years after their parents' divorce (Wallerstein & Lewis, 1998). Effects of the divorce were still apparent. The subjects' childhood memories were of abandonment, terror, and loneliness. Adolescence was, for many, characterized by early sexual activity and drug and alcohol use. The subjects, now in their late 20s and early30s, continue to have some fears of intimacy.

Wallerstein's qualitative studies were limited by a small sample that was selected from a wealthy area and might have exaggerated the long-term impact on children (Amato, 2003). The respondents had been referred to a mental health clinic, and many of the children's parents suffered from mental health ailments; these children might have had more problems than other children even if they had been from intact homes. The conclusion that children of divorce can experience long-term negative effects, however, is borne out by other research.

Baker, Barthelemy, and Kurdek (1993) found that fifth- and sixth-grade children of divorce were less likely to be popular with their peers and were more at risk for long-term maladjustment. Canadian research found that children who lived through a parental divorce had lower levels of self-efficiency, self-esteem, and social support and had less effective coping styles (Kurtz, 1994).

Younger children of divorce have more problems in school than children in intact homes. Most of the problems are related to the poverty often associated with single motherhood (Duncan, Brooks-Gunn, & Klebanov, 1994). Even when the student's race, socioeconomic status, sex, age, and ability are held constant, however, adolescents from divorced homes are 1.7 times more likely to drop out of school (McNeal, 1995).

Among adolescent boys, higher rates of delinquency and incarceration were found for those who had divorced parents (Matlock et al., 1994). A study in Great Britain found that adolescent children of divorce were more likely to impregnate or conceive children out of wedlock than were their peers from intact homes (Russell, 1994). A very high correlation exists between parental divorce and incidence of depression among daughters (Rodgers, 1994).

A research project in New Zealand followed 935 children over 15 years. Children of divorce were found to have more frequent illegal drug usage, more and earlier premarital sexual activity, and more disruptive behaviors. Most, but not all, of the correlation was explained by the socioeconomic status of the parents (Fergusson, Horwood, & Lynsky, 1994). Higher divorce rates also appear to be correlated with higher suicide rates (Krull & Trovato, 1994; Lester & Abe, 1993; McCall & Land, 1994).

The negative effects of divorce appear to extend into adulthood. Adults who grew up in divorced, single-parent families report less solidarity with their parents, see them less often, and perceive less support from their parents. Although these findings apply more strongly to noncustodial parents, they apply to custodial parents also (White, 1994). Relationships with parents suffer even if the divorce occurs after the young persons have left the home (Aquilino, 1994).

RESILIENCE

Emery's (1999) third conclusion is that, in spite of the stressors and risks, most children of divorce are **resilient.** Most "bounce back" to function as well on commonly used measures of adjustment as do those from married-couple households.

Resilient: Marked by an ability to recover quickly from misfortune.

This seems to contradict the research about risks, but it actually does not. Those studies must be interpreted with some care. Although differences between children of divorce and those in intact families are consistently found, the differences are generally relatively small and can easily be exaggerated, sometimes for political purposes by persons who endorse the "family decline" position (Coltrane & Adams, 2003). On the other hand, some in the "glad it changed" category may seek to minimize the impact of divorce on children. The minority of children who do have significant negative reactions can bring down the average scores for the whole group of children of divorce.

Also, even a doubling of risk may only affect a small minority of the group. McLanahan and Sandefur (1994) found that teen pregnancy and dropping out of school were about twice as common in children of divorce as in children of married-couple families. Although this is a significant difference between the two categories of children, most in each group neither drop out nor get pregnant.

In addition, most of the studies find correlations, but that does not prove causal relationships between parents' divorce and negative child outcomes. Much of what appears to be the result of divorce itself might be the result of the conflict that occurs before the divorce. Many of the problems were present in some of the children before the divorce occurred (Emery, 1999). Amato and Booth (1996) found that marital quality is related to parent-child relationships as much as 12 years before the parental divorce occurs. Children who live with significant amounts of marital conflict for long periods of time would likely be troubled even if their parents did not separate. Some problems might be the result of a self-fulfilling prophesy resulting from attitudes held by teachers, counselors, neighbors, and others about the impact of divorce (Smith, 1990; Amato & Keith, 1991; Dawson, 1991).

DISTRESS WITHOUT DISORDERS

Emery's (1999) fourth point confirms Wallerstein's finding of long-lasting effects. Even when there is little overall difference between children of divorce and others in terms of particular measured disorders, there is, nonetheless, some distress and even pain associated with a parental breakup. Not all people who have distress show that by dropping out of school, using drugs, or engaging in risky sexual behavior. Although resilient, children of divorce still have to deal with issues that children in married-couple households do not.

Laumann-Billings and Emery (1999) found that half of a divorced group of college students worried about events, such as graduation, where both parents would be in attendance. Only 10% of students from married parents had such concerns. Twenty-nine percent of the divorce group wondered whether their fathers really loved them; 10% of the children of married couples were concerned about that. Forty-six percent from the divorce group, compared with 19% from married families, wished they could have spent more time with their fathers. While these matters might not indicate serious problems in the children of divorce, Emery (1999) concluded, they are matters that we might prefer our children would not have to worry about.

DIVERSE OUTCOMES IN CHILDREN OF DIVORCE

Emery's (1999) final conclusion was that child outcomes following divorce depend on a variety of circumstances. Perhaps most important is the relationship between the child and the residential parent. Whether the mother or father is the residential parent makes little difference in the child's adjustment (Guttmann & Lazar, 1998).

Compared to married parents, divorced custodial parents "have fewer rules, dispense harsher disciplining, provide less supervision, and engage in more conflict with their children" (Amato, 2000:1279). Children have poorer adjustment if their divorced custodial parent is depressed. Good parenting skills and parental adjustment of the custodial parent predict better outcomes for the children.

It is helpful if the primary parent gets along well with the child, provides proper supervision, and is authoritative rather than authoritarian or permissive. As with other families, resilience is most likely when there is parental competence, shared values, good communication, and parental receptiveness toward the child (Daly, 1999; Hauser et al., 1989; McCubbin et al., 1999; Pett et al., 1999). Evidence suggests that the noncustodial parent's level of contact and involvement with their children, and parenting cooperation between the former spouses, reduces risk for children (Bronstein, et al., 1994).

Children's adjustment is also related to the amount of parental conflict, both before and after the divorce (Vandervalk et al., 2004). Some marriages are high in conflict before the divorce occurs, while others appear to have very little conflict before the breakup. Children subject to high levels of predivorce conflict handle the divorce relatively well. They actually did better as adults than did children whose high-conflict

Noncustodial parents' contact and involvement with their children, and parenting cooperation between the former spouses, reduces risk for children.

parents remained together. Children whose parents had low-conflict marriages before divorce, by contrast, suffered a great deal more. The divorce came as unexpected and unwelcome. It affected their ability to trust and to form relationships of their own well into adulthood. In fact, children whose low-conflict parents divorced had higher divorce rates in their own adult marriages (Amato & Booth, 1996; Booth, 1999; Booth & Amato, 2001).

Conflict during and after the divorce has the opposite effect. Children whose parents have acrimonious conflict over such issues as child custody, child support, and visitation, have poorer parent-child relationships. Such children are more likely to have emotional and behavioral problems (Johnston, 1994). The impact is particularly destructive to the child if the conflict includes domestic violence or child maltreatment (Ayoub, Deutsch, & Maraganore, 1999).

Children's adjustment is also related to economic standing. When income differences are taken into account, much of the disadvantage of children of divorce statistically goes away. Parenting quality, however, suffers in lower-income families, and the children consequently suffer (Emery, 1999). Furthermore, both divorced parents and stepparents are less likely than never-divorced parents to believe that older parents have a responsibility to provide significant economic assistance to children as they make the transition to adulthood (Aquilino, 2005).

The child's relationship with the noncustodial parent might also affect his or her adjustment. Many studies find that frequency of visitation and perceived closeness with the noncustodial parent do not matter much in the child's long-term resilience. After a survey of all available data, however, Emery (1999) concluded that children will adjust better if they have a good relationship with both parents. After a review of 63 studies, Amato and Gilbreth (1999) concluded that authoritative parenting on the part of noncustodial fathers improves their children's academic achievements and reduces other difficulties.

Not all adjustment-related influences come directly from parents. Children who use active coping skills do better than those who withdraw or avoid dealing with problems (Sandler, 1994). Getting social support from their peers helps children cope with parental divorce (Samera & Stolberg, 1993). At least some school-based support programs and other therapeutic interventions can benefit children of divorce (Emery et al., 1999). Finally, children who blame themselves for their parents' divorce are more poorly adjusted (Bussell, 1995).

REMARRIAGE AND STEPFAMILIES

Most men and women reenter the singles scene after divorce, although the idea of "dating" is awkward for those who have been married for some time. Many eventually do so to relieve loneliness, reassure their self-worth, enjoy themselves, and meet intimate needs (Weiss, 1975). Formerly married persons who date or cohabit have better adjustments than those who do not (Tschann, Johnston, & Wallerstein, 1989), but doing so quickly after divorce can disturb the relationship with his or her children (Rodgers & Conrad, 1986). Those who cohabited before their first marriage are more likely to engage in postmarital cohabitation, although cohabiting seems to make remarriages less stable (Wu, 1995).

REMARRIAGE AND COHABITATION AFTER DIVORCE

The United States and Western Europe have always had high rates of remarriage. In earlier times, the remarriages followed death of a spouse; in the postindustrial era, the remarriages have more typically followed divorce (Cherlin, 1992; Furstenberg, 1990). Remarriage rates have gone down somewhat since 1970, partly because of the increased incidence of postmarital cohabitation, but still about 70% of divorced men and 60% of divorced women eventually remarry. About half of remarriages involve creating a stepfamily with minor children (Wineberg & McCarthy, 1998).

National data reveal that, in 1995, only 53.7% of marriages were first marriages for both partners. Both partners had been divorced in 19.7% of marriages, while 21.9% were remarriages for one of the partners. Remarriages involving widows or widowers are only a small percentage of the total (see Table 9.2).

Within five years of divorce, 53% of women have cohabited; after ten years, 70% have done so. Most also remarry; 54% remarry within five years, and 75% do so within ten years (Bramlett & Mosher, 2002).

A variety of factors, including gender, influence the probability of remarriage. Men are more likely to remarry or cohabit, and do so more quickly, than women (Wu & Schimmele, 2005). Longer life expectancy and age hypergamy work against women in the marriage market. It might also be true that fewer women want to remarry.

The younger a woman is at divorce, the more likely she is to remarry, but age is not a factor in probability of remarriage for men (Ahlburg & De Vita, 1992; Bumpass, Sweet, & Martin, 1990). However, a divorced person of any age is more likely to marry than is a person the same gender and age who has never married (Goode, 1993).

Studies about the impact of having children on the likelihood of remarriage are mixed (Bump-ass, Sweet, & Martin, 1990). Bramlett and Mosher (2002) found that, one year after divorce, slightly more women with two or more children had remarried (18%) than had women without children; after ten years, however, 77% of childless women had remarried, compared with 70% of those with two or more children. Nonresident fathers who are involved with their children are more likely to remarry than are other men (Stewart, Manning, & Smock, 2003).

Race and ethnicity make a considerable difference in remarriage rates. While 58% of White women have remarried after five years, 44% of Hispanics and only 32% of Blacks have done so. Even ten years after divorce, only 49% of Black women have remarried, compared with 68% of Hispanics and 79% of Whites (Bramlett & Mosher, 2002).

The influence of education on remarriage rates differs by gender. For women, remarriage rates rise with educational levels until college graduation, but then go down with further education.(Bramlett & Mosher, 2002). For men, the higher the educational level, the higher the remarriage rates (Bumpass, Sweet, & Martin, 1990).

The mate-selection process is different the second time around. For one thing, it appears to be quicker. Divorced persons are sexually intimate sooner in a relationship than never-married persons. They also spend less time dating and have shorter engagements before marriage than never-married singles (O'Flaherty & Eels, 1988).

TABLE 9.2. PERCENT DISTRIBUTION OF MARRIAGES BY PREVIOUS MARITAL STATUS

Wife's Previous Status	Husband's Previous Status		
	Never Married	Divorced	Widowed
Never Married	53.7	10.9	0.3
Divorced	11.0	19.7	1.3
Widowed	0.5	1.4	1.2

Source: Centers for Disease Control and Prevention. 1995. Monthly Vital Statistics Report 43(12). Table 7.

Remarriages are likely to be somewhat less homogamous than first marriages. The age difference for remarriages is about twice that for first marriages, and the age gap increases with the age of the groom. Educational differences are also greater in remarriages (U.S. National Center for Health Statistics, 1990), and religious differences are probably greater as well (Lamanna & Riedmann, 1994).

Interviews revealed that remarried couples see marriage differently than those in their first marriages. They have different perceptions of love and believe that they are more likely to leave a bad marriage than couples in their first marriage (Furstenberg & Spanier, 1984).

Remarried couples also report having a more flexible household division of labor and more shared decision making (Furstenberg, 1980). Although financial problems are common, remarried partners are less likely to think of money as "ours," and more as "his" and "hers," than is the case in first marriages (Fish-man, 1983).

Several studies have compared the quality of remarriages with that of first marriages (Coleman, Ganong, & Fine, 2000). In general, such studies find little or no difference in terms of marital happiness or satisfaction (White & Booth, 1985; Vemer et al., 1989; Glenn, 1990, 1991). MacDonald and DeMaris (1995) found, contrary to expectation, that there was less marital conflict in remarriages; the least conflict was found in the double remarriages. Other studies, however, find lower relationship quality in remarriages (Brown & Booth, 1996).

Remarried spouses are more likely to openly express criticisms, anger, and irritation than first-married couples (Bray & Kelly, 1998), and they report somewhat higher levels of tension and disagreement (Hobart, 1991). The most common source of disagreement is matters dealing with children (Pasley et al., 1993; Clingempeel et al., 1994).

While some studies find a slight negative effect on marital satisfaction from the presence of children (White & Booth, 1985), others find a slight positive effect (Vemer et al., 1989). Kurdek (1999) concluded that children born to first marriages lowered the marital quality more than did having stepchildren in remarriages. MacDonald and DeMaris (1995) found that, in the early years of remarriages with stepchildren, there was less marital conflict than in families with biological children only. Over time, however, the couples with stepfamilies began to have more conflict.

All things considered, remarriages appear able to achieve about the same level of marital satisfaction as first marriages (Coleman & Ganong, 1990). In stepfamilies, both men and women adjust better if they bring children of their own into the new houshold; women adjust better when the only children in the household are hers (Coberly, 1996).

Although subsequent marriages are about as happy as first ones, they are not as stable. Overall, they are about 10% more likely to end in divorce than are first marriages (Furstenberg, 1987; Martin and Bumpass, 1989), and those that end do so more quickly. The same factors that predict the end of first marriages (e.g., age, race and ethnicity, religion, educational level) are at work in second marriages (Bramlett & Mosher, 2002).

It seems inconsistent that remarriages are as happy as first ones while being less stable. Part of the reason for this apparent discrepancy is that those who have divorced once will recognize a bad marriage more quickly than first marrieds and consider it more acceptable to terminate the marriage by divorce (White & Booth, 1985; Booth & Edwards, 1992).

Lynn White and Alan Booth (1985) addressed the apparent inconsistency between happiness and stability in remarriages. They noted that remarriage containing stepchildren are more likely to end in divorce than those that do not. Some couples who are generally satisfied with their marriage and their partner are dissatisfied with the entire family group that includes the stepchildren. They might have high marital satisfaction but low family satisfaction, a situation that sometimes leads to divorce.

White and Booth (1985) found that when only one partner was in a remarriage, divorce rates were about the same as for first marriages. Marriages that were remarriages for both partners were about twice as likely to break up as first marriages. To put this in perspective, Wilson and Clarke (1992) found that couples who entered double remarriages between ages 25 and 44 still had lower divorce rates than those who entered first marriages as teenagers.

The Queen and the Magic Mirror.

The image of stepparents is often negative. We all remember the "wicked stepmother" in fairy tales.

STEPFAMILIES

Andrew Cherlin (1978) referred to remarriage as an "incomplete institution." Role conflict is more common in stepfamilies. Conflict over parenting roles is especially common in stepfamilies compared to first marriage families

(Grizzle, 1999). The media, the culture, and the society reinforce a view of family life that is based on the intact nuclear family (Coleman & Ganong, 1997). The image of stepparents is often negative, as evidenced by the "wicked stepmother" often found in fairy tales. Even in contemporary films, stepfamilies tend to be depicted in negative ways (Leon & Angst, 2005).

Stepfamilies differ from intact families in several ways. Stepfamilies lack a shared family history, have more stress, are less cohesive, and have more loyalty conflicts (Visher & Visher, 1988). Further, stepfamily relationships can become extremely complicated, as Figure 9.5 illustrates.

Section (a) of Figure 9.5 depicts an intact nuclear family, living in one household. Section (b) symbolizes the effect of a divorce in which the children live with their mother in their primary household. They visit their father regularly in what could be called a secondary household. This results in a binuclear family. Both adults (A1 and A2) are heads of a household that, at least part of the time, includes the two children (C1 and C2).

In section (c), matters get considerably more complicated. The children's mother and father each remarry. Each new spouse is also a divorced parent. Children C1 and C2 remain part of the secondary household of their father, but that household now serves as the primary household of a new stepmother (A3), stepbrother (C3), and stepsister (C4). In addition, the primary household for C1 and C2 is now the secondary household of their stepfather's children, C5 and C6, who regularly visit their own father.

Section (d) of Figure 9.5 represents a still more complicated situation. Both of C1 and C2's birth parents become birth parents with their new spouses. This adds half brother (C7) and half sister (C8) to their secondary household. It also adds C9 and C10 to their primary household. Rather than existing in discrete household units, these stepfamilies have formed **remarriage chains** that connect them across households (Cherlin, 1996).

The roles of all the individuals in section (d) are not clear, nor is it clear exactly how many families are represented, nor what kinship term everyone should call everyone else. Imagine how complicated the diagram would be if the families of origin of each of the adults were included, especially if these adults had also been children of divorce. The lack of institutional support for stepfamilies is reflected in the absence of role names. It is more difficult to know how to behave toward someone when the role relationship is unclear (Beer, 1992).

Boundary ambiguity: Uncertainty about who is considered part of a particular family system, or what roles the members should play.

Figure 9.5 seems confusing; that is the point. Many real-life stepfamilies are confusing. Systems theorists would point out that stepfamilies have more potential for subsystem conflict. In addition, stepfamilies are often characterized by **boundary ambiguity,** which leaves family membership and interaction guidelines unclear. Unlike intact nuclear families, stepfamilies have both pre-existing subsystems, consisting of adults and children, and subsystems that cross the boundaries of the new stepfamily.

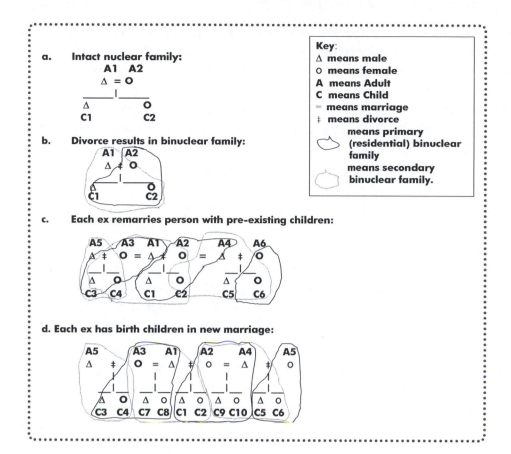

FIGURE 9.5.

Complexity of
Stepfamilies and
Remarriage Chains

Such things as flight plans and dinnertime rituals must be negotiated. So must financial matters. Resource distribution is complicated by the obligations established in the entire remarriage chain. A stepfamily might have child-support payments coming in through the mother and going out through the stepfather, in addition to two or more paychecks and child allowances and decisions about who pays what.

Stepfathers typically assume at least some financial responsibility for the new household without reducing the amount of child support due to his biological children. The more children there are in the new household, especially if they are new biological children, the less frequent in-person contact a father has with his nonresident children (Manning & Smock, 1999).

Even though they have suffered though a divorce, a biological parent and his or her child have established a script that defines their roles and prescribes certain behavioral boundaries. Introduction into the household of another adult, who might have his or her own set of boundaries in mind, requires considerable boundary and role negotiation. Stepparents and biological parents generally think that the stepparent should assume an active parental role. Stepchildren, by contrast, think the stepparent should be less like a parent and more like a friend (Fine et al., 1998). This is reflected in the practice of calling the stepparent by his or her first name, as equals in a relationship typically do, rather than using a title that signifies a dominant-subordinate relationship.

The law is not particularly helpful in establishing stepfamily boundaries nor in defining the role of stepparents (Hans, 2002). For the most part, the law ignores the stepparent-stepchild relationship. Often, the stepparent has no legal right to the child's school records or to be involved in such matters as making legal medical decisions for the child (Malia, 2005). Even criminal incest laws often do not apply to the stepparent-stepchild relationship, although child-abuse laws generally do apply because the stepparent is in a position of authority over the child (Chambers, 1990).

There is a lack of research on the well-being of stepfathers. Mothers in stepfamilies, however, fare almost as well as mothers in first marriages. Never-married mothers and those who have divorced but not remarried are least happy and well off (Demo & Acock, 1996).

Even if they have a long-term relationship with a stepchild, stepparents generally have no parental rights in the event that they divorce the child's biological parent. In most states, the stepparents have no more legal standing to get custody, or even visitation, than would a stranger. There are also no grounds to expect them to pay child support (Chambers, 1990).

Research on behavioral problems and adjustment of stepchildren gets mixed results. Overall, children in intact homes have the fewest behavior problems and the best life adjustment, while those in divorced-single homes have more problems and poorer adjustment. Children in remarried families are often found to be more like divorced children with single parents (Amato, 2000). When differences are found, children in stepfamilies generally are between the other two groups in behavior problems and adjustment (Pasley, Ihinger-Tallman, & Lofquist, 1994).

Research has attempted to understand how children, especially adolescents, are parented in stepfamilies. Studies consistently find that stepparents are less active in both support (warmth, acceptance, and nurturance) and control (supervision and discipline) than are biological parents (Amato, 1987; Fine, Voydanoff, & Donnelly, 1993; Kurdek & Fine, 1993).

Adolescent adjustment is somewhat lower when stepparents punish more (Fine, Donnelly, & Voydanoff, 1991) and somewhat higher when stepparents are perceived by stepchildren to exhibit warmth (Fine & Kurdek, 1992). In stepfather families, better adolescent adjustment is found when mothers are the primary disciplinarians and the stepfathers play only a small part in discipline (Bray, 1988). Consistency in the scripted boundaries of the biological unit apparently eases adjustment for the child.

As is true in intact families, better child adjustment is generally found with parents using authoritative than with authoritarian parenting styles. Crosbie-Burnett and Giles-Sims (1994) found better adolescent adjustment when the stepparent had a parenting style high in supportive behaviors but low in control behaviors.

SUMMARY AND CONCLUSION

With the exception of those societies with stable high-divorce systems, industrialization had the nearly universal effect of increasing the divorce rate. This was true for the United States, where the divorce rate was nearly always higher than in most of Europe.

Over time, divorce in the United States became both more common and easier to get. Divorce in the postindustrial era is usually conducted under no-fault provisions, which replaced the traditional adversarial system. The United Stated today could be called a "postdivorce society," which affects family bonds, inequality, and structural and cultural factors.

A host of variables is associated with divorce rates, including geographical mobility, individualism, race, age at marriage, cohabitation, educational level, and income level. Most persons see the cause of their own divorce, however, in more personal terms that are constructed in terms compatible with social acceptability.

Divorce is a long process with several stages of detachment from the previous role relationships: legal, emotional, legal, economic, coparental, community, and psychic. Adults suffer from divorce, but so do children. Most children of divorce adjust, but divorce is associated with risks such as school problems, delinquency problems, and relationship problems. Most children are resilient, but they still suffer some distress. Several factors, such as economic hardship, determine how well the parents deal with divorce, and support from extrafamilial sources influence children's adjustment.

Almost half of marriages are now remarriages for one or both partners, and many involve children. In spite of the difficulties, remarriages are about as happy as first marriages, but they are more likely to end in divorce. Presence of stepchildren, especially adolescents, is one contributor to remarriage instability. Stepfamilies are different from intact nuclear families

---

FAMILES IN THE NEWS   *CANADIAN COUPLE MARRIED BUT CAN'T DIVORCE*

Two Toronto women got married a week after Ontario's court legalized same-sex marriage. Although they were together for almost ten years prior to their marriage, they separated five days later. Now they want to get divorced—but can't.

Same-sex marriage has been legalized in Ontario, Quebec, British Columbia, and the Yukon. But the national Canadian Divorce Act has not been changed to allow same-sex couples to legally divorce.

The 3,000 same-sex couples who wed last year are, at least temporarily, unable to divorce. Changes in the divorce law are expected soon. Some suggested that the couple's rapid request for divorce was done primarily to test the divorce law. But Martha McCarthy, a lawyer for one of the women, said that, just like any other couple, they parted over differences.

The names of the unhappily wed women have not been released. One shielded her identity to avoid the "stigma" of being associated with Canada's first same-sex divorce case.

Source: Summarized from Colin Campbell. "Gay Pair Seeks Canada's First Same-Sex Divorce." *New York Times,* July 22, 2004. *http://nytimes.com*

in several ways, including their complexity. Some ways of constructing stepparent/stepchild relationships are more effective than are others.

In conclusion, divorce rates in the United States have declined slightly since 1980. Still, millions of adults and children are directly affected every year. The divorce rate is a response to a number of social variables, but the rate itself affects schools, the workforce, and other social factors. In some respects, the United States has become a high-divorce rate society but is attempting to deal with the issue using low-rate solutions.

Rethinking in Context Should the government take steps to try to lower the divorce rate? If so, what should those steps be? What might be the consequences of getting rid of no-fault divorce? Should couples have to get counseling before divorcing? Should joint custody be considered? At what age should children's preferences be honored in making custody decisions? What could schools do to ease the adjustment of children in stepfamilies?

INTERNET SITES

Several scholarly articles on children of divorce, from a variety of perspectives
http://www.futureofchildren.org/cad
The Children of Separation and Divorce Center
http://www.divorceabc.com
Links to several divorce sites
http://www.divorceinfo.com
The Stepfamily Network
http://stepfamily.net
A feminist view of divorce
http://www.backlash.com/book/divorce.html
Alliance for Non-Custodial Parents Rights
http://www.ancpr.org/sitemap.htm
Men's perspective on divorce and custody issues
http://www.vix.com/men/single-dad.html
Advocates for divorce reform
http://www.divorcereform.org

QUESTIONS FOR REVIEW, REFLECTION, AND DISCUSSION

1. According to William J. Goode, did divorce increase or decrease as a result of industrialization? Why?
2. When did the first "no fault" divorce law become effective? In what state did this occur?
3. What is the difference between the crude divorce rate and the refined divorce rate?
4. What is the association between age at marriage and divorce?
5. What's the difference between emotional divorce, legal divorce, and economic divorce?
6. How is divorce viewed in your family, in your culture, and in your religion?

ADDITIONAL READINGS

Amato, P. R. (2005). The impact of family formation change on the cognitive, social, and emotional well-being of the next generation. *The Future of Children, 15,* 75–96.

Bastaits, K., Ponnet, K., & Mortelmans, D. (2014). Do divorced fathers matter? The impact of parenting styles of divorced fathers on the well-being of the child. *Journal of Divorce and Remarriage, 55,* 1–27.

Brown, S. L. (2006). Family structure transitions and adolescent well-being. *Demography, 43,* 447–461.

Hetherington, E. M. (2006). The influence of conflict, marital problem solving and parenting on children's adjustment in nondivorced, divorced and remarried families. In A. Clarke-Stewart & J. Dunn (Eds.), *Families count. Effects on child and adolescent development* (pp. 203–237). Cambridge, NY: Cambridge University Press.

Kanewischer, E. J. W., & Harris, S. M. (2015). Deciding not to un-do the 'I do': Therapy experiences of women who consider divorce but decide to remain married, *Journal of Marital and Family Therapy,* 41(3), 367–380.

UNIT 5

FAMILY
VIOLENCE

KEY TERMS

Physical Child Abuse

Physical Discipline

Permissive Parenting

Authoritative Parenting

Authoritarian Parenting

10

PARENT-CHILD AGGRESSION

Association with Child Abuse Potential and Parenting Styles

By Christina M. Rodriguez

Christina Rodriguez, "Parent-child Aggression: Association with Child Abuse Potential and Parenting Styles," Violence and Victims, vol. 25, no. 6, pp. 728-741. Copyright © 2010 by Springer Publishing Company. Reprinted with permission. Provided by ProQuest LLC. All rights reserved.

In 2006, over 900,000 children were substantiated victims of child abuse and neglect in the United States, and physical abuse constituted 16% of those reports (U.S. Department of Health & Human Services [DHHS], 2008). Others estimate that physical abuse may actually range from over 23% (King, Trocme, & Thatte, 2003) up to nearly 30% of all cases of child maltreatment (Jones & McCurdy, 1992). More troubling are estimates based on anonymous parent report that severe physical assault toward children is in fact 5–11 times greater than official reports (Straus, Hamby, Finkelhor, Moore, & Runyan, 1998). Thus, physical abuse remains a critical concern even considering only those cases that rise to the exacting substantiation standards of child protective services, an agency that received an estimated 3.3 million referrals in 2006 (DHHS, 2008) while simultaneously witnessing steady declines in rates of substantiation (see King et al., 2003, for discussion).

Physical child abuse is typically defined as non-accidental injury to a child (Child Abuse Prevention, Adoption and Family Services Act of 1988), implying the resultant harm was intentional. However, physical abuse often arises when parents unintentionally escalate their administration of physical discipline (Herrenkohl, Herrenkohl, & Egolf, 1983; Whipple & Richey, 1997). Physical discipline has been defined as "the use of physical force with the intention of causing a child to experience pain, but not injury, for the purpose of correction or control of the child's behavior" (Straus, 2000, p. 1110). Physical discipline toward children is virtually universal in this country, with nearly 94% of American parents indicating they had employed physical discipline by the time their child was 3 or 4 (Straus & Stewart, 1999).

Distinguishing between physical abuse and physical discipline is both challenging and controversial. In a review of 8,000 substantiated cases of physical abuse, injurious and non-injurious child maltreatment were comparable with regard to child, parent, and socioeconomic characteristics (Gonzalez, Durrant, Chabot, Trocme, & Brown, 2008). Parents who are physically abusive also apply excessive, unreasonable physical discipline toward their children (Veltkamp & Miller, 1994; Whipple & Webster-Stratton, 1991). Parent–child aggression has been linked to negative behaviors in the recipients, whether the parental behavior is expressed as child abuse (e.g., Edwards, Holden, Felitti, & Anda, 2003; Runyon, Deblinger, Ryan, & Thakkar-Kolar, 2004) or corporal punishment (e.g., see Gershoff, 2002, for review). Consequently, a number of researchers recommend any form of physical parent–child aggression be conceptualized on a physical discipline—child abuse continuum (Graziano, 1994; Greenwald, Bank, Reid, & Knutson, 1997; Rodriguez & Richardson, 2007; Salzinger, Feldman, Hammer, & Rosario, 1991; Straus, 2001a, 2001b; Whipple & Richey, 1997), with mild physical discipline at one endpoint and extreme physical abuse at the other; harsh physical discipline could thus escalate to abuse somewhere along the continuum.

Given such a conceptualization, research relying on confirmed perpetrators of physical abuse would provide insight to a valuable endpoint of the continuum but a potentially restricted component of parent—child aggression. Maltreatment may be undetected by or unreported to protective services (Sedlak & Broadhurst, 1996), and the complex process of substantiation (King et al., 2003) typically yields high false negative rates (see DeGarmo, Reid, & Knutson, 2006, for discussion). Parents identified by protective services likely represent a selective, potentially atypical, fraction of those engaging in abusive parent–child aggression. Moreover, conclusions founded solely on substantiated perpetrators are not optimal when considering approaches intended to prevent abuse. Many abused children never encounter the social services system, and in order to better prevent child abuse, studying those not identified by the system (either low risk or at-risk) can provide a glimpse into how sub-abusive discipline can escalate to child abuse further along the continuum.

One popular line of research concentrates on pinpointing those beliefs and characteristics predictive of a parent's risk to physically maltreat a child (Milner, 1986, 1994), estimating the likelihood a parent will become abusive. This likelihood, termed child abuse potential, is estimated by such measures as the Child Abuse Potential Inventory (CAPI) which incorporates interpersonal and intrapersonal difficulties as well as inflexible attitudes regarding children observed in parents who physically abuse their children (Milner, 1986). Scores on the CAPI distinguish substantiated child abusers from comparison groups (Milner, Gold, & Wimberley, 1986) and predict which parents are likely to become abusive (Milner, Gold, Ayoub, & Jacewitz, 1984). CAPI scores also demonstrate an association with observed coercive parenting styles (Haskett, Scott, & Fann, 1995; Margolin, Gordis, Medina, & Oliver, 2003).

Although the CAPI (Milner, 1986) is widely regarded as a leading instrument to assess child abuse risk, the measure does not explicitly elicit any information regarding actual discipline practices in general or maltreatment behaviors in particular. Indeed, as noted above, the CAPI taps a range of personal issues and attitudes toward children that are characteristics of abusive parents. In contrast, epidemiological surveys have utilized such instruments as the Parent—Child Conflict Tactics Scale (CTSPC; Straus et al., 1998) to determine the frequency of actual behaviors implemented toward children during parent—child conflict. Remarkably little research has yet evaluated the association between child abuse potential and reports of actual parent–child physical aggression, either increased use of physical discipline or physically abusive behaviors. One study utilizing a modified earlier version of the Conflict Tactics Scale (Straus, 1979) determined if child abuse potential was related to a parent's personal history of maltreatment (Caliso & Milner, 1992), but one's own aggressive behavior toward a child was still not assessed. Although measures of child abuse potential should relate to parent–child physical aggression, their actual association has not been studied empirically.

Furthermore, relatively little research has evaluated the connections between parenting styles and child abuse potential or parent–child aggression. Baumrind's (1966) classic conceptualization of parenting style characterizes parental control as generally manifest in three broad styles: permissive (in which the parent exerts minimal control over the child with few demands); authoritarian (in which the parent enforces control of the child by ensuring unquestioned adherence to absolute standards); and authoritative (in which adherence to rules is a cooperative endeavor between parent and child but the parent remains firm in setting standards). Although authoritarian parenting style appears potentially beneficial in some ethnic minority groups (e.g., African American and Chinese American families; Baumrind, 1972; Chao, 1994), authoritative parenting is typically considered optimal whereas permissive and authoritarian parenting are generally construed as dysfunctional approaches (Baumrind, 1966, 1996).

Conceptually, authoritarian parenting would be expected to relate to child abuse risk, supported by empirical research that observational indices of authoritarian parenting are associated with child abuse potential scores (Haskett et al., 1995). Likewise, although parenting style was not measured specifically, child abuse potential was positively associated with coercive parenting approaches and negatively associated with sensitive and consistent parenting in a community sample of parents (Margolin et al., 2003). Overall, however, the pattern of associations between actual physically abusive behavior and physical discipline, child abuse potential, and different disciplinary styles has not yet been adequately clarified. Indeed, although researchers in this field are more apt to concentrate on authoritarian styles, permissive parenting styles are also considered problematic (Arnold, O'Leary, Wolff, & Acker, 1993; Baumrind, 1996) but the literature has not yet explored how permissive styles may relate to child abuse potential. Permissive parenting which results in minimal oversight could conceptually be consistent with neglectful parenting. Given that neglect is often identified in families who engage in physical abuse (DHHS, 2008), it is possible abuse risk relates to permissive parenting styles as well, particularly because the personal issues and attitudes captured by the CAPI may not be unique to physical abuse.

Presumably, parent–child aggression, in the form of both frequent physical discipline and physical maltreatment, would be expected to relate to increased physical child abuse potential and dysfunctional parenting styles. Therefore, the purpose of the present investigation was to evaluate whether child abuse potential, parent–child discipline and abuse, and dysfunctional parenting styles (particularly more authoritarian approaches) would be intercorrelated. Furthermore, parents engaging in parent–child aggression indicative of child maltreatment specifically were expected to demonstrate greater child abuse potential and more maladaptive disciplinary styles. Such associations would provide additional construct validity for the leading measure of abuse risk, the CAPI, as well as lending some insight into how abuse risk and parent–child aggression relate to differing parenting styles. To evaluate these hypotheses, three independent studies were examined, two with low-risk community samples of parents and a third with a clinical at-risk sample of parents of children with externalizing behavior disorders (given that children with behavior problems exhibit behaviors resulting in more frequent discipline incidents that exacerbate abuse risk; Wolfe, 1999).

METHODS

INSTRUMENTS ACROSS ALL STUDIES

The *Child Abuse Potential Inventory* (CAPI; Milner 1986) includes 160 statements to which respondents agree or disagree. Designed to screen for physical child abuse, the CAPI assesses rigidity and intrapersonal and interpersonal difficulties characteristic of identified physically abusive parents. Only 77 items comprise the Abuse Scale score and its six underlying factors, with the remaining statements serving as items for experimental scales or as measures of distortion biases. The factors within the Abuse Scale include: Distress, Rigidity, Unhappiness, Problems with Child and Self, Problems with Family, and Problems with Others.

With regard to internal consistency of the Abuse Scale score, the CAPI manual reports split-half reliability ranging from.96 (for control groups) to.98 (for abuse groups) and Kuder-Richardson reliability coefficients ranging from.92 (for control groups) to.95 (for abuse groups), suggesting high internal consistency for community, at-risk, and abusive samples (Milner, 1986). Retest reliabilities range from.91 after one day to.75 after 3 months (Milner, 1986). In terms of predictive validity, studies have indicated a correct classification rate of 81.4% of confirmed child abusers and 99% of comparison parents, with an overall pattern indicating that a lower cut-off score leads to classification rates in the low-90s% range and that a higher cut-off score leads to greater false-negatives of child abusers (Milner, 1994).

The *Parent-Child Conflict Tactics Scale* (CTSPC; Straus et al., 1998) is a revision of an epidemiological survey of family violence, the Conflict Tactics Scale (Straus, 1979). The CTSPC contains 22 items in which a parent reports on the frequency with which they have engaged in a series of behaviors arising from parent–child conflicts (response categories as follows: 0 = this has never happened; 1 = once in the past year; 2 = twice in the past year; 3 = 3–5 times in the past year; 4 = 6–10 times in the past year; 5 = 11–20 times in the past year; 6 = more than 20 times in the past year; 7 = not in the past year, but it happened before). Responses are scored based on the frequency range reported by the parent: responses of 0, 1, and 2 correspond to scores of 0, 1, and 2, respectively; a score of 4 (the midpoint) is assigned for a parent selecting the 3–5 times category; a score of 8 is assigned to the 6–10 times category; a score of 15 is assigned for the 11–20 times category; and a score of 25 is given for the final category, 20 or more times in the past year.

Thirteen of the CTSPC items directly address varying levels of physical tactics applied toward children, comprising a subscale entitled Physical Assault (with subcategories of minor assault/corporal punishment, severe assault/physical maltreatment, and very severe assault/ severe physical maltreatment). Given the subcategories, actions tapped by the Physical Assault subscale range from spanking, slapping, or pinching up to beating or burning. In addition to the Physical Assault subscale, four items of the CTSPC comprise the Non-Violent Discipline subscale (including such actions as removal of privileges and "time-out") and five items contribute to the Psychological Aggression subscale (involving such behaviors as verbal threats and yelling). Although the CTSPC Physical Assault scale was of most interest, some intriguing results emerged regarding the Psychological Aggression scales and will be reported and discussed. In addition to analyses using the three subscales, physical maltreatment in particular was isolated by computing a classification score based on parents' report of ever using any of severe assault/physical maltreatment (three items) or very severe assault/ severe physical maltreatment (four items) behaviors; respondents indicating that they had engaged in any of the seven maltreatment items were categorized in a CTS Maltreatment group whereas those reporting none of these behaviors were categorized in a CTS No Maltreatment group.

Straus and colleagues (1998) report moderate internal consistency at .55 for the Physical Assault scale, .60 for the Psychological Aggression scale, and .70 for the Nonviolent Discipline scale. These moderate reliability coefficients likely reflect the diverse behaviors included in the measure as well as the very low reported frequency of many of the items (Straus et al., 1998). The authors provide supportive evidence of construct and discriminant validity, and some indication of modest correlations among subscales (Straus et al., 1998).

The *Parenting Scale* (Arnold et al., 1993) was utilized to identify parents' dysfunctional parenting styles. Thirty items present parents with a typical parent–child conflict situation and asks them to indicate their response to the situation along a 7-point scale, with two opposing reactions at endpoints of each scale. The Parenting Scale yields a Total score intended to indicate overall dysfunctional parenting style. Based on the original factor analysis (Arnold et al., 1993), this general dysfunctional parenting style subsumes three separate response styles: Overreactivity (representing a harsh, angry discipline style, consistent with an authoritarian parenting style), Laxness (reflecting a permissive style of parenting), and Verbosity (in which parents rely on verbal persuasion even when ineffective). However, a subsequent normative sample with 785 parents of 2- to 12-year-old children (Collett, Gimpel, Greenson, & Gunderson, 2001) indicated that a new factor analysis did not support a separate Verbosity factor. Consequently, for the purposes of the present study, the Overreactivity and Laxness subscales were targeted as the most potentially meaningful parenting styles to test the hypotheses. Scores are computed by summing across items for the scale and dividing by the number of items, with higher scores indicative of more dysfunctional parenting styles. An example of an Overreactivity item would offer a prompt, such as "When my child misbehaves" and then asks the parent to select between, "I handle it without getting upset," versus, "I get so frustrated and angry that my child can see I'm upset." An example of a Laxness item would prompt, "When I say my child can't do something" followed by the two choices, "I let my child do it anyway," versus, "I stick to what I said."

Internal consistency reported by the test authors for the Total score is moderately high at .84, with Laxness and Overreactivity at .83 and .82, respectively (Arnold et al., 1993), which are comparable to those reported in the more recent normative study (Collett et al., 2001). Over a 2-week period, test–retest reliability was relatively high for the Total, Laxness, and Overreactivity scores, at .84, .83, and .82, respectively (Arnold et al., 1993). In addition, scores were significantly related to clinical observations of parent–child interactions (Arnold et al., 1993).

STUDY 1

Participants. In the first study, 327 parents of children younger than 12 responded to an online parenting study. The mean age of these parents was 30.48 years (standard deviation [*SD*] = 6.22 years), with the majority of respondents female (84%), married (91%), with an average of 1.89 children (*SD* = 1.1). Respondents identified themselves as Caucasian (84.7%), African American (5.2%), Hispanic (4.0%), Asian (3.7%), American Indian/ Alaskan Native (1.2%), or Other (1.2%). The mean annual family income was $54,299, with a median of $45,000 that likely more accurately represents the sample because of some outliers. Participants reported on their highest educational attainment: 1.5% not high school graduates, 18.7% high school graduates, nearly 30% with some college or vocational degree, 37% college degree, and 12.8% graduate school.

Procedures. Study procedures were approved by the university institutional review board. Selected World Wide Websites devoted to parenting (e.g., www.ibaby.com, www. parentsoup. com, www.parenting.com) were targeted for an online parenting study. Links to a webpage for the parenting study were advertised on bulletin boards at these sites. Interested parents linked to the study website, which first presented them with an on-line consent form. Participants were then presented with a series of measures, including the CAPI, Parenting Scale, and CTSPC, which they could complete anonymously. Upon completion of this 60-minunte study, respondents received a gift certificate code for $5 redeemable toward the purchase of an item sold online. Each participant's data was independently screened for accuracy and consistency in responding, with any questionable or incomplete files purged from the data set. For example, any respondent who obtained an elevated score on any of the three CAPI response bias indices was purged from the dataset (*n* = 38). Any files judged remotely questionable (uniform responding on any measure; *n* = 24) or largely incomplete (*n* = 8) were also removed from the data set, yielding 327 verified participants eligible for analyses with complete data on these three measures.

STUDY 2

Participants. Participants in this second community sample were 115 parents of children between ages 7 and 12; mothers ($n = 86$) and fathers ($n = 29$) were recruited for a larger parenting study conducted in a session in their home. The mean age of parents was 37.62 years ($SD = 7.91$ years), and the majority of parents in this sample (83.5%) reported they were living with a partner, with an average of three children. Based on self-identification, 92.2% described themselves as Caucasian, 6.1% as Hispanic, approximately 1% as Native American, and about 1% as "Other." The mean annual family income was $50,067 per year, with a median of $45,000. Nearly all participants (93.9%) reported graduating from high school, with 7.8% no education past high school; 46.1% reported they attended vocational school or some college, 28.6% obtained a college degree, and 11.3% reported a graduate school degree.

Procedures. The study protocol was approved by the university institutional review board and the local school district. Parents in this second study were recruited from their child's school from notices/consent forms sent home about a study on factors affecting parenting and discipline. Interested parents returned a contact information sheet from which a 90-minute session was scheduled in their home for them to complete the larger study on a laptop computer. By using a computer, the participants were able to enter their responses to the questions anonymously and efficiently. Part of this study included the CAPI, the Parenting Scale, and the CTSPC, which were extracted for the present analyses. Parents received $10 as compensation for their time involved participating in this larger study.

STUDY 3

Participants. A clinical sample of parents constituted the third sample, with participants from a parenting study focusing on mothers of 7- to 12-year-old children with diagnosed externalizing behavior problems. In this study, 74 mothers participated, with a mean age of 40.65 years ($SD = 10.53$ years). Of these parents, 71.6% reported they were currently living with a partner, and they had an average of three children in the home. Based on self-report, the majority of the sample was Caucasian (82.4%), with 12.2% of Hispanic origin, 2.7% American Indian/ Alaskan Native, 1.4% African American, and 1.4% Asian. The mean annual family income was $41,016, with a median of $35,000. Most of the sample had graduated from high school (83.6%); 22% had no education beyond high school, 43.2% obtained vocational training or some college, 12.2% attained a college degree, and 5.4% attained a graduate degree.

Procedures. Study procedures were approved by the university institutional review board. Mothers were recruited from flyers distributed to mental health agencies and school psychologists working with children with behavior problems. Participants for this parenting study had to be a mother of a child age 5–12 who was receiving mental health services for a diagnosed externalizing behavior problem. Interested parents meeting these criteria were scheduled for a 2-hour session in their home for a larger parenting and discipline study of at-risk children. Parent responses were entered anonymously onto a laptop computer, with the series of questionnaires including the CAPI, the Parenting Scale, and the CTSPC. Mothers received $20 for participating in this larger study.

RESULTS

PRELIMINARY ANALYSES: COMPARISON TO PREVIOUS NORMS AND CORRELATIONS

All statistical analyses were conducted using the SPSS for Windows 15.0 statistical package. Means and standard deviations for the three measures for all three studies appear in Table 10.1. The obtained sample CAPI Abuse Scale means in Studies 1 and 2 were comparable to the normative sample mean of 91.0 reported in the manual (Milner, 1986), with 14.5% of sample 1 and 15.2% of sample 2 obtaining scores above the clinical cut-off. In contrast, the sample of parents raising children with behavior problems in Study 3, considered an at-risk sample, obtained scores on the CAPI Abuse Scale significantly higher than the normative mean ($t(73) =$ 5.16, $p \leq .001$). Although definitive normative means are not reported by the test authors for the Parenting Scale scores (Arnold et al., 1993), the obtained scores for the community samples in Studies 1 and 2 are comparable to those reported in the normative study (individual means per school grade are reported, ranging from 2.77 to 2.94; Collett et al., 2001). In contrast, Parenting Scale scores for Study 3 were comparable to those reported by the test authors for a clinical sample of mothers raising behavior problem children ($M = 3.1$; Arnold et al., 1993). For the CTSPC, the epidemiological results present mean scores on the Physical Assault, Psychological Aggression, and Non-Violent Discipline scales only for those who had engaged in at least one of the behaviors in the past month (Straus et al., 1998). Consequently, those means would be considerably higher than those obtained in the present investigation's three studies. For comparison purposes, however, the epidemiological means were 46.0 for Non-Violent Discipline, 21.7 for Psychological Aggression, and 13.4 for Physical Assault (Straus et al., 1998).

Although not part of the research questions for this paper, the correlations between the Parenting Scale Overreactivity and Laxness Scales ranged from $r = .33$ and .38 (both $p < .001$) for the two community samples of Studies 1 and 2, consistent with other community samples ($r = .36$; Prinzie, Onghena, & Hellinckx, 2007); for the Study 3 at-risk sample, the association between the two Parenting Scale scores was $r = .62$ ($p < .001$); although generally not reported, one study that included parents raising hard to manage toddlers reported a correlation of $r = .58$ (Slep & O'Leary, 1997). With regard to correlations within the CTSPC, Physical Assault scores correlated with the Non-Violent Discipline scores ranging from $r = .08$ to .26 and with the Psychological Aggression scores from $r = .27$ ($p < .05$; Study 3) to .62 ($p < .001$; Study 2); the Non-Violent Discipline scores were correlated with the Psychological Aggression scores ranging from $r = .21$ ($p = .07$) to .37 ($p < .001$). Correlations between the scales of CTSPC have not been traditionally reported and are greatly impacted by sampling characteristics.

TABLE 10.1: MEANS, STANDARD DEVIATIONS, AND CORRELATIONS

	M	SD	CAPI Abuse Scale (r)	Parenting Overreactivity (r)	Parenting Laxness (r)
CAPI Abuse Scale					
Study 1	92.58	73.31			
Study 2	94.74	83.38			
Study 3	146.28	92.18			
Parenting Scale Overreactivity					
Study 1	2.54	.86	.54**		
Study 2	2.86	.89	.51**		
Study 3	3.06	.93	.50**		
Parenting Scale Laxness					
Study 1	2.32	.84	.16*		
Study 2	2.59	.71	.25*		
Study 3	2.83	1.01	.49**		
CTSPC Physical Assault					
Study 1	9.84	17.36	.39**	.37**	.13[a]
Study 2	7.48	11.23	.32**	.43**	.08
Study 3	10.49	16.07	.33*	.37**	.24[a]
CTSPC Nonviolent Discipline					
Study 1	49.65	26.44	−.01	.10	−.08
Study 2	51.18	25.51	.08	.10	−.03
Study 3	59.76	24.64	−.14	−.15	−.27[a]
CTSPC Psychological Aggression					
Study 1	13.08	14.53	.43**	.56**	.14[a]
Study 2	18.56	16.96	.33**	.58**	.18
Study 3	27.46	21.41	.29*	.48**	.16

Note. CAPI = Child Abuse Potential Inventory; CTSPC = Parent—Child Conflict Tactics Scale.
[a]Because the significance level was reduced to α =.01, these correlations were observed only at $p \le .05$.
*$p \le .01$. **$p \le .001$.

CORRELATIONAL ANALYSES

Correlations among the measures were examined (see Table 10.1). Given the number of correlations of interest, a more conservative significance level of.01 per study was adopted for these analyses.

CAPI and Parenting Scale Correlations. An examination of the pattern of these relationships indicates that across the three samples, CAPI Abuse Scale scores were significantly positively correlated with Parenting Scale scores (Overreactivity and Laxness). However, the CAPI Abuse Scale scores appear to be more strongly correlated with Overreactivity than with Laxness scores, with the exception of the third study sample. Indeed, for Study 1, the CAPI Abuse Scale correlation with Overreactivity was significantly stronger ($T_2 = 6.62$, $p < .001$) than the CAPI correlation with Laxness (based on Steiger's [1980] recommendations regarding Williams' formula for comparing dependent correlations). Similarly, for Study 2, the difference between the CAPI Abuse Scale-Overreactivity and CAPI Abuse Scale-Laxness correlations were also significantly different ($T_2 = 2.74$, $p < .01$). Only the third sample of at-risk parents demonstrated an association between CAPI Abuse Scale and Laxness ($r = .49$) virtually equivalent to the CAPI Abuse Scale association with Overreactivity ($r = .50$).

CAPI and CTSPC Correlations. With respect to the association between the CAPI and the CTSPC scales, across all three studies, abuse potential was not significantly correlated with reported CTSPC Non-Violent Discipline tactics. Interestingly, the overall pattern of associations suggests the CAPI Abuse Scale scores were related to reported use of Psychological Aggression virtually comparable to the use of Physical Assault actions.

CTSPC and Parenting Scale Correlations. Turning to the associations between the Parenting Scale and the CTSPC, Parenting Scale scores were not significantly related to the CTSPC Non-Violent Discipline items. However, for the at-risk sample of Study 3, more use of permissive parenting approaches was marginally associated with lower use of CTSPC Non-Violent discipline tactics (marginal given the reduced significance level). Across all three studies, Parenting Scale Overreactivity scores were significantly associated with the general parent–child aggression assessed by the CTSPC Physical Assault scale. Furthermore, across studies the Parenting Scale Overreactivity scores were also significantly associated with the CTSPC Psychological Aggression, in all cases of higher magnitude than with the Physical Assault scale. The Parenting Scale Laxness scores were not significantly correlated with either the CTSPC Physical Assault or Psychological Aggression scales across all three studies (although for the at-risk sample of Study 3, Laxness was marginally associated with greater frequency of physical assault behaviors).

MALTREATMENT CLASSIFICATION GROUP DIFFERENCES

Parents were classified into maltreatment groups based on their responses to only the maltreatment items on the CTSPC. Differences between these two groups for each study appear in Table 10.2. For Study 1, 6.1% of the sample endorsed at least one item of maltreatment.

Those parents classified into the Maltreatment Group obtained significantly higher CAPI Abuse Scale scores and Parenting Scale scores than those who reported no instances of administering physical maltreatment toward their children. For Study 2, 20% of the parents in this community sample were classified into the Maltreatment Group. Those parents indicating they had engaged in any physical maltreatment obtained higher CAPI Abuse Scale scores and higher Parenting Scale Overreactivity scores than those who did not report such tactics. The obtained difference between the two groups was in the expected direction for the Parenting Scale Laxness scores, but was only marginally significant ($p = .067$). In Study 3, 17.6% of parents were classified into the Maltreatment Group. Again, the Maltreatment group differed from the No Maltreatment Group on the CAPI Abuse Scale and the Parenting Scale Overreactivity scores but not on the Laxness scores.

TABLE 10.2: MEANS, STANDARD DEVIATIONS, AND GROUP COMPARISONS BETWEEN CTSPC MALTREATMENT VERSUS NO MALTREATMENT GROUPS

	Study 1			Study 2			Study 3		
	M	*SD*	*t*[a]	*M*	*SD*	*t*	*M*	*SD*	*t*
CAPI Abuse Scale									
No Maltreatment Group	88.41	70.02	4.13***	83.90	71.72	2.87**	138.36	95.55	2.84**
Maltreatment Group	156.60	93.08		138.09	110.89		221.92	100.81	
Parenting Overreactivity									
No Maltreatment Group	2.48	.84	4.51***	2.71	.85	3.76***	2.94	.91	2.45*
Maltreatment Group	3.36	.87		3.46	.87		3.62	.89	
Parenting Laxness									
No Maltreatment Group	2.28	.81	3.62***	2.53	.66	1.91	2.77	.94	1.07
Maltreatment Group	2.97	1.11		2.84	.84		3.10	1.33	

Note. CAPI = Child Abuse Potential Inventory; CTSPC = Parent–Child Conflict Tactics Scale.
[a] *t*-test statistic for between group differences.
*$p \leq .05$. **$p \leq .01$. ***$p \leq .001$.

DISCUSSION

The current investigation included three independent studies to evaluate the connections among child abuse potential, physical discipline and child abuse, and dysfunctional parenting style. Two studies involved lower risk community samples whereas the third study involved an at-risk group of parents. Overall, the results suggest a pattern of associations whereby parent–child physical aggression in various forms is associated with both dysfunctional parenting style (particularly more authoritarian approaches) and child abuse potential.

Across all studies, reported physically aggressive behavior in general, inclusive of corporal punishment, was significantly associated with increased child abuse potential. Furthermore, parents who reported they had engaged in behavior that would be considered physical maltreatment obtained significantly higher CAPI scores than those who did not report ever using any of those tactics. These findings lend support to the construct validity of the CAPI and are consistent with findings regarding the ability of the CAPI to distinguish physically abusive parents and predict future abuse (Milner, 1994). Consequently, child abuse potential appears associated with the actual reported use of corporal punishment in addition to physical maltreatment behaviors specifically.

Similarly, as hypothesized, results from all three studies suggest that overall parent–child aggression is related to dysfunctional, overreactive, authoritarian parenting. Similar results were obtained in the comparison of those parents who had engaged in some type of physical maltreatment behavior versus those who had not. In contrast, parent–child aggression in general was not significantly correlated with permissive parenting approaches in any of the samples. However, an examination of group differences for those parents who specifically engaged in maltreatment behaviors indicated that lax parenting was indeed more frequently reported in the first community sample but only marginally in the second community sample. Given that permissive parenting is considered problematic (Baumrind, 1966, 1996), notably with respect to behavior problems (Arnold et al., 1993), it is intriguing to find the marginal correlation of permissive parenting style to general parent–child aggression observed only in the at-risk sample of parents raising children with behavior problems. The reduced power in this last sample may complicate identifying significance. However, it may be this finding reflects that parents raising children with behavior problems are inconsistent, vacillating between permissive and overreactive discipline strategies (as evidenced by their strong correlation in that sample). Overall, this pattern does suggest that greater inquiry into the link between permissive parenting practices and parent–child aggression may be warranted, especially in at-risk samples.

Interestingly, although not the main focus of this investigation, across all three samples, greater child abuse potential was also significantly associated with parents' use of psychological aggression although not with the use of non-violent discipline. This connection of the CAPI (which targets physical abuse risk) to psychological aggression likely underscores the intersection between instances of physical maltreatment and psychological maltreatment (e.g., Claussen & Crittenden, 1991). Yet it is also notable that dysfunctional parenting style scores (namely Overreactivity) were more strongly related to psychological aggression than with parent–child physical aggression. Given that earlier studies have linked parental verbal aggression to psychosocial problems in children (e.g., Vissing, Straus, Gelles, & Harrop, 1991), further study of psychological aggression may prove insightful to understanding the correlates of emotional maltreatment (see Glaser, 2002, for review of emotional abuse). Potentially, an authoritarian parenting style may involve psychological aggression tactics that precede and escalate into physical discipline encounters. An interesting avenue for future research could pursue investigating such a progression, although the design of such a study would be admittedly challenging.

Additionally, as anticipated, greater child abuse potential was also significantly associated with dysfunctional disciplinary style across the studies. For the two community samples, this association largely reflected the strength of an overreactive, authoritarian discipline style, consistent with prior research (e.g., Haskett et al., 1995; Margolin et al., 2003). However, for the third at-risk clinical sample, child abuse potential was also strongly associated with a lax discipline approach. As noted earlier regarding the findings on parent–child aggression, perhaps for at-risk samples both authoritarian and permissive dysfunctional parenting styles are associated with abuse risk. The nature of some of the personal problems and attitudes captured by the CAPI items could readily be associated with more neglectful parenting, which is consistent with the under-involved, permissive approach tapped by the Parenting Scale Laxness scale. Future studies should consider whether other at-risk parents demonstrate a similar pattern of abuse risk relating to harsh as well as permissive discipline styles.

A number of limitations to the present study should be acknowledged. Although the current investigation drew from three separate samples of parents in order to minimize the limitations of a single given study, all three are limited by their reliance on parental self-report. All of the studies obtained information from parents anonymously but parents' responses may still be susceptible to underreporting. Therefore, some of these findings may actually reflect conservative estimates of physical discipline use, maltreatment, and abuse risk. Optimally, a study that involves child abuse potential, discipline style, and parent–child aggression could be supplemented by observations of parent–child behavior (e.g., see Haskett et al., 1995 study of abuse potential and observations), although self-report for such constructs is typical because of the inherent difficulty of observing such behaviors. Furthermore, data were gathered from a single source (the parent), which may amplify observed associations. Nonetheless, meaningful distinctions were detected among different parenting styles and aggression types using three measures with no item overlap.

In addition, the nature of the individuals who participated across studies should also be considered given that, despite compensation for participation, the samples involved parents who were willing to participate in a research study. Again, this issue may have led to more conservative estimates of the variables of interest. Yet a considerable minority of the first two community samples obtained clinically elevated CAPI scores, suggesting that abuse risk is apparent even among populations not identified as at-risk (e.g., as compared to Sample 3). Moreover, greater ethnic diversity in the sample distribution should be a goal in future research, and the online sample of the first study appears relatively better educated than either of the two subsequent studies. Although the third sample included at-risk parents, a more thorough investigation with other potential secondary prevention groups would be useful. Indeed, a research design with at-risk samples, accompanied by a group of parents who have been substantiated for abuse, could provide a comparison of how such issues may differ across different risk groups.

Overall, in order to advance prevention efforts, future research should continue to investigate how different parenting styles may relate to physical abuse risk and parent–child aggression.

Progressive approaches to prevention could identify which parenting strategies could be modified that may in turn decrease the incidence of not only abusive parent–child aggression but perhaps aggressive tactics more broadly, including psychological aggression. Identification of the salient parenting attitudes and behaviors linked to varying levels and manifestations of parent–child aggression may help clarify how best to intervene on the continuum of behaviors that emerge during parent–child conflicts.

REFERENCES

Arnold, D. S., O'Leary, S. G., Wolff, L. S., & Acker, M. M. (1993). The Parenting Scale: A measure of dysfunctional parenting in discipline situations. *Psychological Assessment, 2,* 137–144.

Baumrind, D. (1966). Effects of authoritative parental control on child behavior. *Child Development, 37,* 887–907.

Baumrind, D. (1996). The discipline controversy revisited. *Family Relations, 45,* 405–414.

Baumrind, D. (1972). An exploratory study of socialization effects on black children: Some Black-White comparisons. *Child Development, 43,* 261–267.

Caliso, J. A., & Milner, J. S. (1992). Childhood history of abuse and child abuse screening. *Child Abuse & Neglect, 16,* 647–659.

Chao, R. K. (1994). Beyond parental control and authoritarian parenting style: Understanding Chinese parenting through the cultural notion of training. *Child Development, 65,* 1111–1119.

Claussen, A., & Crittenden, P. (1991). Physical and psychological maltreatment: Relations among types of maltreatment. *Child Abuse & Neglect, 15,* 5–18.

Collett, B. R., Gimpel, G. A., Greenson, J. N., & Gunderson, T. L. (2001). Assessment of discipline styles among parents of preschool through school-age children. *Journal of Psychopathology and Behavioral Assessment, 23,* 163–170.

DeGarmo, D. S., Reid, J. B., & Knutson, J. F. (2006). Direct laboratory observations and analog measures in research definitions of child maltreatment. In M. Feerick, J. F. Knutson, P. Trickett, & S. Flanzier (Eds.), *Child abuse and neglect: Definitions, classifications, and a framework for research* (pp. 293–328). Baltimore : Brooks.

Edwards, V. J., Holden, G. W., Felitti, V. J., & Anda, R. F. (2003). Relationship between multiple forms of childhood maltreatment and adult mental health in community respondents: Results from the adverse childhood experiences study. *American Journal of Psychiatry, 160,* 1453–1460.

Gershoff, E. T. (2002). Corporal punishment by parents and associated child behaviors and experiences: A meta-analytic and theoretical review. *Psychological Bulletin, 128,* 539–579.

Gonzalez, M., Durrant, J. E., Chabot, M., Trocme, N., & Brown, J. (2008). What predicts injury from physical punishment? A test of the typologies of violence hypothesis. *Child Abuse & Neglect, 21,* 752–765.

Glaser, D. (2002). Emotional abuse and neglect (psychological maltreatment): A conceptual framework. *Child Abuse & Neglect, 26,* 697–714.

Graziano, A. M. (1994). Why we should study subabusive violence against children. *Journal of Interpersonal Violence, 9,* 412–419.

Greenwald, R. L., Bank, L., Reid, J. B., & Knutson, J. F. (1997). A discipline-mediated model of excessively punitive parenting. *Aggressive Behavior, 23,* 259–280.

Haskett, M. E., Scott, S. S., & Fann, K. D. (1995). Child abuse potential inventory and parenting behavior: Relationships with high-risk correlates. *Child Abuse & Neglect, 19,* 1483–1495.

Herrenkohl, R. C., Herrenkohl, E. C., & Egolf, B. P. (1983). Circumstances surrounding the occurrence of child maltreatment. *Journal of Consulting and Clinical Psychology, 51,* 424–431.

Jones, E. D., & McCurdy, K. (1992). The links between types of maltreatment and demographic characteristics of children. *Child Abuse & Neglect, 16,* 201–215.

King, G., Trocme, N., & Thatte, N. (2003). Substantiation as a multiplier process: The results of a NIS-3 Analysis. *Child Maltreatment, 8,* 173–182.

Margolin, G., Gordis, E. B., Medina, A. M., & Oliver, P. H. (2003). The co-occurrence of husband-to-wife aggression, family-of-origin aggression, and child abuse potential in a community sample. *Journal of Interpersonal Violence, 18,* 413–440.

Milner, J. S. (1986). *The Child Abuse Potential Inventory: Manual* (2nd ed.). Webster, NC: Psyctec.

Milner, J. S. (1994). Assessing physical child abuse risk: The Child Abuse Potential Inventory. *Clinical Psychology Review, 14,* 547–583.

Milner, J. S., Gold, R. G., Ayoub, C., & Jacewitz, M. M. (1984). Predictive validity of the Child Abuse Potential Inventory. *Journal of Consulting and Clinical Psychology, 52,* 879–884.

Milner, J. S., Gold, R. G., & Wimberley, R. C. (1986). Prediction and explanation of child abuse: Cross-validation of the Child Abuse Potential Inventory. *Journal of Consulting and Clinical Psychology, 54,* 865–866.

Prinzie, P., Onghena, P., & Hellinckx, W. (2007). Reexamining the Parenting Scale: Reliability, factor structure, and concurrent validity of a scale for assessing the discipline practices of mothers and fathers of elementary-school-aged children. *European Journal of Psychological Assessment, 23,* 24–31.

Rodriguez, C. M., & Richardson, M. J. (2007). Stress and anger as contextual factors and pre-existing cognitive schemas: Predicting parental child maltreatment risk. *Child Maltreatment, 12,* 325–337.

Runyon, M. K., Deblinger, E., Ryan, E. E., & Thakkar-Kolar, R. (2004). An overview of child physical abuse: Developing an integrated parent-child cognitive-behavioral treatment approach. *Trauma, Violence, & Abuse, 5,* 65–85.

Salzinger, S., Feldman, R. S., Hammer, M., & Rosario, M. (1991). Risk for physical child abuse and the personal consequence for its victims. *Criminal Justice and Behavior, 18,* 64–81.

Sedlak, A. J., & Broadhurst, D. D. (1996). *Third national incidence study of child abuse and neglect: Final report.* Washington, DC : U.S. Dept of Health and Human Services.

Slep, A. M., & O'Leary, S. G. (1997). *Pre-emptive parenting: Relations with discipline style and child behavior.* Poster presented at the annual conference of the Association for the Advancement of Behavior Therapy, Miami, FL.

Steiger, J. H. (1980). Tests for comparing elements of a correlation matrix. *Psychological Bulletin, 87*, 245–251.

Straus, M. A. (1979). Measuring intrafamily conflict and violence: The Conflict Tactics Scales. *Journal of Marriage and Family, 41*, 75–88.

Straus, M. A. (2000). Corporal punishment and primary prevention of physical abuse. *Child Abuse & Neglect, 24*, 1109–1114.

Straus, M. A. (2001a). *Beating the devil out of them: Corporal punishment in American families and its effects on children.* New Brunswick, NJ: Transaction.

Straus, M. A. (2001b). New evidence for the benefits of never spanking. *Society, 38*, 52–60.

Straus, M. A., Hamby, S. L., Finkelhor, D., Moore, D. W., & Runyan, D. (1998). Identification of child maltreatment with the Parent-Child Conflict Tactics Scales: Development and psychometric data for a national sample of American parents. *Child Abuse & Neglect, 22*, 249–270.

Straus, M. A., & Stewart, J. H. (1999). Corporal punishment by American parents: National data on prevalence, chronicity, severity, and duration, in relation to child and family characteristics. *Clinical Child and Family Psychology Review, 2*, 55–70.

United States Department of Health and Human Services. (2008). *Child Maltreatment 2006.* Washington, DC: Government Printing Office.

Veltkamp, L. J., & Miller, T. J. (1994). *Clinical handbook of child abuse and neglect.* Madison, CT : International Universities Press.

Vissing, Y. M., Straus, M. A., Gelles, R. J., & Harrop, J. W. (1991). Verbal aggression by parents and psychosocial problems of children. *Child Abuse & Neglect, 15*, 223–238.

Whipple, E. E., & Richey, C. A. (1997). Crossing the line from physical discipline to child abuse: How much is too much? *Child Abuse & Neglect, 5*, 431–444.

Whipple, E. E., & Webster-Stratton, C. (1991). The role of parental stress in physically abusive families. *Child Abuse and Neglect, 15*, 279–291.

Wolfe, D. A. (1999). *Child abuse: Implications for child development and psychopathology.* Thousand Oaks, CA: Sage.

QUESTIONS FOR REVIEW, REFLECTION, AND DISCUSSION

1. Define "physical child abuse" and "physical discipline"?
2. What parenting styles were conceptualized by Baumrind? Explain the styles. How do they differ from each other?
3. What types of parenting characteristics are typically associated with child abuse risk?
4. Is spanking acceptable in your family? Why or why not?

ADDITIONAL READINGS

Baumrind, D. (1991). The influence of parenting style on adolescent competence and substance use. *The Journal of Early Adolescence, 11*, 56–95.

Baumrind, D. (2013). Authoritative parenting revisited: History and current status. In E. Larzelere, A. S. Morris, & A. W. Harrist (Eds.), *Authoritative parenting. Synthesizing nurturance and discipline for optimal child development* (pp. 11–34). Washington, DC: American Psychological Association.

Chan, T. W., & Koo, A. (2011). Parenting style and youth outcomes in the UK. *European Sociological Review, 27*, 385–399.

Fréchette, S., Zoratti, M., & Romano, E. (2015). What is the link between corporal punishment and child physical abuse? *Journal of Family Violence, 30*(2), 135–148.

Lee, S. J., Altschul, I., Gershoff, E. T. (2015). Wait until your father gets home? Mother's and father's spanking and developmental of child aggression, *Children and Youth Services Review, 52*, 158–166.

KEY TERMS

Intimate Partner Violence

Sociobiological Perspective

Psychodynamic Perspective

Evolutionary Perspective

Psychological Trait Theories

Victim Theory

Learned Helplessness

Cycle of Violence

Investment Theory

Dyadic Stress

Symbolic Interactionism

Traumatic Bonding Theory

Power Theory

Resource Theory

Exchange Theory

Cultural Approval of Violence

Subculture of Violence

Feminist Theory

Family Violence Perspective

Deterrence Theory

Family Stress Theory

Environmental Stress Theory

General Systems Theory

Theory of Gender and Power

Ecological Theory

Gender and Violence

Multiracial Feminisms and Social Exchange Theory

Economic Exclusion / Male Peer Support Model

Social Etiological Model

Contextual Framework

11

THEORETICAL PERSPECTIVES ON INTIMATE PARTNER VIOLENCE

By Stella M. Resko

Understanding the causes of violence against women is important for those who seek to prevent, predict, or intervene to avert the occurrence of violence within intimate relationships (Cunningham, et al., 1998). Theories are important because they influence the actions chosen to address the problem (Bowman, 2003) and frame the general population's understanding of a social issue (Jasinski, 2001). In general, violence against women is a field where the link between theory and practice has been quite explicit (Holtzworth-Monroe & Saunders, 1996). Theory development has proceeded from a wide range of disciplines including criminology, law, psychiatry, psychology, public health, social work, sociology, and women's studies (Jasinksi, 2001; O'Neil, 1998). As Table 11.1 indicates, theorists have developed numerous explanations about the causes and correlates of partner violence that serve as a tremendous foundation for research and practice (See also Bell & Naugle, 2008; Jasinski, 2001; Kurst-Swanger & Petcosky, 2003, O'Neil, 1998).

Stella M. Resko, "Theoretical Perspectives on Intimate Partner Violence," Intimate Partner Violence and Women's Economic Insecurity, pp. 35-64, 203-237. Copyright © 2010 by LFB Scholarly Publishing. Reprinted with permission.

TABLE 11.1: THEORETICAL EXPLANATIONS OF INTIMATE PARTNER VIOLENCE

MODEL OR THEORY	EXPLANATION
Micro Level Analysis	
Sociobiological Perspective (Greene, 1999)	Focuses on how biological and environmental factors interact and influence the perpetration of violence; Focuses on the role of genetics, endocrine function brain injury or dysfunction, and neurotransmitters.
Psychodynamic Perspective (Browne & Herbert, 1997)	Based on Freudian theory; views violence as the result of internal conflicts, abnormal aggressive tendencies, and abnormal death instinct.
Evolutionary Perspective (Daly & Wilson, 1997; Wilson & Daly, 1993)	Violence against women is related to natural selection; aggression functions to control female sexuality to the male's reproductive advantage.
Psychological Trait Theories (Dutton, 2007)	Attributes intimate violence to individual variation in personality traits; individuals who are hostile, for example, tend to be more violent.
Victim Theory (Loseke & Cahill, 1984)	Views intimate partner violence in terms of the victim's characteristics (e.g. low self, esteem, ineffective coping skills); "blaming the victim."
Learned Helplessness (Walker, 1978)	Approach advanced by Lenore Walker suggesting women stay in abusive relationships because constant abuse strips them of the will to leave.
Cycle of Violence (Walker, 1979)	Approach that suggests violence occurs in a cycle that consists of three phases: the tension building phase, the incident of abuse, and the "honeymoon" period, during which the abuser was apologetic and remorseful.
Investment Theory (Choice & Lamke, 1997; Johnson, 1992; Rusbelt & Martz, 1995; Truman-Schram et al., 2000)	Views willingness to stay in a relationship as the balance of rewards over costs for staying involved in the relationship as compared to the balance of rewards over costs for leaving.
Dyadic Stress (Barnett et al., 2005)	A violent partner's behavior is viewed as a response to the behavior of the other partner and is maintained by the interactions of both partners to preserve the homeostatic balance of the relationship.
Symbolic Interactionism (Bersani & Chen, 1988; Gelles & Straus, 1979)	Focuses on perpetrator-victim interactions from the subjective viewpoint of an actor's meaning or definition of these interactions.
Traumatic Bonding Theory (Dutton & Painter, 1993)	Explains intimate partner violence in terms of the unique relationship that develops between victim and abuser.

TABLE 11.1: THEORETICAL EXPLANATIONS OF INTIMATE PARTNER VIOLENCE

MODEL OR THEORY	EXPLANATION
Micro Level Analysis	
Power Theory (Finkelhor, Gelles, Hotaling, and Straus 1983; Straus, Gelles & Steinmetz, 1980; Straus and Hotaling 1980)	Explains violence in terms of the natural power differentials within the family and within male-female relationships. Suggests that partners who lack power will more likely to be abusive.
Resource Theory (Fox et al. 2002; Goode, 1971; Kaukinen, 2004; McCloskey, 1996)	Power differentials influence the propensity to use violence. Male violence is considered a resource of last resort when other resources are unavailable or proved ineffective.
Exchange Theory (Farmer & Tiefenthaler, 1997; Gibson-Davis, et al, 2005b; Riger & Krieglstein, 2000; Worden, 2002)	Explains intimate violence in terms of the interactions between victim and perpetrator from a cost-benefit point of view. Predicts violence would decrease as women's economic resources increase because in gaining resources, women also gain power.
Macro Level Analysis	
Cultural Approval of Violence (Pagelow, 1984; Straus, Gelles, & Steinmetz, 1980)	Assumes that violence is the product of widespread social approval; violence is so generally acceptable that low levels are considered "normative."
Subculture of Violence (Bersani & Chen, 1988; Wolfgang and Ferracuti, 1967)	Certain groups within society may be more likely than other groups to accept the use of violence in specific situations; In these subcultures violence is viewed as acceptable and even encouraged.
Feminist Theory (Dobash & Dobash 1979; Schecter, 1982; Yllo & Bograd, 1988)	Focuses on gender inequality of power; Patriarchal formulations attribute violence to male privilege and power; Patriarchy gives men the "right" to dominate and control women.
Family Violence Perspective (Gelles, 1972; 1993; Straus, Gelles, & Steinmetz, 1980)	Views violence as affecting all family relationships including parent-child, siblings, spouses, etc; the nature of the family structure is at the root of violence.
Deterrence Theory (Pate & Hamilton, 1992; Sherman et al., 1992)	Assumes that the low costs of intimate violence make it easy to abuse a partner and get away with it. Views formal controls, informal controls or both types of controls as effective strategies to deter potential offenders
Family Stress Theory (Farrington, 1980; 1986; Fox et al., 2002)	Explains domestic violence in terms of the characteristics of the family, such as privatization and social isolation, which make it susceptible to violence.

Continued

Continued from page 233

TABLE 11.1: THEORETICAL EXPLANATIONS OF INTIMATE PARTNER VIOLENCE

MODEL OR THEORY	EXPLANATION
Environmental Stress Theory (Gelles, 1972)	Individuals in low-income groups must confront more negative life events as compared to those of higher economic status while they have fewer resources to do so.
Multidimensional Analysis	
General Systems Theory (Giles-Sims, 1983; Straus, 1973)	Domestic violence results from a positive complex feedback system that operates at the individual, family, and societal levels.
Theory of Gender and Power (Raj et al., 1999)	Links gender, power, and violence; Addresses the sexual division of labor, sexual division of power within relationships, and culturally bound social norms.
Ecological Theory (Carlson, 1984; Heise, 1998; Shobe & Dienemann, 2007)	Violence as a multifaceted phenomenon caused by a mixture personal, situational, and sociocultural factors; emphasizes embedded levels of causality.
Gender and Violence (Anderson, 1997)	Combines the feminist and family violence perspectives with resource theory. Suggests women and men view violence differently and violence is one means of constructing masculinity.
Multiracial Feminism and Social Exchange Theory (Worden, 2002)	Combines social exchange theory with multiracial feminism; Exchange theory explains the actual processes of power while multiracial feminism highlights an understanding of race, ethnicity and gender and the relationships of these factors to economic resources.
Economic Exclusion/Male Peer Support Model (DeKeseredy, Alvi & Schwartz, 2006; DeKeseredy & Schwartz, 1993; 2002)	View intimate partner violence, rape and other forms of male-to-female victimization as legitimate and effective means for men to repair their "damaged" masculinity. Framework takes account of micro and macro level factors such as the patriarchal social structure, male-peer support, membership in social groups, alcohol use, and lack of deterrence.
Social Etiological Model (Jasinski, 2000)	Incorporates individual and structural factors; abuse is considered the result of structural inequality where individuals use violence to gain or regain control; the organization of the family is viewed as a factor contributing to violence.

TABLE 11.1: THEORETICAL EXPLANATIONS OF INTIMATE PARTNER VIOLENCE	
MODEL OR THEORY	**EXPLANATION**
Contextual Framework (Bell & Naugle, 2008)	Integrative framework that considers contextual factors associated with intimate partner violence including distal factors (e.g. childhood abuse, attachment style), proximal factors (e.g. partner's demands), motivating factors (e.g. substance use, relationship satisfaction), behavioral repertoire (e.g. coping skills, emotion regulation skills), discriminative stimuli (i.e. environmental cues), verbal rules (e.g. beliefs about violence, and women), and consequences of violence.

Central to the debate on the etiology of domestic violence has been a discussion regarding the importance of gender and patriarchy (Anderson, 1997; Barnett et al 2005; Hagen & Davis, 1992; Gelles, 1993). Feminist theory has been one of the dominant frameworks explaining intimate partner violence although it has not been without challengers. Feminist theory views intimate partner violence as a consequence of a patriarchal society that promotes male coercive power and domination over females (Bowker, 1983; Dobash & Dobash, 1979; O'Leary, 1999; Pagelow, 1984; Stets, 1988). Abuse is viewed as a consequence of a culture that supports the domination of men over women through sexism and economic inequality (Dutton, 1994; Goodyear-Smith, et al., 1999; Harrell, 1991; Levesque et al., 2000; Ronfeldt, Kimerling & Arias, 1998; Yllo, 1993). Feminist theory incorporates the notion that economic inequalities between men and women contribute to the legitimization of male domination and abuse of females (Fagan et al, 1994; Schneider, 2000). Economic and social processes operate directly and indirectly to support a male dominated social order and family structure. From this perspective, intimate partner violence is a product of the male and female sex roles, which are inherently imbalanced. The central theoretical argument is that patriarchy leads to the subordination and oppression of women and causes the historical pattern of systematic violence directed against wives (Dobash & Dobash 1979; Pagelow 1984; Yllo, 1993). Feminist theory suggests that because patriarchal social norms incorporate and accept male violence, power and violence is sustained at the societal level (Berk et al., 1983; Dobash & Dobash, 1979, 1984, 1988; Dutton, 1994; Pagelow, 1984; Yllo & Bograd, 1988).

In addition to the theoretical debate surrounding the role of gender, more recent discussions have focused on the role of socioeconomic status. Theorists have begun to recognize the inability of most theoretical explanations of intimate partner to include socioeconomic factors. These theories have not, to date, adequately incorporated socioeconomic variables (Meier, 1997; Moore, 1997; Raphael 2001; and Riger & Krieglstein, 2000). Although explanations for intimate partner violence that explicitly integrate socioeconomic factors are relatively rare, there is an emerging body of theoretical literature that has, to some extent, incorporated economic factors in their explanation. The following section explores these emerging efforts to incorporate economic factors in theoretical explanations of intimate partner violence and the empirical evidence for these frameworks.

EXCHANGE THEORIES

Social exchange theories are a particularly appealing framework because they explicitly allow for consideration of financial resources (Riger & Krieglstein, 2000; Worden, 2002). Exchange theory focuses on the structure of social relationships and the flow of benefits through social interaction. The early roots of exchange theory can be traced to utilitarian economics and classical anthropology, while more recent attention has come from behavioral psychology and sociology (Turner, 2003; Molm, 2001). Traditionally, social exchange theory has focused on positive or rewarding outcomes and did not examine punishment or power based on the capacity to punish (Molm, 1997). Early theorists, such as Homans ([1961] 1974) and Blau (1964), explicitly excluded punishment and coercive power from their scope of social exchange theory while Emerson (1962; 1972a 1972b) did so implicitly (Molm, 1997). Only more recently has attention focused on relations of dependence characterized by unequal power and conflict (Molm, 1997; 2001) and specifically intimate partner violence (Worden, 2002).

TABLE 11.2: ASSUMPTIONS OF SOCIAL EXCHANGE THEORY (MOLM, 1997)

ACTORS

Actors behave in ways that increase outcomes they positively value and decrease outcomes they negatively value.

RESOURCES

Every class of valued outcomes obeys a principle of satiation (in psychological terms) or diminishing marginal utility (in economic terms).

STRUCTURE OF EXCHANGE

Exchange relations develop within structures of mutual dependence.

PROCESS OF EXCHANGE

Exchange transactions: Benefits obtained from others are contingent on benefits given in exchange.

Exchange relations: Actors engage in recurring, interdependent exchanges with specific partners over time.

The central premise of exchange theory is that human behavior is in essence an exchange (Homans, 1961 [1974]). Virtually all social exchange theories are premised explicitly on four core assumptions (Table 11.2; Molm, 1997). These basic concepts focus on the actors involved in the exchange, the exchange resources, the structure of the exchange, and the process of exchange. The first assumption brings attention to how actors are dependent on one another for outcomes they value. The mutual dependence on one another for valued resources provides the structural basis for their power over each other (Molm, 2001; Molm, Quist, & Wisely, 1994). Following the "principle of least interest," the partner who has the more resources is less dependent on the relationship (Homans, 1961 [1974]). The second assumption highlights how actors are self-interested, seeking to increase outcomes they positively value and decrease outcomes they negatively value (Molm, 2001; Molm & Cook, 1995; Molm, Quist, & Wisely, 1994). While humans are not perfectly rational, they do engage in calculations of costs and benefits in social transactions and attempt to make some benefit from their social transactions with others (Turner, 2003). The third assumption captures the basic premise of exchange theory that social relations are formed and maintained because actors provide reciprocal benefits over time. Actors engage in recurring, mutually contingent exchanges with specific partners over time (Molm & Cook, 1995). The final assumption suggests that all outcomes of value follow a principal of satiation or as described in economic terms as diminishing marginal utility.

Gelles' (1983) work represents one of the earliest efforts to systematically use exchange theory to examine domestic violence (Worden, 2002). Drawing on social exchange theory and to a lesser extent social control theory, Gelles proposed an exchange/social control model of domestic violence. Gelles accepted the basic premise of exchange theory that "human interaction is guided by the pursuit of rewards and the avoidance of punishments" (p.157). Following Blau (1964), Gelles believed that an individual who receives a reward is obligated to reciprocate any gain and furnish benefits to the individual who provided them with the gain. From an exchange perspective, the interaction generally will continue if reciprocity is maintained. Gelles, however, argued that unlike other social interactions, familial relations cannot always be easily broken off. Anger, resentment, conflict, and violence may result from the imbalanced relationship (Gelles). Additionally, Gelles accepted the premise of social control theory that individuals must have control mechanisms to prevent deviant behavior (Bersani & Chen, 1988).

Social control theory contends that deviant criminal behavior will occur in the absence of societal controls to sanction the behavior. Social control is exerted to prevent violence within the family and the absence of effective social controls over family relations decreases the costs of one family member being violent toward another. Combining exchange and social control theory, Gelles (1983) derives the following proposition of family violence: "People hit and abuse other family members because they can" (p.157). Gelles expands this basic concept by stating three principles:

1. Family members are more likely to use violence in the home when they expect that the costs of being violent are less than the rewards.
2. The absence of effective social controls over family relations decreases the costs of one family member being violent toward another.
3. Certain social and family structures serve to reduce social control in family relations, and therefore reduce the costs and/or increase the rewards of being violent.

Gelles suggests violence is compounded by the private nature of institutions like the family and the reluctance of the courts and other institutions to intervene and assist in reducing the cost of the violence. Cultural approval of the use of violence increases the rewards for violent behavior (Jasinski, 2001). Gelles's exchange/social control framework specifically focuses on inequalities when the male partner maintains higher status positions and earns more money. From this perspective, women's economic dependency on men contributes to violence by enabling men to batter without fearing the loss of the relationship (Riger & Krieglstein, 2000) or economic or social sanctions (Gelles, 1983). This theory would predict that violence would decrease when women's economic resources increase because, in gaining greater resources, women have also gained power.

More recently, theorists have extended the exchange perspective and integrated insights from bargaining theory in economics. Similar to earlier exchange perspectives, this theory posits that increasing a woman's economic resources empowers her to either bargain for a better situation for herself within the relationship or threaten to leave the relationship altogether and deprive the man of her company and financial contribution (England & Farkas, 1986; Farmer & Tiefenthaler, 1997; Gibson-Davis, et al, 2005b). A woman's employment and earnings give her a stronger position from which to negotiate with her partner to stop violent or threatening behavior. Bargaining with a partner is conducted with an undertone marked by the possibility of ending the relationship and the viability of each partner's alternative options (Gibson-Davis et al., 2005b). These options or threat points refer to what an individual has to fall back on if the relationship dissolves. This could include, how much one earns, access to other income or support or alternative options for other partners (England & Farkas, 1986). Bargaining power is, therefore, increased if a person has access to assistance from family or friends, social services, or laws which would provide generous divorce settlements (Farmer & Tiefenthaler, 1997).

From the perspective of Farmer and Tiefanthaler (1997), even if a woman does not use a service designed to help women experiencing abuse, simply its availability improves her well-being because it increases her threat-point. Farmer and Tiefenthaler's economic analysis of intimate partner violence suggests that while some women use domestic violence services to facilitate leaving a relationship others use services even though they are not in a position to leave their abuser. The latter group uses services to decrease violence by increasing their 'threat points.'

Supporting evidence of social exchange/bargaining frameworks can be found in the work of Tauchen et al. (1991). Tauchen and colleagues examined data from a sample of 125 women who had been physically abused by an intimate male partner. Their results suggest that violence decreases as women's economic resources increases, although there was an exception for high-income couples where the woman earns most of the income. Farmer and Tiefenthaler (1997) found similar results in their analysis of data from the Domestic Violence Experience in Omaha, Nebraska (1986–1987) and the Charlotte North Carolina Spouse Replication Project (1987–1989). Their results indicated that women who are employed experienced fewer incidences of physical abuse. Within the Charlotte sample, a woman with an additional $1,000 in monthly take-home income experienced six fewer incidences of violence (Farmer & Tiefenthaler, 1997).

Research that has evaluated the effect of a woman's income on the likelihood that she leaves a violent relationship has also been consistent with a social exchange bargaining framework. For example, Pagelow (1981) finds that a woman's access to resources has an effect on whether she leaves a violent husband. Strube and Barbour (1983) examined factors related to the decision to leave an abusive relationship and found that economic dependence played one of the most important roles in the decisions to remain in abusive relationships. Their findings that the more psychologically committed the women were to the relationship, the less likely they were to leave are also in line with the bargaining perspective. Strube and Barbour (1984) later replicated their study with 251 subjects and found that the length of relationship, employment status, and material hardship were consistent.

RESOURCE THEORY

Resource theory is a social psychological framework for understanding social interactions and relationships. It is closely related to social exchange theory and some researchers have suggested resource theory and exchange theories are conceptually equivalent (e.g. Avakame, 1999; McCloskey; 1996). Some scholars describe these frameworks as separate theories (e.g. Bersani & Chen, 1988; Kurst-Swanger, & Petcosky, 2003; Loue, 2001), while others, including myself, view resource theory as one perspective situated within the framework of exchange theory (e.g. Hesse-Biber & Williamson, 1984; Jasinksi, 2001). Like social exchange theory, this framework points to resource deficits as significant risk factors of intimate partner violence and focuses attention on the balance or imbalance of resources within the couple as underlying the use of violence (Fox, et al., 2002; Goode, 1971; Kaukinen, 2004; McCloskey, 1996). In contrast to exchange theory, this framework has not been as fully elaborated (Hesse-Biber & Williamson, 1984) and makes slightly different predictions about intimate partner violence.

Resource theory was first articulated as a framework for studying power within the family by Wolfe (1959) and was subsequently elaborated by Blood and Wolfe (1960). Blood and Wolfe (1960) perceived a close relationship between power and resources. From their perspective, power is viewed as the potential ability of one individual to influence the behavior of another. Resources are conceptualized broadly to include anything one individual can offer to another to help that person satisfy needs or attain goals (Hesse-Biber, & Williamson, 1984). The work of Goode (1971) represents one of the earliest applications of resource theory to violence within intimate partnerships. Goode (1971) characterized resources that can be used to exert power within intimate relationships into four groups: economic variables; prestige and respect; force and its threat; and likeability, attractiveness, friendship, and love (Goode, 1971).

Goode (1971) argued that individuals who possess economic resources, prestige, and likeability/love generally will not feel the need to use threats or overt force. Thus, male violence is a resource of last resort, when other resources are unavailable or have proved ineffective (Goode, 1971). Building on the work of Goode (1971), Allen and Straus (1980) describe violence as the "ultimate resource" that will be invoked by a person who lacks other resources used to derive power within relationships. Specifically, comparative resources theory suggests a status inconsistency hypothesis where the risk of male violence is heightened in couples in which the female's economic contribution meets or exceeds the male's contribution to their economic well being (Allen & Straus, 1980; Atkinson, Greenstein & Lang, 2005; Fox et al., 2002; Goode, 1971). Additionally, resource theory suggests that in couples with male superiority in earnings in work history, male violence might be more likely if violence is construed as a privilege of his greater resource contribution and simultaneously as a reflection of his partner's relative economic vulnerability (Fox et al., 2002). Resource theory contends that the power differential between partners influences the propensity towards violence (Anderson, 1997). The most powerful people tend to abuse the least powerful individuals; therefore, the less power a female has, as compared to her partner, the greater the risk of abuse.

From this perspective intimate violence occurs when a man loses his instrumental and symbolic role as a breadwinner (Gibson-Davis, et al., 2005b). As women become more economically independent, men may resort to an available resource—namely violence—to compensate for both their labor market difficulties and for their frustrations when women become chief breadwinners (Fox, et al., 2002; Hornung, McCullough & Sugimoto, 1981; Macmillan & Gartner, 1999; McCloskey, 1996). The Family Violence Option (FVO), motivated by a concern that forcing a woman to work may increase her risk of abuse, is consistent with the resource perspective (Gibson-Davis et al., 2005b).

Empirical support for resource theory can be found in studies that indicate men with lower levels of income, prestige, and income are more likely to abuse their wives (Allen & Strauss, 1981; Hoffman, Demo, & Edwards, 1994; Hornung, McCullough, & Sugimoto, 1981; Hotaling and Sugarman, 1986; McCall & Shields, 1986; Okun, 1986). Hornung, McCullough and Sugimoto (1981) analyzed the link between marital violence and the occupational and educational match between partners. They found higher rates of violence among couples where the woman's occupational status exceeded the man's status. Conversely, lower rates of violence were found in couples where men's resources far exceeded those of his wife. Allen and Strauss (1981) had similar results in their examination of college students' reports of violence between their parents. Male perpetrated violence was more likely when the woman's economic resources were much higher than her husband's resources.

More recent studies have indicated support of relative resource theory when measures of status inconsistency were used to compare the men's resources to that of their female partner (Atkinson, Greenstein & Lang, 2005). McCloskey (1996) examined the effect of socioeconomic factors to "determine whether it is the strain of economics or gender related economic power that give rise to domestic violence" (p. 452). Although occupational disparity was unrelated to domestic violence, when women's economic resources approached or exceeded their partner's they were more likely to be abused. These findings may suggest that when men's contributions of resources to the family are lower than their wife's contribution marital tension can increase as a result of perceived failures in fulfilling gender roles. Fox et al.'s (2002) analysis of the National Survey of Families and Households revealed some evidence supporting this position, although their evidence offered stronger support for hypotheses related to stress theory. Macmillan and Gartner's (1999) findings on spousal violence from a nationally representative sample of Canadian women revealed that patterns of employment in marital relationships had large and consistent effects on risks of spousal violence. The results indicated that the effect of one partner's employment is conditioned by the employment status of the other partner. Women's labor force participation lowered the risk of spousal abuse when their male partners were employed, but substantially increased the risk when their male partners were not employed.

A growing body of empirical and theoretical work has also integrated feminist insights into resource theory. Anderson (1997) proposed a gender and violence theory in an effort to combine feminist and family violence perspectives and integrate them with resource theory. Anderson's approach attempts to integrate family violence researchers' focus on how structural inequalities increase the propensity for intimate violence with feminist insights about gender and power. This knowledge is then incorporated into resource theorists' view that individuals who have relatively few resources, as compared with their partner, may engage in domestic violence as a means to affirm their power within the relationship. Anderson's analysis of the first wave of the National Survey of Families and Households suggested that while gender, per se, was not a significant predictor of violence, risk factors for intimate partner violence differed by gender. Resource theory was supported by the strong inverse relationship between couple's earnings and men's perpetration of violent acts although it was also contradicted by the weaker and less consistent finding that higher levels of education may be linked to more violence among men (Anderson). The integration of gender theory with resource explanations of intimate violence was also supported by the finding that a man's lower relative income status was associated with higher rates of male violence, whereas the opposite pattern existed for women (Anderson).

Situated within the resource and power theory frameworks, Raj and colleagues (1999) proposed the theory of gender and power to explain intimate abuse within heterosexual relationships. Their approach considers the influence of socioeconomic factors and attempts to be more sensitive to culture and gender than traditional explanatory models. The theory of gender and power initially emerged from Connell's (1987) work developing a social theory of gender relations. Since this beginning, the theory of gender and power has been operationalized to examine issues related to women's health (Wingood & DiClemente, 1992) and now more recently intimate partner violence against women (Raj, et al., 1999).

The theory of gender and power focuses on three structures that influence the culturally-bound roles of men and women. These structures include: (1) the sexual division of labor, (2) sexual division of power within relationships, and (3) culturally bound social norms. The sexual division of labor explicitly addresses socioeconomic factors related to the experience of intimate partner violence by bringing attention to the gender-based allocation of work manifested through segregation of unpaid work such as housework and childcare, inequalities in wages and educational attainment between men and women (Raj, et al., 1999). According to the structure of labor, women may be more susceptible to direct or indirect financial incentives to maintain a relationship with an abusive partner when the economic disparity between men and women increases. The sexual division of power incorporates imbalances created through control, authority, and coercion in heterosexual relationships. The structure of cathexis encompasses the culturally bound social norms that govern the roles of men and women in relationships. This structure dictates, within a given cultural context, which behaviors are considered appropriate for individuals in various social roles (Raj, et al., 1999). Accepting normative roles and behaviors may diminish women's power within a relationship and could potentially block means for women to resist abuse (Raj, et al., 1999).

Raj and colleagues (1999) found partial support for the theory of gender and power in explaining intimate partner violence within a community based sample of low-income African-American women. Their results indicate that economic challenges might limit women's abilities to effectively resist violence from their male partners. Consistent with earlier research by Hornung, McCullough, and Sugimoto (1981), McCloskey (1996), and Raj, et al. (1999) found support for the notion that women's greater relative economic power increases men's likelihood of being abusive. The strongest predictors of intimate partner violence were variables related to gender-based power differentials in the relationship.

More recently, Riger and Krieglstein (2000) have integrated resource theory with feminist insights that highlight how the desire for male dominance could potentially spark a "backlash" should women gain economic resources. According to the backlash hypothesis, abuse may increase as a violent-prone man attempts to compensate for their relative loss of dominance. As Riger and Krieglstein (2000) point out, the lack of longitudinal data on violence against women has made it difficult to fully test this theory. Despite this limitation, there has been some evidence from cross-sectional studies indicating support for the feminist backlash hypothesis.

Atkinson, Greenstein, and Lang (2005) analyzed the first wave of the National Survey of Families and Households. Their results suggest that husband's relative earnings are negatively and significantly related to the likelihood of abuse primarily when men adhere to traditional ideologies of women's employment. Relative resources had little effect on the likelihood of abuse when husbands held more egalitarian attitudes toward women. Examining data from the 1999 Canadian General Social Survey, Kaukinen (2004) found some support that supported the backlash hypothesis. Kaukinen concluded that while status compatibilities favoring women were not related to increased risk of physical violence, they were associated with an increased risk of emotional abuse.

Evidence that domestic violence is a barrier to employment for some women is also in line with the backlash approach (Gibson-Davis et al, 2005b). In some relationships, the man may resent a woman's economic independence and therefore take steps to sabotage her employment (Honeycutt, Marshall, & Weston, 2001; Lein, Jaquet, Lewis, Cole, & Williams, 2001; Raphael, 2001; Romero, Chavkin, Wise & Smith, 2003). Research has documented that abusers can hinder labor force participation by turning off an alarm clock, inflicting bruises that mar a woman's appearance, undermining her self confidence, or harassing her at her place of employment (Moe & Bell, 2004; Riger et al., 2000; Sable, Libbus, Huncke, & Anger, 1999; Tolman & Rosen, 2001). The findings of Brush (2000) for example, indicate that education and training can precipitate or aggravate controlling behaviors of intimate partners.

McCloskey (1996) similarly noted that when a woman's economic resources approached or exceeded their partner's they were more likely to be abused. In contrast, Avakame's (1999) study of rape victimization did not find support for the backlash hypothesis. Unemployed women were more likely to be raped than women working outside the home were and in contrast to the backlash hypothesis, employed women were less likely to be raped by an intimate partner. It is possible however that these findings may be due to the focus on rape and the use of survey data that collected in the context of a crime survey.

STRESS THEORIES

Stress is considered a significant risk factor for violence against women (Farrington, 1986; Jasinski, 2001; Kurst-Swanger & Petcosky, 2003; Pagelow, 1984). Although stress has received inconsistent attention within the domestic violence literature, it has been the focus of several theorists who generally taken two paths: the family stress perspective and the environmental stress perspective. The first approach focuses on individuals within the family and the characteristics that make families particularly prone to stress. In contrast, the environmental stress perspective examines the structural characteristics of society that result in a disparate distribution of opportunities.

Although violence has long been viewed as problem for families with increased levels of stress (Kurst-Swanger & Petcosky, 2003), Farrington (1980; 1986) is one of the first researchers to specifically focus on the role stress plays in family violence. Following general stress theorists, Farrington (1986) suggests stress is a multidimensional concept that involves both objective and subjective components. The objective component involves a stressor stimulus or series of stressor stimuli and the objective reality that stressor stimulus has on the individual, independent of any cognitive perception or interpretation on the part of the individual. The subjective element relates to the definition of the situation arrived at by the individual or social system. Stress is then viewed as a discrepancy between the demand posed by the objective and/or subjective demands of a stressor stimulus and the coping behavior(s) drawn from the individual's or social system's response capabilities (Farrington, 1986).

From this perspective violence is not likely to be the most frequent response to stress (Farrington, 1986). It is also neither a necessary nor a sufficient condition for violence to occur (Farrington, 1986). With the exception of Cano and Vivian (2001), most researchers (e.g. Farrington, 1986; Straus, 1990c), do not argue that stress directly causes violence. A number of important precipitating and mediating variables operate to determine whether a particular individual will respond to stress or the frustration resulting from an unresolved stress experience in a violent manner (Farrington, 1986; Straus, 1990c). Mediating factors can include the sex of the actor, socioeconomic position, past experiences with violent behavior, and the extent to which violence is viewed as an acceptable response to a stressful situation within the actor's family and subculture (Farrington, 1986), norms related to the legitimacy of violence within the family (Farrington, 1986; Straus, 1990c), and the involuntary nature of family membership (Straus, 1990c).

Families are often not adequately equipped with the necessary resources to manage demanding situations (Farrington, 1986; Straus, 1990b). The family stress theory suggests that diminished economic resources may lead to conflict in intimate relationships (Holtzworth-Munroe et al 1997; Riggs et al., 2000; Straus, 1990c; Straus et al., 1980). Work related stressors such as unemployment and chronic poverty may be particularly stressful situations for men. These stressors, leading to frustration, in turn may heighten the risk of husband to wife violence (Gelles & Cornell, 1990; Jasinski, 2001; Riggs et al, 2000). When demands are intolerable, violence may be an acceptable response to the stressful situation (Jasinski, 2001).

Stress frustration theories would suggest that violence is particularly prevalent in relationships in which both partners are unemployed or work long hours, household income is low, and neither has a high school educational attainment (Kaukinen, 2004). Stress theories also predict that newer relationships, young age, cohabitation instead of marriage, and the presence of young children would heighten the risk of abuse (Kaukinen, 2004).

The environmental stress theory assumes that stress and frustration elicit abusive behavior and holds that violence in human relations arises from institutionalized inequalities between people along age, race, gender, and social class lines (Gil, 1986). Exposure to social stress varies significantly across gender, age, marital status, and occupational status (Turner, Wheaton, & Lloyd, 1995) with those from lower SES groups experiencing greater amounts of environmental stress (Gil, 1970; McLeod & Kessler, 1990; Parke & Collmer, 1975). The unequal distribution of opportunities, along with stressors associated with poverty (e.g. financial worry, poor health, crowded living conditions) produces high levels of frustration in lower class families (Farrington, 1980; Straus, 1980a). Additionally, while low income groups must confront more negative life events as compared to those of higher economic status, they have fewer resources to do so (Farrington, 1986; Gelles, 1993; Gil, 1970; MacEwen & Barling, 1988). Individuals with financial means can simply purchase relief from their problems, which keeps them from festering and presenting as violence (Schwartz, 1988).

Environmental stress is a central concept of the social structural theory of violence (Gelles, 1972; See Table 2.4). The social structural theory views violence as generally a response to stress, frustration, or to threats to identity. Violence is rarely an "irrational attack" (Gelles, 1972). This approach recognizes that stress is differentially distributed in social structures (Gelles, 1972). Families that have less education, occupational status, and income are more likely to encounter stressful events and have stressful family relations as compared to families with higher education, occupational status, and income. Additionally the ability to cope with stress is unevenly distributed and the families that encounter the most stress have the fewest resources to deal with it (Gelles, 1972).

Findings that violence is more common among lower income couples and couples experiencing bouts of unemployment (Greenfeld, et al; Rennison & Welchans, 2000; Tjaden & Thoennes, 1998) are consistent with the view of environmental stress theories. Additional support can also found in the work of Cunradi, Caetano, and Schafer (2002). Their examination of the 1995 National Alcohol Survey linked low socioeconomic status with increased risks of intimate partner violence, although the relative influence on the probability of violence varied across racial/ethnic groups and by perpetrator gender. Income made a greater contribution to the probability of violence than education or employment status category (Cunradi, Caetano, & Schafer, 2002).

Fox et al. (2002) tested both family stress theory and resource theory in their study of the impact of household economic indicators on the risk of violence against women in intimate relationships. Their results provided greater support for family stress theory as they concluded that men's and women's preferences for their spouse's additional employment hours are important in predicting man to woman violence (Fox et al., 2002). In addition, the risk of violent victimization was elevated for employed women whose jobs render them exhausted and irritable, who feel not working is not an option, who work in lower level, blue-collar jobs, when there is an increased reliance on women's income, or women's working is a sign of financial problems (Fox et al., 2002).

ECOLOGICAL THEORIES

Ecological theories conceptualize violence as a multifaceted phenomenon caused by a combination of personal, situational, and sociocultural factors. Ecological theories of intimate partner violence are grounded in Bronfenbrenner's (1977, 1979) early work that focused on a child's development within the context of the system of relationships that form his or her environment. Bronfenbrenner's ecological model is one of the best-known and most often cited theories explaining human development (Edleson & Tolman, 1992). Ecological explanations of violence were initially developed by Garbarino (1977) and Belsky (1980) in efforts to help explain child abuse and neglect. Since these beginnings, ecological frameworks have been applied to intimate partner violence by a variety of theorists including Carlson (1984), Edleson and Tolman (1992), Heise, (1998), and Riger, et al. (2002).

Although ecological approaches have been conceptualized in a variety of ways, they share the notion of embedded levels of causality and draw on several levels of analysis (Edleson & Tolman, 1992; Heise, 1998). Carlson's (1984) work represents an early application of an ecological framework to domestic violence. Heise's (1998) more recent efforts, like Belsky (1980), used the ecological model as a heuristic tool to organize empirical research. Both models are represented visually as four concentric circles although they each adopted different terminology. The following paragraphs outline how Carlson (1984) and Heise (1998) integrated socioeconomic factors into the four levels of their ecological explanation of intimate partner violence.

The innermost circle of Carlson's model represents individual factors that each person brings to the relationship. Individual factors include "attitudes, values and beliefs learned in one's family of origin; personal resources, skills and abilities; subjective perceptions of reality and views of the world; and personal weaknesses, problems, and pathologies" (Carlson, 1984, p. 572). Carlson (1984) describes several socioeconomic factors at the individual level including occupational status, income, and education. At this level, Carlson (1984) also highlights the importance of resources that each partner brings to a relationship and incorporates insights gleaned from resource theory (Allen & Straus, 1980) and status incompatibility frameworks (Hornung, McCullough & Sugimoto, 1981). The first level of Heise's model focuses on personal history or ontogenic factors. Socioeconomic factors are not included in this level of Heise's (1998) model. Heise concluded that income, education level, and occupying the role of a housewife were not consistently related to victimization of women (p. 267).

The second level of analysis in Carlson's (1984) model focuses on the nature of the family including the family role structure and familial interactions. At the family level, socioeconomic factors relate to the division of labor within the family. While the family division of labor has been traditionally quite rigid and based primarily on an individual's sex, significant changes have begun (Carlson, 1984). Carlson (1984) attributes these changes in part to the tremendous influx of women in the workforce and women's greater decision-making roles within the family.

The second level of Heise's model describes the microsystem or "immediate context of abuse" (p. 269). Similar to Carlson (1984), Heise emphasizes factors related to the family and male dominance and control of decision-making authority and economic resources. Heise suggests empirical support for these factors can be found in Levinson's (1989) cross-cultural research and Straus et al's (1980) analysis of the 1975 National Family Violence Survey. Levinson concluded that male economic and decision-making authority in the family was one of the strongest predictors of societies that demonstrate high levels of violence against women. Straus and colleagues (1980) reported that wife abuse occurred in about 11% of couples with a clearly dominant husband as compared to 3% of couples where the women had relatively equal influence on decision-making. Heise highlights the work of Levinson (1989) and Kalmuss (1984) suggesting that male control of wealth in the family increases the risk of abuse. Levinson (1989) noted that wife abuse was most frequent in societies in which men control the wealth, while Kalmuss (1984) report similar findings in the U.S. According to their analysis of a nationally representative data set, a wife's economic dependence on her husband—defined as the wife being unemployed outside the home, the presence of children under age five, and the husband earning 75% of the income—was a significant predictor of severe wife-beating (Kalmuss, 1984). Heise presents evidence suggesting that socioeconomic factors contribute to conflicts in violent marriage. Noting the work of Hotaling and Sugarman (1990), Heise suggests that marital conflicts often involve disagreements related to the division of labor and a wife's educational attainment exceeding that of her husband.

Carlson's third level of analysis outlines social structural causes of domestic violence related to major institutions in society. In the broadest sense these institutions are reflected by economic indicators such as the strength of the economy, overall unemployment rates, and the distribution of goods in society (Carlson, 1984). Carlson notes that the structural theory of intrafamily violence (Gelles & Straus, 1979) is relevant at this level of the social ecology as it highlights the impact of unemployment and the stress and material deprivation associated with it. This approach recognizes societal resources are not equitably distributed across all social groups. Structural inequalities cause deprivation to be differentially distributed across families with those at the bottom of the socioeconomic ladder leading more stressful deprived lives. Research has documented the role of economic factors and particularly unemployment in contributing to marital conflict (Carlson, 1984). Carlson suggests that socioeconomic factors appear to contribute to violence through the stress and tension created by insufficient material resources.

In the exosystem, the third level of Heise's (1998) analysis, low socioeconomic position and unemployment emerged as factors linked to intimate partner violence. Heise notes that family income has been a consistent risk factor for violence in general population surveys and multiple studies as indicated by Hotaling and Sugarman's (1986) case-comparison study. Heise also calls attention to similar evidence that has emerged from cross-cultural research. Heise (1998) notes that unemployment has been linked with violence although it is not clear whether being unemployed, in itself, increases the risk of violence. "It may not be the lack of income, but rather some other variable that accompanies the experience of living in poverty, such as crowding or hopelessness, that is significant" (Heise, 1998, p 274).

The fourth level of Carlson's model is the sociocultural level of analysis and focuses on societal norms, cultural values, and belief systems that affect members of society. Carlson (1984) addresses sexism, sex-role stereotyping, general acceptance of violence and the norms about a family in general. In relation to socioeconomic factors, Carlson discusses the impact of sexism manifested in the labor market that makes it difficult for women to obtain and maintain jobs and receive equal pay for equal work.

The fourth level of analysis in Heise's (1998) model is the macrosystem. In an approach similar to Carlson (1984), Heise (1998) refers to the broad cultural values and beliefs that influence the other layers of the social ecology. Specifically she addresses conceptions of masculinity, rigid gender roles at the societal or individual levels, sense of male entitlement over women, approval of physical chastisement of women and a cultural ethos that condones violence as a means to resolve interpersonal disputes. Heise (1998) does not explicitly discuss socioeconomic factors at this level although such factors as rigid gender roles relate to work and the labor market.

One positive feature of ecological frameworks is the ability to recognize multiple causes of intimate partner violence by factors operating at different levels of analysis (Carlson, 1984; Edleson & Tolman, 1992, and Heise, 1998). As the description of Carlson (1984) and Heise's (1998) framework exemplifies, socioeconomic factors were included at both individual and broader levels of analysis. Perhaps the most serious challenge of an ecological theory is that it does not provide clear direction on how various factors, once identified, should be weighted (Carlson, 1984). As Carlson (1984) noted, it is reasonable to assume that the contributions of all factors are not equally important and that particular factors are not equally important across different situations.

ECONOMIC EXCLUSION/MALE PEER SUPPORT MODEL

The economic exclusion/male peer support model conceptualizes violence as a multifaceted phenomenon caused by a combination of micro- and macro-level factors (see Fig. 12.1). This framework has emerged relatively recently and is grounded in the theoretical work by DeKeseredy and Schwartz (1993), Sernau (2001), and Young (1999). The economic exclusion model contends that major economic transformations, such as the shift from a manufacturing to a service based economy, stagnating wages, and downsizing and outsourcing of jobs, led to an increase in formal labor market exclusion. These changes have contributed to alarmingly high unemployment rates and a class of "postmodern serfs" composed of underemployed, deskilled, and disposable service workers (DeKeseredy, Alvi, & Schwartz, 2006).

In the face of these changes, being an economic provider is still fundamental to most men's self identity and part of women's expectations (Edin, 2000; Kenney 2006; Lichter, Batson, & Brown,

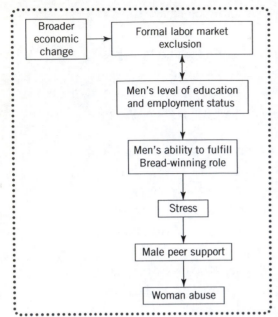

FIGURE 11.1

Economic exclusion/ male peer support model (DeKeseredy & Schwartz, 2002; DeKeseredy, Alvi, & Schwartz, 2006).

2004). Consequently, more men are left to cope with the stress of being unable to be a "good breadwinner" and they often turn to their male peers for support (DeKeseredy, Alvi, & and Schwartz, 2006). Male peer support has been described as the attachments to male peers and the resources through which these men perpetuate and legitimate violence against women (DeKeseredy, 1990). Male peer support models initially were used to examine violence against women and the influence of memberships in primary social groups that subscribe to patriarchal ideologies. They have been used to explain rape and sexual assault against college women (Schwartz & DeKeseredy, 1997), women in public housing (DeKeseredy and Schwartz, 2002) as well violence perpetrated by men in the military (Morris, 1996; Rosen, Kaminski, Palmley, Knudson & Fancher, 2003) and male student athletes (Crosset, Ptacek, McDonald, & Benedict, 1996).

The male peer support model takes account of a number of factors including a patriarchal social structure, male peer social support, membership in social groups, alcohol use, and lack of deterrence. Expanding the traditional social bond theory of crime and delinquency, Godenzi, Schwartz, and DeKeseredy (2001) argue that deviance is a culturally relative construct and that some behaviors defined by scholars as 'deviant' are in fact acts of conformity to the norms that are conventional within certain communities or social groups. Within these groups men feel pressured to adopt values associated with violence against women (Godenzi, Schwartz, & DeKeseredy, 2001). Male peer support groups provide positive reinforcement and social rewards for behavior the group considers appropriate (DeKeseredy & Schwartz, 1993). In addition there is a lack of punishment and deterrence. Violence against women is seen as a legitimate and effective means to repair "damaged" masculinity. Peers also serve as role models because many of them beat their own intimate partners.

While a limited number of studies have tested the economic exclusion/male peer support model, it is consistent with the larger body of research that has concluded the risk of domestic violence is exacerbated when economic differentials favor women. Empirical evidence that focuses on male peer support has also emerged. Schwartz & DeKeseredy's (2000) analysis of a national representative sample from Canada suggests that informational peer support for abusive behavior was a significant predictor of male perpetrated sexual abuse during dating. The authors conclude that informational support provides men with guidance and advice that encourages sexual, physical, and psychological assault on dating partners. Focusing on data from 713 U.S. servicemen, Rosen and colleagues (2003) examined both individual and group-level predictors of intimate partner violence, specifically focusing on factors associated with the cultural environment of a small military group. Consistent with a male-peer support framework, lower leadership support (vertical cohesion), a culture of hypermasculinity (operationalized as increased group disrespect), and lower support for spouses were significantly associated with an increased risk of intimate partner violence.

SUMMARY OF THE THEORETICAL LITERATURE

The recent efforts reviewed above provide encouraging evidence that theorists are beginning to address the connection between intimate partner violence and socioeconomic factors. Reviewing these efforts has also brought attention to areas that should receive attention in order to improve our theoretical understanding of the relationship between intimate partner violence and socioeconomic factors. The need for clarity is an issue that requires attention. Many frameworks explaining intimate partner violence consist of similar ideas and subsequently lack theoretical clarity. The distinction between social exchange theory and resource theory, for example, is rarely well articulated. This lack of agreement is indicative of the need to recognize and explore the discrepancies within the theoretical literature. Theoretical clarity will be particularly useful in order to empirically test a theory.

Additionally, the empirical evidence in support of these theories is another primary concern. Developing a comprehensive and useful theory requires ongoing empirical investigation (quantitative and qualitative) (Bersani & Chen, 1988). While the theoretical literature explaining intimate partner violence is large, the empirical data in support of these theories is quite meager (Margolin, Sibner, & Gleberman, 1988). The lack of empirical evidence is particularly pronounced when considering theories that integrate socioeconomic factors. Contributions to the theoretical literature would be strengthened with the addition of empirical evidence. The work of Yick (2001) and Riger and Krieglstein (2000), for example, represent ambitious attempts at theory development. While these are valuable contributions to the development of scientific knowledge, they leave much of what we 'know' at the level of theoretical speculation (Farrington, 1986). For this reason it is imperative that there be greater empirical investigation in terms of testing the utility of theoretical models and looking specifically at the relationships between socioeconomic factors and violence. There remain many questions about the relationship of socioeconomic factors and violence, which can only be answered through additional investigation.

Empirical investigations rarely test more than one theory and we are often limited in our ability to evaluate the relative utility of explanations (Margolin, Sibner, & Gleberman, 1988). Future research might benefit from studies that test more than one theory at a time. Fox and colleagues (2002) provide an example of how this can be particularly useful. Their analysis of the National Survey of Families and Households revealed evidence supporting both family stress and resource theory. The evidence was not equal as the results provided stronger support for the family stress model (Fox et al., 2002). Findings that provided 'partial support' for the theory tested (e.g. Anderson, 1997; Raj et al, 1999), may be enhanced if multiple frameworks are compared.

A final concern is the extent to which theories of intimate partner violence have successfully impacted violence prevention and intervention programs (Bell & Naugle, 2008; Whitaker et al., 2006). While many theoretical explanations intimate partner violence have played a significant role in influencing prevention and intervention strategies (Holtzworth-Munroe & Saunders, 1996), to date these programs have made relatively little impact on reducing the rates of intimate partner violence perpetration over time (Babcock, Green & Robie, 2004; Bell and Naugle, 2008). Although small effect sizes may result in part from methodological factors including the research design, selection of outcome measures, and high attrition rates (Babcock et al., 2004), the effectiveness of these programs may be limited by field's limited theoretical and empirical understanding of the complexity of intimate partner violence perpetration (Bell and Naugle, 2008).

REFERENCES

Allen, C. M., & Straus, M. A. (1980). Resources, power and husband-wife violence. In M. A. Straus, & G. T. Hotaling (Eds.), *The Social Causes of Husband-Wife Violence* (pp. 188–208). Minneapolis: University of Minnesota Press.

Anderson, K. L. (1997). Gender, status, and domestic violence: An integration of feminist and family violence approaches. *Journal of Marriage and the Family, 59*, 655–669.

Atkinson, M. P., Greensten, T. N., & Lang, M. M. (2005). For women breadwinning can be dangerous: Gendered resource theory and wife abuse. *Journal of Marriage and the Family, 67*(5), 1137–1148.

Avakame, E. F. (1999). Females labor force participation and rape: An empirical test of the backlash hypothesis. *Violence Against Women, 5*(8), 926–949.

Babcock, J. C., Green, C. E., & Robie, C. (2004). Does batterers' treatment work? A meta-analytic review of domestic violence treatment. *Clinical Psychology Review, 23*(8), 1023–1053.

Barnett, O., Miller-Perrin, C. L., & Perrin, R. D. (2005). *Family violence across the lifespan: an introduction.* Malibu, CA: Sage Publications.

Bell, K. M. & Naugle, A. E. (2008). Intimate partner violence theoretical considerations: Moving towards a contextual framework. *Clinical Psychology Review, 28*(7), 1096–1107.

Berk, R., Berk, S. F., Loseke, D., & Rauma, D. (1983). Mutual combat and other family violence myths. In D. Finkelhor, R. J. Gelles, G. T. Hotaling & M.A. Straus (Eds.), *The Dark Side of Families: Current Family Violence Research.* (pp. 197–212). Beverly Hills, CA: Sage Publications.

Bersani, C., & Chen, H. T. (1988). Sociological perspectives in family violence. In V. B. Van Hasselt, R. L. Bellack & R. L. Morrison (Eds.), *Handbook of Family Violence* (pp. 57–86). New York: Plenum Press.

Blau, P. M. (1964). *Exchange and power in social life.* New York: J. Wiley.

Blood, R. O., & Wolfe, D. M. (1965). *Husbands & Wives: The Dynamics of Married Living.* New York: Free Press.

Bowker, L. H. (1983). *Beating Wife-Beating.* Lexington, MA: Lexington Books.

Bowman, C. G. (2003). Theories of domestic violence in the African context. *American University Journal of Gender, Social Policy and the Law, 11*(2), 847–863.

Bronfenbrenner, U. (1977). Toward an experimental ecology of human development. *American Psychologist, 32*(7), 513–531.

Bronfenbrenner, U. (1979). *The Ecology of Human Development: Experiments by Nature and Design.* Cambridge, MA: Harvard University Press.

Brush, L. D. (2000). Battering, traumatic stress, and welfare-to-work transition. *Violence Against Women, 6*(10), 1039–1065.

Cano, A., & Vivian, D. (2001). Life stressors and husband-to-wife violence. *Aggression and Violent Behavior, 6*(5), 459–480.

Carlson, B. E. (1984). Causes and maintenance of domestic violence: An ecological analysis. *Social Service Review, 58(4)*, 569–587.

Crosset, T., Ptacek, J., Mcdonald, M., & Benedict, J. (1996). Male student-athletes and violence against women: A survey of campus judicial affairs offices. *Violence Against Women, 2*(2), 163–79.

Cunningham, A., Jaffe, P. G., Baker, L., Dick, T., Malla, S., Mazaheri, N., et al. (1998). *Theory-derived explanations of male violence against female partners: Literature update.* London: London Family Court Clinic.

Cunradi, C. B., Caetano, R., & Schafer, J. (2002). Socioeconomic predictors of intimate partner violence among white, black, and Hispanic couples in the United States. *Journal of Family Violence, 17*(4), 377–389.

DeKeseredy. W.S., Alvi, S. & Schwartz, M. D. (2006). Curbing woman abuse and poverty: Is 'Wedfare' the cure? *Critical Criminology, 14*(1),23–41.

DeKeseredy, W. S., & Schwartz, M. D. (1993). Male peer support and woman abuse: An expansion of DeKeseredy's model. *Sociological Spectrum, 13*(4), 393–413.

Dobash, R. E., & Dobash, R. (1979). *Violence against Wives: A Case against the Patriarchy.* New York: Free Press.

Dobash, R. E., & Dobash, R. P. (1984). The nature and antecedents of violent events. *British Journal of Criminology , 24* (3), 269–288.

Dobash, R. E., & Dobash, R. (1988). Research as social action: The struggle for battered women. In K. Yllo, & M. Bograd (Eds.), *Feminist Perspectives on Wife Abuse* (pp.51–74). Newbury Park, CA: Sage.

Dutton, D. G., & Painter, S. (1993). Emotional attachments in abusive relationships: A test of traumatic bonding theory. *Violence and Victims,* 8(2), 105–120.

Dutton, D. G. (1994). Patriarchy and wife assault: The ecological fallacy. *Violence and Victims, 9*(2), 167–182.

Edin, K. (2000). What do low-income single mothers say about marriage? *Social Problems, 47*(1), 112–133.

Edleson, J. L., & Tolman, R. M. (1992). *Intervention for Men Who Batter: An Ecological Approach.* Newbury Park, CA: Sage Publications.

Emerson, R. M. (1962). Power-dependence relations. *American Sociological Review, 27*(1), 31–41.

England, P., & Farkas, G. (1986). *Households, Employment, and Gender: A Social, Economic, and Demographic View.* New York: Aldine Publishing Co.

Fagan, J., and Browne. (1994). Violence between spouses and intimates: Physical aggression between women and men in intimate relationships. In A. J. Reiss & J. A. Roth (Eds.), *Understanding and Preventing Violence: Vol. 3.* (pp. 115–292). Washington, DC: National Academy Press.

Farmer, A. & Tiefenthaler, J. (1997). An economic analysis of domestic violence. *Review of Social Economy*, 55(3), 337–359.

Farrington, K. (1980). Stress and family violence. In M. A. Straus, & G. T. Hotaling (Eds.), *The Social Causes of Husband-Wife Violence* (pp. 94–114). Minneapolis: University of Minnesota Press.

Farrington, K. (1986). The application of stress theory to the study of family violence: Principles, problems and prospects. *Journal of Family Violence, 1*(2), 131–149.

Fox, G. L., Benson, M. L., DeMaris, A. A., & Van Wyck (2002). Economic distress and intimate violence: Testing family stress and resources theories. *Journal of Marriage and the Family, 64*(3), 793–807.

Garbarino, J. (1977). The human ecology of child maltreatment: A conceptual model for research. *Journal of Marriage and the Family, 39*, 721–736.

Gelles, R. J. (1972). *The Violent Home: A Study of Physical Aggression between Husbands and Wives.* Beverly Hills, CA: Sage Publications.

Gelles, R. J. (1983). An exchange/social control theory. In D. Finkelhor, R. J. Gelles, G. T. Hotaling & M. A. Straus (Eds.), *The Dark Side of Families: Current Family Violence Research* (pp. 151–165). Beverly Hills, CA: Sage Publications. Monstrosity

Gelles, R. J. (1993). Family violence. In R. L. Hampton, T. Gullotta, G. Adams, E. H. Potter III & R. P. Weissberg (Eds.), *Family Violence: Prevention and Treatment* (1st ed., pp. 1–25). Newbury Park, CA Sage Publications.

Gelles, R. J., & Cornell, C. P. (1990). *Intimate Violence in Families* (2nd ed.). Newbury Park, CA: Sage Publications.

Gelles, R. J., & Straus, M. A. (1979). Violence in the American family. *Journal of Social Issues, 35*(2), 15–39.

Gibson-Davis, C. M., Edin, K., & McLanahan, S. (2005). High hopes but even higher expectations: The retreat from marriage among low-income couples. *Journal of Marriage and Family, 67*(5), 1301–1312.

Gibson-Davis, C. M., Magnuson, K., Gennetian, L. A., Duncan, G. J. (2005). Does employment protect women from domestic violence *Journal of Marriage and the Family, 67*(5), 1149–1168.

Gil, D. G. (1986). Sociocultural aspects of domestic violence. In M. Lystad (Ed.), *Violence in the Home: Interdisciplinary Perspectives* (pp. 124–149). New York: Brunner/Mazel.

Godenzi, A., M. D. Schwartz, et al. (2001). Toward a gendered social bond/male peer support theory of university woman abuse. *Critical Criminology*, 10(1), 1–16.

Goode, W. J. (1971). Force and violence in the family. *Journal of Marriage and the Family, 33*(4), 624–636.

Goodyear-Smith, F. A. & Laidlaw, T.M. (1999). Aggressive acts and assaults in intimate relationships: towards an understanding of the literature. *Behavioral Sciences & the Law* 17(3), 285–304.

Greenfeld, L. A., Rand, M. R., Craven, D., Klaus, P. A., Perkins, C., & Warchol, G. (1998). *Violence by intimates: Analysis of data on crimes by current or former spouses, boyfriends, and girlfriends*. Washington, DC: U.S. Dept. of Justice, Office of Justice Programs, Bureau of Justice Statistics.

Hagen, J. & Davis, L. V. (1992). Working with women: Building a policy and practice agenda. *Social Work, 37*(6), 495–502.

Harrell, A. (1991). *Evaluation of court-ordered treatment for domestic violence offenders: Summary and recommendations*. Washington D.C.: Urban Institute.

Heise, L. L. (1998). Violence against women: An integrated ecological framework. *Violence Against Women, 4*(3), 262–290.

Hesse-Biber, S., & Williamson, J. (1984). Resource theory and power in families: Life cycle considerations. *Family Process, 23*(2), 261–278.

Hoffman, K. L., Demo, D. H., & Edwards, J. N., (1994). Physical wife abuse in a non-western society: An integrated theoretical approach. *Journal of Marriage and the Family, 56*(1), 131–146.

Holtzworth-Munroe, A., & Saunders, D. G. (1996). Men who batter: Recent history and research. *Violence and Victims, 11*(4), 273–276. Homans, G. C. (1974). *Social Behavior: Its Elementary Forms* (Rev. ed.). New York: Harcourt, Brace, Jovanovich.

Honeycutt, T. C., Marshall, L. L., & Weston, R. (2001). Toward ethnically specific models of employment, public assistance, and victimization. *Violence Against Women, 7*(2), 126–140.

Hornung, C. A., McCullough, B. C., & Sugimoto, T. (1981). Status relationships in marriage: Risk factors in spouse abuse. *Journal of Marriage and the Family, 43*(3), 675–692.

Hotaling, G. T., & Sugarman, D. B. (1986). An analysis of risk markers in husband to wife violence: The current state of knowledge. *Violence and Victims, 1*(2), 101–123.

Jasinski, J. L. (2001). Theoretical explanations for violence against women. In C. M. Renzetti, J. L. Edleson & R. K. Bergen (Eds.), *The Sourcebook on Violence Against Women* (pp. 5–22). Thousand Oaks, CA: Sage Publications.

Kalmuss, D. (1984). The intergenerational transmission of marital aggression. *Journal of Marriage and the Family, 46*(1), 11–19.

Kaukinen, C. (2004). Status compatibility, physical violence, and emotional abuse in intimate relationships. *Journal of Marriage and the Family, 66*(2), 452–471.

Kenney, C. (2006). The power of the purse: Allocative systems and inequality in couple households. *Gender and Society, 20*(3), 354–381.

Kurst-Swanger, K., & Petcosky, J. L. (2003). *Violence in the Home: Multidisciplinary Perspectives*. Oxford: Oxford University Press.

Lein, L., Jacquet, S. E., Lewis, C. M., Cole, P.R. & Williams, B.B. (2001). With the best of intentions: Family violence option and abused women's needs. *Violence Against Women, 7*(2), 193–210.

Levesque, D. A., Gelles, R. J., Velicer, W. F. (2000). Development and validation of a stages of change measure for men in batterer treatment. *Cognitive Therapy and Research, 24*(2), 175–199.

Levinson, D. (1989). *Family Violence in Cross-Cultural Perspective.* Newbury Park, CA.: Sage Publications.

Lichter, D. T., Batson, C. D., & Brown, J. B. (2004). Welfare reform and marriage promotion: The marital expectations and desires of single and cohabiting mothers. *Social Service Review, 78*(1), 2–25.

Loue, S. (2001). *Intimate Partner Violence: Societal, Medical, Legal, and Individual Responses.* New York: Kluwer Academic/Plenum Publishers.

MacEwen, K. E., & Barling, J. (1988). Multiple stressors, violence in the family of origin, and marital aggression: A longitudinal investigation. *Journal of Family Violence, 3*(1), 73–87.

Macmillan, R., & Gartner, R. (1999). When she brings home the bacon: Labor-force participation and the risk of spousal violence against women. *Journal of Marriage and the Family, 61*(4), 947–958.

Margolin, G., John, R. S., & Foo, L. (1998). Interactive and unique risk factors for husbands' emotional and physical abuse of their wives. *Journal of Family Violence, 13*, 315–344.

McCall, G. J. & Shields, N. M. (1986). Social and structural factors in family violence. In M. Lystad (Ed.), *Violence in the Home: Interdisciplinary Perspectives.* (pp. 98–123). New York: Brunner/Mazel.

McCloskey, L. A. (1996). Socioeconomic and coercive power within the family. *Gender & Society, 10*(4), 449–463.

McLeod, J. D., & Kessler, R. C. (1990). Socioeconomic status differences in vulnerability to undesirable life events. *Journal of Health and Social Behavior, 31*(2), 162–172.

Meier, J. (1997). Domestic violence, character, and social change in the welfare reform debate. *Law & Policy, 19*(2), 205–263.

Mihalic, S. W., & Elliott, D. (1997). A social learning theory model of marital violence. *Journal of Family Violence, 12*(1), 21–47.

Moe, A. M. & Bell, M. P. (2004). *Abject economics: The effects of battering and violence on women's work and employability.* Violence Against Women 10(1), *29–55.*

Molm, L. D. (1997). *Coercive Power in Social Exchange.* Cambridge, UK: Cambridge University Press.

Molm, L. D. (2001). Theories of social exchange and exchange networks. In G. Ritzer, & B. Smart (Eds.) *Explorations in Social Theory,* (pp. 260–272). Thousand Oaks, CA: Sage Publications.

Molm, L. D., & Cook, K. S. (1995). Social exchange and exchange networks. In K. S. Cook, G. A. Fine & J. S. House (Eds.), *Sociological Perspectives on Social Psychology* (pp. 209–235). Boston: Allyn & Bacon.

Molm, L. D., Quist, T. M., & Wisely, P. A. (1994). Imbalanced structures, unfair strategies: Power and justice in social exchange. *American Sociological Review, 59*, 98–121.

Moore, A. M. (1997). Intimate violence: Does socioeconomic status matter? In A. Carderelli (Ed.), *Violence Between Intimate Partners* (pp. 90–100). Boston: Allyn & Bacon.

Okun, L. (1986). *Woman Abuse: Facts Replacing Myths.* Albany: State University of New York Press.

O'Leary, K. D. (1999). Psychological abuse: A variable deserving critical attention in domestic violence. *Violence and Victims, 14*(1), 3–23.

O'Neill, D. (1998). A post-structuralist review of the theoretical literature surrounding wife abuse. *Violence Against Women, 4*, 457–490.

Pagelow, M. D. (1981). *Woman-battering: Victims and Their Experiences*. Beverly Hills, CA: Sage Publications.

Pagelow, M. D. (1984). *Family Violence*. New York: Praeger.

Parke, R. D., & Collmer, C. W. (1975). Child abuse: An interdisciplinary analysis. In M. Hetherington (Ed.), *Review of Child Development Research* (5, pp. 1–102). Chicago: University of Chicago Press.

Pilkington, B. F. (2000). Persisting while waiting to change: Women's lived experiences. *Health Care for Women International, 21*, 501–516.

Raj, A., Silverman, J. G., Wingood, G. M., & Diclemente, R. J. (1999). Prevalence and correlates of relationship abuse among a community-based sample of low-income African American women. *Violence Against Women, 5*(3), 272–291.

Raphael, J. (2000). *Saving Bernice: Battered Women, Welfare, and Poverty*. Boston: Northeastern University Press.

Raphael, J. (2001). Domestic violence as a welfare to work barrier. In C. M. Renzetti, J. L. Edleson & R. K. Bergen (Eds.), *The Sourcebook on Violence Against Women* (pp. 443–456). Thousand Oaks, CA: Sage Publications.

Riger, S., Ahrens, C. & Blickenstaff, A. (2000). Measuring interference with employment and education reported by women with abusive partners: Preliminary data. *Violence & Victims, 15*(2), 161–172.

Riger, S., & Krieglstein, M. (2000). The impact of welfare reform on men's violence against women. *American Journal of Community Psychology, 28*(5), 631–647.

Riggs, D. S., Caulfield, M. B., & Street, A. E. (2000). Risk for domestic violence: Factors associated with perpetration and victimization. *Journal of Clinical Psychology 56*(10), 1289–1316.

Romero, D, Chavkin, W, Wise, P., & Smith, L. (2003). Low-income mothers' experience with poor health, hardship, work, and violence: implications for policy. *Violence Against Women*, 9(10), 1231–1244.

Ronfeldt, H. M., Kimerling, R., & Arias, I. (1998). Satisfaction with relationship power and the perpetration of dating violence. *Journal of Marriage and the Family*, 60(1), 70–78.

Rosen, L. N., Kaminski, R. J., Moore Palmley, A., Knudson, K., H., & Fancher, P. (2003). The effects of peer group climate on intimate partner violence among married male U.S. army soldiers. *Violence Against Women, 9*(9), 1045–1071.

Sable, M. R., Libbus, M. K., Huneke, D., & Anger, K. (1999). Domestic violence among AFDC recipients: Implications for welfare-to-work programs. *Affilia, 14*(2), 199–216.

Schneider, E. M. (2000). *Battered Women & Feminist Lawmaking*. New Haven: Yale University Press.

Schwartz, M. D. (1988). Ain't got no class: Universal risk theories of battering. *Contemporary Crises, 12*(4), 373-392.

Schwartz, M.D. and DeKeseredy, W.S. (2000). Aggregation bias and womanabuse: Variations by male peer support, region, language and school type. *Journal of Interpersonal Violence,* 15, 555–565.

Sernau, S. (2001). *Worlds Apart: Social Inequalities in a New Century.* Thousand Oaks, CA: Pine Forge Press

Stets, J. E. (1988). *Domestic Violence and Control.* New York: Springer-Verlag.

Straus, M. A. (1980a). In Straus, M. A., Gelles, R. J, & Steinmetz S. K. (Eds.), *Behind Closed Doors: Violence in the American Family* (1st ed.). Garden City, NY: Anchor Press/ Doubleday.

Straus, M. A. (1990c). Physical Violence in American Families: Risk Factors and Adaptations to Violence in 8,145 Families. In M. A. Straus, & R. J. Gelles (Eds.), (pp. xxii, 622). New Brunswick, NJ: Transaction Publishers.

Straus, M.A., Gelles, R. J. & Steinmetz, S. K. (1980). *Behind Closed Doors: Violence in the American Family.* New York: Doubleday/Anchor.

Strube, M. J., & Barbour, L. S. (1984). Factors related to the decision to leave an abusive relationship. *Journal of Marriage & Family, 46,* 837.

Strube, M. J., & Barbour, L. S. (1983). The decision to leave an abusive relationship: Economic dependence and psychological commitment. *Journal of Marriage & the Family,* 45(4), 785–793.

Tauchen, H.V., Witte, A. D., & Long, S. K. (1991). Domestic violence: A nonrandom affair. *International Economic Review,* 32(2), 491–511.

Tjaden, P. G., & Thoennes, N. (1998, November). Prevalence, incidence, and consequences of violence against women: Findings from the national violence against women survey. *Research in Brief* (NCJ 172837). Washington, DC: U.S. Dept. of Justice, Office of Justice Programs, National Institute of Justice.

Tolman, R. M., & Rosen, D. (2001). Domestic violence in the lives of women receiving welfare: Mental health, substance dependence, and economic well-being. *Violence Against Women, 7*(2), 141–158.

Turner, J. H. (2003). *The Structure of Sociological Theory* (7th ed.). Belmont, CA: Wadsworth Thomson Learning.

Whitaker, D. J., Morrison, S., Lindquist, C., Hawkins, S. R., O'Neil, J. A., Nesius, A. M., et al. (2006). A critical review of interventions for the primary prevention of perpetration of partner violence. *Aggression and Violent Behavior,* 11(2), 151–166.

Wingood, G. M., & DiClemente, R. J. (1992). Culture, gender and psychosocial influences on HIV-related behavior of African-American female adolescents: Implications for the development of tailored prevention programs. *Ethnicity and Disease, 2*(4), 381–388.

Wolfe, D. M. (1959). Power and authority in the family. In D. Cartwright (Ed.), *Studies in Social Power* (pp. 99–118). Ann Arbor: University of Michigan Press.

Worden, H. A. (2002). *The effects of race and of class on women's experience of domestic violence.* Thesis (Ph. D.), Boston University.

Yick, A. G. (2001). Feminist theory and status inconsistency theory: Application to domestic violence in Chinese immigrant families. *Violence Against Women, 7*(5), 545–562.

Yllö, K. (1993). Through a feminist lens: Gender, power, and violence. In R. J. Gelles, & D. R. Loseke (Eds.), *Current Controversies on Family Violence* (pp. 47–62). Newbury Park, CA: Sage Publications.

Yllö, K., & Bograd, M. L. (1988). *Feminist Perspectives on Wife Abuse.* Newbury Park, CA: Sage Publications.

Young, J. (1999). *The Exclusive Society.* London: Sage.

QUESTIONS FOR REVIEW, REFLECTION, AND DISCUSSION

1. What two theories do you think are most similar? How are why are they similar? How do they differ from each other?
2. What is the difference between micro-level theories and macro-level theories?
3. What do you think is meant by multidimensional level of analysis?
4. Gelles combined what two theories? What did combining those two theories allow him to do?
5. What is the "principle of least interest"?
6. How is women's labor-force participation associated with spousal abuse?
7. Do you know of anyone who has experienced intimate partner violence? Think about that person's experience and identify the theory or theories that best reflect that particular situation.

ADDITIONAL READINGS

Johnson, M. P. (2011). Gender and types of intimate partner violence: A response to an anti-feminist literature review. *Current Controversies on the Role of Gender In Partner Violence, Aggression and Violent Behavior, 16*(4), 289–296.

Johnson, M. P., Leone, J. M., & Xu, Y. (2014). Intimate terrorism and situation couple violence in general surveys: Ex-spouses required, *Violence Against Women, 20*(2), 186–207.

Newton, T.L., Burns, V. E., Miller, J. J., & Fernandez-Botran, G. R. (2016). Subjective sleep quality in women with divorce histories: The role of intimate partner victimization, *Journal of Interpersonal Violence, 31*(8), 1430–1452.

Nybergh, L., Enander, V., & Krantz, G. (2016). Theoretical considerations of men's experiences of intimate partner violence: An interview-based study, *Journal of Family Violence, 31*(2), 191–202.

Vu, H. S., Schuler, S., Hoang, T. A., & Quach, T. (2014). Divorce in the context of domestic violence against women in Vietnam, *Culture, Health & Sexuality, 16*(6), 634–647.

UNIT 6

STRESS AND WELL-BEING

KEY TERMS

Stress

Stressor

Normative Family Stressors

Nonnormative Family Stressors

Morphogenesis

Morphostasis

ABC-X Model

Double ABC-X Model

Vulnerability-Stress-Adaptation Model

Avoidance

Minimization

12

MODELS OF FAMILY STRESS AND COPING

By Chris Segrin and Jeanne Flora

Stress is an inevitable part of family life. Although there are few certainties in the modern family, it is safe to assume that all families will experience stress and that coping with stressors will be an ongoing activity in all families. Why is stress such a ubiquitous part of family life? In some cases, families generate stressors of their own through problematic interactions among themselves (Pearlin & Skaff, 1998). Most parents who have raised an adolescent child and most people who can remember their family interactions during adolescence have experienced such stressors. In other cases family members encounter problems in their roles outside of the family boundary (e.g., student, employee, and friend) that can adversely impact relationships and activities within the family (Pearlin & Skaff). This happens, for example, when a parent gets laid off at work. For reasons such as these, it has been argued that 'All stressors either begin or end up in the family" (Olson, 1997, p. 261).

In this selection we attempt to answer a number of fundamental questions about the role and impact of stress on family relationships. For example, what are the different types of stressors that families must deal with? Do all stressful events have a negative impact on the family? Through examining various models of family stress we attempt to explain the process by which families respond to stress. Questions about the role of communication in addressing arid managing stressors are taken up as well. There are also a number of important questions about the family's response to stress. How do families cope with stressors? Exactly how does social support from the family help to deal with stressful experiences and situations? The answers to these questions reveal complex and intriguing associations between the family and the stressors they face.

When studying the effects of stress on the family, it is important to distinguish stress from stressors. Olson, Lavee, and McCubbin (1988) define *family stressors* as "discrete life events or transitions that have an impact upon the family unit and produce, or have the potential to produce, change in the family social system" (p. 19). On the other hand, *family stress* is the response of the family to the stressor; it involves the tensions that family members experience as a result of the stressor (McCubbin et al., 1980). When do stressors produce stress? According to family systems theorists families develop a requisite variety of rules of transformation (Burr & Klein, 1994). This means that families usually have enough rules for how to handle different situations that they are able to transform inputs (e.g., stressors) into outputs in such a way that their basic needs, functions, and goals can be sustained. The family experiences stress when they do not have the requisite variety of rules to meet the challenges of certain stressors. In other words, they do not have the means to handle the change that is necessitated by the stressor while still fulfilling their basic goals and functions.

People often think of family stressors and stress in negative terms. However, it is important to keep in mind that stress can stimulate growth and important transitions for families. Successfully managing stress can fundamentally alter family relationships and interactions, sometimes in a very positive way. At the same time, stress can sometimes permanently damage, and even destroy, family relationships. Often the key to explaining the consequences of stressors on the family can be found in a careful examination of their communication behaviors. Stress can alter family communication patterns; but family communication patterns can equally alter the family's experience and reaction to a stressor.

TYPES OF FAMILY STRESSORS

There are an almost infinite number of events or situations that families might find stressful. One useful way to think about family stressors is to consider those that are normative or predictable versus those that are nonnormative or unpredictable (Cowan, 1991). *Normative family stressors* involve those changes or progressions in family life that occur for most families, usually coming with the passage of time. These involve, for example, marriage, birth of the first child, and death of an elderly family member. Normative stressors are viewed as ubiquitous in that they occur in most families, and expectable because they can easily be anticipated (McCubbin et al., 1980). *Nonnormative family stressors,* on the other hand, are difficult to foresee because they happen somewhat at random, and do not occur in every family. These include, for example, the serious illness of a child, involuntary separations from the family, and divorce. Because of the random nature of nonnormative stressors, they are often experienced as more traumatic for family members. At the same time, the ability to see normative stressors impending on the horizon does not necessarily lessen their impact on the family environment.

It is important to understand that the distinction between normative and nonnormative family stressors is imperfect. The "normative" family stressors that accompany progression through the family life cycle may not really be normative in modern society. Untimely death, divorce, and childlessness mean that many families never experience some of the stressors that are commonly considered to be normative. Similarly, those stressors that are characterized as "nonnormative" may not be as unpredictable as once thought. At least some "unpredictable" family stressors such as marital distress and divorce are clearly foreshadowed in couple's communication behaviors.

Both normative and nonnormative family stressors contribute to what family systems theorists refer to as *morphogenesis* (Olson et al., 1979). That is the tendency of a family to develop and change over time. The inevitability of normative family stressors implies that there will always be morphogenetic forces impinging on all families. During periods of relative calm, families also experience *morphostasis,* which is the tendency to remain at a steady state, or follow the status quo. The experience of both normative and nonnormative stressors typically disrupts morphostatic tendencies and at least temporarily engages morphorgenetic tendencies of the family.

Another useful way of understanding and classifying family stressors was developed by Adams (1975). Adams argued that there are two distinct dimensions to family stressors. The first has to do with how *temporary versus permanent* the family stressor is. Some stressors such as raising an adolescent child are inherently temporary. By necessity, such stressors will eventually pass. Other stressors, such as the death of a family member, are permanent. These are stressors that the family will bear over the long run. Keep in mind that temporary and permanent really represent end points on a continuum. There are of course many stressors, such as long-term illness, that fall somewhere in between these two extremes. The second conceptual dimension proposed by Adams concerns the *voluntary versus involuntary* nature of family stressors. As strange as it may sound at first, family members sometimes voluntarily enter into situations that can be very stressful. For example, a married couple may undergo a period of separation or seek a divorce on their own volition. Other stressors such as infertility or raising a troubled child are more involuntary in nature. Like the temporary–permanent dimension, voluntary and involuntary are best viewed as end points on a continuum. Some stressors like early retirement or optional layoff from work might be viewed as a situation that is a response to both voluntary and involuntary forces. It may be tempting to conclude that voluntary stressors are easier to cope with than those that are involuntary because people often have some control over them. However, voluntary stressors carry with them more personal responsibility and blame that can create considerable mental anguish for family members.

A more recent theory of family stress conceptualizes stress as occurring at one of three different levels of abstraction (Burr & Klein, 1994). Burr and Klein based their conceptualization of different levels of stress on group theory and the theory of logical types (Watzlawick, Weakland, & Fisch, 1974). Group theory explains how change can occur within a system that as a whole stays constant. The theory of logical types explains how members experience a metamorphosis whereby they move from one logical level to a higher one. Combining elements of these theories, Burr and Klein (1994) proposed a developmental theory of family stress based on different logical levels of stress and with the assumption that families will first try to adjust very specific concrete processes in order to deal with stress before resorting to more fundamental and abstract changes to the family system.

Level I stress causes the family to cope by changing its role expectations or rules. If changes in these role expectations or rules are effective at handling the stressor, the family is assumed to enter into a period of recovery as they gain mastery over the stressor. Burr and Klein (1994) suggest that for many families, the birth of a child represents a Level I stressor. In most families, husbands and wives have to assume a new role (i.e., father and mother) and certain rules may need to be enacted to address the stressor (e.g., someone needs to feed the child when she or he wakes up in the morning). For most families, such changes are sufficient for effectively coping with the stressor. When Level I processes are unsuccessful, the family is in a more difficult situation, characterized as Level II stress.

When families encounter *Level II stress* rearranging rules and making simple changes in roles are not sufficient to allow the family to effectively deal with the stressor. Rather, the family must make more fundamental changes, usually in their approach to relating to each other. For example, when a family attempts to handle the stress of raising an adolescent child, they may develop new rules such as a curfew and make role adjustments such as having the child assume responsibility for some household chores. If this approach is not effective, the family may need to rethink its approach to discipline, responsibility, and the way that they relate to the child. Instead of just assuming that the parents' rules and intentions will automatically be followed, they may need to reconsider how they relate to the child, perhaps by now creating adverse consequences when rules and obligations are not followed. This may change the fundamental nature of the parent—child relationship from caretaker and provider to authority figure and enforcer. When such Level II processes are ineffective, the family is in an even more difficult situation, characterized as Level III stress.

The experience of *Level III stress* causes the family to question its most basic assumptions, and the very fabric of the family is in trouble (Burr & Klein, 1994). The family's most basic orientation and philosophy of life must be examined, and often changed or discarded. Returning to our example of raising the adolescent child, assume that the child is involved in criminal activity, charged with assault, and sentenced to a juvenile detention facility. In this case, the parents may feel overwhelmed and defeated, despite their best efforts at raising the child. They may have to psychologically relinquish at least part of their relationship with and emotional connection to their child in order to cope with the severe stressor that they are experiencing. In this case, the very nature of what it means to be a family and a parent is called into question, reexamined, and altered in response to the stressor. The idea that parents are ultimately responsible for the actions of their children may have to be abandoned. Burr and Klein note that in Level III stress, families often have to deal with fundamental questions of whether people are good or bad, their spiritual beliefs, and how much emotional distance from family members is necessary and desirable.

MODELS OF FAMILY STRESS

THE ABC-X MODEL

Perhaps the premier model of family stress was developed and described by Hill (1949) as part of his now-classic research on the stress of separation and reunion following World War II. During World War II many men were enlisted into the military and shipped overseas as part of their military service, often leaving their wives and children behind to face an uncertain future. During the war, many women entered the work force for the first time and earned their own salaries. When the war ended and soldiers came home many families had yet another set of adjustments to make. Adopting a systems perspective, Hill realized that the stress experienced by the family was not just the result of a particular event such as the husband's departure from the home due to active military duty. Rather, there were a number of systemic variables that seemed to influence which families experienced high degrees of stress and which managed without as much difficulty.

The ABC-X model gets its name from four interrelated factors that are theorized to describe the experience of family stress. The A factor represents the *event or situation* that the family encounters. This interacts with the B factor which is the family's *resources*. The event or situation also interacts with the C factor, the family's *perception* of the event. Collectively the A, B, and C factors produce the *stress or crisis* reaction which is the X factor. Hill's ABC-X model is depicted in Figure 12.1.

STRESSFUL EVENTS OR SITUATIONS (A)

In the family context, stressful events have been described as "an occurrence that provokes a variable amount of change in the family system" (McKenry & Price, 2000, p. 6). Notice how McKenry and Price's definition of the stressful event is focused on *change*. The underlying assumption is that anything that alters the status quo has the potential to produce stress. Most families develop routines that allow for smooth functioning without having to constantly renegotiate roles, argue over rules, and so forth. When stressful events occur, these routines are upset. Roles that used to be functional for the family are now lost or seriously altered. Rules that used to ensure family harmony and well-being may now have to be adjusted or broken once the event or situation is encountered. McKenry and Price also note that not all "stressful" events or situations are negative. Even positive events can produce stress in the family. The inheritance of a large sum of money from a distant relative or a job promotion can each be associated with stress.

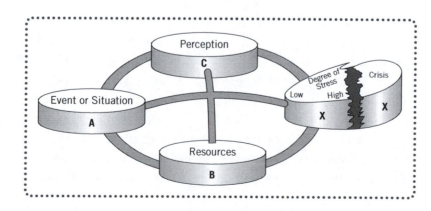

FIGURE 12.1.

Hill's (1949) ABC-X Model of Family Stress

Remarkably, the stress associated with these seemingly positive events or situations can sometimes be as disruptive to family functioning as the stress from what are ordinarily viewed as negative events such as the death of a family member or the loss of a family member's job. Later in this selection we discuss one common classification scheme for stressful family events based on their predictability or unpredictability.

FAMILY RESOURCES (B)

Resources are traits, abilities, and qualities of individual family members, the family system, and the greater community in which the family is embedded that can be used to address the demands imposed by the event or situation (McCubbin & Patterson, 1985). Family systems theorists generally feel that resources reside in individuals, the collective family unit, and the societal ecosystem in which the family is a part. Family resources can mitigate the ill effects of many situations. For example, if a family member is laid off at work, but other family members have good jobs and incomes, these resources can lessen the potentially negative impact of the situation on the family. Therefore, family scientists say that resources may act as a *buffer* against the potentially negative consequences of stressful events. On the other hand, some families may lack resources to protect against the negative effects of certain events. Consider for example a rural farm family that is isolated and has few close friends or relatives. Even a fairly modest event such as the brief hospitalization of one of the parents has the potential to create substantial turmoil for the family and the care of their farm. In this way, family scientists suggest that the lack of resources can create a *vulnerability* to stress when certain events or situations are encountered.

FAMILY PERCEPTION (C)

The family's perception is their appraisal, assessment, or definition of the event or situation. How people appraise life events and situations is strongly tied to how stressed they are in response to those situations (Lazarus & Launier, 1978). There is remarkable variation in how different families appraise the same event. For instance, in some families the departure of a young adult child might be a time of intense sadness. Parents may fear the loss of the child's companionship, worry about how the child will make it on his or her own, and lament missed opportunities for interaction with the child that may never be recaptured. However, other families may view this as a celebration, fueled by pride in the child's successful transition to adulthood and independence, or by a "good riddance" attitude. The great American songwriter John Mellencamp once wrote, "There is nothing more sad or glorious than generations changing hands." This statement is an elegant account of both the dualism inherent in many family events as well as of the dramatic range of feelings that family members might have concerning a given event. Families that cope best with stressful events are those who are able to recast or reframe the event in a positive light. This allows family members to (a) clarify issues, hardships, and tasks and render them more manageable; (b) decrease the intensity of emotional burden created by the event; and (c) encourage members to carry on with the family's fundamental tasks (McCubbin & Patterson, 1985; McKenry & Price, 2000). There are many different ways of looking at the same event. Like resources, positive appraisals can buffer against the ill effects associated with potentially stressful events.

STRESS AND CRISIS (X)

The X factor in Hill's ABC-X model is the stress and crisis actually experienced by the family. This is thought to be a product of the event, the family's resources, and the family's perceptions of the event. The family's stress experience is their reaction or response to the event or situation (filtered through their resources and perceptions). Stress and crisis are two different types of reaction to challenging events and situations. Crisis is an overwhelming disturbance in the family's equilibrium that involves severe pressure on and incapacitation of the family system (Boss, 1988; McKenry & Price, 2000). When a family is in a state of crisis they are in genuine disorder and are unable to function normally or effectively. Customary roles and routines are often abandoned and boundaries are dramatically changed when a family is in crisis. Alternatively, stress denotes a change in the family's steady state. So long as these changes do not overtax the family's resources and coping skills, there may be no negative outcomes for the family. As McKenry and Price note, crisis is a dichotomous variable. The family is either in a state of crisis or not. Stress is a continuous variable. A family can experience varying degrees of stress. Because stress merely represents a change or disturbance in the family's normal state and routines, it is easy to see why stress is not inherently bad. Many families may benefit from some stress. The experience of stress can sometimes cause families to abandon harmful practices as when family members try to prepare healthy meals after one family member had a heart attack.

THE DOUBLE ABC-X MODEL

Hill's (1949) *ABC-X* model of family stress has been very influential over the past 50 years (Huang, 1991). However, the model was refined by McCubbin and Patterson (1982) in recognition of the fact that family stress unfolds over time, and that families develop new perceptions and new resources after they initially experience the event or situation. Accordingly, McCubbin and Patterson developed the double *ABC-X* model of family stress. This expanded version of the original ABC-X model is depicted in Figure 12.2. As evident in Figure 12.2, the double ABC-X model is divided into precrisis and postcrisis stages. The variables in the precrisis stage are identical to Hill's (1949) original ABC-X model (i.e., stressor, resources, perception, and crisis). The postcrisis factors were included to better explain how and why families adapt to the stressful situation once it is encountered.

McCubbin and Patterson (1982) note that stressors rarely occur in isolation from other problems. Often stressful events are associated with other issues, events, and situations that are themselves stressful to the family. These authors suggest that there are several types of stressors that contribute to stress pileup in the family. First, the *initial stressor event* has its own set of hardships that can move the family into a state of crisis. Second, *family life changes* are often ongoing at the time that the initial event is experienced and happen regardless of the initial stressor. Finally, *consequences of family coping* efforts often bring on an additional set of stressors. For example, if a child is diagnosed with a serious illness, that illness could function as an initial stressor on the family. At the same time that the family is dealing with this stressor, they may also be in the process of launching their oldest child and caring for an aging grandparent. These family life changes only further compound the family's stress over the sick child. If an overwhelmed parent turns to heavy drinking in order to cope with the demands of these stressors to soothe his or her nerves, this coping mechanism may bring on further stressors such as a drunk driving conviction, missed work, and failure to meet other obligations due to intoxication. Collectively, all of these different stressors that come in the wake of the child's illness constitute stressor pileup and potentially make a bad situation even worse. In a study of families with autistic or communication-impaired children, stress pileup proved to be the most consistent and strongest predictor of family adjustment (Bristol, 1987). Menees and Segrin (2000) found that children who were exposed to the stress of an alcoholic parent were anywhere from two to four times more likely than children without an alcoholic parent to have been exposed to additional family stressors such as parental

FIGURE 12.2.
McCubbin and Patterson's (1982) Double ABC-X Model of Family Stress

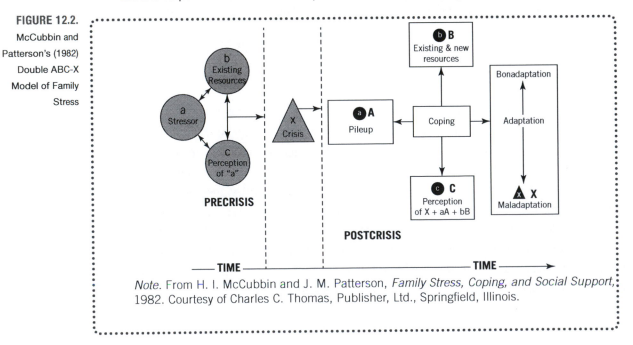

Note. From H. I. McCubbin and J. M. Patterson, *Family Stress, Coping, and Social Support,* 1982. Courtesy of Charles C. Thomas, Publisher, Ltd., Springfield, Illinois.

separation, divorce, or unemployment. These findings illustrate McCubbin and Patterson's point that family stressors rarely occur in isolation and that the pileup of stressors has a major impact on family outcomes.

EXISTING AND NEW RESOURCES (bB)

In the double ABC-X model there are two types of family resources. The first are the family's existing resources at the time of the initial stressor. These are available at the time of initial impact and allow the family to minimize the immediate consequences of the stressor and, in the best case scenario, prevent the family from entering into a state of crisis. The second set of resources is characterized as *coping resources* (McCubbin & Patterson, 1982). These are personal, family or social resources that are developed or strengthened in response to the initial stressor. Coping resources might include social support that is mobilized after the initial stressor, or new skills that the family develops in order to handle the initial stressor. Recall from the discussion of stress pileup that sometimes these post-crisis-coping efforts may bring on new stressors as well. Ideally, the family's postcrisis resources will be factors that help to minimize the negative effects of the stressful event or situation, while allowing the family to effectively adapt to this new challenge in their lives.

PERCEPTION (cC)

The double C factor in the double ABC-X model (McCubbin & Patterson, 1982) is the family's perception of (a) the initial stressor event and (b) the stress or crisis produced by that event, as well as any stress pileup that followed. Like the original C factor, this factor entails the family's perception and definition of the situation that they find themselves in. McCubbin and Patterson state that the family's postcrisis perceptions involve religious beliefs, redefining the original situation, and endowing the situation with meaning. Over time, people tend to look at many stressful situations differently from when they first encountered them. When families reframe an event in a more positive light, the amount of stress that they experience may be minimized. For instance, if a troubled adolescent is picked up by the police and jailed for theft, the family may initially be shocked and upset. The parents may feel like failures and fear for their child's future. However, as time progresses, the family may reframe the initial stressor in more positive terms. For instance, they may feel that contact with the criminal justice system might be a "wake-up call" for the troubled adolescent. Perhaps he or she might be required to enroll in a drug treatment program because the theft was committed so that the adolescent could get money to buy drugs. They may feel that this will scare the child and put him or her back on track, away from a life of crime. In this way, the family is seeing new meaning and even some potential benefits to what was originally a stressful and shocking event. The double C factor in this model is an explicit recognition of the fact that perceptions are not static. They evolve and change over time.

FAMILY CRISIS AND ADAPTATION (xX)

The double X factor in the model is the family's ultimate adaptation to the crisis. McCubbin and Patterson (1982) define adaptation as "the process of stimulus regulation, environmental control, and balancing to achieve a level of functioning, which preserves family unity and enhances the family system and member growth and development" (p. 45). Stimulus regulation and environmental control involve literally taking control of the situation that produced the initial stress and the surrounding environment (e.g., immediate family, extended family, and local community) in which the family exists. In stimulus regulation, the family selectively lets in or shuts out demands that are imposed by the stressful event. In some cases they may have to resort to denial in order to accomplish stimulus regulation. In environmental control the family tries to influence the type and quality of demands that are placed on them. Balancing entails making accommodations or compromises in order to adjust to the stressor and perhaps assimilating the stressful event or situation into their daily lives and routines. Some stressors such as the death or chronic illness of an immediate family member are permanent and often unchanging in their nature. These require family members to make equally permanent changes in the structure of their roles and routines, thereby assimilating the stressor into the fundamental fabric of the family's life. Unlike the X factor in the precrisis state (crisis), the X factor in the postcrisis state (adaptation) is really a continuum. The family's degree of adaptation can range from maladaption (from the French word "mal," meaning bad or poorly) on the low end to bonadaptation (from the French word "bon," meaning good) on the high end. A family in a state of maladaption is in crisis. However, a family in a state of bonadaptation is probably functioning *better* after the stressor than before. Bonadaptation implies that the demands on the family unit are matched by the resources that they have available (McCubbin & Patterson). For some families that mobilize their resources and reframe stressful events in a positive light, the experience can lead to a form of hypercoping in which the family functioning is literally improved following the stressor.

ADDITIONAL CONCEPTS IN THE DOUBLE ABC-X MODEL

Proponents of the double ABC-X model of family stress often use concepts in addition to events, resources, perceptions, and stress in order to understand how families function under stress. McCubbin and Patterson (1982) suggest that vulnerability and regenerative power are useful for understanding how families defend themselves against a crisis and how they recover from a crisis. *Vulnerability* is the family's ability to prevent stressors from creating a crisis situation. As we mentioned earlier in this section, the family's resources (B) play a major role in determining their vulnerability. For the most part, the more resources the family has available, the lower their vulnerability is. *Regenerative power* is the family's ability to bounce back and recover from a crisis. Like certain lizards that can rapidly regrow a severed tail, some families have a remarkable ability to recover from states of crisis. This concept is similar to what some refer to as resiliency (Olson et al., 1988). According to the double

ABC-X model, those families with good resources, optimistic perceptions, and functional coping responses should have high regenerative power. Finally, research on the double ABC-X model has highlighted the role of *boundary ambiguity* (McCubbin & Patterson). Boundary ambiguity occurs when family members are unsure about who is in or out of the system and who occupies what roles. When a father goes off to war, for example, the remaining family members may be uncertain about who will take over the family functions that were previously taken care of by the now absent father. Perhaps a close relative will spend more time with the family and help out. This may raise questions about how to treat that person. Is he or she now a member of the immediate family? These sorts of questions and dilemmas can be stressful for the family and contribute to stressor pileup.

THE ROLE OF FAMILY COMMUNICATION IN THE ABC-X AND DOUBLE ABC-X MODELS

Although not explicitly labeled as a component of either model, family communication plays an important role in both the ABC-X and the double ABC-X models. In most cases, family communication could be viewed as a resource (B) that could help to buffer against the ill effects of stress or as a vulnerability factor in the case of families with poor communication. Family communication plays a vital role in processes such as social support, coping, information exchange, and problem solving. A study of stress among intergenerational farm families revealed that participants, especially members of the older generation, saw family communication (e.g., showing positive feelings) as a resource for coping with their stress (Weigel & Weigel, 1993). For families that have clear, direct, open, and responsive styles of communication, that pattern of behavior literally becomes a resource on which they can draw during times of stress. Alternatively, families with ambiguous, indirect, and minimal communication patterns would be more vulnerable to the experience of stressful events and situations. This is because they would have a hard time mobilizing the family resources that would allow them to effectively cope with and respond to the demands imposed by the stressful event. In extreme cases, these problematic family communication patterns can become stressors in their own right, Dysfunctional family communication patterns such as expressed emotion and communication deviance can function as a stressor that exacerbates the course of certain mental health problems experienced by family members.

The beneficial effect of family communication as a resource in times of stress is illustrated in a study on the transition to parenthood among adolescent African American and Latino couples (Florsheim et al., 2003). These researchers followed 14- to 19-year-old mothers and their partners as they became first-time parents. Most were still living in their family of origin. They found that young parents who had good relationships with their own parents, as indexed by supportive interactions and minimal conflict for example, maintained good relationships with their partner and exhibited lower risk for parental dysfunction (i.e., parental stress and child abuse potential). Despite the fact that these young couples were experiencing a major life stressor, good communication and relationships with their parents and each other proved to be associated with better outcomes for the family.

Another important role of family communication in the ABC-X models is in the process of perception (C). The family's perception or definition of a stressor is theorized to play a vital role in their ultimate reaction and adaptation to the event or situation. Family perceptions develop largely as a result of the family's communication about the stressful event. According to the theory of symbolic interaction, shared realities are created through interaction with other people. What does a parent's layoff from work mean to a young child? What does a mother's diagnosis of breast cancer mean to her adolescent children? Answers to questions such as these emerge as a product of the family's communication about the stressor. Particularly for younger family members who may not understand the stressful event, there is at best a vague notion of what the stressor implies for the family. In healthy families, parents and children talk about the meaning and impact of the stressor. Often parents may try to shield their younger children from the stress that could be associated with the event or situation. In so doing, they minimize the potentially aversive impact of the event on the young children by trying to offer a benign definition or perception of the situation. Of course, this tactic can be taken too far such that family members remain in the dark about the true meaning of the stressor to their own detriment. In either case, however, the ultimate family perception of the event is created, shaped, revised, and sustained through family communication.

OLSON'S SYSTEMS MODEL OF FAMILY STRESS

One of the major models of family functioning was developed by Olson and his colleagues and is centered around the twin concepts of adaptability (or flexibility) and cohesion (Olson, 1993; Olson et al., 1979). The most functional families according to this approach are those that are balanced in their adaptability and cohesion. However, there is some evidence indicating a linear relationship among adaptability, cohesion, and positive family outcomes (Farrell & Barnes, 1993). This perspective has been fruitfully extended to the domain of family stress and has produced a number of predications about families that are best able to handle stressors. One of the more fundamental hypotheses from this perspective is that families will adjust their levels of adaptability and cohesion in response to situational stressors and changes that result from progression through the family life cycle (Olson, 1983; Olson & McCubbin, 1982). Even though moderate amounts of adaptability and cohesion are optimal for family functioning, there are times when it is best for the family to at least temporarily alter their adaptability and cohesion in response to stressful events. Naturally, healthy families will make adjustments in response to environmental stressors. On the other hand, dysfunctional families often remain rooted at extremes on the adaptability and cohesion dimensions, unable to make adjustments in response to stressors. For example, a healthy family with moderate degrees of adaptability and cohesion might find it most helpful to increase their cohesion (in the direction of enmeshment) and increase their adaptability (in the direction of chaos) after a member of the immediate family is seriously injured in a car accident. The increased cohesion facilitates the exchange of social and emotional support. The heightened adaptability allows family members to assume each other's roles and cover for each other so that they can simultaneously attend to the injured family member while still taking care of routine family business. Of course, in a functional family, these extreme levels of adaptability and cohesion that allow the family to effectively cope with the stressor would be expected to subside as the impact of the stressor event declines. Ultimately, such families would be expected to return to "normal" levels of adaptability and cohesion as they adjust to the stressor. Olson and McCubbin are quick to point out that the most functional changes in response to stress are those that are moderate, such as a shift from flexible to structured, as opposed to a dramatic shift from chaotic to rigid.

A related prediction rooted in this perspective is that troubled families will either not change their adaptability and cohesion when stressed or make dramatic changes from one extreme to the other (Olson et al., 1979). As we mentioned earlier, some dysfunctional families are unable to adjust their levels of adaptability and cohesion in response to stressors. However, there are some dysfunctional families that dramatically swing from, say, disengaged all the way to enmeshed upon experiencing a stressful event or situation. These families come across as unstable and may be somewhat chaotic. These wild swings in adaptability and cohesion can themselves become a source of stress, potentially contributing to stress pileup. According to Olson and his associates, the most functional families will make temporary adjustments in their adaptability and cohesion in order to meet the demands of a stressor, but these adjustments are moderate, not dramatic.

What allows families to make the necessary changes in their adaptability and cohesion in order to effectively cope with stressful events? Olson (1993) suggests that family communication skills facilitate movement and adjustment along the adaptability and cohesion continua. Families with positive communication skills such as clear messages, effective problem solving, supportive statements, and demonstration of empathy are hypothesized to be able to alter their adaptability and cohesion in response to stressors. Alternatively, families that do not listen well to each other, who use indirect messages, and who are excessively critical of each other are expected to be locked into one particular level of adaptability and cohesion, usually at one of the extremes, unable to change when they encounter a stressful event or situation.

Earlier we mentioned that families need to adjust their adaptability and cohesion in response to both situational stressors and ordinary progressions through the family life cycle. In other words, a married couple with two adolescent children may need to function at a level of adaptability different from that of a retired couple with no children. Research has consistently shown that well-functioning families at different stages in the family lifestyle tend to exhibit predictably different levels of adaptability and cohesion (Olson et al., 1988; Olson & Lavee, 1989). For example, the majority of young couples without children are moderately high in both their cohesion and adaptability. Once children become part of the family, the situation changes considerably. Families with young children tend to be more structured in their adaptability, while showing slight decreases in cohesion. When teenagers become part of the picture, this pattern is even more accentuated. A much greater percentage (60%) of families with teens are separated in their cohesion compared to young couples without children (29%; Olson & Lavee, 1989). Older couples whose children have left home tend to exhibit adaptability levels that are comparable to those of young couples without children, and cohesion levels that are comparable to those of families with teens, but lower than those of young couples without children. As families progress through the life cycle and respond to the different stresses and strains that are imposed by these developmental challenges, they make moderate adjustments in their adaptability and cohesion. In functional families these changes are a natural part of the family life cycle. However, dysfunctional families show a greater tendency to remain stuck at one level of adaptability and one level of cohesion, unable to adjust in order to adequately meet the demands of the changing family life cycle.

Olson's (1997) systems model of family stress also predicts that families will first draw on internal resources before using external resources to manage family stress. Internal resources can be found within the family system. These include such things as social support, good communication, tangible assistance with tasks, financial resources that the family has, and the use of special skills that family members can use to manage the stressor. External resources are located outside the family system and include such things as community-based assistance programs, professional counseling or therapy, and law enforcement intervention. Using this knowledge, one could accurately assume that families who tap into external resources (e.g., calling the police to help settle domestic disputes or visiting the community food bank to get food) are under a great degree of stress. Contact with these external agencies suggests that they were unable to bring resolution to their problems or meet the demand of the stressor with the resources that they had within the family system. It implies that the family has effectively exhausted its internal resources for addressing the stressor.

THE VULNERABILITY—STRESS—ADAPTATION MODEL OF MARRIAGE

Thus far we have examined several models of family stress that take a systemwide perspective to understanding the family's experience of and response to stress. A more recent addition to the roster of family stress models was proposed by Karney and Bradbury (1995) in their vulner ability-stress-adaptation model of marriage. This model differs from other family stress models in some important ways. First, this is a model that is specific to the marital subsystem. Second, unlike those models that begin with the stressful event or experience, Karney and Bradbury's model explicitly assumes that marital partners have preexisting vulnerabilities that color husbands' and wives' reactions to stress. Finally, the model assumes that the presence of stress affects the stability and satisfaction of the marriage. In other words, the quality of this family subsystem is partially a function of the stress that the couple experiences. The vulnerability—stress—adaptation model is depicted in Figure 12.3.

In the vulnerability—stress—adaptation model, *stressful events* are assumed to have an impact on *adaptive processes* in the marriage (depicted as path A in Figure 12.3). Adaptive processes are those behaviors that spouses exchange, such as positive communication and problem solving, that allow them to adjust to their roles within the marriage and to cope with challenges that they encounter. The experience of stress tends to have a negative influence on these processes (Karney & Bradbury, 1995), which can then threaten the quality of the

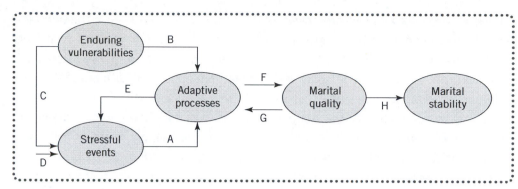

FIGURE 12.3.

Karney and Bradbury's Vulnerability—Stress— Adaptation Model of Marriage

Note. From "The Longitudinal Course of Marital Quality and Stability: A Review of Theory, Method, and Research," by B.R. Karney and T.N. Bradbury, 1995, *Psychological Bulletin, 118,* p. 23. Copyright 1995 by the American Psychological Association. Reprinted with permission.

marriage. The model also assumes that spouses bring with them certain backgrounds or *enduring vulnerabilities* that influence both adaptive processes (path B) and the experience of stressful events (path C). Enduring vulnerabilities are backgrounds and traits that husbands and wives bring into their marriage. Consider, for example, poor Communication skills as an enduring vulnerability. First, people with poor communication skills will presumably have a harder time adjusting to their role as husband or wife. Negotiating expectations, clarifying preferences, and blending into extended family systems are all interpersonal tasks that present challenges to people with poor communication skills. At the same time, the model predicts that people with poor skills will actually experience more stressful events. This phenomenon is characterized as the stress generation effect (Segrin, 2001a). Someone with poor communication skills may experience excessive arguments with his or her partner and have a hard time creating positive interactions and experiences within the marriage. The net result of this enduring vulnerability is that the couple may actually experience more stressful events.

Similar to the double ABC-X model (McCubbin & Patterson, 1982), Karney and Bradbury's (1995) model assumes that adaptive processes will influence the likelihood of encountering stressful events (path E). Couples with good adaptive processes can cope well with stressful events and keep them from piling up. On the other hand, couples with poor adaptive processes will respond to stress in such a way as to actually increase the probability of experiencing more stressful events. Karney and Bradbury note that this sets up a vicious cycle in which stressful events tax the couple's capacity for adaptation, which in turn contributes to worsening of the events, which only serves to further hinder the couple's capacity for adaptation. These adaptive processes play a vital role in the vulnerability—stress—adaptation model because they are seen as proximal and reciprocal causes of *marital quality* (paths F and G). Marital quality is the couple's overall evaluation of and satisfaction with their marriage. Marriages that have good adaptive processes (i.e., the partners exchange positive behaviors, have rewarding interactions, and adjust well to tasks in the marriage) are assumed to have higher quality than those with poor adaptive processes. At the same time, the quality of the marriage is assumed to influence adaptive processes. Naturally, partners who are happy with their marriage are more likely to exchange positive behaviors, treat each other graciously, and work hard at solving marital problems compared to partners who are unhappy with their marriage. In this way, marital quality can actually enhance couples' adaptive processes.

Ultimately, the vulnerability—stress—adaptation model assumes that marital quality is a proximal predictor of *marital stability* (path H). Marital stability simply refers to the duration of the marriage, and in particular, whether the couple stays together. Research findings generally show that marital satisfaction has stronger effects on marital stability than on most other variables that have been examined as potential predictors of marital stability (Karney & Bradbury, 1995). However, Karney and Bradbury are quick to point out that this effect is still only moderate in magnitude. They suggest that this may be due to the fact that most unstable (i.e., broken-up) marriages are marked by dissatisfaction, but not all stable (i.e., in tact) marriages are marked by satisfaction.

FAMILY COPING WITH STRESS

The concept of coping or adaptation figures prominently in most theoretical models of family stress. Family coping involves the active strategies and behaviors that families enact in order to manage and adapt to stressful situations (McCubbin & Dahl, 1985). In the ABC-X model, coping is considered to be a family resource, and in the double ABC X model coping is assumed to influence stress pileup, resources, perceptions, and adaptation to the stressor (McCubbin & Patterson, 1982). Family coping has a powerful impact on the relationship between stressful events and the family's stress reaction to those events. There are a number of hypotheses that explain this relationship (McCubbin et al., 1980). First, effective family coping behaviors are thought to decrease vulnerabilities to stressors. Second, family coping strategies can strengthen or maintain family resources such as cohesiveness, organization, and adaptability. Third, effective coping in the family can reduce or eliminate stressor events and their negative consequences. Finally, family coping behaviors may actively alter the environment by changing social circumstances surrounding the stressor and its experience.

TAXONOMIES OF FAMILY COPING STRATEGIES

There is a wide range of coping strategies that families will enact when they encounter stressors. These run from tactics that are generally helpful for reducing the ill effects of the stressor to strategies that can actually worsen the impact of the stressor. For example, psychologists Robert and Anita Plutchik developed a taxonomy of eight basic strategies that families use to cope with stress (Plutchik & Plutchik, 1990). *Mapping* is coping with a problem by trying to obtain more information about it. *Avoidance* involves coping with a problem by removing the family members from situations that produce the stressor. Families that use *help seeking* cope with stress by asking for help from other family members, neighbors, coworkers, or experts. *Minimization* is an attempt to cope by psychologically reducing the importance, significance, or seriousness of the stressor. Some families cope through *reversal* in which they act the exact opposite of how they feel. For example, the angrier they get with someone, the more polite and generous family members may behave toward that person. When families cope with *blame* they try to make themselves feel good by assigning responsibility for the problem to other people or external factors. *Substitution* is a coping strategy in which families employ indirect methods to solve a problem. Substitution is most often used when there are no direct methods for dealing with a problem. For example, family members who feel stressed out by their jobs and school will often take a pleasant vacation. Quitting work or school is not an option, but the vacation allows the family time to relax and at least temporarily escape the stressor. Finally, *improving shortcomings* is a technique that families use when they carefully consider how they contributed to the stressor and then try to improve aspects of their lives in order to deal with the stressor and prevent its reoccurrence. Note that not all of these coping strategies involve actual behaviors. Sometimes family members will cope with a stressor not by acting or communicating but by denying the problem or changing the way that they think about it.

For Plutchik and Plutchik (1990), communication is a fundamental element of families' efforts at coping with stressful events. They observe that "for every problem, however small or large, there are many possible solutions…. it has been our experience that most people tend to use one style of communication most of the time. When this particular style does not work, they become angry and frustrated rather than simply switching to an alternative approach" (p. 36). Plutchik and Plutchik are suggesting here that effective coping almost always entails some flexibility in the substance and style of family members' interactions following the stressor. Families that are locked into one style of communicating are, in the long run, going to have more trouble coping with stressors than are families that can adjust their style of interaction to meet the demands of the situation.

A complementary taxonomy of family coping methods was developed by Burr and Klein (1994) in which they identified seven highly abstract strategies that have emerged from research on family coping. Each of these strategies is in turn associated with a number of less abstract, or more specific, strategies. Burr and Klein's (1994) taxonomy is summarized in Table 12.1. One noteworthy aspect of this taxonomy is Burr and Klein's explicit recognition of family communication as an actual coping strategy (see also Olson, 1997). They find that certain positive communication behaviors such as being open and honest, carefully listening to each other, and paying careful attention to each other's nonverbal behaviors can function as effective coping mechanisms for family members in times of stress. Presumably many of these communication tactics work by putting family members "on the same page" as they are confronted with a stressor. When family members misunderstand each other, the effects of a stressor can be intensified. These communication strategies substantially decrease the likelihood of such an occurrence. It is also worth noting that what Burr and Klein refer to as "communication" is actually a collection of strategies, some associated with message production (e.g., exchanging information and being honest) and some with message reception (e.g., listening and being sensitive).

When most people think about coping with a problem, they tend to think about the things that we do to lessen the impact of a stressor and to effectively resolve the difficulties that it presents. However, researchers agree that family coping strategies can have both positive and negative effects (McCubbin et al., 1980; Plutchik & Plutchik, 1990). Recall from our discussion of the double ABC-X model that certain coping strategies can lead to stress pileup. This happens when family coping literally becomes a source of stress. How does this happen? McCubbin et al. suggest that there are at least three ways that family coping strategies can actually be a source of stress. First, some coping strategies may indirectly damage the family system. If a family tries to shield its children from the crimeridden neighborhood in which they live by sending them to an exclusive private school on the other side of town, the exorbitant tuition that they pay may actually create financial hardships that effectively become a family stressor in their own right. Second, some family coping strategies cause direct harm to the family system. When family members turn to drugs or alcohol as a means of coping with hardship they may experience secondary stressors that are directly linked to these behaviors such as drunk driving convictions and missed work. Third, some family coping mechanisms create further stress by interfering with the adaptive behaviors that could enhance the family's well-being. For example, some family members may use denial as a coping mechanism. Unfortunately this will do nothing to motivate family members to pursue effective solutions to the problem that plagues them. In the meantime, the problem may actually worsen. It is clear that effective coping strategies certainly have the potential to greatly minimize the negative effects of stressors. At the same time, there are some families that employ coping strategies that are literally antagonistic to effective solutions to their problems. In such cases the coping strategies literally produce more stressors, contributing to stress pileup.

As families cope with the stressors that they encounter, they directly and indirectly teach coping mechanisms to their children (Chambers, 1999; Kliewer, Fearnow, & Miller, 1996). Kliewer et al. suggest that one way this happens is through *coaching*. In coaching, parents directly instruct their children on how to handle the various problems they encounter. Coaching might entail explaining the meaning of the stressor to the child and recommending concrete methods for addressing the stressor. This advice is often consistent with the parents' own preferred coping styles. Another mechanism by which families transmit coping strategies to their children is through *modeling*. Social learning theory explains how children will pick up behaviors by observing their parents enact those behaviors, especially when there are positive outcomes connected to the coping behaviors. Kliewer and her associates found that mothers who used less active coping strategies had daughters who also used less active coping strategies. Mothers who modeled avoidant coping methods also had sons who reported more avoidant coping strategies. These results suggest that children will often pick up their parents' preferred mechanisms for coping by simply observing them in stressful situations. So, if a parent comes home from a difficult day at work and proceeds to drink large amounts of alcohol and then starts to exhibit a more pleasant mood, children who repeatedly observe this coping strategy would be very likely to eventually enact the same behaviors when they are stressed.

TABLE 12.1: BURR AND KLEIN'S CONCEPTUAL FRAMEWORK OF FAMILY COPING STRATEGIES	
HIGHLY ABSTRACT STRATEGIES	**MODERATELY ABSTRACT STRATEGIES**
• Cognitive	• be accepting of the situation and others • gain useful knowledge • change how the situation is viewed or defined (reframe)
• Emotional	• express feelings and affection • avoid or resolve negative feelings and disabling expressions of emotion • be sensitive to others' emotional needs
• Relationships	• increase cohesion (togetherness) • develop increased trust • increase cooperation • increase tolerance of each other
• Communication	• be open and honest • listen to each other • be sensitive to nonverbal communication
• Community	• seek help and support from others • fulfill expectations in organizations
• Spiritual	• be more involved in religious activities • increase faith or seek help from God
• Individual Development	• develop autonomy, independence, and self-sufficiency • keep active in hobbies

Note: From W.R. Burr, and S.R. Klein. *Reexamining Family Stress: New Theory and Research,* p. 133, copyright © 1994 by Sage Publications. Reprinted with permission of Sage Publication, Inc.

FAMILY COPING AND STRESS APPRAISAL

Psychologists refer to the assessment of stressors and the degree to which they are threatening as *primary appraisal* and to assessment of coping resources for dealing with those stressors as *secondary appraisal* (Lazarus, 1966). Presumably family coping strategies are effective either when they alter primary appraisals by removing the stressor or making it seem less threatening or when they alter secondary appraisals by enhancing perceptions of family members' ability to handle the stressor (Wills, Blechman, & McNamara, 1996). Consistent with this notion, a study of dual-worker couples revealed that the best predictor of marital adjustment was not the hardships that they experienced but rather their communication (a coping resource) and their relational efficacy (i.e., the couple's appraisal of their ability to deal with problems; Meeks, Arnkoff, Glass, & Notarius, 1986). Menees (1997) also found that children of an alcoholic parent had highest self-esteem when they coped with stressors via family problem solving and ventilation. Young people who engage in family problem solving work together with their parents to address their stressors. Although it may seem ironic that this would be an effective strategy in children of alcoholics, the fact that the stressor emerged from the family of origin makes that same family an especially powerful force for shaping the child's primary and secondary appraisals. Ventilation is a coping strategy that involves talking with other people to get things out in the open rather than keep them to oneself. This sort of coping may engage other people and solicit input from them that could be vital in altering primary and secondary appraisals for the better. Sometimes just talking to other people about a problem can make the problem seem not so bad.

COMMUNAL COPING

Many of the family coping strategies covered earlier in this section could be enacted by family members individually. However, there are many cases where families (e.g., parents and their children and wives and their husbands) cope with problems together as a unit. This phenomenon is known as *communal coping*. Communal coping refers to appraising and acting on a problem in the context of a relationship by pooling resources and efforts to address the problem (Lyons, Mickelson, Sullivan, & Coyne, 1998). According to Lyons and associates, the key to communal coping is that family members perceive the stressor as "our" problem versus "my" or "your" problem. Furthermore, they decide as a unit that the problem is "our" responsibility. Seeing the stressor as "our" problem reflects an appraisal that is communal rather than individual in nature. Seeing the required action as "our" responsibility implies that coping strategies and solutions will be enacted by the family as a whole rather than by just one person in the family. Lyons et al. explain that the process of communal coping can be broken down into three main components. The first component is a *communal coping orientation*. This is the belief that the family must join together in order to effectively address the problem. Second, communal coping involves *communication about the stressor*. Because communal coping is inherently social, family members must discuss the details of how the problem happened, what they think can be done to address it, and how it will affect the family, for example. Finally, there must be some *cooperative action* in communal coping. This simply means that family members collaborate to develop strategies and enact remedies to deal with the stressor.

Research findings consistently show that communal coping is very effective and is generally associated with positive outcomes for families dealing with stressors. For example, pregnant women experience fewer symptoms of depression to the extent that their partners (e.g., spouses and family members) use active prosocial coping strategies such as joining together to deal with the problems that they experience (Monnier & Hobfoll, 1997). Men's success in adjusting to and recovering from a heart attack is dependent on the efforts of their wives who create changes in the couple's diet and daily routine, as well as the couple's ability to work together to make lifestyle changes (Coyne, Ellard, & Smith, 1990).

Sometimes one subunit in the family can work together to shield other family members from the ill effects of stress. During the 1980s there was a severe economic downturn in rural economy that had devastating effects on families and their farms. Family scientists Rand and Katherine Conger studied how rural families coped with the stressor imposed by these austere circumstances (Conger & Conger, 2002). They found that children and adolescents in the family do not experience stress directly as a result of the economic conditions but rather through the responses of their parents to the financial hardships facing the family. Consequently, if husbands and wives exhibited strong social support toward each other, they were generally unlikely to show outward signs of emotional distress and their children therefore did not experience significant trauma as a result of the family's financial hardships. Conger and Conger theorized that if parents can contain their emotional distress and interpersonal conflicts, while maintaining their parenting skills (e.g., being nurturant and involved with the children), their children can weather the storm without any real adjustment problems or emotional distress of their own. One way that rural families pulled together during the terrible farm economy was to maintain close ties between the parents while simultaneously demonstrating affection, warmth, and minimal hostility toward the children. In these cases the parents worked together to provide a positive atmosphere for their children so that the children could prosper developmentally despite the adverse circumstances that faced the family.

FAMILY SOCIAL SUPPORT

Social support is one of the most important and fundamental forms of family communication. It could be argued that a primary function of the family is to provide social support to its members. People often view the family as the last bastion of social support when support from anyone else cannot be found during times of stress. The beneficial effects of social support have been conclusively established over decades of scientific research. The availability of social support significantly enhances people's general well-being and happiness in addition to their ability to withstand a variety of major stressors such as serious illness (Coyne & Smith, 1994). On the other hand, people who lack available social support appear to be at risk for developing a range of physical and mental health problems.

Social support is enacted through interpersonal communication and sometimes through instrumental behaviors. Its beneficial effects appear to result from several socialpsychological processes. According to the *buffering model* (Cohen & Wills, 1985) social support mitigates the ill effects of stress by reducing the appraised threat and reducing the stress response that typically follows physical or psychological threat. Supportive communication allows people to work through their emotional reactions to stressful events and to develop relief-generating reappraisals that alleviate or minimize stress (Albrecht, Burleson, & Goldsmith, 1994; Burleson & Goldsmith, 1998). The *main effect model* holds that involvement in caring relationships provides a generalized source of positive affect, self-worth, and belonging that keeps psychological despair at a minimum (Cohen, Gottlieb, & Underwood, 2000). The family is an especially likely source of such caring relationships.

In the family context most acts of social support could be classified into one of three general categories (Wills et al., 1996). *Emotional support* is the availability of a family member with whom one can discuss problems, concerns, and feelings. Ordinarily, a provider of emotional support is a good listener who is not critical, blaming, or judgmental. Sometimes a family member who provides emotional support need not do anything more than listen and be available. *Instrumental support* is offered when a family member provides assistance with various tasks. In the family, this might mean help with household chores, a ride to school, or assistance with auto repairs. When family members provide *informational support* they give guidance, feedback, and resource information that is helpful in addressing a problem. Parents are often providers of informational support to their children. So, for example, when a child attends his or her first formal high school dance, parents may offer suggestions on things like an appropriate suit or dress to wear, places to go out to dinner, and where to go to buy flowers. This kind of information can greatly reduce the stress of such an experience by helping to reduce uncertainty.

Social support from the family has a number of beneficial effects for maintaining well-being in the face of a variety of stressors and life circumstances. For instance, social support from the family is negatively related to substance abuse in adolescents (Wills, 1990; Wills et al., 1996). Among adults, family social support is positively associated with life satisfaction, health, and positive mood (Walen & Lachman, 2000). Family social support is also positively associated with intentions to behave in less risky ways among HIV-positive gay men (Kimberly & Serovich, 1999). For young adults with an alcoholic parent, family social support was significantly associated with increased self-esteem (Menees, 1997). Just as the presence of family social support can enhance well-being and buffer against the negative effects of stress, the lack of supportive relationships in the family can be detrimental to well-being. Children who do not receive very much social support from their families are more harmful to others, uncooperative, withdrawn, and exhibit higher levels of hopelessness (Kashani, Canfield, Borduin, Soltys, & Reid, 1994).

There can be no question that social support from the family can have a number of beneficial effects for family members. But what are the mechanisms that produce these positive effects? Family researchers believe that there are numerous pathways between family social support and positive outcomes (Wills, 1990). One basic function of social support is to *reduce negative affect*. When people are aware of the availability of social support from their family, they may worry less about problems and perceive them as more manageable. When people do become sad or anxious, readily available social support from family members can help to minimize these feelings. Also, family social support may *promote health-protective behaviors*. Wills suggests that family networks aid people in both recognizing symptoms and seeking medical attention when illness is suspected. One common explanation for why married men are generally healthier than unmarried men is because their wives point out their symptoms of illness and urge them to seek medical attention. Conversely, people with little social support available are more likely to be involved in health-damaging behaviors such as smoking, alcohol, or drug use. Additionally, family social support can *promote positive affect*. As we mentioned earlier, the main effect model for social support holds that family social support causes us to feel valued and cared for. This promotes a positive emotional state, feelings of belonging to a group or community, and feeling appreciated by others. Family social support may be associated with leisure experiences, enjoyment of shared activities, and help with instrumental tasks, all of which promote a positive mood in the recipients of the social support.

CONCLUSION

We begin this selection by examining different ways of classifying family stressors. Clearly "family stress" is not a generic phenomenon. Issues such as whether the stressor is normative versus unpredictable, temporary versus permanent, or voluntary versus involuntary can have a substantial effect on the extent to which the family experiences stress as result of exposure to various stressors. Family scientists have developed a number of theoretical models to explain how families experience and respond to stress. These include the ABC-X and double ABC-X models, along with the systems and vulnerability—stress—adaptation models. Although each of these models differs in the components and mechanisms that are specified to explain family stress, each is useful for understanding how family communication influences and is influenced by stress. For example, in the ABC-X model, family communication could certainly be thought of as a resource. In Olson's (1997) systems model, communication is the mechanism that allows family to alter their adaptability and cohesion to appropriately respond to the stressor. Finally, in Karney and Bradbury's (1995) vulnerability—stress—adaptation model, marital communication could be an enduring vulnerability as well as an adaptive process. In all models, there is a possibility that family communication itself could be the stressor or at least generate stressors. Coping involves the strategies that families use to deal with stressors. Like stressors themselves, coping strategies are diverse ranging from functional to dysfunctional and individual to communal. Many involve specific types of communication and messages exchanged between family members in order to address the stressor. Finally, we discuss social support as a fundamental and important type of family communication that is vital for responding to stressful events.

There are few family processes as consequential as the family's means and mechanisms for dealing with stress. All families will experience stress. Some families respond to stress in a ways that make them a stronger and more competent social structure. However, stress literally defeats and destroys other families. What differentiates those families that grow from those that fall apart in the face of stress is the nature of the family's communication, coping tactics, and their predisposition to attack problems instead of each other. Supportive communication in the family is vital as it relates to physical and mental health problems.

QUESTIONS FOR REVIEW, REFLECTION, AND DISCUSSION

1. What is the difference between stress and stressor?
2. What is the difference between morphogenesis and morphostasis?
3. What is meant by normative and non-normative stressors? Provide examples of both types of stressors.
4. Explain each component of the ABC-X model.

ADDITIONAL READINGS

Boss, P. (1992). Primacy of perception in family stress theory and measurement, *Journal of Family Psychology, 6*(2), 113–119.

Boss, P., Bryant, C.M., & Mancini, J. A. (2017). *Family stress management: A contextual approach, Third Edition.* Los Angeles, CA: Sage.

Chappel, A., Suldo, S., & Ogg, J. (2014). Associations between adolescents' family stressors and life satisfaction, *Journal of Child & Family Studies, 23*(1), 76–84.

Neppl, T. K., Senia, J. M., & Donnellan, M. B. Effects of economic hardship: Testing the family stress model over time, *Journal of Family Psychology, 30*(1), 12–21.

Vaughn-Coaxum, R., Smith, B. N., Iverson, K. M., & Vogt, D. (2015). Family stressors and postdeployment mental health in single versos partners parents deployed in support of the wars in Afghanistan and Iraq, *Psychological Services, 12*(3), Special Section: Military/Veteran Children and Families. 241–249.

White, R.M.B., Liu, Y. , & Nair, R. L. (2015). Longitudinal and integrative tests of family stress model effects on Mexican origin adolescents, *Developmental Psychology, 51*(5), 649–662.

KEY TERMS

Median

Poverty, Poverty Line

Economic Inequality

Poverty Trap

Temporary Assistance for Needy
Families (TANF)

Aid to Families with Dependent Children (AFDC)

Earned Income Credit (EIC)

Medicaid

Special Supplemental Food Program for
Women, Infants, and Children (WIC)

13

POVERTY AND ECONOMIC INEQUALITY

By Timothy Taylor

Timothy Taylor, "Poverty and Economic Inequality","
Microeconomics: Economics and the Economy, pp.
260-269. Copyright © 2014 by Textbook Media.
Reprinted with permission.

The labor markets that determine what workers are paid don't take into account how much income a family needs to afford necessities like food, shelter, clothing, and health care. Market forces don't worry about what happens to families when a major local employer goes out of business. Market forces don't take time to contemplate whether those who are earning higher incomes should pay an even higher share of taxes.

However, labor markets do create considerable inequalities of income. In 2011, the median American family had income of $50,054 (the median is the level where half of all families had more than that level and half had less). However, top executives at many companies earned much more. In 2011, for example, Stephen Hemsley of UnitedHealthcare received total compensation of $101 million. The point here is not to pick on Hemsley, who received most of that compensation through stock options that had built up over years. Nor is the intention to pick on corporate executives: certain athletes, entertainers, and others can have extremely high incomes, too. But the amounts are still amazing. Hemsley's $101 million was equal to the combined income of more than 2,000 typical families.

At the other extreme, about 9.5 million U.S. families were classified by the federal government as being below the poverty line in 2011. Think about the practical aspects for a family of three—perhaps a single mother with two children—attempting to pay for the basics of life on perhaps $15,000 per year. After paying rent, health care, clothing, and transportation, such a family might have $6,000 to spend each year on food. Spread over 365 days per year, the food budget for the entire family would be about $17 per day. Most cities have upscale restaurants where $17 will buy you an appetizer for one.

Such comparisons of high and low incomes raise issues of economic inequality and poverty. While these two issues are often mentioned in the same breath, they are not the same. **Poverty** is measured by the number of people who fall below a certain level of income—called the **poverty line**—that defines the income needed for a basic standard of living. Economic **inequality** compares the share of the total income (or wealth) in society that is received by different groups; for example, comparing the share of income received by the top 10% to the share of income received by the bottom 10%. This chapter first explores the issues of poverty in detail: how the U.S. government defines poverty, the trade-offs between assisting the poor without discouraging work, and how U.S. antipoverty programs work. The chapter then moves to a discussion of inequality: how economists measure inequality, why inequality has changed in recent decades, the range of possible government policies to reduce inequality, and the danger of a trade-off that too great a reduction in inequality may reduce incentives for producing output.

poverty: Falling below a certain level of income needed for a basic standard of living.

poverty line: The specific amount of income needed for a basic standard of living.

inequality: When one group receives a higher share of total income or wealth than others.

DRAWING THE POVERTY LINE

In the United States, the official definition of the poverty line traces back to a single person: Mollie Orshansky. In 1963, Orshansky was working for the Social Security Administration, where she published an article called "Children of the Poor" in a highly useful and dry-as-dust publication called the *Social Security Bulletin*. Orshansky's idea was to define a poverty line based on the cost of a healthy diet. Her previous job had been at the U.S. Department of Agriculture, where she had worked in an agency called the Bureau of Home Economics and Human Nutrition, and one task of this bureau had been to calculate how much it would cost to feed a nutritionally adequate diet to a family. Orshansky found evidence that the average family spent one-third of its income on food. Thus, she proposed that the poverty line be the amount needed to buy a nutritionally adequate diet, given the size of the family, multiplied by three. The current U.S. poverty line is essentially the same as the Orshansky poverty line, although the dollar amounts are adjusted each year to represent the same buying power over time.

The current U.S. poverty lines, based on family size, appear in Exhibit 13-1. Exhibit 13-2 shows the U.S. poverty rate over time; that is, the percentage of the population below the poverty rate in any given year. The poverty rate declined through the 1960s, rose in the early 1980s and early 1990s, dropped a bit in the mid-1990s, and then rose sharply. Exhibit 13-3 compares poverty rates for different groups in 2011. Poverty rates are relatively low for whites, for the elderly, for the well educated, and for male-headed households.

POVERTY IN LOW-INCOME COUNTRIES

The World Bank sets two poverty lines that it applies to low-income countries around the world. One poverty line is set at an income of $1.25/day per person; the other is at $2/day. By comparison, the U.S. poverty line of $17,916 annually for a family of three works out to $16.36 per person per day. Clearly, many people around the world are far poorer than Americans. China and India both have more than a billion people, Nigeria is the most populous country in Africa, and Egypt is the most populous country in the Middle East. In all four of those countries, a substantial share of the population subsists in dire poverty on less than $2/day. Indeed, nearly half the world lives on less than $2.50 a day, and about 80 percent of the world lives on less than $10/day.

Country	Share of Population below $1.25/Day	Share of Population below $2/Day
Brazil (2009)	6%	10%
China (2008)	13%	29%
Egypt (2008)	2%	15%
India (2010)	32%	68%
Mexico (2008)	1%	5%
Nigeria (2010)	68%	84%

Size of Family Unit	Weighted Average Thresholds (Poverty Threshold)
One person (unrelated individual)	$11,484
Under 65 years	$11,702
65 years and over	$10,788
Two people	$14,657
Householder under 65 years	$15,139
Householder 65 years and over	$13,609
Three people	$17,916
Four people	$23,021
Five people	$27,251
Six people	$30,847
Seven people	$35,085
Eight people	$39,064
Nine people or more	$46,572

EXHIBIT 13.1.

The U.S. Poverty Line in 2011

If a family, given its size, had less than the amount of income shown in the table, then it was considered officially "poor" or "in poverty."

EXHIBIT 13.2.

The U.S. Poverty Rate

since 1960

The poverty rate fell
dramatically during the
1960s, rose in the early
1980s and early 1990s,
dropped a bit in the
mid-1990s, and then rose
sharply.

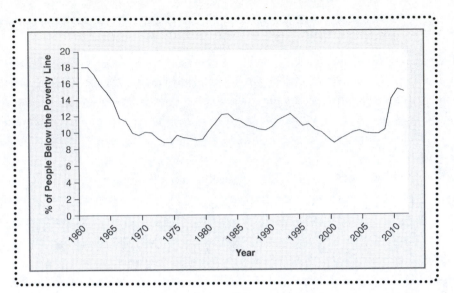

EXHIBIT 13.3.

Poverty Rates by

Group, 2011

Poverty rates are lower for
men than for women, lower
for whites than for blacks
or Hispanics, and lower for
those of prime working age
than for those earlier in life.

Group	Poverty Rate
Females	16.3%
Males	13.6%
White	12.8%
Black	27.6%
Hispanic	25.3%
Under age 18	21.9%
Ages 18–24	20.6%
Ages 25–34	15.9%
Ages 35–44	12.2%
Ages 45–54	10.9%
Ages 55–59	10.7%
Ages 60–64	10.8%
Ages 65 and older	8.7%

The concept of a poverty line raises many tricky questions. In a vast country like the United States, should the same national poverty line apply in all states? After all, the median household income varies considerably across states, and prices of some basic goods like housing are quite different between states. The poverty line is based on cash income, which means it doesn't take into account government programs that provide assistance to the poor in a non-cash form, like Medicaid that provides health insurance to the poor or food stamps that can be exchanged for food in grocery stores. Should the poverty line be adjusted to take the value of such programs into account? (These programs and other welfare programs will be discussed in detail later in this chapter.) Perhaps rather than just updating Molly Orshansky's poverty line from the early 1960s, the concept of what poverty means in the twenty-first century should be rethought from scratch?

Government statisticians at the U.S. Census Bureau have ongoing research programs to address questions like these. But any poverty line will be somewhat arbitrary, and it is useful to have a poverty line whose basic definition doesn't change much over time. If Congress voted every few years to redefine completely what poverty means, then it would be difficult to compare poverty rates over time. After all, would a lower poverty rate mean that the definition had been changed, or that people were actually better off?

THE POVERTY TRAP

A conflict lies at the heart of assisting the poor. When people are provided with food, shelter, health care, income, and other necessities, such assistance may reduce their incentives to work. For example, consider a program to fight poverty that works in this reasonable-sounding manner: the government provides assistance to the poor, but as the poor earn income to support themselves, the government reduces the level of assistance it provides. With such a program, every time a poor person earns $100, the person also loses $100 in government support. As a result of such a program, the person will experience no net gain to working. Economists call this problem the **poverty trap**.

For a concrete example of the poverty trap, consider the situation faced by a single mother with two children, as illustrated in Exhibit 13-4. First consider the labor-leisure budget constraint faced by this family in a situation without government assistance to the poor. Assume that the mother can earn a wage of $8 per hour. By working 40 hours a week, 50 weeks a year, let's say that her utility-maximizing choice is to work a total of 2,000 hours per year and earn $16,000. Now suppose that a government antipoverty program is created that guarantees every family with a single mother and two children $18,000 in income. With this program, each time the mother earns $1,000, the government will deduct $1,000 of its support.

poverty trap:
When antipoverty programs are set up so that government benefits decline substantially as people earn more income—and as a result, working provides little financial gain.

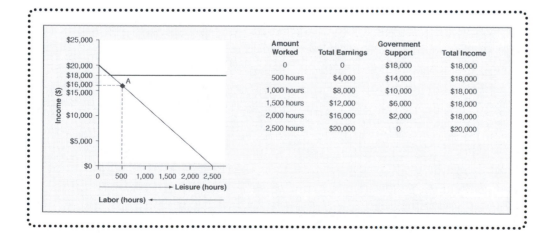

EXHIBIT 13.4.

The Poverty Trap in Action

The original choice is 500 hours of leisure, 2,000 hours of work at point A, and income of $16,000. With a guaranteed income of $18,000, this family would receive $18,000 whether it provides zero hours of work or 2,000 hours of work. Only if the family provides, say, 2,300 hours of work does its income rise above the guaranteed level of $18,000—and even then, the marginal gain to income from working many hours is small.

Amount Worked	Total Earnings	Government Support	Total Income
0	0	$18,000	$18,000
500 hours	$4,000	$14,000	$18,000
1,000 hours	$8,000	$10,000	$18,000
1,500 hours	$12,000	$6,000	$18,000
2,000 hours	$16,000	$2,000	$18,000
2,500 hours	$20,000	0	$20,000

The new budget line, with the antipoverty program in place, is the heavy line that is flat at $18,000 and then upward sloping at the far left of the budget line. If the mother doesn't work at all, she receives $18,000, all from the government. If she works full time, giving up 40 hours per week with her children, she still ends up with $18,000 at the end of the year. Only if she works, say, 2,300 hours in the year—which is an average of 44 hours per week for 50 weeks a year—does household income rise to $18,400. But even in this case, all of her year's work means that household income rises by only $400 over the income she would receive if she did not work at all.

Clearly, this kind of government antipoverty program creates a powerful incentive not to work. Indeed, the poverty trap is even stronger than this simplified example shows because a working mother will have extra expenses like transportation and child care that a nonworking mother will not face—making the economic gains from working even smaller. Moreover, those who don't work fail to build up job experience and contacts, which makes working in the future even less attractive.

The bite of the poverty trap can be reduced by designing the antipoverty program so that instead of reducing government payments by $1 for every $1 earned, payments are reduced by some smaller amount, instead. Exhibit 13.5 illustrates a government program that guarantees $18,000 in income, even for those who do not work at all, but then reduces this amount by 50 cents for each $1 earned. The new, higher budget line in the figure shows that with this program in place, additional hours of work will bring some economic gain. However, this type of program raises some issues as well. First, even if it does not eliminate the incentive to work by reducing government payments by $1 for every $1 earned, enacting such a program may still reduce the incentive to work. For example, at least some people who would be working 2,000 hours per year without this program might decide to work fewer hours but still end up with more income—that is, their choice on the new budget line would be like S, above and to the right of the original choice P. Of course, others may choose a point like R, which involves the same amount of work as P, or even a point to the left of R that involves more work. The second major issue

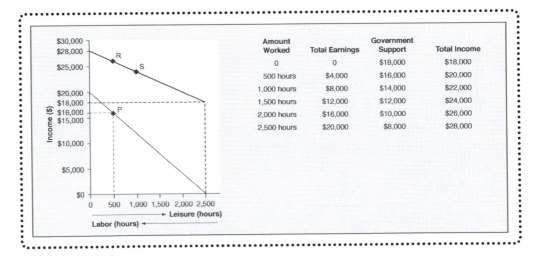

Amount Worked	Total Earnings	Government Support	Total Income
0	0	$18,000	$18,000
500 hours	$4,000	$16,000	$20,000
1,000 hours	$8,000	$14,000	$22,000
1,500 hours	$12,000	$12,000	$24,000
2,000 hours	$16,000	$10,000	$26,000
2,500 hours	$20,000	$8,000	$28,000

is that when the government phases out its support payments more slowly, the antipoverty program costs the government more money. Still, it may be preferable in the long run to spend more money on a program that retains a greater incentive to work, rather than spending less money on a program that nearly eliminates any gains from working.

The next section will consider a variety of U.S. government support programs that are focused specifically on the poor, including welfare, food stamps, Medicaid, the earned income tax credit, and more. Although these programs vary from state to state, it is generally a true statement that in many states from the 1960s into the 1980s, if poor people worked, their level of income barely rose—or did not rise at all—after the reduction in government support payments was factored in. One major issue with rethinking antipoverty programs in the last decade or two is to find ways to combine assistance for the poor with incentives to work—and to declaw the poverty trap.

THE SAFETY NET

The U.S. government has implemented a number of programs to assist those below the poverty line and those who have incomes just above the poverty line, who are referred to as the **near-poor**. As a group, such programs are nicknamed the **safety net**, in recognition of the fact that they offer some protection for those who find themselves without jobs or income.

near-poor: Those who have incomes just above the poverty line.

safety net: Nickname for the group of government programs that provide assistance to the poor and the near-poor.

TEMPORARY ASSISTANCE FOR NEEDY FAMILIES

From the Great Depression of the 1930s until 1996, the United States' most visible antipoverty program was Aid to Families with Dependent Children (AFDC), which provided cash payments to mothers with children who were below the poverty line. This program was often just called "welfare." In 1996, Congress passed and President Bill Clinton signed into law the Personal Responsibility and Work Opportunity Reconciliation Act, more commonly called the welfare reform act. The new law replaced AFDC with Temporary Assistance for Needy Families (TANF).

TANF brought several dramatic changes in how welfare operated. Under the old AFDC program, states set the level of welfare benefits that they would pay to the poor, and the federal government guaranteed to chip in some of the money as well. Thus, the federal government's welfare spending would rise or fall depending on the number of poor people and on how each state set its own welfare contribution. Under TANF, however, the federal government gives a fixed amount of money to each state. The state can then use the money for almost any program with an antipoverty component: for example, the state might use the money to give cash to poor families, or to reduce teenage pregnancy, or even to raise the high school graduation rate. However, the federal government imposes two key requirements. First, if states are to keep receiving the TANF grants, they must impose work requirements so that most of those receiving

TANF benefits are working (or attending school). Second, no one can receive TANF benefits with federal money for more than a total of five years over his or her lifetime. The old AFDC program had no such work requirements or time limits.

TANF attempts avoid the poverty trap by requiring that welfare recipients work and by limiting the length of time they can receive benefits. In its first few years, the program was quite successful. The number of families receiving payments in 1995, the last year of AFDC, was 4.8 million. By 2002, the number of families receiving payments under TANF was 2.0 million—a decline of more than half.

TANF benefits to poor families vary considerably across states; for example, in 2011 the highest monthly payment in California to a single mother with two children was $638, while in Tennessee the highest monthly payment to that family was $185. Total spending on TANF was $33 billion in 2011, split about evenly between the federal and state governments.

EARNED INCOME CREDIT (EIC)

The *earned income credit (EIC)* is a method of assisting the working poor through the tax system. For every $1 in earned income, a family with children receives a tax refund. The amount of the tax break increases with the amount of income earned, up to a point. In 2012, for example, a single parent with two children would have received a tax refund of 40 cents for every dollar earned up to an income level of $12,570—for a total tax refund of $5,028. The earned income credit has often been popular with both economists and the general public because of the way it effectively increases the payment received for work.

What about the danger of the poverty trap that every additional $1 earned will reduce government support payments by close to $1? To minimize this problem, the earned income credit is phased out slowly. For a single-parent family with two children in 2012, the credit is not reduced at all (but neither is it increased) as earnings rise from $12,570 to $16,350. Then, for every $1 earned above $16,350, the amount received from the credit is reduced by 32 cents, until the credit phases out completely at an income level of $41,952.

In recent years, the EIC has become the single most expensive government program for providing income assistance to the poor and near-poor, costing about $62 billion in 2012. In 2012, the EIC provided benefits to about 27 million families and individuals, and on average is worth about $2,200 per family with children. One reason that the welfare reform bill of 1996 worked as well as it did in the years just after its passage is that the EIC was greatly expanded in the late 1980s and again in the early 1990s, which increased the returns to work for low-income Americans.

FOOD STAMPS

Food stamps are a federally funded program, started in 1964, in which poor people receive coupons each month that they can use in grocery stores to buy food. The amount of food stamps for which a household is eligible varies by income, number of children, and other factors, but in general, households are expected to spend about 30% of their own income on food, and if 30% of their income is not enough to purchase a nutritionally adequate diet, then those households are eligible for food stamps.

Food stamps contribute to the poverty trap. For every $100 earned, the government assumes that a family can spend $30 more for food and thus reduces eligibility for food stamps by $30. This decreased food stamp benefit is not a complete disincentive to work—but combined with how other programs reduce benefits as income increases, it doesn't help. However, the food stamp program does try to address the poverty trap with its own set of work requirements and time limits for recipients.

Why give food stamps and not just cash? Part of the political support for food stamps comes from a belief that since food stamps must be spent on food, they can't be "wasted" on other forms of consumption. But from an economic point of view, the belief that food stamps must increase spending on food seems wrong-headed. After all, say that a poor family is spending $2,500 per year on food, and then it starts receiving $1,000 per year in food stamps. The family might react to the food stamps by spending $3,500 per year on food (income plus food stamps), or it might react by continuing to spend $2,500 per year on food but use the $1,000 in food stamps to free up $1,000 that can now be spent on other goods. Thus, it is reasonable to think of food stamps as an alternative method, along with TANF and the earned income credit, of transferring income to the working poor.

Indeed, anyone eligible for TANF is also eligible for food stamps, although states can expand eligibility for food stamps if they wish to do so. In some states, where TANF welfare spending is relatively low, a poor family may receive more in support from food stamps than from TANF. In 2012, about 46 million people received food stamps at an annual cost of about $78 billion. The average monthly benefit was about $133 per person per month—thus, a qualifying mother with two children might receive $4,788 per year in food stamp benefits.

MEDICAID

Medicaid is a federal-state joint program enacted in 1965 that provides medical insurance for certain (not all) low-income people, including the near-poor as well as those below the poverty line, and focusing on low-income families with children, the low-income elderly, and the disabled. About one-third of Medicaid spending is for low-income mothers with children; an increasing share of the program funding in recent years has gone to pay for nursing home costs for the elderly poor. States must provide a basic level of benefits under Medicaid, but they are free to provide higher levels if they wish.

In the past, a common problem has been that many low-paying jobs pay enough to a breadwinner so that a family could lose its eligibility for Medicaid, yet the job doesn't offer health insurance benefits either. Thus, a poor parent considering such a job might choose not to work rather than to lose health insurance for his or her children. In this way, health insurance can become a part of the poverty trap. Many states recognized this problem in the 1980s and 1990s and expanded their Medicaid coverage to include not just the poor but also the near-poor earning up to 135% or even 185% of the poverty line. Some states also guaranteed that children would not lose coverage if their parents worked. These expanded guarantees cost money to the government, of course, but they also helped to encourage those on welfare to enter the labor force.

Medicaid spending totaled $389 billion in federal and state spending in 2010, which is roughly triple the total combined spending of TANF, the earned income tax credit, and food stamps. Of the 62 million or so people who are eligible for Medicaid, only about 40% are below the poverty line because the program focuses on certain groups like families with children and the elderly, whether they are poor or near-poor, but the program has not traditionally focused on providing health insurance to all people below the poverty line.

OTHER SAFETY NET PROGRAMS

The safety net includes a number of other programs: government-subsidized school lunches and breakfasts for children from low-income families; the Special Supplemental Food Program for Women, Infants, and Children (WIC), which provides food assistance for pregnant women and newborns; the Low Income Home Energy Assistance Program, which provides help with home heating bills; housing assistance, which helps pay the rent; and Supplemental Security Income, which provides cash support for the elderly poor.

There is no straightforward answer to the problem of ensuring that the poor have a decent standard of living while also providing incentives to work. TANF tries to use work requirements and time limits. The earned income credit attempts to increase the incentives for work. Medicaid has been expanded to be widely available to the near-poor as well as the poor. But with all of these programs, and food stamps as well, there comes a point where, as families earn more money, their government support payments are reduced, which inevitably reduces the incentives for the poor and near-poor to work. The poverty trap can be loosened, but it cannot be abolished.

MEASURING INCOME INEQUALITY

Economic inequality involves comparing those with high incomes, middle incomes, and low incomes—not just looking at those below or near the poverty line. In turn, measuring income inequality means dividing up the population into various groups and then comparing the groups, a task that can be carried out in several ways.

INCOME DISTRIBUTION BY QUINTILES

quintiles:
Dividing a group into fifths, a method often used to look at distribution of income.

One common way of measuring income inequality is to rank all households by income, from lowest to highest, and then to divide all households into five groups with equal numbers of people—known as **quintiles**. This calculation allows measuring inequality by comparing what share of the total income is earned by each quintile.

U.S. income distribution by quintile appears in Exhibit 13-6. In 2005, for example, the bottom quintile of the income distribution received 3.4% of income; the second quintile received 8.6%; the third quintile, 14.6%; the fourth quintile, 23.0%; and the top quintile, 50.4%. The final column of the table shows what share of income went to households in the top 5% of the income distribution: specifically, 22.2% in 2005. Over time, from the late 1960s to the early 1980s, the top fifth of the income distribution typically received between 43–44% of all income. However, the share of income that the top fifth received then began to rise. Using the quintile measure, income inequality has increased in recent decades.

It can also be useful to divide the income distribution in ways other than quintiles—for example, into tenths or even into percentiles (that is, hundredths). A more detailed breakdown can provide additional insights. For example, the last column of Exhibit 13-6 shows the income received by the top 5% of the income distribution. From 1980 to 2011 the share of income going to the top fifth increased by 7 percentage points (from 44.1% in 1980 to 51.1% in 2011). Over this same time, the share of income going to the top 5% increased by 5.8 percentage points (from 16.5% in 1980 to 22.3% in 2011). Thus, the increased share of income going to the top fifth has been mostly accounted for by the increased share of income going to the top 5% of the income distribution.

CLEARING IT UP

SEPARATING POVERTY AND INCOME INEQUALITY

Poverty can change even when inequality does not move at all. Imagine, for example, a situation in which income for everyone in the population declines by 10%. Poverty would rise, since a greater share of the population would now fall below the poverty line income level. However, inequality would be the same because everyone suffered the same proportional loss. Conversely, a general rise in income levels over time would keep inequality the same but reduce poverty.

It's also possible for economic inequality to change without affecting the poverty rate. Imagine a situation in which a large number of people who already have high incomes increase their incomes by even more. Inequality would rise as a result—but the number of people below the poverty line would remain unchanged.

Year	Lowest Quintile	Second Quintile	Third Quintile	Fourth Quintile	Highest Quintile	Top 5%
1967	4.0	10.8	17.3	24.2	43.6	17.2
1970	4.1	10.8	17.4	24.5	43.3	16.6
1975	4.3	10.4	17.0	24.7	43.6	16.5
1980	4.2	10.2	16.8	24.7	44.1	16.5
1985	3.9	9.8	16.2	24.4	45.6	17.6
1990	3.8	9.6	15.9	24.0	46.6	17.6
1995	3.7	9.1	15.2	23.3	48.7	21.0
2000	3.6	8.9	14.8	23.0	49.8	22.1
2005	3.4	8.6	14.6	23.0	50.4	22.2
2010	3.3	8.5	14.6	23.4	50.3	21.3
2011	3.2	8.4	14.3	23.0	51.1	22.3

...

ENDNOTES

1. Kennedy 1999, 214–19.
2. National Bureau of Economic Research 2010; U.S. Bureau of Labor Statistics 2010b.
3. Condon and Wiseman 2013.
4. Markoff 2012.
5. Fischer and Hout 2006, 154–56; U.S. Census Bureau 2011a.
6. Klein 2012, 89–93; Gill, Glazer, and Thernstrom 1992, 22; OECD 2011b.
7. U.S. Census Bureau 2012f.
8. Auerbach and Kellermann 2011.
9. These poverty statistics rely on the official U.S. poverty measure. Specifically, this measure has two components: poverty thresholds and the definition of family income that is compared with these thresholds. The measure was originally devised by Mollie Orshansky, a researcher at the Social Security Administration, in the early 1960s. She constructed poverty thresholds by calculating what it cost to feed a family on a low-cost food plan and then multiplying this amount by three, since families at the time spent close to a third of their incomes on food. Thresholds have been updated yearly for inflation using the consumer price index (CPI). The poverty threshold for a four-person family in 2011 was $22,811. The definition of family resources used to compare with the thresholds is gross annual cash income. A family and its members are considered poor if their income falls below the poverty threshold for a family of that size and composition. This poverty measure is not without its critics, as many think the threshold is too low, and others point out that it imperfectly measures people's incomes, because it leaves out near-cash government transfers like housing subsidies and food assistance vouchers. See Iceland 2013 for a fuller discussion of poverty measurement issues.
10. Blank 1997, 2009.
11. Congressional Budget Office, 2012.
12. Piketty and Saez 2003, 29; Piketty and Saez 2013.
13. Levine 2012, summary page.
14. Wolff 2013, 1.
15. Iceland 2013 also has an extended discussion of these issues.
16. Blank 2009, 76.
17. Blank 2009, 64–68.
18. U.S. Bureau of Labor Statistics 2011a, 7.
19. Grusky and Weeden 2011.
20. Bluestone and Harrison 2000, 190–97; Harrison and Bluestone 1990.
21. Duhigg and Bradsher 2012.
22. Stangler 2012.
23. Richtel 2005.
24. Danziger and Gottschalk 1995, 130–31.
25. Bernstein et al. 2000, table 1.
26. See Osterman 1999; Blank 2009, 77–78.

27. Duncan and Trejo 2011a.
28. Lindsey 2009, 48.
29. Congressional Budget Office 2011, xii.
30. Grusky and Weeden 2011, 95.
31. Congressional Budget Office 2011, 18–19.
32. Freeland 2011.
33. National Bureau of Economic Research 2010; U.S. Bureau of Labor Statistics 2010b.
34. Bosworth 2012; U.S. Bureau of Labor Statistics 2012a.
35. A discussion of these issues is also included in Iceland 2013.
36. Rajan 2010.
37. Sherman 2011.
38. Wolff, Owens, and Burak 2011, 134 and 150–51; Food Research Action Center 2012, 3.
39. Schoen 2012.
40. Rampell 2012.

REFERENCES

Auerbach, David I., and Arthur L. Kellermann. 2011. "A Decade of Health Care Cost Growth Has Wiped Out Real Income Gains for an Average US Family." *Health Affairs* 30 (9): 1–7.

Bernstein, Jared, Elizabeth C. McNichol, Lawrence Mishel, and Robert Zahradnik. 2000. *Pulling Apart: A State-by-State Analysis of Income Trends.* Center on Budget and Policy Priorities and Economic Policy Institute Report, Washington, D.C., January.

Blank, Rebecca. 1997. "Why Has Economic Growth Been Such an Ineffective Tool against Poverty in Recent Years?" In *Poverty and Inequality: The Political Economy of Redistribution,* edited by Jon Neil. Kalamazoo, MI: W. E. Upjohn Institute for Employment Research.

____. 2009. "Economic Change and the Structure of Opportunity for Less-Skilled Workers." In *Changing Poverty, Changing Policies,* edited by Maria Cancian and Sheldon Danziger. New York: Russell Sage Foundation.

Bluestone, Barry, and Bennett Harrison. 2000. *Growing Prosperity: The Battle for Growth with Equity in the Twenty-First Century.* Boston: Houghton Mifflin.

Bosworth, Barry. 2012. *Economic Consequences of the Great Recession: Evidence from the Panel Study of Income Dynamics.* Center for Retirement Research at Boston College Working Paper, CRR WP 2012–4.

Condon, Bernard, and Paul Wiseman. 2013. "Millions of Middle-Class Jobs Killed by Machines in Great Recession's Wake." Associated Press, as reported in *Huffington Post,* January 23. Available at www.huffingtonpost.com/2013/01/23/middle-class-jobs-machines_n_2532639.html (accessed January 30, 2013).

Congressional Budget Office. 2011. *Trends in the Distribution of Household Income between 1979 and 2007.* October report.

Congressional Budget Office. 2012. "Trends in the Distribution of Household Income between 1979 and 2009." Presentation to the NBER Conference on Research in Income and Wealth, August 6. Available at www.cbo.gov/sites/default/files/cbofiles/attachments/ Trends_in_household_income_forposting.pdf (accessed February 6, 2013).

Danziger, Sheldon H., and Peter Gottschalk. 1995. *America Unequal.* Cam-bridge, MA: Harvard University Press.

Duhigg, Charles, and Keith Bradsher. 2012. "How U.S. Lost Out on iPhone Work." *New York Times*, Business Day, January 22.

Duncan, Brian, and Stephen J. Trejo. 2011. *Low-Skilled Immigrants and the U.S. Labor Market.* IZA Discussion Paper no. 5964, September.

Fischer, Claude S., and Michael Hout. 2006. *Century of Diff erence: How America Changed in the Last One Hundred Years.* New York: Russell Sage Foundation.

Freeland, Chrystia. 2011. "The Rise of the New Global Elite." *Atlantic*, January /February. Available at www.theatlantic.com/magazine/archive/2011/01/the-rise-of-the-new-global-elite/308343/?single_page = true (accessed February 11, 2013).

Gill, Richard T., Nathan Glazer, and Stephan A. Thernstrom. 1992. *Our Changing Population.* Englewood Cliff s, NJ: Prentice-Hall.

Grusky, David B., and Kim A. Weeden. 2011. "Is Market Failure behind the Takeoff in Inequality?" In *The Inequality Reader: Contemporary and Foundational Readings in Race, Class, and Gender.* 2nd ed., edited by David B. Grusky and Szonja Szelényi. Boulder, CO: Westview Press.

Iceland, John, and Gregory Sharp. 2013. "White Residential Segregation in U.S. Metropolitan Areas: Conceptual Issues, Patterns, and Trends from the U.S. Census, 1980 to 2010." *Population Research and Policy Review* 32 (5): 663–86.

Kennedy, David M. 1999. *Freedom from Fear: The American People in the Depression and War, 1929–1945.* New York: Oxford University Press.

Klein, Herbert S. 2012. *A Population History of the United States.* 2nd ed. New York: Cambridge University Press.

Levine, Linda. 2012. *The U.S. Income Distribution and Mobility: Trends and International Comparisons.* Congressional Research Service Report 7–5700, November 29.

Lindsey, Duncan. 2009. *Child Poverty and Inequality: Securing a Better Future for America's Children.* New York: Oxford University Press.

Markoff , John. 2012. "The iEconomy, Part 5: Artifi cial Competence: Skilled Work, without the Worker." *New York Times*, August 18.

National Bureau of Economic Research. 2010. *Business Cycle Dating Committee Report, September 20, 2010.* NBER, Cambridge, MA. Available at www.nber.org/cycles/sept2010.pdf (accessed January 30, 2013).

OECD. 2011b. "Health at a Glance 2011: OECD Indicators." Health Status Figure 1.1.1. Available at www.oecd.org/els/healthpoliciesanddata/healthataglance2011.htm#B5 (accessed July 30, 2012).

Osterman, Paul. 1999. *Securing Prosperity.* Princeton, NJ: Princeton University Press.

Piketty, Thomas, and Emmanuel Saez. 2003. "Income Inequality in the United States, 1913–1998." *Quarterly Journal of Economics* 118 (1): 1–39.

Rajan, Raghuram G. 2010. *Fault Lines: How Hidden Fractures Still Threaten the World Economy.* Princeton, NJ: Princeton University Press.

Rampell, Catherine. 2012. "Majority of New Jobs Pay Low Wages, Study Finds." *New York Times,* August 30. Available at www.nytimes.com/2012/08/31/business/majority-of-new-jobs-pay-low-wages-study-finds.html?hp (accessed February 12, 2013).

Richtel, Matt. 2005. "Outsourced All the Way." *New York Times,* June 21. Available at www.nytimes.com/2005/06/21/business/worldbusiness/21outsource.html?pagewanted=all (accessed February 11, 2013).

Schoen, C., R. Osborn, D. Squires, M. Doty, R. Pierson, and S. Applebaum. 2011. "New 2011 Survey of Patients with Complex Care Needs in Eleven Countries Finds That Care Is Often Poorly Coordinated." *Health Affairs* 30 (12): 2437–48.

Sherman, Arloc. 2011. *Poverty and Financial Distress Would Have Been Substantially Worse in 2010 without Government Action, New Census Data Show.* Center on Budget and Policy Priorities Research Report, November 7.

Stangler, Cole. 2012. "Obama Jobs Council Packed with Outsourcing Companies." *Huffington Post,* July 12. Available at www.huffingtonpost.com/2012/07/12/obama-jobs-council-outsourcing_n_1666443.html (accessed February 11, 2013).

U.S. Bureau of Labor Statistics. 2011a. *Highlights of Women's Earnings.* U.S. BLS Report no. 1031, July.

U.S. Census Bureau. "Table A-2. Percent of People 25 Years and Over Who Have Completed High School or College, by Race, Hispanic Origin and Sex: Selected Yeas 1940 to 2011." Educational Attainment data, CPS Historical Time Series Tables. Available at www.census.gov/hhes/socdemo/education/data/cps/historical/index.html (accessed January 18, 2013).

Wolff, Edward N. 2013. "The Asset Price Melt-Down and the Wealth of the Middle Class." Census Brief prepared for the Projection US2010. Available at http://www.s4.brown.edu/us2010/Data/Report/report05012013.pdf (accessed May 8, 2013).

Wolff, Edward N., Lindsay A. Owens, and Esra Burak. 2011. "How Much Wealth Was Destroyed in the Great Recession?" In *The Great Recession,* edited by David B. Grusky, Bruce Western, and Christopher Wimer. New York: Russell Sage Foundation.

QUESTIONS FOR REVIEW, REFLECTION, AND DISCUSSION

1. Do you think it is useful to have a poverty line whose basic definition does not change much over time? Why or why not?
2. What is the difference between Temporary Assistance for Needy Family (TANF) and Aid to Families with Dependent Children (AFDC)?
3. What is the earned income credit (EIC)?

ADDITIONAL READINGS

Chappell, M. (2010). *The war on welfare: Family, poverty, and politics in modern America.* Philadelphia: University of Pennsylvania Press.

Cuesta, L., & Cancian, M. (2015) The effect of child support on the labor supply of custodial mothers participating in TANF. *Children and Youth Services Review, 54,* 49-56.

Levy, Helen. *RSF (2015). Income, poverty, and maternal hardship among older Americans, The Russell Sage Foundation Journal of the Social Sciences, 1(1), 55–77.*

Priemus, H., Kemp, P. A., & Varady, D. P. (2005). Housing vouchers in the United States, Great Britain, and the Netherlands: Current issues and future. *Housing Policy Debate, 16*(3/4), 575–609.

Sweeney, S. (2015). The poor among us: A history of family, poverty and homelessness in New York City. *Journal of Urban Affairs, 37*(2), 225–228.

Tierney, J. (February 18, 2013). Prison and the poverty trap. *The New York Times.*Wu, C., Cancian, M., & Wallace, G. (2014). The effect of welfare sanctions on TANF exits and employment. *Children and Youth Services Review, 36,* 1–14.

KEY TERMS

Great Depression

Great Recession

Gini Coefficient

14

ECONOMIC WELL-BEING

By John Iceland

John Iceland, "Economic Well-Being," A Portrait of America: The Demographic Perspective, pp. 83-95, 99-101, 105-106. Copyright © 2014 by University of California Press. Reprinted with permission.

The growth of the U.S. economy over the long haul has been exceptional. This growth has been accompanied by rising living standards—meaning that children could generally expect to earn more, in real terms, than their parents. Increasing standards of living have also been accompanied by the widespread dissemination of wondrous household appliances and consumer products, including—over just the last hundred years or so—automobiles, radios, televisions, dishwashers, microwave ovens, personal computers, smart phones, and tablets. The health of the population has also improved, and life expectancies have grown longer. Far fewer people in the United States die of disease or abject poverty today than a century ago.

This general pattern of economic growth has been accompanied by considerable volatility. Recurring booms and busts are a central feature of capitalism and, therefore, of the American economy. The Great Depression of the 1930s represented perhaps the most serious downturn: lasting about ten years, and with unemployment reaching as high as 25 percent, it produced considerable hardship and poverty across the country. Many people's faith in the laissez-faire economic system was shaken, leading a substantial majority of Americans to support Franklin Delano Roosevelt's vigorous attempts, in the form of his New Deal programs, to moderate the system's excesses. These efforts yielded the creation of regulatory structures like the Securities and Exchange Commission and the introduction of many crucial elements of the social safety net still in existence today, such as Social Security, welfare, and federally funded unemployment insurance. Nevertheless, the sustained sluggishness of the economy led some at the time to believe that the country had reached the end of economic growth and rising living standards. Commenting on the popular mood in the depths of the Depression, historian David Kennedy writes:

> But the worm of doubt about the New Deal's effectiveness and even its ultimate purposes also began to gnaw at others, including liberals. As 1935 opened, some ten million persons, more than 20 percent of the work force, still remained jobless. The country seemed to flounder, without a workable remedy to the afflictions from which it had been suffering now for half a decade. . . . In a summary report to Hopkins [a Roosevelt adviser] on New Year's Day 1935, Hickok [an American journalist] rehearsed her worries about a "stranded generation": men over forty with halfgrown families, people who might never get their jobs back.[1]

The Great Recession of 2007–9, while not nearly as severe as the Great Depression (unemployment reached a high of 10 percent during the recession), was nevertheless the gravest economic downturn over the nearly seventy intervening years. It was longer than previous recessions, the unemployment rate rose more sharply, and the pace of recovery was slower than after most previous ones.[2] Relatively high and persistent unemployment, stagnant wages, and growing income inequality again led many to question whether broadly shared economic prosperity was a thing of the past. For example, one news story from 2013, which echoes the picture seventy-five years earlier, reported:

> Five years after the start of the Great Recession, the toll is terrifyingly clear: Millions of middle-class jobs have been lost in developed countries the world over. And the situation is even worse than it appears. Most of the jobs will never return, and millions more are likely to vanish as well, say experts who study the labor market. . . . They're being obliterated by technology. Year after year, the software that runs computers and an array of other machines and devices becomes more sophisticated and powerful and capable of doing more efficiently tasks that humans have always done. For de -cades, science fiction warned of a future when we would be architects of our own obsolescence, replaced by our machines; an Associated Press analysis finds that the future has arrived.[3]

Has our prophesied decline finally arrived? How entrenched is slow growth and rising inequality and poverty? What explains current trends in inequality? Is inequality even necessarily a bad thing for our economy? These are the questions I address in this chapter. I begin with a brief historical review of economic trends in the United States. I then track recent changes in economic growth, income inequality, and poverty and discuss the forces that help explain these patterns. I compare U.S. trends with those in other wealthy countries and end with a discussion of the overall effect of inequality on individuals and society.

RISING LIVING STANDARDS

The U.S. economy has generally grown briskly over time. Economic growth and rising living standards are a function of forces that boost productivity: mainly continued human and capital investment and technological improvements. Agricultural production, for example, is far more efficient today than it used to be as a result of plant breeding, pesticides, fertilizers, and modern farm equipment. Manufacturing is likewise becoming increasingly efficient. As one newspaper article describing changes in high-tech industries pointed out: "At the Philips Electronics factory on the coast of China, hundreds of workers use their hands and specialized tools to assemble electric shavers. That is the old way. At a sister factory here in the Dutch countryside, 128 robot arms do the same work with yoga-like flexibility. Video cameras guide them through feats well beyond the capability of the most dexterous human. . . . And they do it all without a coffee break—three shifts a day, 365 days a year."[4]

Greater economic productivity generally leads to higher standards of living because it lets workers produce more for the same amount of work. This means greater profit for owners and typically higher wages for workers. Figure 14.1 shows the pattern of per capita economic growth from 1790 to 2011 using a common indicator, the gross domestic product (GDP). GDP measures the market value of all goods and services produced in a country in a given period of time. Real GDP per capita rose from $1,025 in 1790 to $5,557 in 1900 to $42,671 in 2011 (in constant 2005 dollars). We see dips in GDP per capita during the Great Depression, the more recent Great Recession, and in other periodic economic downturns. Nevertheless, the overall upward slope is striking.

Increases in GDP per capita show up in other concrete ways as well. Whereas just over 10 percent of the population had toilets in their homes (i.e., indoor plumbing in general) in 1890, by 1970 inside toilets were pretty much universal. In 1900 virtually no one owned a car; by 1920, 25 percent of households had a car, by 1930 this

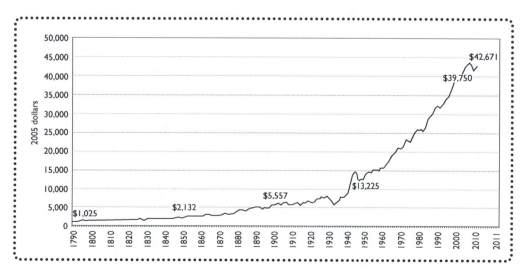

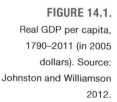

FIGURE 14.1.
Real GDP per capita, 1790–2011 (in 2005 dollars). Source: Johnston and Williamson 2012.

FIGURE 14.2.

Median household
income, 1967–2011 (in
2011 dollars). Source:
U.S. Census Bureau
2012k.

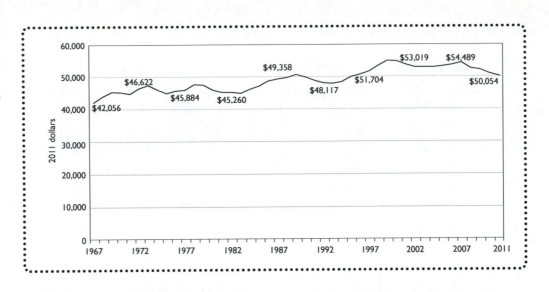

figure was up to 50 percent, and today over 90 percent of American households own a car. Because of growing incomes, Americans today do not need to devote as great a proportion of their income to purchasing basic necessities such as food and instead now devote considerably more to recreational activities.[5] Growing standards of living are associated with improvements in health as well. The average life expectancy at birth in the United States rose from about 35 years in 1789, to 49 years in 1900, 64 years in 1940, and 79 years in 2010.[6] The U.S. population has likewise become more educated. Whereas in 1940 just one-quarter of the population of ages 25 and over had earned a high school diploma, and only 5 percent had four or more years of college, by 2012, 88 percent of the population had completed high school, and 31 percent had four or more years of college.[7] Educational gains have in turn helped fuel economic productivity and growth.

Reflecting these trends, figure 14.2 shows the increase in household income over the past forty-five years. Median household income rose from $42,056 in 1967 to $49,358 in 1987, before reaching its peak of $54,932 in 1999. Median household income fell in the 2001 recession, much as it did in other recessions. However, unlike after past recessions, the economic recovery in the years after 2001 did little to boost the median household income. There was a further sharp drop in household incomes after the 2007–9 recession, and again incomes have yet to recover. Unfortunately, the 2000s stand out as the only decade during the period when household incomes did not rise. Increasing health care costs are putting a further dint to households' purchasing power, and the amount businesses spend on health care may be putting downward pressure on wages.[8]

Trends in poverty tell a fairly similar story: while poverty declined rapidly in the 1960s and into the early 1970s, it has mainly fluctuated with the business cycle since. The 2000s stand out as a decade with little respite from increasing poverty (see Figure 14.3).[9] There is some disconnect between the trends shown in Figure 14.1

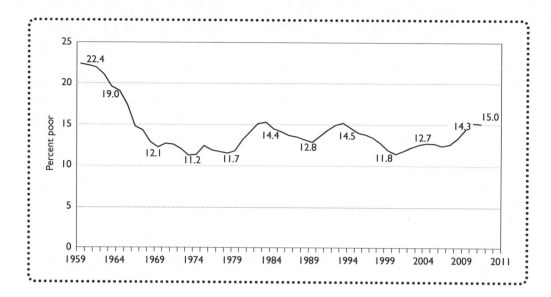

FIGURE 14.3.
Poverty rates,
1959–2011. Source:
DeNavas-Walt, Proctor,
and Smith 2012, table
B2.

(GDP per capita) and Figures 14.2 and 14.3 (income and poverty): while all measures show a dip during recessions, the upward climb in GDP per capita, especially during the 2000s, occurred even while median household incomes were stagnant or declining and poverty for the most part increased. Thus, income and poverty have been less responsive to economic growth than in previous decades. One of the main culprits of this disconnect is the growing level of income inequality.[10]

GROWING INCOME INEQUALITY

Even though per capita GDP has risen over time, some Americans have benefited more from economic growth than others. Figure 14.4 shows the trend in family income by where families stood in the income distribution. Between 1947 and the late 1970s, families along all points of the income distribution experienced increases in income. For example, between 1947 and 1979, the income of families at the 20th

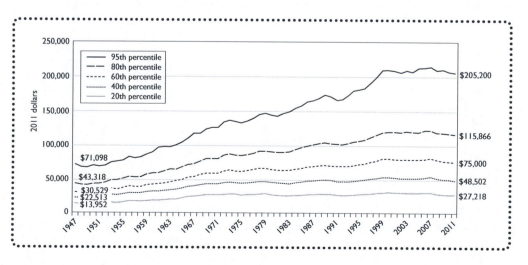

FIGURE 14.4.
Family incomes, by
quintile, 1947–2011 (in
2011 dollars). Source:
U.S. Census Bureau
2012c.

percentile of the income distribution increased from $13,952 to $28,471 (in 2011 dollars). Thereafter, income at this percentile stagnated, such that by 2011 it stood at just $27,218. The increase in income is most striking for the top 5 percent of earners. Family income at the 95th percentile was $71,098 in 1947, before rising to $146,516 in 1979 and $205,200 in 2011, even after a small dip in wake of the 2007–9 recession. Data from other sources indicate that the top 1 percent have enjoyed the largest increase of all. For example, after-tax income increased by 155 percent among the top 1 percent from 1979 to 2009, compared with a still large increase of 58 percent for the rest of this quintile (i.e., households in the 81st to 99th percentile), which in turn experienced a larger increase than other quintiles.[11]

One common summary measure of inequality is the Gini coefficient. It ranges from 0 to 1, with 0 indicating that all families have the same income and 1 indicating that one family possesses all income. Figure 14.5 shows that the Gini coefficient actually declined modestly in the years after 1947 (from 0.376) to a low of 0.348 in 1968. It remained fairly stable for the next decade before beginning a marked increase. The Gini reached its high point of 0.450 in the final year shown, 2011, indicating that inequality is as high as it has ever been over the sixty-four years covered in Figure 14.5. Taking a longer view, one study that examined tax records from 1913 to 2011 found that the share of national income going to the top 10 percent and top 1 percent of Americans was very high in the early decades of the twentieth century (reaching a peak in 1928 shortly before the Great Depression), then declined sharply during World War II (when wage controls were put in place for the war effort), and have been drifting upward ever since. The share of income going to top earners is now approaching the earlier 1928 peak level.[12] As a report by the nonpartisan Congressional Research Service aptly summarized, "These, among other measures of dispersion, have led analysts to conclude that inequality has increased in the United States as a result of high-income households pulling further away from those lower in the distribution."[13]

FIGURE 14.5.

Gini coefficient for inequality in family income, 1947–2011.

Note: The sharp increase in the Gini coefficient in the early 1990s was due to the redesign in the survey used to collect household income data. Higher numbers mean more inequality. Source: U.S. Census Bureau 2012b.

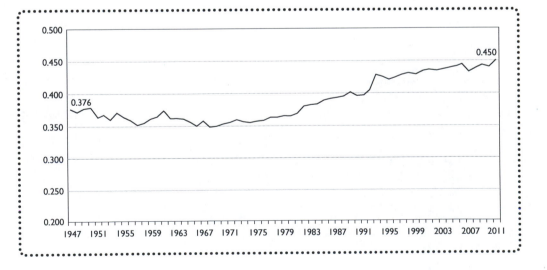

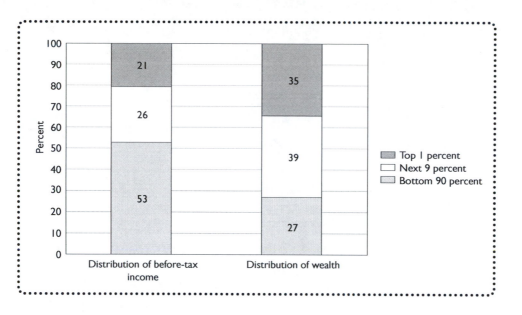

FIGURE 14.6.

Distribution of income
and wealth, 2007.

Source: Stone, Trisi, and
Sherman 2012, 12; original
data from Wolff 2010.

Wealth inequality is even greater than income inequality. Wealth includes a wide array of assets, such as homes, savings accounts, retirement accounts, and other kinds of stocks and bonds. Many Americans have no wealth or savings at all, while others can live entirely off the interest earned from their wealth. Figure 14.6 shows that the top 1 percent of households earn 21 percent of all income but hold 35 percent of the nation's wealth. Conversely, the bottom 90 percent of the population earns 53 percent of the nation's income but possesses only 27 percent of its wealth. In addition, median wealth as a whole plummeted from 2007 to 2010 as a result of the Great Recession. Not all people were equally affected: the middle class, which lost considerable home equity wealth after the housing bubble burst, was hardest hit. As a result, inequality in people's net worth rose steeply between 2007 and 2010, as did the racial and ethnic disparity in wealth.[14]

There are a number of plausible explanations for why inequality has increased over the past few decades.[15] The most prominent include the increasing demand for high-skill workers due to technological changes; globalization and international trade; the decline in unionization; the rising salaries for people who are considered "superstars"; and changes in government policies that have favored the affluent. Regarding the first of these, some have argued that technological advancements since the 1970s have led to "skill-biased technological change" (SBTC), which calls upon workers to be increasingly familiar with computers or high-tech equipment and machinery. The increased demand for more-skilled workers drove up wages for people with higher levels of education during a time when demand for less-skilled workers, such as those employed in blue-collar manufacturing jobs, fell.[16]

Strong evidence for this perspective comes from the effects that education has on changing patterns of employment and wages. Labor force participation rates of college-educated men have held steady, while those of men with a high school diploma

FIGURE 14.7.

Percentage of change
in median usual weekly
earnings, by educational
attainment and gender,
between 1979 and 2010.

Source: U.S. Bureau of
Labor Statistics, 2011a,
chart 3.

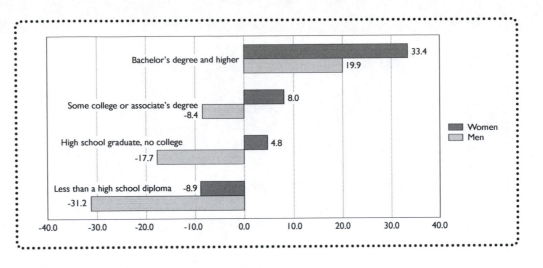

have declined. Women of all educational levels have experienced increases in work over the past three decades, though increases were highest among the most educated women.[17] Meanwhile, while weekly wages among less-skilled men declined by 31 percent between 1979 and 2010, such earnings grew by 20 percent among men with a bachelor's degree or higher (see Figure 14.7). Among women, high school dropouts also saw a decline in wages (9 percent), while those with a college education experienced a large increase (33 percent).[18] The importance of receiving a college degree has occurred during a time when the price of a college education has also increased significantly, making it more difficult for low-income students to attend college. Some argue that colleges could be doing more to meet increased consumer demand and expand the number of slots available to prospective students.[19]

Globalization and international trade may have contributed to growing wage inequality, as U.S. workers increasingly compete with workers around the world. Highly skilled U.S. workers often have a comparative advantage in the global economy because of the high quality of postsecondary education in the United States and because many multinational corporations are headquartered there. Conversely, less-skilled American workers are at a disadvantage given the lower production costs and wages in other parts of the globe. This has, at least in part, contributed to continued deindustrialization in the United States, which began in the second half of the twentieth century, when many manufacturing jobs were outsourced to lower-wage countries such as China and Mexico.[20]

One good example of this phenomenon is Apple computers, which employed 43,000 people in the United States and 20,000 overseas in 2012—a small fraction of the over 400,000 workers General Motors employed in the United States in the 1950s. An additional 700,000 people work for Apple's contractors, engineering, building, and assembling various Apple products such as iPhones and iPads, and nearly all of these jobs are staffed by foreign companies in Asia, Europe, and elsewhere overseas.[21] Apple has considerable company in this trend. Between 2001 and 2012, General Electric lost

37,000 American jobs and added 25,000 overseas (though some of the job losses are due to the sale of NBC to Comcast); likewise, Xerox, Boeing, and American Express also increased their overseas workforce during these years, in jobs ranging from manufacturing to call service centers.[22]

Outsourcing is not confined to large corporations either. As one news story reported:

> Philip Chigos and Mary Domenico are busy building a children's pajama business. They are refining patterns, picking fabrics and turning the basement of their two-bedroom apartment into an office. Then there is the critical step of finding the right seamstresses in China. Instead of looking for garment workers in this city, they plan to have their wares manufactured by low-cost workers overseas. In doing so, they've become micro-outsourcers, adopting a tactic of major American corporations, which are increasingly sending production work abroad. A growing number of mom-and-pop operations, outsourcing experts say, are braving a host of potential complications and turning to places like Sri Lanka, China, Mexico and Eastern Europe to make clothes, jewelry, trinkets and even software programs. "We'd love it to say 'made in the U.S.A.' and use American textiles and production," Mr. Chigos said of his product. But, he said, the cost of that would be 4 to 10 times what was planned. "We didn't want to sell our pajamas for $120."[23]

In addition to globalization, the decline of unions has also contributed to growing inequality in the United States over the past few decades. The proportion of the workforce that is unionized has been falling since the 1950s, and this decline accelerated after the mid-1970s.[24] Only 12 percent of workers were in unions in 2011, down from 29 percent in 1975.[25] Nonunionized workers typically are paid lower wages and have less job security.[26] There has been much debate on whether immigration has contributed to inequality, but studies on the whole suggest that immigration has served to depress the wages of native low-skill workers by only a small amount.[27]

The tax burden on high earners has also fallen over the past several decades, and the distributive effect of government transfers may have also declined. For example, proportionately the wealthy pay substantially less in taxes than they did a generation ago. The top individual tax rate was reduced from 70 percent at the start of Ronald Reagan's first term to a low of 28 percent by the end of his term in 1988. Through most of the 2000s, it was at 35 percent, and legislation in 2013 increased it to 39.6 percent. Estate taxes, dividend taxes, and capital gains taxes (all of these taxes are paid disproportionately by wealthy individuals) have also been reduced since 1980, whereas Social Security and Medicare taxes, which place a relatively larger burden on the middle class, have increased.[28] The distribution of government transfers has also shifted, moving away from low-income households. In 2007, households in the bottom income quintile received 35 percent of transfer payments, down from 50 percent in 1979.[29] Many growing programs, such as Social Security and Medicare, benefit middle-class Americans.

Several possible reasons account for the spectacular rise in the incomes of the top 1 percent. Some have noted the large increases in pay among corporate executives. The general increase in the size and complexity of businesses may have contributed to this. However, probably more important are changes in corporate governance that have allowed executives to essentially pay themselves more—at the expense of their workers—including with lucrative stock options. Board members who set the pay of CEOs often serve at the pleasure of the CEO, leading to an incentive to provide a high compensation package. As David Grusky and Kim Weeden write, the change in pay-setting practices "[is] rather like asking a professor's students to decide on the professor's pay in advance of receiving their grades. When the fox is guarding the henhouse, one has to believe that the fox's interests are better served than those of the hens."[30]

Some also argue that "superstars," such as actors, athletes, and musicians, make more than they used to, perhaps because globalization and rising living standards have increased consumer demand and the amount that people at successful enterprises can earn. Also more lawyers and financial professionals are in the top 1 percent than in the past, indicating that their specialized services have become increasingly valued and rewarded (in line with more general SBTC arguments above). Lastly, the growing importance of the financial sector in generating profits has led to large pay increases among those working in this sector. Deregulation may have helped increase these profits.[31] As one article noted, "After a down year in 2008, the top 25 hedge-fund managers were paid, on average, more than $1 billion each in 2009, quickly eclipsing the record they had set in pre-recession 2007."[32]

...

THE GREAT RECESSION

The Great Recession of 2007–9 was the deepest economic downturn since the Great Depression of the 1930s.[33] Overall, the nation's output (GDP) declined by 8 percent from the end of 2007 to mid-2009. Households lost one-quarter of their wealth over the two-year period, and a third of those losses were attributable to declining home values. (Homes are the most valuable asset for many families.) The nation's economy lost 8.5 million jobs, going from a peak of 138.1 million jobs in December 2007 to a low of 129.6 million jobs in February 2010. The unemployment rate peaked at 10.0 percent.[34]

The precipitating cause of the 2007–9 recession was the bursting of a large housing bubble. This shook the banking system, which then nearly brought all economic activity to a halt.[35] The crisis, however, had a number of other underlying causes, including rising inequality, the loosening of bank lending rules, and the rise of mortgage securitization with too little regulatory oversight. Rising inequality was an important factor, because rising per capita GDP in the 2000s meant that the affluent were enjoying increasing purchasing power even while much of the middle class was not. This helped produce debt-fueled housing consumption, as many households took out large mortgages or borrowed from their home equity.

Deregulation of the banking industry over the years led banks to offer riskier loans at high interest rates to people who could not afford them. The banks would then bundle and sell these mortgages as securities to investors—many of whom did not fully understand the risk associated with these investments. As a rising number of ordinary people defaulted on their home mortgage loans, the housing market collapsed and the value of the securities, and housing, plunged.[36] Banks stopped lending, many businesses went bankrupt, and a deep recession ensued.

In addition to rising unemployment, poverty increased, from 12.3 percent in 2006 to 15.0 percent in 2011, even with an increase in government spending (in the form of unemployment insurance payments, food assistance, and the economic stimulus, among other initiatives) that was aimed at boosting the economy and reducing hardship.[37] Food insecurity rose, and household wealth declined markedly. For example, households saw an average decline of 39 percent in their home equity from 2007 to 2009.[38]

These numbers translated into real hardship for people across the country. As one news story reported:

> The poor stayed poor and the rich got richer, but the middle slipped a few more rungs down the economic ladder. . . . For Ray Bober, 45, of Pittsburgh, whose unemployment benefits ran out this year after a family printing business failed several years ago, the dismal economy takes a toll every time he sends out another resume that goes nowhere. "You have to learn to roll with the punches and laugh a little; it's very depressing," he said. "It takes a toll, especially this long. You want to reach out and shake your fist in the air and blame someone, but you can't. The way it is, is the way it is. There's nothing you can do about it but stay in the fight."[39]

A story on the rise of part-time work after the recession provides another anecdote of the struggles many have continued to face, even years later:

> Some of these new, lower-paying jobs are being taken by people just entering the labor force, like recent high school and college graduates. Many, though, are being filled by older workers who lost more lucrative jobs in the recession and were forced to take something to scrape by.
>
> "I think I've been very resilient and resistant and optimistic, up until very recently," said Ellen Pinney, 56, who was dismissed from a $75,000-a-year job in which she managed procurement and supply for an electronics company in March 2008. Since then, she has cobbled together a series of temporary jobs in retail and home health care and worked as a part-time receptionist for a beauty salon. She is now working as an unpaid intern for a construction company, putting together bids and business plans for green energy projects, and has moved in with her 86-year-old father in Forked River, N.J. "I really can't bear it anymore," she said, noting that her applications to places like PetSmart and Target had gone unanswered. "From every standpoint—my independence, my sense of purposefulness, my self-esteem, my life planning—this is just not what I was planning."[40]

···

CONCLUSION

The United States has experienced a tremendous amount of economic growth over time. The population has become better educated and more productive, leading to impressive increases in our standards of living. Americans are much better housed, fed, and clothed than a century ago. They have at their disposal many consumer products that would have been unimaginable to their ancestors. Nevertheless, this growth has been punctuated by periods of economic instability and high unemployment, the most notable being the Great Depression of the 1930s, when unemployment reached a peak of 25 percent and the foundations of the entire market system seemed under siege. More recently, increasing inequality, the deep recession of the late 2000s, and the subsequent sluggish recovery have ushered in another period of gloom. Our economic history suggests that periods of economic growth interrupted by sometimes-painful decline will likely continue.

One issue of growing concern is the increase in income inequality since the 1970s. The incomes of middle- and low-income households have stagnated in recent years, even while those at the top have continued to grow; the incomes of the top 1 percent in particular have increased markedly. Levels of wealth inequality are even greater than income inequality, where the top 1 percent of the country owns over 35 percent of its wealth. Growing inequality has likely been propelled by a number of factors, including skill-biased technological change (SBTC), which has prompted a greater demand for workers with high levels of education and skill to fill the kinds of higher-tech jobs that are available. Globalization may have also contributed to growing wage inequality, as many manufacturing jobs— and increasingly other kinds of jobs—have been outsourced to places with lower labor costs, such as China, India, and Mexico. Highly skilled U.S. workers are still faring well because of the high quality of postsecondary education in the United States, along with the fact that many multinational corporations are headquartered in the United States. Declines in unionization, increases in the cost of college, changes in the tax code that have favored the wealthy, the rise of finance, and changes in corporate governance that have produced higher salaries for CEOs (at the expense of workers) may all have played a role in exacerbating inequality in recent years.

The United States has one of the highest GDPs per capita in the world, and it remains well above the average among **OECD** countries. Nevertheless, inequality is also more prevalent in the United States, indicating that it is a country with larger extremes of wealth and poverty than most of its peers. Economic mobility also appears to be no greater in the United States than in a number of other wealthy countries. It should be noted that increasing inequality is a challenge that most OECD countries are facing,

Editorial Commentary: Organization for Economic Cooperation and Development (OECD): Forum whereby governments with market economies work with each other in an effort to promote economic growth. They also work with non-members. Retrieved from https://usoecd.usmission.gov/mission/overview.html on December 6, 2016

since some of the forces that have increased inequality in the United States (such as globalization) are affecting many other nations as well.

Some argue that inequality is not necessarily a bad thing, because the profit motive of our market system provides an incentive for innovative economic activity. Such activity spurs growth and rising living standards—often for everyone. The opportunity for talented and hard-working people to strike it rich also embodies the ideals of a meritocratic society. Others counter that while some inequality based on these principles is fine, both individuals and society do worse when inequality gets out of hand. Low-income individuals obviously suffer from both the absolute deprivation (in the form of very low wages) and relative deprivation (such as embarrassment and stigma) that can accompany low economic achievement. Society may suffer if inequality is high enough to impede economic growth, given that a significant portion of economic activity is based on the consumption of goods and services by a vibrant middle class. Inequality can also potentially stifle economic mobility if low-income individuals do not have the resources necessary to invest in their own education and skills. This is why inequality coupled with the rising cost of postsecondary education has been so troubling to many Americans.

These issues are often cyclical—often pushed to the background in good economic times and thrust to the foreground during bad ones. How the U.S. economy continues to rebound after the lost decade of the 2000s will thus be of intense interest to all Americans.

QUESTIONS FOR REVIEW, REFLECTION, AND DISCUSSION

1. When did the Great Recession occur? What happened? How did the Great Recession impact families?
2. How were banks involved in the Great Recession? How did that affect families?
3. Do you know of any families that were affected by the Great Recession? What happened to them? Were they able to bounce back? If so, how?
4. What does greater economic productivity lead to and how might that affect families?

ADDITIONAL READINGS

Afifi, T., Davis, S., Merrill, A.F., Coveleski, S., Denes, A., & Afifi, W. (2015). In the wake of the Great Recession: Economic uncertainty, communication, and biological stress responses in families. *Human Communication Research, 41*(2), 268–302.

Cherlin, A., Cumberworth, E., Morgan, S. P., Wimer, C. (2013). The effects of the Great Recession on family structure and fertility, *Annals of the American Academy of Political and Social Science, 650,* 214–231.

Eamon, M.K., & Wu, C.F. (2013). Employment, economic hardship, and sources of assistance in low-income, single-mother families before versus during and after the Great Recession, *Journal of Poverty, 17*(2), 135–156.

Schneider, D., Harknett, K., & McLanahan, S. (2016). Intimate partner violence in the Great Recession. *Demography, 53*(2), 471–505.

Schneider, D., & Hastings, O. P. (2015). Socioeconomic variation in the effect of economic conditions on marriage and nonmarital fertility in the United States: Evidence from the Great Recession, *Demography, 52*(6), 1893–1915.

Schneider, W., Waldfogel, J., Brooks-Gunn, J. (2015). The Great Recession and behavior problems in 9-year old children. *Developmental Psychology, 51*(11), 1615–1629.

UNIT 7

HEALTH
AND AGING

KEY TERMS

Health Care

Mortality

Life Expectancy

Migration

Immigrants

15

HEALTH AND MORTALITY

By John Iceland

Few issues have been more contentious than the state of our nation's health and health care system. People differ in their views on how to best deliver quality care while containing health care costs that threaten to overwhelm federal and state budgets. As a way of providing a firm factual footing for these discussions, the National Academies convened an expert panel of researchers to report on the health of Americans in comparison with people in a number of peer countries. The report, released in 2013, was ominously titled *U.S. Health in International Perspective: Shorter Lives, Poorer Health.* Indeed, the panel concluded: "The United States is among the wealthiest nations in the world, but it is far from the healthiest. Although life expectancy and survival rates in the United States have improved dramatically over the past century, Americans live shorter lives and experience more injuries and illnesses than people in other high-income countries."[1]

The findings were widely reported in the press, and naturally the public weighed in with their opinions on why the United States fares so poorly. Some pointed to the health care system. One tweet sent in to CNN read: "America has made healthcare most difficult to access even for the middle class. Imagine the poor. That's what greed does!" Others pointed to obesity and the environment: "We invented the term #supersize" and "I moved from Europe to the U.S. about six months ago. First observation after a visit to the supermarket: fruits and vegetables way too expensive; cheap products stuffed with fats and sugars. In short, if you want to kill off a whole population, slow but sure, I couldn't come up with a better strategy." CNN commentator Steve Cray added, "They [the National Academies panel] needed 18 months to determine the problem! It will take me less than a minute:

obesity, sedentary lifestyle, a for-profit healthcare system controlled by insurance and pill-pushing pharmaceutical companies that try to limit preventative healthcare."[2]

Many of these observations hold at least some truth. There is no single reason why health in the United States is worse than in other countries; rather, it is a confluence of factors, including disparities in people's access to health care, individual health behaviors, and the physical and social environment.[3] The rest of this chapter provides an in-depth discussion of these and related issues. First, I document recent patterns and trends in health and mortality in the United States. I review evidence on health disparities by gender, race, and socioeconomic status and describe their origins. I discuss the aging of the American population and the strains this puts on the health care system and the U.S. budget. I end by systematically describing why the health of Americans lags behind their peers in other developed countries.

PATTERNS AND TRENDS IN HEALTH AND MORTALITY

Let's start with the good news. In many important respects the health of Americans has improved. Figure 15.1 shows that life expectancy at birth grew from 66 years in 1950 to 76 in 2010 for men and from 71 to 81 for women. This kind of gradual health improvement shows up in other ways. In 1970, the infant mortality rate was 20 (indicating that 20 infants out of 1,000 died before their first birthday). By 2011, this figure was less than a third as large, at 6.[4] As a National Center for Health Statistics reported in an examination of mortality patterns over the 1935 to 2010 period, "Although there were year to year exceptions, the last 75 years witnessed sustained declines in the risk of dying in the United States."[5] Decreases in death rates occurred for men and women, all age groups, and for all racial and ethnic groups. The number

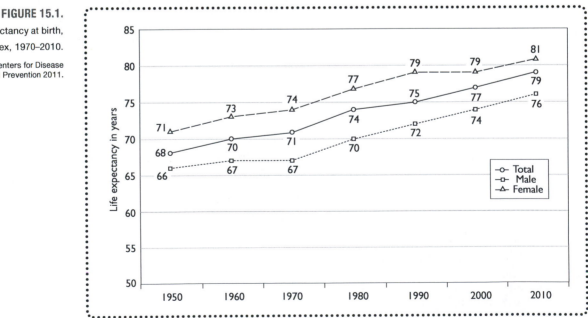

FIGURE 15.1.

Life expectancy at birth, by sex, 1970–2010.

Source: Centers for Disease Control and Prevention 2011.

of Americans living to see their hundredth birthday has risen from 32,000 to 53,000 from 1980 to 2010. The centenarian population increased by a greater percentage (66 percent) than the increase in the population as a whole (36 percent).[6]

Why women live longer than men is not fully understood, but part of the reason may be biological (the female advantage in life expectancy is found among a majority of animals), and part is due to environmental and behavioral factors. Men consume more tobacco, alcohol, and drugs than women, and they are more likely to die from accidents and intentional injuries (homicides, suicides, and in war). The slight narrowing of the gender gap in life expectancy in the United States and other developed countries since the 1970s is likely a function of a reduction in lifestyle differences. Women, for example, are more likely to smoke than they used to be, and this has contributed to a decline in the gender mortality gap.[7]

Health outcomes vary considerably by race and Hispanic origin. The life expectancy among whites was 79 in 2010, four years more than the life expectancy among blacks (75). This gap, however, is narrower than in the past, especially since 1990 (see Figure 15.2).[8] This trend applies to both men and women, though the black-white gap among women (3 years) is narrower than among men (5 years).[9] The persistence of significant health disparities between blacks and whites—but the narrowing of the gap in recent years—shows up in other ways, including age-adjusted death rates, cause-specific death rates, infant mortality, and disability.[10] The higher rates of disease and death among blacks compared with whites reflect the earlier onset of illness, the greater severity of diseases, and lower rates of survival.[11] A final finding of note in the figure is that, contrary to what one might expect given socioeconomic differentials across groups, Hispanics have a higher life expectancy (81) than both blacks and whites. This "Hispanic health paradox" is discussed in more detail shortly. The Centers for Disease Control do not publish life expectancy figures for Asians, but other data indicate that

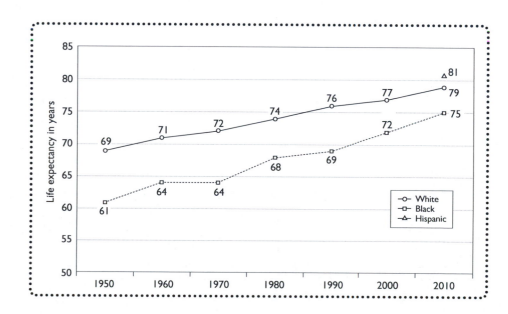

FIGURE 15.2.

Life expectancy at birth, by race and Hispanic origin, 1950–2010. Note: The Centers for Disease Control and Prevention time series for Hispanic life expectancy does not begin until 2006.

Source: Centers for Disease Control and Prevention 2011.

Asians are not disadvantaged when it comes to health outcomes and in fact often fare better than whites.[12] For example, the infant mortality rate for babies born to Asian mothers (4.5 per 1,000 live births) is lower than among non-Hispanic whites (5.5). Finally, it should be noted that statistics for pan-ethnic groups mask some variation across origins within a given group. For example, regarding Hispanics, the infant mortality rate among Puerto Ricans (7.3) is higher than among Mexicans (5.6) and Cubans (4.9).[13]

Health and mortality are strongly associated with socioeconomic status. Figure 15.3 shows the differences in health outcomes by levels of education. (These patterns are also observed across income groups.) Only 30 percent of people who graduated from college report that their health is not excellent or very good, compared with 77 percent of those who did not finish high school. Disability is likewise less prevalent among those with a college degree, as are obesity, diabetes, and infant mortality.[14] Socioeconomic status has also been linked to an even wider array of health problems, including low birth weight, cardiovascular disease, hypertension, arthritis, cancer, and depression.[15] Contrary to the narrowing of the racial health gap, the strength of the relationship between socioeconomic status and health has increased in recent decades, with growing gaps in mortality, life expectancies, and the prevalence of disabilities by educational attainment.[16]

What explains these socioeconomic health disparities? Education, income, and occupational status can all affect one's health. Better-educated people tend to have greater access to information and resources that promote health—no small matter when considering the complexity of diagnosing and treating health problems and navigating through our health care system. People with higher levels of education also tend to have a greater sense of control over their lives, are more likely to plan ahead, and are better able to draw upon useful social networks that can provide advice and assistance during difficult times.[17] Obtaining a higher level of education also increases one's earning power and probability of landing a high-status, stable job, which in turn also lead to better health and lower mortality.

FIGURE 15.3.

Health, by educational attainment, 2000s. Note: The percentage of those without excellent or very good health refers to self-reported health among respondents ages 25 to 74; activity limitation refers to respondents age 25 and over; the percentage of obese respondents refers to those age 20 and over with a body mass index greater than or equal to 30 kg.

Source: Braveman et al. 2010, table 2.

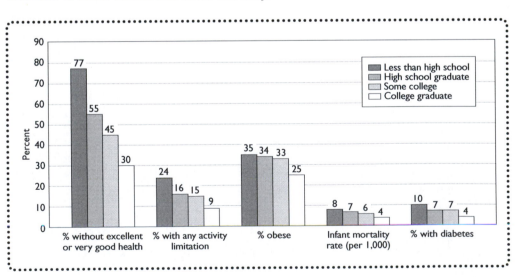

With regard to income, people with fewer resources may not have the means to purchase health care insurance that provides access to better health services. More than 60 percent of the uninsured are in low-income families. Although many poor individuals may be eligible for Medicaid, many do not end up enrolling. As a result, low-income individuals are less likely to see a physician and get preventative screening.[18] In addition, lower-income families may not have the resources to access quality housing, schooling, recreation, and nutrition that can enhance health. For example, poorer neighborhoods are more likely to be located near highways, industrial areas, and toxic waste sites, since land is cheaper in those areas. Families of low socioeconomic status (SES) are more likely to live in crowded and noisy environments, which can lead to, among other conditions, hypertension. The struggle to get by can be stressful, and this can affect both physical and mental health.

Similarly, people employed in lower-status occupations often have jobs that expose them to greater physical risk. For example, some blue-collar jobs involve exposure to toxic substances or to physical activity that can lead to injury and disability.[19] In contrast, people in higher-status professions have more control over their own working environment and are generally less likely to lose their job.[20]

In addition to the direct ways in which SES may contribute to poorer health, a number of indirect pathways have also been identified, including behavior and lifestyle, which might account for half of the earlier mortality among lower-SES individuals. Those with less education and income are more likely to smoke and drink heavily, are less likely to exercise and eat nutritiously, and are thus more likely to be overweight. Low-income individuals and their children have less access to safe, well-lit places to walk, bike, and play, and these all contribute to less healthy living.[21]

The following story on the growing poverty in the United States in the wake of the Great Recession illustrates the health challenges faced by poor individuals:

> Millions of workers and their families are similarly vulnerable to such mundane changes as a slight decline in the number of hours per workweek or an extra few cents per gallon in the cost of gasoline. . . . One such person is 67-year-old Mary Vasquez, whose Social Security check is $600 and whose rent is $500. A tiny woman, her health broken by cancer, heart attacks, diabetes, high blood pressure and a multitude of other ailments, Vasquez works as a phone operator at a Walmart on the outskirts of Dallas. . . . A large part of her salary went for medical expenses not covered by Medicare or her Walmart healthcare plan; much of the rest went to pay down usurious payday loans she'd accumulated in recent years as her health declined. Sitting in a union hall in the suburb of Grapevine, Vasquez (one of a handful of employees working to unionize her workplace) explains that she skips "mostly breakfast and sometimes lunch." As a diabetic, she is supposed to eat fresh produce. Instead, she says, "a lot of times I buy a TV dinner; we have them on sale for 88 cents. A lot of times, food, I can't pay for."
>
> Another American who struggles to put food on the table is Jorge, a 57-year-old who migrated to the United States from Mexico in 1982. Jorge (who doesn't want his last name used) lives with his wife in the large Chaparral *colonia,* an informal settlement of

trailers, small houses and shanties near Las Cruces, New Mexico. . . . "There's a lot of deterioration of the trailers," Jorge says in Spanish. "In winter, pipes explode because of the freeze. I don't have water right now. Heating is so expensive, with propane gas. Those who have little children, they have to use it, but it's so expensive." A volunteer firefighter, he adds, "We see a lot of accidents with water heaters and explosions with the propane tanks."[22]

These stories illustrate the many factors contributing to the poor health of low-income Americans, including the challenge of paying for health care, the propensity to purchase low-cost and often high-caloric food of dubious nutritional value, and problems with housing conditions that can lead to accidents and poor health.

Regarding racial disparities, the health disadvantage among blacks stems not only from their disadvantaged socioeconomic position but also from racism and residential segregation. Differences in their health outcomes cannot be attributed entirely to SES, because blacks are more disadvantaged than whites even when compared with those in the same income brackets and at the same educational levels. Simple comparisons overlook the multiple SES disadvantages that blacks often face. Blacks have less income and wealth than whites of the same educational backgrounds, and they also live in worse neighborhoods with higher poverty. The differences in the residential circumstances of blacks and whites, rooted in residential segregation, ensure that blacks are more likely to live in neighborhoods with greater social disorder and isolation. These differences reflect the historical legacy of institutional discrimination as well as contemporary racism. Experiences of discrimination can increase stress and hypertension and are predictive of an increased risk of substance abuse to cope with the extra stress.[23]

Given what we know about the association among socioeconomic status, race, and health, why do Hispanics have a higher life expectancy and lower levels of fatal chronic diseases, such as heart disease, cancer, lung disease, and stroke, than both blacks and whites?[24] This unexpected finding has been termed the *Hispanic paradox*. Further deepening the puzzle, immigrants' risk of disability and chronic disease increases with increasing length of residence in the United States, and native-born Hispanics have worse health and lower life expectancies than Hispanic immigrants. A number of explanations have been offered to explain these patterns. Some believe that cultural factors, such as better health habits and strong networks of social support in Hispanic communities help explain it. Thus, according to this view, as Hispanic immigrants and their children acculturate to the poor eating habits of the native population, their health outcomes worsen and their life expectancy declines.[25] Certainly, anecdotal evidence supports the view that Hispanic health behaviors become unhealthier in the United States. As one story in the news described it:

> Becoming an American can be bad for your health. . . . For the recently arrived, the quantity and accessibility of food speaks to the boundless promise of the United States. Esther Angeles remembers being amazed at the size of hamburgers—as big as dinner

plates—when she first came to the United States from Mexico 15 years ago. "I thought, this is really a country of opportunity," she said. "Look at the size of the food!"

Fast-food fare not only tasted good, but was also a sign of success, a family treat that new earnings put in reach. "The crispiness was delicious," said Juan Muniz, 62, recalling his first visit to Church's Chicken with his family in the late 1970s. "I was proud and excited to eat out. I'd tell them: 'Let's go eat. We can afford it now.'"

For others, supersize deals appealed. "You work so hard, you want to use your money in a smart way," said Aris Ramirez, a community health worker in Brownsville, explaining the thinking. "So when they hear 'twice the fries for an extra 49 cents,' people think, 'That's economical.'"

For Ms. Angeles, the excitement of big food eventually wore off, and the frantic pace of the modern American workplace took over. She found herself eating hamburgers more because they were convenient and she was busy in her 78-hour-a-week job as a housekeeper. What is more, she lost control over her daughter's diet because, as a single mother, she was rarely with her at mealtimes.[26]

While these stories seem compelling, there is danger in relying too much on anecdotes, as the evidence supporting the notion that migration to the United States is wholly responsible for causing increasing obesity is actually not overwhelming. Notably, important shifts in nutritional patterns and trends toward inactivity have occurred in countries around the globe in recent years. Barry Popkin, who has written extensively about this *nutritional transition,* notes: "The diet of poor people in rural or urban settings in Asia during the 1960s was simple and rather monotonous: rice with a small amount of vegetables, beans or fish. Today, their eating is transformed. It is common for people in these settings to regularly consume complex meals at any number of away-from-home food outlets—western or indigenous. The overall composition of diets in the developing world is shifting rapidly, particularly with respect to fat, caloric sweeteners, and animal-source foods."[27]

The prevalence of obesity has increased so rapidly in Mexico that the obesity rate there now surpasses the rate in the United States—making Mexico the most obese country in the hemisphere.[28] This suggests that immigrants and their children who are eating less nutritional foods now in the United States would be doing so regardless of whether they had migrated to the United States or not. As one commentator on growing obesity in Mexico put it, "The speed at which Mexicans have made the change from a diet dominated by maize and beans to one that bursts at the seams with processed fats and sugars poses one of the greatest challenges to public health officials."[29]

Factors that have contributed to growing obesity in Mexico and other developing countries include globalization and lifestyle changes. Some of these changes are cultural, in that patterns of food consumption associated with Western countries (the United States in particular) are being diffused throughout the world. Migration networks may have helped diffuse these eating patterns to Mexican communities,[30] but they may have occurred eventually anyway given their rise in countries around the globe. International food trade, commercialization, and marketing have made many new high-calorie foods and beverages with little nutritional value widely available at a relatively low cost. Such foods were initially mainly accessible to wealthier families in urban areas in developing countries, but they are increasingly available to poor families in rural areas as well.[31] Lifestyle changes stem from urbanization and the decline in physical activity in many occupations, both in the United States and abroad. Mechanization at work and in the household has reduced the need for strenuous labor. Many fewer people are employed in physically intensive activities such as farming, mining, and forestry, and an increasing number in the service sector are employed to perform sedentary activities, such as sitting in front of a computer terminal (much as I am as I write this).[32]

A growing consensus suggests that the issue of the Hispanic advantage in life expectancy in the United States is primarily related to *migration*. Specifically, Hispanics who migrate to the United States tend to be healthier than those who stay behind (in other words, immigrants are positively selected for their good health), and immigrants who leave the United States to return to home often do so when their health worsens. Indeed, studies have found that foreign-born Hispanics who left the United States had higher mortality levels than those who remained, and returnees to Mexico were more than three times more likely to rate their health as fair or poor than those who remained in the United States.[33] The Hispanic paradox has thus sometime been referred to as the immigrant paradox, as immigrants from a wide range of countries have longer life expectancies than do native-born Americans, and much of this has been attributed to the selectivity of immigrants more generally.[34] This issue is not fully settled, as it is not clear if migration fully explains the Hispanic health advantage. Research continues on the potentially protective roles that immigrant communities and health behaviors play.[35]

THE AGING OF THE AMERICAN POPULATION AND HEALTH CARE COSTS

Like the population of most developed countries around the world, the U.S. population is gradually aging. This is a function of declining fertility rates, the aging of the relatively large baby boom generation, and declining mortality. Figure 15.4 shows that the median age of the U.S. population dipped slightly from 30 to 28 between 1960 and 1970 because of the lingering effects of the baby boom, before increasing to 37 by 2010. Likewise, the percentage of the population over the age of 65 increased from 9 percent in 1960 to 13 percent in 2010. This is expected to rise to 20 percent by the year 2050. The percentage of the population that is over the age of 65 is lower in the United States than in other countries with low fertility, such as Japan, Germany, and Italy (all of whose percentage over the age of 65 already exceeds 20 percent), but considerably higher than the corresponding percentages in rapidly growing developing countries such as Uganda and Egypt, where 2 percent and 5 percent of the population are over the age of 65, respectively.[36]

The composition of the older population varies by gender and race/ ethnicity. Because of women's longer life expectancies, women made up well over half of the elderly population (57 percent) in 2010, though the narrowing of the male-female life expectancy gap in recent years has reduced the percentage of the older population that is female. (Women made up 59 percent

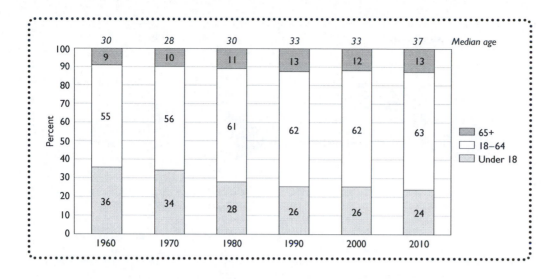

FIGURE 15.4.

Age distribution and median age of the U.S. population, 1960–2010.

Source: Howden and Meyer 2011, figure 4.

of the elderly population in 2000.)[37] Whites currently constitute about 80 percent of the elderly population, but they make up just 63 percent of the total population. Moreover, only about 54 percent of all births in 2011 were to white women, indicative of the very different racial and ethnic composition of the American population by age. By 2030, the projection is that about a third of the elderly population will be ethnic minority group members.[38]

The leading causes of death vary across the life course. The five leading causes of death for the population as a whole in 2010 were heart disease, cancer, chronic lower respiratory disease, stroke, and accidents. However, as shown in Figure 15.5, among children and young adults of ages 1 to 24, the leading causes of death were accidents (unintentional injuries), homicides, and suicides, followed by cancer and heart disease, while among those age 65 and over, the leading causes nearly mirrored the totals for the population as a whole (reflecting the concentration of deaths in this age group): heart disease, cancer, chronic lower respiratory diseases, stroke, and Alzheimer's. Accidents top the list for those age 25 to 44, while cancer was the top killer among people age 45 to 64.[39] Health and mortality vary across states. Life expectancy is longer and health is better in states such as Hawaii, Florida, and Connecticut, and worse in many states of the South, such as Mississippi, Kentucky, and West Virginia, where rates of obesity, diabetes, heart disease, and smoking are relatively high.[40]

One general concern about an aging population is that it can strain government budgets. While the elderly often amass savings during their lifetime in the form of pension plans, savings accounts, mutual funds, and equity in their homes—and they often continue to work even after the age of 65—they are nevertheless often economically dependent on the working-age population. The two main programs that serve the elderly—and whose growth has been met with alarm—are Social Security and Medicare. These two programs cost the federal government $1.3 trillion in 2012, accounting for about 37 percent of federal spending.[41] As many understand it, people

FIGURE 15.5.

Percentage distribution
of five leading causes of
death, by age group, in
the United States, 2010.
Source: Minino and
Murphy 2012, 4.

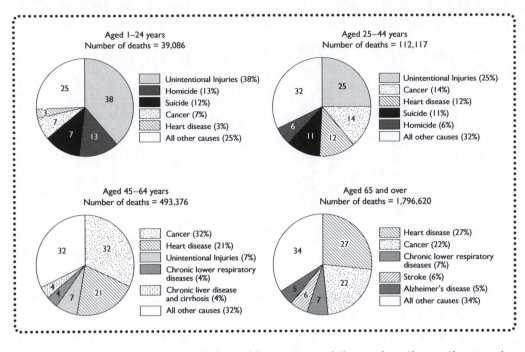

contribute payroll taxes during their working years and then, when they retire, receive in benefits what they paid in. However, the way the program is structured, people who are currently employed pay for current retirees. While a Social Security trust fund was set up to cover future needs, some of these funds have been used to help finance other government programs. In short, because the U.S. population is aging and the number of elderly is swelling compared with the size of the working-age population, the Social Security trust fund is projected to run out of revenue at some point in the next couple of decades (in 2033, according to a recent estimate).[42]

Likewise, the elderly require, on average, much more medical attention than younger people, and health care costs have been soaring well beyond inflation in recent years. The hospital component of Medicare, which accounts for about half of Medicare spending, is financed much like Social Security, through payroll taxes. This trust fund is expected to be depleted by about 2026.[43] Making structural changes to these programs is difficult because they are generally popular and actually quite effective, as Social Security significantly reduces poverty, and Medicare helps provide access to much-needed health care services. Medicare is in fact often better at controlling costs than other kinds of health insurance, as it is able to bargain with doctors and hospitals for lower prices because of the number of people it represents.[44]

While an aging population has put some stress on health care spending, it is important to note that the problem is considerably broader. Our health care system is not well designed to provide efficient care to either young or old Americans. In just the ten years between 1999 and 2009, the average annual premium for employer-sponsored family insurance coverage rose from $5,800 to $13,400, and the average cost per Medicare beneficiary went from $5,500 to $11,900.[45] Our medical spending is high and increasing for many reasons. Part of it has to do with the fact that doctors and hospitals are paid for the tests and procedures they conduct rather than for results (health outcomes). Thus, the incentive is to prescribe many such tests and procedures. Moreover, prices are often vastly inflated and arbitrary. *Time* magazine ran a series of articles on health care costs run amok in the United States:

> When Sean Recchi, a 42-year-old from Lancaster, Ohio, was told last March that he had non-Hodgkin's lymphoma, his wife Stephanie knew she had to get him to MD Anderson Cancer Center in Houston. Stephanie's father had been treated there 10 years earlier, and she and her family credited the doctors and nurses at MD Anderson with extending his life by at least eight years.
>
> Because Stephanie and her husband had recently started their own small technology business, they were unable to buy comprehensive health insurance. For $469 a month, or about 20% of their income, they had been able to get only a policy that covered just $2,000 per day of any hospital costs. "We don't take that kind of discount insurance," said the woman at MD Anderson when Stephanie called to make an appointment for Sean. . . . The total cost, in advance, for Sean to get his treatment plan and initial doses of chemotherapy was $83,900.
>
> Why? The first of the 344 lines printed out across eight pages of his hospital bill— filled with indecipherable numerical codes and acronyms—seemed innocuous. But it set the tone for all that followed. It read, "i acetaminophen tabs 325 mg." The charge was only $1.50, but it was for a generic version of a Tylenol pill. You can buy 100 of them on Amazon for $1.49 even without a hospital's purchasing power.
>
> Dozens of midpriced items were embedded with similarly aggressive markups, like $283.00 for a "CHEST, PA AND LAT 71020." That's a simple chest X-ray, for which MD Anderson is routinely paid $20.44 when it treats a patient on Medicare, the government health care program for the elderly. Every time a nurse drew blood, a "ROUTINE VENIPUNCTURE" charge of $36.00 appeared, accompanied by charges of $23 to $78 for each of a dozen or more lab analyses performed on the blood sample. In all, the charges for blood and other lab tests done on Recchi amounted to more than $15,000. Had Recchi been old enough for Medicare, MD Anderson would have been paid a few hundred dollars for all those tests. By law, Medicare's payments approximate a hospital's cost of providing a service, including overhead, equipment and salaries.[46]

This story helps provide an inkling as to why the health of Americans compares poorly with that of people in other rich countries—the topic to which I now turn.

...

CONCLUSION

Life expectancies in the United States have continued to increase over the last several decades. Infant mortality is down, other age-specific death rates are also down, and mortality from curable diseases has also declined. Nevertheless, significant disparities in health and mortality by ethnicity and socioeconomic status remain. Blacks live shorter lives on average and are more likely to suffer from a number of health conditions than whites. People with relatively low levels of education and income and those who work in low-status occupations likewise suffer from health deficits. However, ethnic disparities have slowly declined in recent years, and socio-economic ones have significantly increased—consistent with broader trends in ethnic and socioeconomic inequality in the United States.

Those with higher levels of education have more information about healthy living and the ability to navigate through our complex health care system, those with higher income have greater access to health care services and healthy homes and neighborhood environments, and those in high-status occupations are less exposed to risky working conditions. Some of the ethnic disparity in health is explained by socioeconomic disparities associated with ethnicity, but minority—especially black—individuals also contend with residential segregation that exacerbates social and health inequality and with discrimination that increases stress and hypertension. Notably, Hispanics have higher life expectancies than both blacks and whites, though at least a significant portion of this health advantage is a function of the selectivity of relatively healthy immigrants who come to the United States (compared with those who stay behind), as well as the selective migration back home of immigrants with worsening health.

With relatively low fertility, declining mortality, and the aging of the relatively large baby boom generation, a growing proportion of the American population is over the age of sixty-five. This has led to greater expenditures on popular and effective programs such as Social Security and Medicare, which has in turn put a greater stress on government budgets. Health expenditures are very high in the United States for a variety of reasons, including the absence of incentives to reduce the number of tests and procedures prescribed by doctors as well as the high cost of these procedures.

Despite the large amount of money spent on health care, Americans suffer from high mortality and worse health than people in other rich countries. The U.S. life expectancy, for example, is below the OECD average even though the United States has a higher GDP per capita than nearly all of the other countries. While the causes of this health deficit are difficult to pinpoint, they are likely rooted in differences in health care accessibility, individual behaviors, social factors, physical and environmental factors, and political and social values across countries.

Editorial Commentary: Remember OECD is the Organization for Economic Cooperation and Development. GDP is the Gross Domestic Product

The National Academies report on these issues offers recommendations for improving health outcomes in the United States, such as setting specific national health objectives. The report provides a concrete list of such objectives, ranging from improving the quality of air, land, and water to expanding community-based preventative services. It also recommends alerting the public about the U.S. health disadvantage to spark a national discussion on these issues, which might help promote a broader campaign on healthy living.[55] Thus, even though the health of Americans currently lags behind that of their peers, many positive steps can be taken to improve health and well-being in the future.

QUESTIONS FOR REVIEW, REFLECTION, AND DISCUSSION

1. Although the United States is one of the wealthiest nations in the world, why isn't it the healthiest?

2. Why do women tend to live longer than men? What impact might that have on families?

3. How are health and mortality associated with socioeconomic status?

4. Do a little research and find out how obesity is assessed and how it is defined.

ADDITIONAL READINGS

Ikram, U. Z., Malmusi, D., Juel, K., Rey, G., Kunst, A. (2015). Association between integration policies and immigrants' mortality: An explorative study across three European countries. *PLOS ONE. 10*(6), 1–14.

Gusmano, M. K., Weisz, D., Rodwin, V. G., Lang, J., Qian, M., Bocquier, A., Moysan, V., & Verger, P. (2014). Disparities in access to health care in three French regions. *Health Policy, 114*(1), 31–40.

Romero-Ortuno, R. (2014). Cross-national disparities in sex differences in life expectancy with and without frailty, *Age and Ageing, 43*(2), 222–228.

Ruiz, J. M., Campos, B., Garcia, J.J. (2016). Special issue on Latino physical health: Disparities, paradoxes, and future directions. *Journal of Latina/o Psychology, 4*(2), 61–66.

Zick, C. D. (2014). Family, frailty, and fatal futures? Own-health and family-health predictors of subjective life expectancy, *Research on Aging, 36*(2), 244–266.

ENDNOTE

1. National Research Council and Institute of Medicine 2013, 1.
2. J. Wilson 2013.
3. National Research Council and Institute of Medicine 2013, 4–6.
4. World Bank 2012.
5. Hoyert 2012, 2.
6. Meyer 2012.
7. Thorslund et al. 2013, 2–3; Preston and Wang 2006, 631.
8. Race and Hispanic origin information is collected from two separate questions. Hispanics can be of any race.
9. Centers for Disease Control and Prevention 2011.
10. Hoyert 2012, 5; MacDorman, Hoyert, and Mathews 2013; Schoeni, Freedman, and Martin 2009.
11. D. R. Williams et al. 2010.
12. Centers for Disease Control and Prevention 2012b, 5–6.
13. Centers for Disease Control and Prevention 2012c.

14. Braveman et al. 2010, table 2.
15. Adler and Newman 2002; Gallup 2012.
16. Hummer and Lariscy 2011, 254; Masters, Hummer, and Powers 2012; Miech et al. 2011; Montez et al. 2011; Olshansky et al. 2012, 1806; Schoeni, Freedman, and Martin 2009.
17. Hummer and Lariscy 2011, 243–45.
18. Peckham and Wyn 2009.
19. Adler and Newman 2002, 61–68; Williams and Mohammed 2008, 136.
20. Hummer and Lariscy 2011, 245.
21. Adler and Newman 2002, 68–69; Hummer and Lariscy 2011, 243.
22. Abramsky 2012.
23. D. R. Williams and Sternthal 2010, S20–S21.
24. Zhang, Hayward, and Lu 2012.
25. Singh and Miller 2004; Osypuk et al. 2009; see also Population Reference Bureau 2013 for a concise discussion of the Hispanic paradox.
26. Tavernise 2013.
27. Popkin 2004, 38.
28. Food and Agriculture Organization of the United Nations 2013, annex table.
29. Lakhani 2013.
30. Riosmena et al. 2012.
31. Popkin, Adair, and Ng 2012.
32. Popkin 2004, 39.
33. Palloni and Arias 2004; Turra and Elo 2008; Riosmena, Wong, and Palloni 2013.
34. Markides and Eschbach 2011, 227; Singh and Miller 2004.
35. Markides and Eschbach 2011, 237.
36. Jacobsen et al. 2011, 3.
37. Werner 2011, 2.
38. Jacobsen et al. 2011, 4–5; Motel and Patten 2013, tables 1 and 11.
39. Minino and Murphy 2012, 2–4.
40. Centers for Disease Control and Prevention 2013.
41. Holzer and Sawhill 2013.
42. Board of Trustees, Federal Old-Age and Survivors Insurance and Federal Disability Trust Funds 2013.
43. Board of Trustees, Federal Old-Age and Survivors Insurance and Federal Disability Trust Funds 2013.
44. Isaacs et al. 2012.
45. Gawande 2009.
46. Brill 2013.
47. United Nations 2012.
48. Caselli et al. 2013, 5.
49. National Research Council and Institute of Medicine 2013, 27–88.
50. Schoen et al. 2011, exhibit 1.

51. National Research Council and Institute of Medicine 2013, 190–238; Preston and Wang 2006; Pampel 2005.
52. National Research Council and Institute of Medicine 2013, 190–238.
53. National Research Council and Institute of Medicine 2013, 155–58.
54. National Research Council and Institute of Medicine 2013, 159.
55. National Research Council and Institute of Medicine 2013, 347–74.

KEY TERMS

Obesity

Food Insecurity

Food Desert

SNAP (Supplemental Nutrition Assistance Program)

CDC (Centers for Disease Control)

16

FOOD INSECURITY AND OBESITY IN RURAL AMERICA

Paradoxes of the Modern Agrifood System

By Keiko Tanaka, Patrick H. Mooney, and Brett Wolff

Keiko Tanaka, Patrick H. Mooney, and Brett Wolff, "Food Insecurity and Obesity in Rural America: Paradoxes of the Modern Agrifood System," Rural America in a Globalizing World: Problems and Prospects for the 2010s, pp. 642-660. Copyright © 2014 by West Virginia University Press. Reprinted with permission.

INTRODUCTION

How can food insecurity, often synonymous with hunger and "obesity," generally considered a sign of overconsumption, co-exist in places that make the United States the breadbasket of the world? The issue of food security is riddled with contradictions. When the United States entered the Great Recession in December 2007, food became more expensive as unemployment increased (US Bureau of Labor Statistics 2012a; 2012b). Meanwhile, more "food" and cropland was diverted to the production of biofuels. Increased economic uncertainty forced more urban households to make difficult spending choices. But what about rural Americans?

For the approximately 80 percent of Americans who live in suburban and urban areas (US Census Bureau 2012), rural America is a mysterious place where farmers supposedly reside and work. They hardly fathom the impact of the Great Recession on rural residents, such as increased rates of food insecurity, obesity, and higher health care costs. In the crevices of the contradiction between food insecurity and obesity we begin to uncover the complexity of food security.

In this chapter, we examine two sets of contradictions surrounding food security. First, in the United States, more people are becoming both hungry and obese. The second contradiction deals with rural areas as places of both food production and food insecurity. We argue that these apparent contradictions lie in a misunderstanding of material reality. In the modern globalized world, gone are the simplistic connections among poverty, economic disadvantage, and hunger. To be food insecure no longer implies going hungry. Obesity is no longer only a problem of the rich, but also of the poor. There is growing evidence that obesity in America is not just a health issue, but also a serious economic and political issue (Carolan 2011; Guthman 2011). The productive capacity of modern agriculture creates large volumes of inexpensive calories, but as Carolan (2011, 58) argues, "cheap food rests upon a cheapened understanding of food . . . In terms of maximizing calorie production, today's food system has been an unqualified success. The global obesity epidemic is testament to this fact."

We contend that the existing literature on rural food insecurity and obesity is insufficient. Odd and often contradictory findings reflect this inadequacy. "Rural" must be treated as more than just a geographical variable. The importance of place and history in shaping key social relationships must be recognized by social scientists in addressing the paradox of food insecurity and obesity in rural America.

THE PARADOX OF HUNGER AND OBESITY IN AMERICA

HUNGER IN THE UNITED STATES

The US Department of Agriculture (USDA) broadly defines a food insecure household as one that, at some point during the last year, could not claim to have "access at all times to enough food for active, healthy life" (Coleman-Jensen et al. 2012, 4). Since 1995, the USDA has collected annual data on household-level food security through a US Census Bureau survey that supplements the Current Population Survey (CPS). The USDA further breaks food insecurity down into "low food security" and "very low food security." Households with low food security reported three to five food insecure conditions on an eighteen-item questionnaire. Households with very low food security reported six or more food insecure conditions.

Since 1995, the overall household food insecurity rate was lowest in 1999 at 10.1 percent (Coleman-Jensen et al. 2012). Between 1998 and 2011, the prevalence of household food insecurity in the United States increased from 11.8 percent to 14.9 percent, or by 5.7 million households. Over the same period, the number of individuals in food insecure households increased from thirty-six million (13.5 percent) to fifty million (16.5 percent), including two million additional children living in food insecure households (Coleman-Jensen et al. 2012). Among food insecure households, the proportion of households with very low food security rose from 29.7 percent in 1999 to 32.8 percent in 2004 and to 35.5 percent in 2005. By 2008, the proportion of very low food security among the overall food insecure population was 39 percent. This indicates that both the overall prevalence of food insecurity has increased, as has its relative severity among food insecure households.

Most food insecure households tend to be food insecure temporarily, say during spates of unemployment or illness when family budgets are constrained (Coleman-Jensen et al. 2012). Other households tend to suffer temporary but recurrent hunger, such as at the end of each month, or annually due to regular seasonal fluctuations in employment and household expenses (e.g., utility bills, medical bills). As Table 16.1 shows, household food insecurity rates vary by household demographics. We summarize the key characteristics of vulnerable groups.

LOW-INCOME HOUSEHOLDS

Low-income households are at greater risk for food insecurity. Approximately one-third of all households with income below 185 percent of the official poverty threshold are food insecure. Each year since 2008, over 40 percent of households with income under the official poverty threshold experience food insecurity at some point of the year. Among households with children, vulnerability is higher.

HOUSEHOLDS WITH CHILDREN, PARTICULARLY THOSE HEADED BY SINGLE MOTHERS

In 2011, one of every five households with children were food insecure at some point in the year, and one of every four children resided in food insecure households (Coleman-Jensen et al. 2012). Both Table 16.1 and Figure 16.1 show a significant rise in food insecurity among households with children after 2008. High vulnerability among children living in single-parent households, particularly those headed by single women, is alarming.

BLACK AND HISPANIC HOUSEHOLDS

Non-Hispanic black and Hispanic households, especially those with children, are distinctly more likely to experience food insecurity than those of non-Hispanic whites. Between 2005 and 2011, the rate of food insecurity among Hispanic households increased by nearly 50 percent. In 2008, the Hispanic population had become the racial and ethnic group most vulnerable to overall food insecurity. However, a higher proportion of non-Hispanic black households continue to experience very low food security.

HOUSEHOLDS IN THE SOUTH AND WEST

Food insecurity prevalence rates vary among regions and among states within regions (Coleman-Jensen et al. 2012). The South and the West have consistently higher rates of household food insecurity than the Midwest and Northeast. Between 2004 and 2011, regional gaps in food insecurity rates shifted unevenly, reflecting regional differences in the rates of economic growth and contraction.

TABLE 16.1: SELECTED CHARACTERISTICS OF FOOD INSECURE HOUSEHOLDS, 2004 TO 2011

	2004	2005	2006	2007	2008	2009	2010	2011
All Households	11.9	11	10.9	11.1	14.6	14.7	14.5	14.9
Household Composition:								
With children < 18 yrs	17.6	15.6	15.6	15.8	21	21.3	20.2	20.6
Married couple	11.6	9.9	10.1	10.5	14.3	14.7	13.8	13.9
Female head, no spouse	33	30.8	30.4	30.2	37.2	36.6	35.1	36.8
Male head, no spouse	22.2	17.9	16.9	18	27.6	27.8	25.4	24.8
Other household with child	17.7	18.9	17.4	16	29.2	32.6	20.8	19
Without children < 18 yrs	8.9	8.5	8.5	8.7	11.3	11.4	11.7	12.2
More than one adult	6.7	6.7	6.5	6.7	9.1	9.2	9.9	9.9
Women living alone	11.8	11	11.3	11.7	14.9	14.7	13.7	15.6
Men living alone	12.3	11.5	11.4	11.2	14	14.5	15	15.5
With elderly	6.5	6	6	6.5	8.1	7.5	7.9	8.4
Elderly living alone	7.3	6.4	5.9	7.3	8.8	7.8	8	8.8
Race/Ethnicity:								
White	8.6	8.2	7.8	7.9	10.7	11	10.8	11.4
Black	23.7	22.4	21.8	22.2	25.7	24.9	25.1	25.1
Hispanic	21.7	17.9	19.5	20.1	26.9	26.9	26.2	26.2
Other	11.1	9.6	9.6	9.6	13.7	13.2	12.7	8.4
With Children:								
White	12.7	11.8	11.3	11.7	15.5	15.7	14.4	15.5
Black	29.2	27.4	26.4	25.9	31.9	32.6	32.9	29.2
Hispanic	26.8	21.6	23.8	23.8	32.1	32.7	30.6	32.3
Other	15.3	12.2	11.3	10.5	17.5	16.8	16.6	15.2
Household Income-to-Poverty Ratio:								
Under 1	36.8	36	36.3	37.7	42.2	43	40.2	41.1
1.85 and over	5.4	6.7	5.3	5.5	13.7	7.6	9.3	7

Sources: Nord, Andrews, and Carlson (2005, 2006, 2007, 2008, 2009); Nord et al. (2010); Coleman-Jensen et al. (2011, 2012).

HOUSEHOLDS IN INNER CITIES AND OUTSIDE METROPOLITAN AREAS

With few exceptions, the prevalence of food insecurity has been consistently higher among rural (or nonmetro) than urban and suburban (or metro) households. Among households with children, the gap between these two residential areas is greater and more consistent (Figure 16.1). Within metropolitan areas, households in principal cities[2] are more vulnerable than those in more prosperous suburbs.

OBESITY IN AMERICA

Overweight and obesity contribute to serious illnesses such as coronary heart disease, hypertension, and Type 2 diabetes. The economic impact of overweight and obesity and associated health problems include high medical costs,[3] as well as lost income, decreased productivity, and absenteeism (CDC 2012a).

CDC monitors the data on obesity and overweight through a series of surveys including the Behavioral Risk Factor Surveillance System (BRFSS), National Health and Nutrition Examination Survey (NHANES), and Youth Risk Behavior Surveillance System (YRBS). CDC (2012c) defines overweight and obesity based on body mass index (BMI), which is calculated from one's weight and height (CDC 2013).

Obesity data are difficult to interpret in order to identify vulnerable groups. Unlike household food insecurity, which tends to be an outcome of low household income, obesity is a result of multiple factors at the individual, family, and community levels, from one's genetics and lifestyle to the available infrastructure for recreation, health care, and food access.

RISING OBESITY RATES

Approximately 35.7 percent of adults and 17 percent of children and adolescents aged two to nineteen are considered obese (Ogden et al. 2012). Between 1985 and 2010, the prevalence of obesity in the United States dramatically increased. Until 1991, no state had a prevalence of obesity more than 20 percent. In 2010, no state had a prevalence of obesity less than 20 percent (CDC 2012b).

HIGHER RURAL OBESITY RATES

In 2005 to 2006, 27.4 percent of rural[4] adult residents were classified as obese compared to 23.9 percent of their urban counterparts (Bennett, Olatoshi, and Probst 2008). In 2003, among children between ten and seventeen years of age, urban children were slightly more likely to be overweight (16 percent) than rural children (15 percent), while more rural children were considered obese (16.5 percent) than urban children (14.5 percent) (Liu et al. 2007).

FIGURE 16.1

Food insecure
households, rural versus
urban, 2004 to 2011.
Sources: Nord, Andrews,
and Carlson (2005, 2006,
2007, 2008, 2009); Nord
et al. (2010); Coleman-
Jensen et al. (2011,
2012)

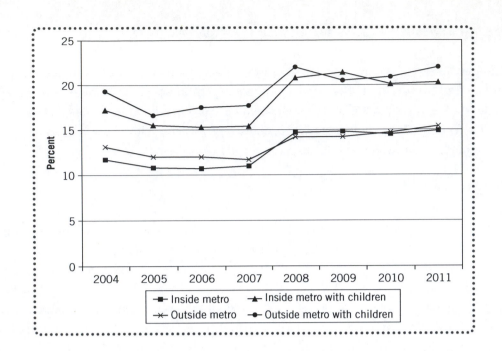

OBESITY RATES AFFECT SOCIOECONOMIC GROUPS DIFFERENTLY

Obesity rates vary among regions and states. By 2011, thirty-nine states had a prevalence of 25 percent or more and twelve had a prevalence of 30 percent or more. The analysis of the NHANES data for 2005 to 2008 paints a complex relationship between obesity and socioeconomic status in adults (Ogden et al. 2010). Most obese male and female adults (approximately forty-two million) are white non-Hispanic with income at or above 130 percent of the poverty level. About fifteen million obese adults are low income at or below 130 percent of the poverty level. Although obesity prevalence among non-Hispanic white men is similar at all income and educational levels, among non-Hispanic black and Mexican American men, obesity prevalence increases as income increases. However, obesity among women decreases as income and education increase. The intersection of gender and race/ethnicity with obesity prevalence is an interesting issue that requires further investigation.

Keep in mind that food insecurity and obesity are neither necessary nor sufficient conditions for causing each other. Although certain groups are at higher risk of both, other groups are at higher risk for one, but not for the other. Variations in the prevalence of household food insecurity and obesity among socioeconomic groups indicate that larger social transformations differentially affect their vulnerability. In the next section, we discuss how key transformations in rural America have contributed to creating paradoxical problems of food insecurity and obesity.

PARADOX OF RURAL AMERICA

Food insecurity and obesity trends clearly indicate that geography does matter. Rural Americans are vulnerable to both food insecurity and obesity. Many rural communities and states with large rural populations are increasingly burdened by the rapidly growing costs of providing adequate services to rural residents experiencing hunger and obesity. Recent rural health literature indicates a growing sense of urgency to understand and address rural hunger and obesity (e.g., NACRHHS 2011; NACo 2008). Unfortunately, many findings from the existing literature are puzzling and sometimes raise more questions than they answer. More importantly, there is an urgent need for good data on rural children.

Following Busch and Lacy (1984), as well as others, we identify four distinct dimensions: *availability*, *accessibility*, *affordability*, and *adequacy*. At the empirical level, these four dimensions of food security closely interact, affecting socioeconomic groups differently. High food insecurity and obesity rates in rural America reflect the unequal spatial distribution of economic, political, social, and cultural capital. We discuss these four dimensions of food security to better understand growing food insecurity and obesity rates in rural America in relation to four interrelated social processes (see Lobao's introduction to this section of this volume).

RURAL AMERICANS DEPEND ON GLOBAL FOOD ECONOMY FOR FOOD AVAILABILITY

Over the last century, rapid transformations in the structure of agriculture and food economies have dramatically altered food availability. Today, technological advances as well as neoliberal trade agreements have enabled easier flow of capital, goods, services, and labor in agricultural and food systems across national borders.

Government policies and programs, particularly subsidization of certain crops, and rapid concentration of food markets among a few corporations facilitated domination by fewer, bigger farms; regional specialization; and our high dependence on an energy intensive distribution system that moves food long distances (Brown and Shaft 2011). Much of our farmland is used to produce raw ingredients for processed food at very low cost or biofuel, rather than nutrient-rich fresh vegetables and fruits. Cheap food becomes a culprit for increasing obesity prevalence in this country and the world. In this food system, only a small portion of the value generated from food production stays in the hands of farmers and the rural communities (Gereffi, Lee, and Christian 2009). Rural Americans are as dependent on grocery stores to purchase food as urban Americans.

Yet, food availability is still geographically determined because the global agricultural and food economy varies enormously between and within most nations. Improved food availability has contributed to the paradox of hunger and obesity in this country, including for rural Americans. To understand this paradox as a geographically situated social process, *community food security* is a useful concept. Community food security expands the measurement of household food security that "concerns the underlying social, economic, and institutional factors within a community that affect the quantity and quality of available food and its affordability or price relative to the sufficiency of financial resources available to acquire it" (Cohen, Andrews, and Kanter 2002, 3). Community food security is a critical element of the environment that shapes individuals' health behaviors and outcomes.

County-based analysis of community food security highlights the complexity of hunger as a spatially and temporally grounded public problem. High rates of food insecure households in rural areas, particularly in the South, alone do not necessarily demonstrate that food availability, per se, in these geographical areas is more limited. Existing work on food accessibility (e.g., Morton and Blanchard 2007) and affordability (e.g., Zimmerman, Ham, and Frank 2008) confirms that readily available foods for urban Americans are surprisingly less available to rural Americans. Accessibility, affordability, and adequacy of available food are important components in assessing community food security.

FOOD ACCESS IS LIMITED IN RURAL AMERICA

Accessibility refers to all members of society being able to obtain the food they need. A *food desert* illustrates the lack of large food retailers within close proximity, and low food accessibility in a given community. Measuring food deserts usually involves spatial identification of urban neighborhoods that are more than one mile, or "walkable distance," from supermarkets and grocery stores. In rural areas, a distance of more than ten miles from a supermarket or grocery store has been used to measure rural food deserts (Morton et al. 2005).

This latter measure reveals 418 food desert counties in the United States. When the unit of analysis for food deserts is at the county level, nearly all food deserts are nonmetro counties, mostly counties with no towns or cities with a population of more than 10,000. Morton and Blanchard (2007) identify common characteristics of these counties, including lower educational attainment, higher poverty, lower median family incomes, higher concentrations of elders, more convenience stores per capita, and smaller grocery stores.

According to Feeding America (2009), communities of color tend to face a higher likelihood of community food insecurity. Most of these high food insecure counties with large percentages of ethnic minorities are located in rural areas.

FOOD IS LESS AFFORDABLE IN RURAL AMERICA

As Busch and Lacy (1984, 2) note, "simply making food available is not enough; one must also be able to purchase it." The Cost of Living Index grocery survey, published by the Council for Community and Economic Research or ACCRA-COLI, is an instrument used to assess food affordability (C2ER 2012). For SNAP (Supplemental Nutrition Assistance Program; the erstwhile food stamp program) allotments, the USDA's Thrifty Food Plan (TFP) is used as a national standard for a nutritious diet at a minimal cost. This TFP is another useful instrument for market basket surveys in documenting geographical variations in the availability of basic goods and services as well as the cost of living.

According to the Current Population Survey (CPS), food secure individuals spend $2.54 per meal on average[5] (Feeding America 2009). Among the 313 counties with the most expensive food costs, the average meal costs $3.12, or 23 percent higher than the national average. Many high-cost meal counties were located in rural areas.

Zimmerman, Ham, and Frank (2008) in Kentucky and Morton and colleagues (2005; 2008) in Iowa suggest that the relationships among poverty, food insecurity, hunger, and obesity in rural America are not directly comparable with those in urban America. Zimmerman, Ham, and Frank (2008) point out that the ACCRA-COLI is based on urban-biased market baskets and neglects expenditures needed to make up for the lack of some basic services such as public water and municipal sewer services in rural Kentucky. Rural residents from eight case study counties in rural Kentucky, on average, needed to drive 28.2 miles round trip to access the items listed in the ACCRA-COLI survey.[6] In their study of rural communities in Iowa, Morton et al. (2004) found that open-country rural residents[7] shop at more stores for groceries and shop more often at superstores or wholesale/discount stores outside their county than in-town rural residents.

Spatial differences in the cost of living also lead to a variation between rural and urban households in their use of nonmarket food exchanges to mitigate food insecurity. The study of two rural and two urban low-income counties in Iowa shows that low-income urban Americans may be more likely to use food redistribution mechanisms organized by government and community groups such as the SNAP, WIC, food pantries, and elder meal programs, while their rural counterparts are more likely to use reciprocal exchange of food with family, friends, and neighbors through gardening, fishing, and/or hunting (Morton et al. 2008). The same study suggests that rural Americans may be more likely to donate foods through these redistribution mechanisms than urban Americans. While food insecure households in urban areas can use cheap public transportation to frequent food redistribution services, many rural households may need to travel long distances, incurring significant costs, to access foods through such institutions.

Residential differences in the use of nonmarket mechanisms to access food illustrate the different ways that family, neighborhood, churches, and communities mitigate hunger among low-income households (Duncan 1999; Lee, Coward, and Netzer 1994; Meert 2000). Morton et al. (2008, 114) point out that "urban density may contribute to the community of strangers providing and depending on public redistribution programs rather than reciprocity relations of friends and kin found in smaller rural places." While a stronger cultural norm of giving (Hofferth and Iceland 1998; Lee, Coward, and Netzer 1994; Meert 2000) may encourage rural Americans to contribute to food banks and meal programs, the lack of anonymity, which encourages food-giving behavior, may also discourage rural low-income households' reception of food through food assistance programs for fear of social stigma. The Feeding America study (2009) finds rural Americans to be less knowledgeable about benefit eligibility. In short, geo-spatial factors such as density and distance continue to reproduce differential socio-spatial patterns of interaction (e.g., anonymity, cohesion) that influence food security (Hofferth and Iceland 1998).

One of the critical findings in the Iowa study is that those who are older, more educated, and have home gardens are more likely to maintain nutritionally adequate diets through consumption of fruits and vegetables. This suggests that participation in the reciprocity economy requires a set of life skills to make gardening a financially and nutritionally effective way for mitigating food insecurity. The attainment and use of such life skills needs further investigation in relation to food adequacy. Long-term approaches to mitigating food insecurity must include not only the facilitation of reciprocal economic mechanisms at the community level, but also transmission of these life skills as cultural capital across generations.

FOOD ADEQUACY REFLECTS UNIQUE INSTITUTIONALIZED RELATIONSHIPS IN RURAL AMERICA

Adequacy refers to balanced diets for the nutritional needs of various segments of the population and implies that food is safe. It may also include a number of cultural, or personal, preferences in an adequate diet. Even among experts, there is considerable disagreement over what constitutes an adequate diet and which foods are safe (Guthman 2011; Nestle 2003).

At the macro level, FAO (2012) uses total availability of calories in a particular nation to estimate food adequacy. That is, whether the total caloric requirements for the entire population, while accounting for varied caloric requirements for diverse population groups (e.g., pregnant women, children, elderly), can be met through that country's food supply. Under this measurement, the United States appears to have plenty of available food and should not be facing food insecurity as a public policy issue.

At the micro level, such measures can be problematic. In measures of per capita consumption, many Americans' extremely high levels of calorie consumption statistically obscure populations that might be deprived of an adequate number of calories. Household surveys, which include food intake indicators, are often used to measure the amount of food actually consumed at the individual or household level. Nutritional status, measured by anthropometric measures (e.g., BMI), is also used to assess dietary deficiencies (Migotto et al. 2005). In many industrialized countries, a somewhat invisible form of food insecurity or malnutrition is constituted not by low caloric intake, but by a high intake of nutritionally inadequate calories.

In community food security assessments, food adequacy is rarely evaluated at both macro and micro levels. If measured, food adequacy is often estimated with a combination of food availability, accessibility, and affordability variables. Health researchers often rely on prevalence rates of obesity and obesity-associated health outcomes (e.g., Type 2 diabetes, hypertension) among residents as an indicator of food adequacy in the community (Dabney and Gosschalk 2003; Drewnowski and Darmon 2005; Liu et al. 2008). Not only do food insecurity and obesity co-exist in rural America, the breadbasket, but also the prevalence of obesity is treated as a sign of food insecurity.

UNDERSTANDING OBESITY IN RURAL AMERICA

The existing literature consistently shows that obesity rates are higher in rural America, particularly in the South. Henderson and Low (2006, 3) point out, "at the state level, per capita spending on obesity-related healthcare was not only higher in rural states, but also accounted for a greater share of the states' total spending on healthcare." Obesity rates among children and adolescents tend to be higher in rural areas, indicating "a reversal of the situation in the United States prior to 1980, when, in general, obesity was more common in children in large metropolitan areas" (Tai-Seale and Chandler 2003, 116).

Yet, comparative analysis of obesity rates between urban and rural adults and children by different social demographic groups depicts a complex picture of how structural changes in the agricultural and food economy affect these groups differently. For example, in 2005, non-Hispanic white, non-Hispanic black, and Hispanic adults in rural areas were significantly more obese than their urban counterparts. However, this was not the case among Asian, Native American, and other ethnic adults (Bennett, Olatoshi, and Probst 2008). Rural residence is correlated with obesity and overweight among white adult men and women, but not among black men and women when controlling for demographic and other mediating variables. However, extremely obese black men are more prevalent in rural areas and large cities (Liu et al. 2008; Tai-Seale and Chandler 2003).

According to Liu et al. (2007), among those aged ten to seventeen, rural children are more likely to be obese than urban children. Among rural children, younger children (aged ten to fourteen), boys, and children in households below the 200 percent poverty threshold and in relatively poor health are at a greater risk of obesity. Rural African American children (23.8 percent) are almost twice as likely to be obese as rural white children (14.5 percent). Significantly higher overweight and obesity rates were found in rural areas among white children, male children, children with family incomes at 200 to 400 percent above the poverty line, and children with self-perceptions of "excellent/very good" health status. This study found no significant residential differences in the impact of race, ethnicity, or poverty level on the risk of obesity among children.

One possible explanation for these differences is that obesity and food insecurity may interact differently for diverse social groups across geographical space. Whether in urban or rural areas, certain institutionalized relationships such as race, ethnicity, and household income appear to consistently play a critical role. In rural areas, however, obesity may not necessarily be an outcome of poverty, particularly for white residents. Other environmental factors may play a role in moderating the interaction, as discussed below.

ENVIRONMENTAL FACTORS

Health researchers use various institutional and environmental factors to examine obesity and overweight rates among rural residents: including physical activity levels (Ahern, Brown, and Dukas 2011; Bennett, Olatoshi, and Probst 2008; Joens-Matre et al. 2008; Liu et al. 2007, 2008); access to health care (Bennett, Olatoshi, and Probst 2008; Liu et al. 2007;

2008); the number of total restaurants, fast food restaurants, and convenience stores (Ahern, Brown, and Dukas 2011); and the frequency of family meals (Liu et al. 2007). According to Bennett, Olatoshi, and Probst (2008), in 2005 rural adults were significantly less physically active while rural children were significantly more physically active; and rural children ate family meals less frequently than urban children. The same study reports that one primary care physician was available to every 1,461 persons in rural counties, in contrast to one physician to every 880 persons in urban counties.

Ahern et al. (2011) examine health outcomes (total age-adjusted mortality rates, adult obesity rates, and adult diabetes rates) of food availability and access variables to infer food adequacy among adults in metro and nonmetro counties. In nonmetro counties, more fast food restaurants per capita were unexpectedly associated with greater diabetes rates but lower obesity rates. These researchers confirmed previous findings that the availability of grocery stores was associated with better health outcomes. Surprisingly, in nonmetro counties, a higher number of grocery stores per capita was associated with higher mortality. In metro counties, direct farm sales per capita were negatively associated with both mortality and diabetes rates. In nonmetro counties, direct farm sales per capita were negatively associated with mortality and obesity rates but positively associated with diabetes rates.

Rather than offering possible explanations, we emphasize that these seemingly anomalous findings in urban-rural comparisons reveal challenges in conceptualizing and measuring the difference of food adequacy in rural areas. These findings require rigorous scrutiny for explanation through collaborative research between health scientists and rural social scientists. Designing instruments to effectively assess food adequacy, both quantitatively and qualitatively, either at the individual and household level or at the community level, is not an easy task because numerous variables (e.g., age, gender, ethnicity, religion, geography, health status) need to be taken into account.

First, these unexpected results in rural counties indicate the limitation of focusing solely on formal market mechanisms, or even formal redistribution mechanisms, for understanding food access and availability. Some of the assumptions about the relationships between food consumption behaviors and health outcomes, taken for granted among urban Americans, may not be applicable to the rural population. A second problem concerns the use of obesity and health outcomes as indicators of food adequacy. Health measures oversimplify how the quality of our individual and family lives is shaped over a lifetime. These limitations often lead to policy and program recommendations that only address temporary challenges of food insecurity. As Morton et al. (2008, 116) emphasize, "neither redistribution nor reciprocity solve the problem of rural food insecurity" because they are insufficient in addressing challenges of attaining nutritionally, culturally, and socially adequate foods at reasonable costs. We must consider the livelihood strategies of households and individuals in a given community for mitigating periodic hunger and malnutrition over time. In this way, we can address structural problems that continuously reproduce food insecurity among the same social groups, if not the same individuals, in the same geographical areas. A concerted effort is necessary among government agencies at different levels, the food industry, community organizations, activist groups, and scholars to revise and/or create new policies and programs such as agricultural subsidies, price supports, regulatory action, institutional feeding, and consumer education.

CONCLUSIONS

The root of the apparent contradictions between food insecurity and obesity and between the rural as a place of both food production and food insecurity comes from a simplistic and anachronistic understanding of food insecurity's relationship to production, distribution, hunger, and poverty. That same outdated vision of what it means to be poor or hungry or food insecure obscures the ways that structural forces and individual choices intertwine in the modern complex of US food inequality. Prevalent popular discourses aimed at helping the hungry and blaming the obese are tragic evidence of this short-sightedness.

The rise of obesity is also, in part, an outcome of macro-structural transformations that limit access, availability, and adequacy in food deserts. This is not a private but a public issue, insofar as the market is inadequate to serve those neighborhoods or communities, who, even collectively, cannot effectively participate in it. Thus we can observe the uneven effects of these unhealthy trends across racial, gender, and class lines, and again across geographical space.

In 2008, total US expenditures on all foods and beverages were estimated at $1,204 billion (USDA-ERS 2012), while obesity-related medical expenditures that same year were estimated at $147 billion (Finkelstein et al. 2009). At the micro level, consumers are encouraged to choose healthier and more nutritious diets and maintain regular physical exercise in order to save on medical costs. At the macro level, how this smart lifestyle by individual residents will eventually translate into actual savings in medical expenditures at the community, state, and federal levels is not very clear. Both food insecurity and obesity are public policy issues tied to the declining minimum wage; the lack of health insurance and family benefits; government subsidization of calorie-dense but nutritionally inadequate crops; the subsequent over-promotion of high-calorie, nutrition-poor diets; and declining neighborhood resources. These issues need to be addressed through a concerted program of environmental and policy interventions.

Existing research on food insecurity and obesity tends to focus on food access and affordability by using spatial and economic data such as the distance that food travels (or food miles), or the distance that people must travel to geographically concentrated food stores and restaurants. Each rural place and area is unique in a more subtle way. The democratization of food policy and economies can provide solutions to those unique local circumstances and many communities are experimenting (e.g., local food policy councils) with diverse efforts to resolve the constellation of problems specific to their community (Mooney, Ciciurkaite, and Tanaka 2012).

More collaborative research is needed between health scientists and rural social scientists to examine the qualitative features of food consumption, particularly surrounding the adequacy of food, and the economics of food choices. Health scientists recognize obesity as an outcome of food environments, but do not always investigate the socioeconomic environment of obese people. Rural sociologists and social scientists examine the socioeconomic environment of obese people, but do not quite find effective ways to incorporate obesity and other health outcomes, as well as other socio-cultural variables, in assessing the qualitative variation of food (in)security. Fruitful collaborations between these two groups of scientists will provide a more nuanced understanding of food insecurity and obesity, highlighting the implications of variable gender, racial, and ethnic dynamics in a diverse rural America.

REFERENCES

Ahern, M., C. Brown, and S. Dukas. Winter 2011. "A National Study of the Association between Food Environments and County-Level Health Outcomes." *Journal of Rural Health* 27 (4): 367–79. http://dx.doi.org/10.1111/j.1748-0361.2011.00378.x. Medline:21967380.

Bennett, Kevin J., Bankole Olatoshi, and Janice C. Probst. 2008. *Health Disparities: A Rural—Urban Chartbook.* Columbia, SC: South Carolina Rural Research Center.

Brown, D., and K. Shaft. 2011. *Rural People and Communities in the 21st Century: Resilience and Transformation.* Malden, MA: Polity Press.

Busch, L., and W.B. Lacy. 1984. *Food Security in the United States.* Boulder, CO: Westview Press.

C2ER. 2012. "Cost of Living Index Manual." Accessed 2 September. http://www.coli.org/surveyforms/colimanual.pdf.

Carolan, Michael. 2011. *The Real Cost of Cheap Food.* London, New York: Routledge.

CDC (Center for Disease Control). 2012a. "Adult Obesity Facts." Accessed 15 March. http://www.cdc.gov/obesity/data/adult.html.

CDC. 2012b. "Obesity Trends among U.S. Adults between 1985 and 2010." PowerPoint presentation. Accessed 10 August. http://www.cdc.gov/obesity/data/adult.html.

CDC. 2012c. "Defining Overweight and Obesity." Accessed 10 August. http://www.cdc.gov/obesity/adult/defining.html.

CDC. 2013. "Body Mass Index." Accessed 11 July. http://www.cdc.gov/healthyweight/assessing/bmi/index.html.

Cohen, B., M. Andrews, and L.S. Kanter. 2002. "Community Food Security Assessment Toolkit." Electronic Publications from the Food Assistance & Nutrition Research Program. Washington DC: USDA Economic Research Service. Accessed 14 February 2012. http://www.ers.usda.gov/publications/efan-electronic-publications-from-the-food-assistance-nutrition-research-program/efan02013.aspx.

Coleman-Jensen, A., M. Nord, M. Andrews, and S. Carison. 2011. *Household Food Security in the United States in 2010.* USDA Economic Research Report Number 125. Washington, DC: USDA. Accessed 15 February 2012. http://ers.usda.gov/publications/err-economic-research-report/err125.aspx.

Coleman-Jensen, A., M. Nord, M. Andrews, and S. Carison. 2012. *Household Food Security in the United States in 2011.* USDA Economic Research Report Number 141. Washington, DC: USDA. Accessed 20 September. http://www.ers.usda.gov/publications/ap-administrative-publication/ap-058.aspx.

Dabney, Betty, and Annie Gosschalk. 2003. "Diabetes in Rural America: A Literature Review." In *Rural Healthy People 2010: A Companion Document to Healthy People 2010*, ed. Larry D. Gamm, Linnae L. Hutchison, Betty J. Dabney, and Alicia Dorsey, 57–72. College Station, TX: The Texas A&M University System Health Science Center, School of Rural Public Health, Southwest Rural Health Research Center. Accessed 3 September 2012. http://www.srph.tamhsc.edu/centers/rhp2010/05Volume1diabetes.pdf.

Drewnowski, A., and N. Darmon. July 2005. "The Economics of Obesity: Dietary Energy Density and Energy Cost." *American Journal of Clinical Nutrition* 82 (1 Suppl): 265S–73S. Medline:16002835.

Duncan, C. 1999. *Worlds Apart: Why Poverty Persists in Rural America*. New Haven, CT: Yale University Press.

FAO. 2012. "Hunger." Accessed 27 September. http://www.fao.org/hunger/en/.

Feeding America. 2009. *Map the Meal Gap 2011. Highlights of Findings*. Chicago, IL: Feeding America.

Finkelstein, Eric A., Justin G. Trogdon, Joel W. Cohen, and William Dietz. September– October 2009. "Annual Medical Spending Attributable to Obesity: Payer-and Service-Specific Estimates." *Health Affairs (Project Hope)* 28 (5): w822–31. http://dx.doi.org/10.1377/hlthaff.28.5.w822. Medline:19635784.

Gereffi, Gary, Joonkoo Lee, and Michelle Christian. July 2009. "US-Based Food and Agricultural Value Chains and Their Relevance to Healthy Diets." *Journal of Hunger & Environmental Nutrition* 4 (3–4): 357–74. http://dx.doi.org/10.1080/19320240903321276. Medline:23144675.

Guthman, Julie. 2011. *Weighing In: Obesity, Food Justice, and the Limits of Capitalism*. Berkeley: University of California Press.

Henderson, J., and S. Low. 2006. "Obesity: America's Economic Epidemic. The Main Street Economist: Commentary on the Rural Economy." *Center for the Study of Rural America* 1 (11): 1–4.

Hofferth, S., and J. Iceland. 1998. "Social Capital in Rural and Urban Communities." *Rural Sociology* 63 (4): 574–98. http://dx.doi.org/10.1111/j.1549-0831.1998.tb00693.x.

Joens-Matre, R.R., G.J. Welk, M.A. Calabro, D.W. Russell, E. Nicklay, and L.D. Hensley. Winter 2008. "Rural-Urban Differences in Physical Activity, Physical Fitness, and Overweight Prevalence of Children." *Journal of Rural Health* 24 (1): 49–54. http://dx.doi.org/10.1111/j.1748-0361.2008.00136.x. Medline:18257870.

Lee, G., R. Coward, and J. Netzer. 1994. "Residential Differences in Filial Responsibility Expectations among Older Persons." *Rural Sociology* 59 (1): 100–9. http://dx.doi.org/10.1111/j.1549-0831.1994.tb00524.x.

Liu, J., K.J. Bennett, N. Harun, and J.C. Probst. Fall 2008. "Urban-Rural Differences in Overweight Status and Physical Inactivity among US Children Aged 10–17 Years." *Journal of Rural Health* 24 (4): 407–15. http://dx.doi.org/10.1111/j.1748-0361.2008.00188.x. Medline:19007396.

Liu, J., K.J. Bennett, N. Harun, J.C. Probst, and R.R. Pate. 2007. *Overweight and Physical Inactivity among Rural Children Aged 10–17: A National and State Portrait*. Columbia, SC: South Carolina Rural Health Research Center.

Meert, H. 2000. "Rural Community Life and the Importance of Reciprocal Survival Strategies." *Sociologia Ruralis* 40 (3): 319–38. http://dx.doi.org/10.1111/1467-9523.00151.

Migotto, Mauro, Benjamin Davis, Gero Carletto, and Kathleen Beegle. 2005. *Measuring Food Security Using Respondents' Perception of Food Consumption Adequacy*. ESA Working Paper No. 05-10. Agricultural and Development Economics Division, the Food and Agriculture Organization of the United Nations. Accessed 15 September 2012. http://www.fao.org/economic/esa/en.

Mooney, Patrick, Gabriele Ciciurkaite, and Keiko Tanaka. 2012. "The Food Policy Council Movement in North America: A Convergence of Alternative Local Agrifood Interests?" Presented at the 13th World Congress for Rural Sociology, Lisbon, Portugal, August.

Morton, L.W., E. Bitto, M. Oakland, and M. Sand. 2004. "Rural Food Access Patterns: Elderly Open-Country and in-Town Residents." *Iowa Food Security, Insecurity, and Hunger*. SP 236. Iowa State University, University Extension. Accessed 20 February 2012. http://www.foodshedproject.ca/pdf/postingtowebsitejanuary2011/grocery%20stores%20and%20hunger.pdf.

Morton, L.W., E. Bitto, M. Oakland, and M. Sand. 2005. "Solving the Problems of Iowa Food Deserts: Food Insecurity and Civic Structure." *Rural Sociology* 70 (1): 94–112. http://dx.doi.org/10.1526/0036011053294628.

Morton, L.W., E. Bitto, M. Oakland, and M. Sand. 2008. "Accessing Food Resources: Rural and Urban Patterns of Giving and Getting Food." *Agriculture and Human Values* 25 (1): 107–19. http://dx.doi.org/10.1007/s10460-007-9095-8.

Morton, L.W., and T.C. Blanchard. 2007. "Starved for Access: Life in Rural America's Food Deserts." *Rural Realities* 1 (4): 1–10.

National Advisory Committee on Rural Health and Human Services (NACRHHS). 2011. *The 2011 Report to the Secretary: Rural Health and Human Services Issues*. Accessed 10 September 2012. http://www.hrsa.gov/advisorycommittees/rural/publications/index.html.

National Association of Counties (NACo). 2008. *Rural Obesity: Strategies to Support Rural Counties in Building Capacity*. Accessed 10 August 2012. http://www.leadershipforhealthy-communities.org/resources-mainmenu-40/reports/235-report98.

Nestle, M. 2003. *Safe Food: Bacteria, Biotechnology, and Bioterrorism*. Berkeley, Los Angeles: University of California Press.

Nord, M., M. Andrews, and S. Carlson. 2005. *Household Food Security in the United States, 2004. Measuring Food Security in the United States*. Washington, DC: USDA Economic Research Service.

Nord, M., M. Andrews, and S. Carlson. 2006. *Household Food Security in the United States, 2005. Measuring Food Security in the United States.* Washington, DC: USDA Economic Research Service.

Nord, M., M. Andrews, and S. Carlson. 2007. *Household Food Security in the United States, 2006. Measuring Food Security in the United States.* Washington, DC: USDA Economic Research Service.

Nord, M., M. Andrews, and S. Carlson. 2008. *Household Food Security in the United States, 2007. Measuring Food Security in the United States.* Washington, DC: USDA Economic Research Service.

Nord, M., M. Andrews, and S. Carlson. 2009. *Household Food Security in the United States, 2008. Measuring Food Security in the United States.* Washington, DC: USDA Economic Research Service.

Nord, M., A. Coleman-Jensen, M. Andrews, and S. Carlson. 2010. *Household Food Security in the United States, 2009.* Washington, DC: United States Department of Agriculture.

Ogden, Cynthia L., Margaret D. Carroll, Brian K. Kit, and Katherine M. Flegal. 1 February 2012. "Prevalence of Obesity and Trends in Body Mass Index among US Children and Adolescents, 1999–2010." *JAMA: Journal of the American Medical Association* 307 (5): 483–90. http://dx.doi.org/10.1001/jama.2012.40. Medline:22253364.

Ogden, Cynthia L., Molly M. Lamb, Margaret D. Caroll, and Katherine M. Flegal. 2010. *Obesity and Socioeconomic Status in Adults: United States, 2005–2008. NCHS Data Brief No. 50.* Washington, DC: US Department of Health and Human Services, Center for Disease Control and Prevention.

Tai-Seale, T., and C. Chandler. 2003. "Nutrition and Overweight Concerns in Rural Areas: A Literature Review." In *Rural Healthy People 2010: A Companion Document to Healthy People 2010*, vol. 2. ed. Larry D. Gamm, Linnae L. Hutchison, Betty J. Dabney, and Alicia Dorsey, 115–30. College Station, TX: The Texas A&M University System Health Science Center, School of Rural Public Health, Southwest Rural Health Research Center.

US Bureau of Labor Statistics. 2012a. "Labor Force Statistics from the Current Population Survey." Unemployment Rate. Accessed 18 July. http://bls.gov/data.

US Bureau of Labor Statistics. 2012b. "Consumer Food Price Index." Accessed 18 July. http://bls.gov/data/.

US Census Bureau. 2012. "Growth in Urban Population Outpaces Rest of Nation, Census Bureau Reports." 26 March press release. http://www.census.gov/newsroom/releases/archives/2010_census/cb12-50.html.

USDA-ERS. 2012. "Food Expenditure." Accessed 20 September. http://ers.usda.gov/data-products/food-expenditures.aspx.

Zimmerman, J.N., S. Ham, and S.M. Frank. 2008. "Does It or Doesn't It? Geographic Difference and the Costs of Living." *Rural Sociology* 73 (3): 463–86. http://dx.doi.org/10.1526/003601108785766561.

QUESTIONS FOR REVIEW, REFLECTION, AND DISCUSSION

1. What is a food insecure household?
2. Have you ever lived in a food insecure household? How long did your household experience food insecurity? What did you do? What happened?
3. What causes obesity?
4. Why are some people in the United States experiencing hunger?
5. What illnesses are associated with obesity?
6. What region of the United States tends to experience higher rates of household food insecurity?
7. Do a little research. Look up CDC (Centers for Disease Control) and find out what they do. In what city is CDC based?
8. Do a little research. Look up the National Health and Nutrition Examination Survey (NHANES). What did you find out about that survey?

ADDITIONAL READINGS

Averett, S.L., Sikora, A., & Argys, L.M. (2008). For better or worse: Relationship status and body mass index, *Economics and Human Biology, 6*, 330–349.

Garasky, S., Stewart, S.D., Gundersen, C., Lohman, B.J., Eisenmann, J.C., 2009. Family stressors and child obesity. *Soc. Sci. Res. 38*(4), 755–766.

Hutson, S., Anderson, M., & Swafford, M. (2015). Applying the post-modern Double ABC-X Model to family food insecurity, *Journal of Family and Consumer Sciences, 107*(1), 19–24.

Kreider, B., Pepper, J.V., Gundersen, C., Jolliffe, D., 2012. Identifying the effects of SNAP (Food Stamps) on child health outcomes when participation is endogenous and misreported. *J. Am. Statistical Assoc. 107*(499), 958–975.

Lytle, L. A., Hearst, M. O., Fulkerson, J., Murray, D. M., Martinson, B., Klein, E., Pasch, K., & Samuelson, A. (2011). Examining the relationships between family meal practices, family stressors, and weight of youth in the family, *Annals of Behavioral Medicine, 41*(3), 353–362.

Ruiz-Castell, M., Muckle, G., Dewailly, É., Jacobson, J. L., Jacobson, S.W., Ayotte, P., Riva, M. (2015). Household crowding and food insecurity among Inuit families with school-aged children in the Canadian Arctic, *American Journal of Public Health, 105*(3), e122–e132.

The, N.S., & Gordon-Larsen, P. (2009). Entry into romantic partnership is associated with obesity, *Obesity, 17*, 1441–1447

Wetherill, M. S., & Gray, K. A. (2015). Farmers' markets and the local food environment: Identifying perceived accessibility barriers for SNAP consumers receiving Temporary Assistance for Needy Families (TANF) in an urban Oklahoma community, *Journal of Nutrition Education and Behavior, 47*(2), 127–133.

Zahra, J., Jago, R., & Sebire, S.J. (2015). Associations between parenting partners' objectively-assessed physical activity and body mass index: A cross-sectional study, *Preventive Medicine Reports, 2*, 473–477.

ENDNOTES

1. The authors thank anonymous reviewers and editors for constructive comments on earlier versions of this chapter. This project was partially funded by the Dr. & Mrs. C. Milton Coughenour Sociology Professorship in Agriculture & Natural Resources in the College of Agriculture at the University of Kentucky.

2. The USDA defines households "in principal cities" as those "within incorporated areas of the largest cities in each metropolitan area" (Nord, Andrews, and Carlson 2005, 9).

3. In 2008, the total medical cost was estimated to be $147 billion (Finkelstein et al. 2009).

4. National health surveillance data collected by the CDC use the USDA-ERS's 2003 Urban Influence Codes (UICs) to categorize rural and urban counties. In the obesity literature under our review, UICs of one and two, or metropolitan areas, were classified as urban. While all other UICs were classified as rural, this is further divided into "micropolitan" rural (UICs three, five and eight), "small rural adjacent to a metro area" (UICs four, six, and seven), and "remote rural" (UICs nine, ten, eleven, and twelve).

5. Based on the assumption of three meals per day, seven days per week, an average cost per meal was calculated by dividing the average dollar amount of weekly food expenditures that food secure individuals reported by twenty-one.

6. In order to determine distances needed to access the goods and services listed in the ACCRA-COI inventory, for each case county Zimmerman, Ham, and Frank (2008) measured the miles driven to access each item from the population center of that county as the starting point. They coded any business located in the population center as zero miles. Then, they calculated the average mileage.

7. Open counties, or noncore, rural counties, are those statistical areas without an urban cluster of at least 10,000 people. In-town rural countries are micropolitan areas, centered on urban clusters of 10,000 or more people.

APPENDICES

APPENDIX A: MARRIAGE RATES BY STATE

Marriage rates by State: 1990, 1995, and 1999–2014
[Rates are based on provisional counts of marriages by state of occurrence. Rates are per 1,000 total population residing in area. Population enumerated as of April 1 for 1990, 2000, and 2010 and estimated as of July 1 for all other years]

State	Marriage rate																	
	2014	2013	2012	2011	2010	2009	2008	2007	2006	2005	2004	2003	2002	2001	2000	1999	1995	1990
Alabama	7.8	7.8	8.2	8.4	8.2	8.3	8.6	8.9	9.2	9.2	9.4	9.6	9.9	9.4	10.1	10.8	9.8	10.6
Alaska	7.5	7.3	7.2	7.8	8.0	7.8	8.4	8.5	8.2	8.2	8.5	8.1	8.3	8.1	8.9	8.6	9.0	10.2
Arizona	5.8	5.4	5.6	5.7	5.9	5.6	6.0	6.4	6.5	6.6	6.7	6.5	6.7	7.6	7.5	8.2	8.8	10.0
Arkansas	10.1	9.8	10.9	10.4	10.8	10.7	10.6	12.0	12.4	12.9	13.4	13.4	14.3	14.3	15.4	14.8	14.4	15.3
California [1]	6.4	6.5	6.0	5.8	5.8	5.8	6.7	6.2	6.3	6.4	6.4	6.1	6.2	6.5	5.8	6.4	6.3	7.9
Colorado	7.1	6.5	6.8	7.0	6.9	6.9	7.4	7.1	7.2	7.6	7.4	7.8	8.0	8.2	8.3	8.2	9.0	9.8
Connecticut	5.4	5.0	5.2	5.5	5.6	5.9	5.4	5.5	5.5	5.8	5.8	5.5	5.7	5.4	5.7	5.8	6.6	7.9
Delaware	6.0	6.6	5.8	5.2	5.2	5.4	5.5	5.7	5.9	5.9	6.1	6.0	6.4	6.5	6.5	6.7	7.3	8.4
District of Columbia	11.8	10.8	8.4	8.7	7.6	4.7	4.1	4.2	4.0	4.1	5.2	5.1	5.1	6.2	4.9	6.6	6.1	8.2
Florida	7.3	7.0	7.2	7.4	7.3	7.5	8.0	8.5	8.6	8.9	9.0	9.0	9.4	9.3	8.9	8.7	9.9	10.9
Georgia	--	--	6.5	6.6	7.3	6.6	6.0	6.8	7.3	7.0	7.9	7.0	6.5	6.1	6.8	7.8	8.4	10.3
Hawaii	17.7	16.3	17.5	17.6	17.6	17.2	19.1	20.8	21.9	22.6	22.6	22.0	20.8	19.6	20.6	18.9	15.7	16.4
Idaho	8.4	8.2	8.2	8.6	8.8	8.9	9.5	10.0	10.1	10.5	10.8	10.9	11.0	11.2	10.8	12.1	13.1	13.9
Illinois	6.2	5.4	5.8	5.6	5.7	5.7	5.9	6.1	6.2	5.9	6.2	6.5	6.6	7.2	6.9	7.0	6.9	8.8
Indiana	7.1	6.6	6.7	6.8	6.3	7.9	8.0	7.0	7.0	6.9	7.8	7.1	7.9	7.9	7.9	8.1	8.6	9.6
Iowa	6.9	7.4	6.8	6.7	6.9	7.0	6.5	6.6	6.7	6.9	6.9	6.9	7.0	7.1	6.9	7.9	7.7	9.0
Kansas	6.1	6.0	6.3	6.3	6.4	6.4	6.7	6.8	6.8	6.8	7.0	6.9	7.3	7.5	8.3	7.1	8.5	9.2
Kentucky	6.9	7.3	7.2	7.5	7.4	7.6	7.9	7.8	8.4	8.7	8.8	9.1	9.0	9.0	9.8	10.9	12.2	13.5
Louisiana	6.9	6.4	5.7	6.4	6.9	7.1	6.8	7.5	--	8.0	8.0	8.2	8.1	8.4	9.1	9.1	9.3	9.6
Maine	7.7	8.3	7.3	7.2	7.1	7.1	7.4	7.4	7.8	8.2	8.6	8.4	8.4	8.6	8.8	8.6	8.7	9.7

State																		
Maryland	9.7	8.4	7.5	7.5	7.0	7.1	6.9	6.9	6.9	6.6	6.5	5.9	5.8	5.7	5.8	5.6	6.5	6.5
Massachusetts	7.9	7.1	6.2	5.8	6.2	5.9	5.6	6.5	6.2	5.9	5.9	5.7	5.6	5.6	5.5	5.5	5.5	5.6
Michigan	8.2	7.3	6.8	6.7	6.7	6.5	6.3	6.2	6.1	5.9	5.7	5.6	5.4	5.5	5.7	5.6	5.8	5.8
Minnesota	7.7	7.0	6.8	6.8	6.6	6.5	6.3	6.0	6.0	6.0	5.8	5.4	5.3	5.3	5.6	5.6	6.0	5.9
Mississippi	9.4	7.9	7.8	6.9	6.5	6.4	6.2	6.1	5.8	5.7	5.4	5.1	4.8	4.9	4.9	5.8	6.7	6.9
Missouri	9.6	8.3	8.1	7.8	7.5	7.3	7.2	7.1	7.0	6.9	6.9	6.8	6.5	6.5	6.6	6.5	6.4	6.7
Montana	8.6	7.6	7.4	7.3	7.1	7.1	7.2	7.5	7.4	7.4	7.5	7.6	7.3	7.4	7.8	7.8	7.4	7.9
Nebraska	8.0	7.3	7.5	7.6	7.9	7.5	7.0	7.1	7.0	6.8	6.8	6.9	6.6	6.6	6.6	6.7	6.3	6.4
Nevada	99.0	85.2	82.3	72.2	69.6	67.4	63.9	62.1	57.4	52.1	48.6	42.3	40.3	38.3	36.9	35.1	32.3	31.9
New Hampshire	9.5	8.3	7.9	9.4	8.5	8.3	8.1	8.0	7.3	7.2	7.1	6.8	6.5	7.3	7.1	6.8	6.9	7.2
New Jersey	7.6	6.5	5.9	6.0	6.4	6.0	5.8	5.9	5.7	5.5	5.4	5.4	5.0	5.1	4.8	4.9	5.1	5.4
New Mexico	8.8	8.8	8.0	8.0	7.6	7.9	6.9	7.4	6.6	6.8	5.6	4.0	5.0	7.7	8.0	6.9	7.3	8.1
New York	8.6	8.0	7.3	7.1	7.6	7.3	6.8	6.8	6.8	6.9	6.8	6.6	6.5	6.5	6.9	7.0	6.9	6.7
North Carolina	7.8	8.4	8.5	8.2	7.4	7.7	7.4	7.3	7.3	7.3	7.0	6.9	6.6	6.6	6.7	6.6	6.5	6.9
North Dakota	7.5	7.1	6.6	7.2	6.5	6.8	7.1	6.9	6.8	6.7	6.6	6.5	6.4	6.5	6.7	6.6	6.3	6.3
Ohio	9.0	8.0	7.8	7.8	7.2	7.0	6.7	6.6	6.5	6.3	6.1	6.0	5.8	5.8	5.9	5.8	5.7	5.8
Oklahoma	10.6	8.6	6.8	--	--	--	--	6.5	7.3	7.3	7.3	7.1	6.9	7.2	6.9	6.9	7.1	7.1
Oregon	8.9	8.1	7.6	7.6	7.5	7.1	7.2	8.1	7.3	7.3	7.2	6.9	6.6	6.5	6.6	6.6	6.3	6.8
Pennsylvania	7.1	6.2	6.1	6.0	5.8	5.7	5.9	5.9	5.8	5.7	5.7	5.5	5.3	5.3	5.3	5.5	5.4	5.8
Rhode Island	8.1	7.3	7.5	7.6	8.1	7.8	7.8	7.7	7.0	6.6	6.4	6.1	5.9	5.8	6.0	6.1	6.2	6.7
South Carolina	15.9	11.9	10.2	10.6	9.9	9.3	9.0	8.2	8.3	7.8	7.9	7.3	7.3	7.4	7.2	7.4	7.1	7.6
South Dakota	11.1	9.9	9.1	9.4	8.9	8.8	8.4	8.4	8.4	8.0	7.8	7.7	7.3	7.3	7.5	7.5	7.0	7.1
Tennessee	13.9	15.5	14.7	15.5	13.5	13.1	11.9	11.4	10.9	10.6	10.1	9.4	8.4	8.8	9.0	8.8	8.4	8.4
Texas	10.5	9.9	9.1	9.4	9.1	8.4	8.1	8.0	7.8	7.6	7.4	7.3	7.1	7.1	7.1	7.3	7.0	6.9
Utah	11.2	10.7	9.6	10.8	10.2	10.4	10.2	9.9	9.8	9.2	9.6	9.0	8.4	8.5	8.6	8.4	7.5	7.3
Vermont	10.9	10.3	10.0	10.0	9.8	9.8	9.7	9.4	8.9	8.6	8.5	7.9	8.7	9.3	8.3	8.2	9.2	8.7
Virginia	11.4	10.2	9.2	8.8	8.8	8.6	8.4	8.3	8.2	7.8	7.5	7.2	6.9	6.8	6.8	6.8	6.7	6.7
Washington	9.5	7.7	7.2	6.9	7.0	6.5	6.5	6.5	6.5	6.5	6.4	6.3	6.0	6.0	6.1	6.3	7.1	7.0
West Virginia	7.2	6.1	7.5	8.7	7.9	8.1	7.5	7.5	7.4	7.3	7.3	7.1	6.7	6.7	7.2	7.0	6.6	6.7
Wisconsin	7.9	7.0	6.7	6.7	6.5	6.3	6.2	6.2	6.1	6.0	5.7	5.6	5.3	5.3	5.3	5.4	5.2	5.7
Wyoming	10.7	10.6	9.9	10.0	10.0	9.5	9.3	9.3	9.3	9.3	9.0	8.6	8.0	7.6	7.8	7.6	7.5	7.7

--Data not available.

1 Marriage data includes nonlicensed marriages registered.

Note: Rates for 2001–2009 have been revised and are based on intercensal population estimates from the 2000 and 2010 censuses.

Source: CDC/NCHS, National Vital Statistics System.

APPENDIX B: NATIONAL MARRIAGE AND DIVORCE RATE

Centers for Disease Control and Prevention

CDC 24/7. Saving Lives, Protecting People™
National Marriage and Divorce Rate Trends

PROVISIONAL NUMBER OF MARRIAGES AND MARRIAGE RATE: UNITED STATES, 2000–2014			
Year	Marriages	Population	Rate per 1,000 total population
2014[1]	2,140,272	308,759,713	6.9
2013[1]	2,081,301	306,136,672	6.8
2012	2,131,000	313,914,040	6.8
2011	2,118,000	311,591,917	6.8
2010	2,096,000	308,745,538	6.8
2009	2,080,000	306,771,529	6.8
2008	2,157,000	304,093,966	7.1
2007	2,197,000	301,231,207	7.3
2006[2]	2,193,000	294,077,247	7.5
2005	2,249,000	295,516,599	7.6
2004	2,279,000	292,805,298	7.8
2003	2,245,000	290,107,933	7.7
2002	2,290,000	287,625,193	8.0
2001	2,326,000	284,968,955	8.2
2000	2,315,000	281,421,906	8.2

[1] Excludes data for Georgia.

[2] Excludes data for Louisiana.

Note: Rates for 2001–2009 have been revised and are based on intercensal population estimates from the 2000 and 2010 censuses. Populations for 2010 rates are based on the 2010 census.

Source: CDC/NCHS National Vital Statistics System.

PROVISIONAL NUMBER OF DIVORCES AND ANNULMENTS AND RATE: UNITED STATES, 2000–2014

Year	Divorces & annulments	Population	Rate per 1,000 total population
2014[1]	813,862	256,483,624	3.2
2013[1]	832,157	254,408,815	3.3
2012[2]	851,000	248,041,986	3.4
2011[2]	877,000	246,273,366	3.6
2010[2]	872,000	244,122,529	3.6
2009[2]	840,000	242,610,561	3.5
2008[2]	844,000	240,545,163	3.5
2007[2]	856,000	238,352,850	3.6
2006[2]	872,000	236,094,277	3.7
2005[2]	847,000	233,495,163	3.6
2004[3]	879,000	236,402,656	3.7
2003[4]	927,000	243,902,090	3.8
2002[5]	955,000	243,108,303	3.9
2001[6]	940,000	236,416,762	4.0
2000[6]	944,000	233,550,143	4.0

[1] Excludes data for California, Georgia, Hawaii, Indiana, and Minnesota.

[2] Excludes data for California, Georgia, Hawaii, Indiana, Louisiana, and Minnesota.

[3] Excludes data for California, Georgia, Hawaii, Indiana, and Louisiana.

[4] Excludes data for California, Hawaii, Indiana, and Oklahoma.

[5] Excludes data for California, Indiana, and Oklahoma.

[6] Excludes data for California, Indiana, Louisiana, and Oklahoma.

Note: Rates for 2001–2009 have been revised and are based on intercensal population estimates from the 2000 and 2010 censuses. Populations for 2010 rates are based on the 2010 census.

Source: CDC/NCHS National Vital Statistics System.

APPENDIX C: REMARRIAGE IN THE UNITED STATES

American Community Survey Reports

By Jamie M. Lewis and Rose M. Kreider Issued March 2015

INTRODUCTION

The context of marriage in the United States involves not only whether and when Americans choose to marry, but also how many times they marry. The majority of recent marriages are first marriages for both spouses. However, divorce rates are higher in the United States compared with European nations,[1] and remarried adults have a higher likelihood of divorce than those in their first marriage.[2]

Some highlights of the report are:

- About half of all men (50 percent) and women (54 percent) aged 15 and over had married only once.
- The proportion of adults that had married only once has decreased since 1996, from 54 percent to 50 percent of men and 60 percent to 54 percent of women.
- Between 1996 and 2008–2012, the share of those that had married twice or three or more times increased only for women aged 50 and older and men aged 60 and older.

---

[1]See Gunnar Andersson, "Dissolution of Unions in Europe: A Comparative Overview," *MPIDR Working Paper*, WP 2003-004, Max Planck Institute for Demographic Research, Rostock, Germany, 2003.
[2]See Diana B. Elliott and Tavia Simmons, "Marital Events of Americans: 2009," *American Community Survey Reports*, ACS-13, U.S. Census Bureau, Washington, DC, 2011.

- Non-Hispanic White men and women are most likely to have married three or more times, while Asian men and women are least likely.[3]
- Those with at least a bachelor's degree are more likely to have married only once (64 percent) than all adults (52 percent).
- The majority of recent marriages (58 percent) are first marriages for both spouses, although 21 percent involve both spouses marrying for at least the second time.
- States with a lower share of ever-married adults who had remarried are concentrated in the Northeast and Midwest, while Southern and Western states generally have a higher share.
- Lake Havasu City-Kingman, Arizona and Prescott, Arizona are among the MSAs with the highest percentage of ever-married adults who had remarried, with about 40 percent or more.

HOW MANY MEN AND WOMEN HAD MARRIED MORE THAN ONCE?

Table C.1 provides a look at some basic measures of marital history by age and sex. A majority of adults aged 15 and over had ever married: two-thirds of men and 72 percent of women. Marital history does differ somewhat by sex, as women tend to marry earlier than men. For example, about 18 percent of women aged 20 to 24 had ever married, compared with 11 percent of men. Marital history is also shown for various age groups since it varies throughout the life course. For example, we would not expect many teens to be married. Indeed, when looking at older age groups, who have had more time to marry, we see that more had done so. For all age groups of women aged 30 and over, the majority had married, as had the majority of men aged 30 and over. Thus, despite concerns of a "retreat from marriage,"[4] this life event continues to be pursued and achieved by most in America.

Although most Americans marry, they do not necessarily remain in a particular marriage for life. In addition to reviewing whether men and women ever marry, information on the number of times they marry and whether they are still in a particular marriage is important. About half of all adults aged 15 and over had married once: 50 percent of men and 54 percent of women (Table C.1). There were 40 percent of men and 37 percent of women still in their first marriage, 13 percent of men and 14 percent of women had married twice, and 4 percent had married three or more times.[5] Age is an important factor relating to remarriage, as older individuals have had more time to see a previous marriage conclude and to remarry. The proportion of men and women married twice is about 20 percent or higher for men and women aged 50 to 69.

---

[3]Individuals who responded to the question on race by indicating only one race are referred to as the *race-alone* population or the group that reported only one race category. This report will refer to the White-alone population as White, the Black-alone population as Black, the Asian-alone population as Asian, and the White-alone, non-Hispanic population as non-Hispanic White unless otherwise noted.

[4]See, for example, Daniel T. Lichter et al., "Race and the Retreat from Marriage: A Shortage of Marriageable Men?" *American Sociological Review*, 57(6):781–799, 1992; and Robert Schoen and Yen-Hsin Alice Cheng, "Partner Choice and the Differential Retreat from Marriage," *Journal of Marriage and Family*, 68(1):1–10, 2006.

[5]The estimates for men and women differ statistically.

TABLE C.1: MARITAL HISTORY FOR PEOPLE 15 YEARS OLD AND OVER BY AGE AND SEX: 2008–2012

Characteristic	Total, 15 years and over	15 to 17 years	18 to 19 years	20 to 24 years	25 to 29 years	30 to 34 years	35 to 39 years	40 to 49 years	50 to 59 years	60 to 69 years	70 years and over
MALE											
Total	115,969,884	6,511,043	3,796,578	10,150,214	10,181,620	9,667,056	9,669,427	20,955,362	19,970,679	13,830,810	11,237,095
Percent											
Never married	33.6	99.5	98.5	89.4	63.4	37.9	24.5	17.4	11.6	6.2	3.7
Ever married	66.4	0.5	1.5	10.6	36.6	62.1	75.5	82.6	88.4	93.8	96.3
Married once	49.9	0.5	1.5	10.4	34.9	56.5	64.2	63.5	60.5	60.3	69.4
Currently married[1]	40.1	0.3	1.4	9.3	30.5	48.4	53.5	50.7	47.3	48.6	51.2
Married twice	13.0	X	X	0.3	1.7	5.2	10.1	16.0	21.6	24.4	20.4
Currently married[1]	10.0	X	X	0.2	1.5	4.5	8.4	12.7	16.5	18.8	15.0
Married three or more times	3.5	X	X	X	0.1	0.4	1.2	3.1	6.3	9.1	6.5
Currently married[1]	2.6	X	X	X	0.1	0.3	0.9	2.3	4.7	6.6	4.6
FEMALE											
Total	124,129,728	6,216,078	3,519,612	10,073,564	10,371,401	9,943,647	10,028,068	21,837,736	21,342,984	15,324,558	15,472,080
Percent											
Never married	27.9	99.4	96.1	81.5	51.7	29.9	19.6	13.7	9.6	5.9	3.9
Ever married	72.1	0.6	3.9	18.5	48.3	70.1	80.4	86.3	90.4	94.1	96.1
Married once	54.5	0.6	3.9	17.8	45.0	61.5	65.7	64.0	61.0	64.0	74.1
Currently married[1]	37.3	0.5	3.6	15.4	37.7	50.3	51.9	47.7	43.1	41.4	28.8
Married twice	14.0	X	X	0.7	3.1	7.8	12.8	18.2	22.3	22.4	17.3
Currently married[1]	9.0	X	X	0.6	2.6	6.3	9.9	13.2	15.3	13.7	6.4
Married three or more times	3.7	X	X	X	0.2	0.7	1.9	4.1	7.0	7.6	4.7
Currently married[1]	2.2	X	X	X	0.1	0.5	1.4	2.8	4.5	4.4	1.7

(For information on confidentiality protection, sampling error, nonsampling error, and definitions, see www.census.gov/acs/www /Downloads/data_documentation/Accuracy/MultiyearACSAccuracyofData2012.pdf)

X Not applicable.

[1] Does not include those currently separated.

Source: U.S. Census Bureau, American Community Survey, 2008–2012.

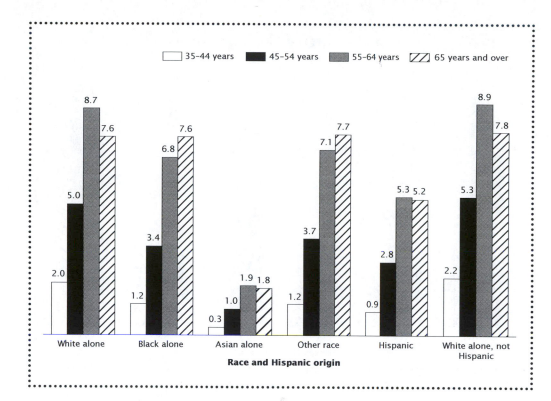

FIGURE C.1.

Percentage of Men Married Three Times or More by Age, Race, and Hispanic Origin: 2008–2012

(For information on confidentiality protection, sampling error, nonsampling error, and definitions, see www.census.gov/ acs/www/Downloads/ data_documentation/ Accuracy/ MultiyearACSAccuracyof Data2012.pdf)

Universe: Men 35 years old and over.

Source: U.S. Census Bureau, American Community Survey, 2008–2012.

WHAT ARE THE CHARACTERISTICS OF THOSE WHO HAD MARRIED MORE THAN ONCE?

Figures C.1 and C.2 show the percentage of men and women aged 35 and over who had married three or more times by age, race, and Hispanic origin. Here, we look at those aged 35 and over to exclude many younger adults who have not had time to remarry, or may not have married at all. As was noted earlier, in general, the proportion who had married three or more times is higher for older age groups. An exception is the 65 and over age group who are less likely than those aged 55 to 64 to have married at least three times.[6] This pattern likely reflects a cohort effect. People born and coming of age at different times encounter varying expectations regarding marriage and divorce. Those who are aged 65 or older today reached marriageable age in the 1950s and early 1960s when divorce rates were stable. As noted previously, divorce rates increased sharply in the 1960s and 1970s during the time when today's 55- to 64-year-olds were young adults.

While overall in 2008–2012, just 4 percent of adults had married three or more times, this varied by race and Hispanic origin. Among men aged 55 to 64, 9 percent of non-Hispanic Whites had married three or more times, compared with 7 percent of Blacks, 2 percent of Asians, and 5 percent of Hispanics, who may be of any race. The pattern for women aged 55 to 64 is similar, with 9 percent of non-Hispanic White women married at least three times, compared with 4 percent of Black women, 2 percent of

FIGURE C.2.

Percentage of Women
Married Three Times
or More by Age, Race,
and Hispanic Origin:
2008–2012

(For information
on confidentiality
protection, sampling
error, nonsampling
error, and definitions,
see www.census.gov/
acs/www/Downloads/
data_documentation/
Accuracy/MultiyearACS
Accuracyof
Data2012.pdf)

Universe: Women 35
years old and over.

Source: U.S. Census
Bureau, American
Community Survey,
2008–2012.

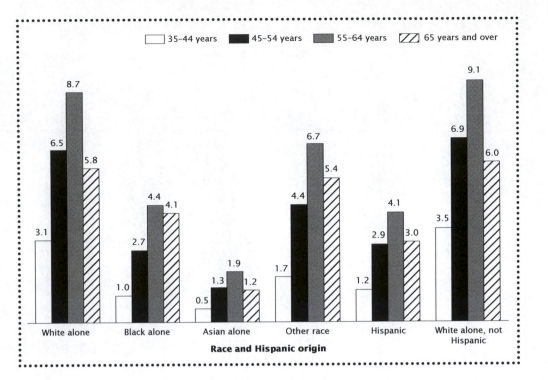

Asian women, and 4 percent of Hispanic women.[7] This pattern, in which non-Hispanic Whites are most likely to have married three or more times and Asians least likely, is observed not only for both women and men but also for each age group.

APPENDIX D: HOW THE CENSUS BUREAU MEASURES POVERTY AND [2015]* POVERTY GUIDELINES

Following the Office of Management and Budget's (OMB) Statistical Policy Directive 14, the Census Bureau uses a set of money income thresholds that vary by family size and composition to determine who is in poverty. If a family's total income is less than the family's threshold, then that family and every individual in it is considered in poverty. The official poverty thresholds do not vary geographically, but they are updated for inflation using Consumer Price Index (CPI-U). The official poverty definition uses money income before taxes and does not include capital gains or noncash benefits (such as public housing, Medicaid, and food stamps).

*Pages 172–174 have been updated to reflect 2015 data from the US Census Bureau.
Copyright in the Public Domain.

INCOME USED TO COMPUTE POVERTY STATUS (MONEY INCOME)

- Includes earnings, unemployment compensation, workers' compensation, Social Security, Supplemental Security Income, public assistance, veterans' payments, survivor benefits, pension or retirement income, interest, dividends, rents, royalties, income from estates, trusts, educational assistance, alimony, child support, assistance from outside the household, and other miscellaneous sources.
- Noncash benefits (such as food stamps and housing subsidies) **do not** count.
- Before taxes
- Excludes capital gains or losses.
- If a person lives with a family, add up the income of all family members. (Non-relatives, such as housemates, do not count.)

MEASURE OF NEED (POVERTY THRESHOLDS)

Poverty thresholds are the dollar amounts used to determine poverty status.
Each person or family is assigned one out of 48 possible poverty thresholds
Thresholds vary according to:
- Size of the family
- Ages of the members

The same thresholds are used throughout the United States (do not vary geographically).

Updated annually for inflation using the Consumer Price Index for All Urban Consumers (CPI-U).

Although the thresholds in some sense reflect families needs,
- They are intended for use as a statistical yardstick, not as a complete description of what people and families need to live.
- Many government aid programs use a different poverty measure, the Department of Health and Human Services (HHS) poverty guidelines, or multiples thereof.

Poverty thresholds were originally derived in 1963-1964, using:
- U.S. Department of Agriculture food budgets designed for families under economic stress.
- Data about what portion of their income families spent on food.

COMPUTATION

If total family income is less than the threshold appropriate for that family,
- The family is in poverty.
- All family members have the same poverty status.

- For individuals who do not live with family members, their own income is compared with the appropriate threshold.

If total family income equals or is greater than the threshold, the family (or unrelated individual) is not in poverty.

Example

Family A has five members: two children, their mother, father, and great-aunt.

Their threshold was $28,498 in 2013. (See poverty thresholds for 2013 near the end of this reading).

Suppose the members' incomes in 2013 were:

APPENDIX D TABLE 1.	
Mother	$10,000
Father	9,000
Great-aunt	10,000
First Child	0
Second Child	0
Total Family Income	$29,000

Compare total family income with their family's threshold:

Income / Threshold = $29,000 / $28,498 = 1.02

Since their income was greater than their threshold, Family A is not "in poverty" according to the official definition.

The income divided by the threshold is called the **Ratio of Income to Poverty**.
—Family A's ratio of income to poverty was 1.02.

The difference in dollars between family income and the family's poverty threshold is called the **Income Deficit** (for families in poverty) or **Income Surplus** (for families above poverty)
—Family A's income surplus was $502 (or $29,000 - $28,498).

People Whose Poverty Status Cannot Be Determined

Unrelated individuals under age 15 (such as foster children):
- Income questions are asked of people age 15 and older.
- If someone is under age 15 and not living with a family member, we do not know their income.
- Since we cannot determine their poverty status, they are excluded from the "poverty universe" (table totals).

People in:

- Institutional group quarters (such as prisons or nursing homes)
- College dormitories
- Military barracks
- Living situations without conventional housing (and who are not in shelters)

Authority Behind Official Poverty Measure

The official measure of poverty was established by the Office of Management and Budget (OMB) in Statistical Policy Directive 14

To be used by federal agencies in their statistical work.

Government aid programs do not have to use the official poverty measure as eligibility criteria.

- Many government aid programs use a different poverty measure, the Department of Health and Human Services (HHS) poverty guidelines, or variants thereof.
- Each aid program may define eligibility differently.

Official poverty data come from the Current Population Survey (CPS) Annual Social and Economic Supplement (ASEC), formerly called the Annual Demographic Supplement or simply the "March Supplement."

2015 POVERTY GUIDELINES

ONE VERSION OF THE [U.S.] FEDERAL POVERTY MEASURE

The following figures are the 2014 HHS poverty guidelines which are scheduled to be published in the Federal Register on January 22, 2015. (Additional information will be posted after the guidelines are published.)

APPENDIX D TABLE 2. 2015 POVERTY GUIDELINES FOR THE 48 CONTIGUOUS STATES AND THE DISTRICT OF COLUMBIA	
Persons in family/household	**Poverty guideline**
For families/households with more than 8 persons, add $4,160 for each additional person.	
1	$11,770
2	15,930
3	20,090
4	24,250
5	28,410
6	32,570
7	36,730
8	40,890

APPENDIX D TABLE.3 2015 POVERTY GUIDELINES FOR ALASKA

Persons in family/household	Poverty guideline
For families/households with more than 8 persons, add $5,200 for each additional person.	
1	$14,720
2	19,920
3	25,120
4	30,320
5	35,520
6	40,720
7	45,920
8	51,120

APPENDIX D TABLE.4: 2015 POVERTY GUIDELINES FOR HAWAII

Persons in family/household	Poverty guideline
For families/households with more than 8 persons, add $4,780 for each additional person.	
1	$13,550
2	18,330
3	23,110
4	27,890
5	32,670
6	37,450
7	42,230
8	47,010

The separate poverty guidelines for Alaska and Hawaii reflect Office of Economic Opportunity administrative practice beginning in the 1966-1970 period. Note that the poverty thresholds— the original version of the poverty measure—have never had separate figures for Alaska and Hawaii. The poverty guidelines are not defined for Puerto Rico, the U.S. Virgin Islands, American Samoa, Guam, the Republic of the Marshall Islands, the Federated States of Micronesia, the Commonwealth of the Northern Mariana Islands, and Palau. In cases in which a Federal program using the poverty guidelines serves any of those jurisdictions, the Federal office which administers the program is responsible for deciding whether to use the contiguous-states-and-D.C. guidelines for those jurisdictions or to follow some other procedure.

The poverty guidelines apply to both aged and non-aged units. The guidelines have never had an aged/non-aged distinction; only the Census Bureau (statistical) poverty thresholds have separate figures for aged and non-aged one-person and two-person units.

Programs using the guidelines (or percentage multiples of the guidelines—for instance, 125 percent or 185 percent of the guidelines) in determining eligibility include Head Start, the Supplemental Nutition Assistance Program (SNAP), the National School Lunch Program, the Low-Income Home Energy Assistance Program, and the Children's Health Insurance Program. Note that in general, cash public assistance programs (Temporary Assistance for Needy Families and Supplemental Security Income) do NOT use the poverty guidelines in determining eligibility. The Earned Income Tax Credit program also does NOT use the poverty guidelines to determine eligibility. For a more detailed list of programs that do and don't use the guidelines, see the Frequently Asked Questions (FAQs).

The poverty guidelines (unlike the poverty thresholds) are designated by the year in which they are issued. For instance, the guidelines issued in January 2014 are designated the 2015 poverty guidelines. However, the 2015 HHS poverty guidelines only reflect price changes through calendar year 2014; accordingly, they are approximately equal to the Census Bureau poverty thresholds for calendar year 2014. (The 2014 thresholds are expected to be issued in final form in September 2015; a preliminary version of the 2014thresholds is now available from the Census Bureau.)

The poverty guidelines may be formally referenced as "the poverty guidelines updated periodically in the *Federal Register* by the U.S. Department of Health and Human Services under the authority of 42 U.S.C. 9902(2)."

EDITOR'S NOTE

DIFFERENCE BETWEEN THE POVERTY GUIDELINES AND THE POVERTY THRESHOLDS

Poverty thresholds are used for calculating all official poverty population statistics — for instance, figures on the number of Americans in poverty each year. They are updated each year by the Census Bureau. The poverty thresholds were originally developed in 1963-1964 by Mollie Orshansky of the Social Security Administration.

The poverty guidelines are a simplified version of the federal poverty thresholds used for administrative purposes — for instance, determining financial eligibility for certain federal programs. They are issued each year in the Federal Register by the Department of Health and Human Services (HHS).

EXAMPLES OF PROGRAMS THAT USE THE HHS POVERTY GUIDELINES

The HHS poverty guidelines, or percentage multiples of them (such as 125 percent, 150 percent, or 185 percent), are used as an eligibility criterion by a number of federal programs, including those listed below. For examples of major means-tested programs that do not use the poverty guidelines, see the end of this response.

APPENDIX D TABLE.5: POVERTY THRESHOLDS FOR 2013 BY SIZE OF FAMILY AND NUMBER OF RELATED CHILDREN

SIZE OF FAMILY UNIT	WEIGHTED AVERAGE THRESHOLDS	RELATED CHILDREN UNDER 18 YEARS								
		NONE	ONE	TWO	THREE	FOUR	FIVE	SIX	SEVEN	EIGHT
One person (unrelated)	11,888									
Under 65 years............	12,119	12,119								
65 years and over........	11,173	11,173								
Two people..................	15,142									
Households under 65 years......................	15,679	15,600	16,057							
Households 65 years and over....................	14,095	14,081	15,996							
Three people...............	18,552	18,222	18,751	18,769						
Four people................	23,834	24,028	24,421	23,624	23,707					
Five people.................	28,265	28,977	29,398	28,498	27,801	27,376				
Six people..................	31,925	33,329	33,461	32,771	32,110	31,128	30,545			
Seven people..............	36,384	38,349	38,588	37,763	37,187	36,115	34,865	33,493		
Eight people................	40,484	42,890	43,269	42,490	41,807	40,839	39,610	38,331	38,006	
Nine or more...............	48,065	51,594	51,844	51,154	50,575	49,625	48,317	47,134	46,842	45,037

Department of Health and Human Services:
- Community Services Block Grant
- Head Start
- Low-Income Home Energy Assistance Program (LIHEAP)
- PARTS of Medicaid (31 percent of eligibles in Fiscal Year 2004)
- Hill-Burton Uncompensated Services Program
- AIDS Drug Assistance Program
- Children's Health Insurance Program
- Medicare – Prescription Drug Coverage (subsidized portion only)
- Community Health Centers
- Migrant Health Centers
- Family Planning Services
- Health Professions Student Loans — Loans for Disadvantaged Students
- Health Careers Opportunity Program
- Scholarships for Health Professions Students from Disadvantaged Backgrounds
- Job Opportunities for Low-Income Individuals
- Assets for Independence Demonstration Program

Department of Agriculture
- Supplemental Nutrition Assistance Program (SNAP) (formerly Food Stamp Program)
- Special Supplemental Nutrition Program for Women, Infants, and Children (WIC)
- National School Lunch Program (for free and reduced-price meals only)
- School Breakfast Program (for free and reduced-price meals only)
- Child and Adult Care Food Program (for free and reduced-price meals only)
- Expanded Food and Nutrition Education Program

Department of Energy
- Weatherization Assistance for Low-Income Persons

Department of Labor:
- Job Corps
- National Farmworker Jobs Program
- Senior Community Service Employment Program
- Workforce Investment Act Youth Activities

Department of Treasury
- Low-Income Taxpayer Clinics

Corporation for National and Community Service:
- Foster Grandparent Program
- Senior Companion Program

Legal Services Corporation:
- Legal Services for the Poor

Most of these programs are non-open-ended programs — that is, programs for which a fixed amount of money is appropriated each year. A few open-ended or "entitlement" programs that use the poverty guidelines for eligibility are the Supplemental Nutrition Assistance Program (formerly Food Stamps), the National School Lunch Program, certain parts of Medicaid, and the subsidized portion of Medicare – Prescription Drug Coverage.

Some state and local governments have chosen to use the federal poverty guidelines in some of their own programs and activities. Examples include financial guidelines for child support enforcement and determination of legal indigence for court purposes. Some private companies (such as utilities, telephone companies, and pharmaceutical companies) and some charitable agencies also use the guidelines in setting eligibility for their services to low-income persons.

Major means-tested programs that do not use the poverty guidelines in determining eligibility include the following:
- Supplemental Security Income (SSI)
- Earned Income Tax Credit (EITC)
- State/local-funded General Assistance (in most cases)
- Some parts of Medicaid
- Section 8 low-income housing assistance
- Low-rent public housing